Cane Reapers

Chinese Indentured Immigrants In Guyana

3rd Revised Edition

by

Trev Sue-A-Quan, Ph.D.

Vancouver, British Columbia

Cane
Press

Published by

Cane Press

240 Woodstock Avenue E.
Vancouver, B.C. V5W 1N1
Canada
Canereapers@Lycos.com

First Printing 1999
Second Revised Edition 2003
Third Revised Edition 2017

Sue-A-Quan, Trev, 1943-
Cane Reapers: Chinese Indentured Immigrants in Guyana / by Trev Sue-A-Quan - 3rd Revised Edition

Includes bibliographical references.

ISBN 978-0-9733557-3-4

Other books by the author:

Cane Ripples: The Chinese in Guyana (2003)
ISBN 978-0-9733557-1-9
Cane Rovers: Stories of the Chinese-Guyanese Diaspora (2012)
ISBN 978-0-9733557-2-7

Website: Chinese in Guyana: Their Roots
www.rootsweb.com/~guycigtr

FOREWORD

When God wishes to send blessings upon a person, He first sends a little **mishap** and sees how well he can take it.

Poverty is *not a disgrace*; disgrace lies in poverty without **ambition**
— *Chinese Proverbs*

These two proverbs (which I found among the "Maxims" listed at the end of Margery Kirkpatrick's (née Ting-A-Kee) earlier book (1993) on aspects of Chinese immigrant life in British Guiana) seem to me to apply aptly to Dr. Sue-A-Quan's newly researched account of the life and times of Chinese indentured immigrants in Guyana from their arrival aboard the *Glentanner* and *Lord Elgin* in early January 1853 through the end of the immigration period (1879) and on to our own later twentieth century day.

The book reveals that in that century and a half the "mishaps," such as the high mortality on a sea journey sometimes nearly 6 months long, and their sufferings in the plantation and alien environment of Demerara indeed seem "little" when compared with the "blessings" that the Chinese community increasingly received with the advancing decades. These blessings they spiritually recognized in their own building of (an Anglican) St. Saviour's Church, to worship in their own language, as early as 1875, and they materially demonstrated through the success of their business skills as middlemen shopkeepers and upper-level merchants and property owners.

In that same period too their "ambition" defeated the visual disgrace of "poverty" through the muscular efforts of their first generation, such as is evidenced in the creation in 1865 of the Hopetown settlement (25 miles up the Demerara River). For their future generations they made the young avail themselves of more than basic education. The efforts at Hopetown had produced a going charcoal business, which, though it eventually failed, typified the industry which was going to flourish later in shops and laundries and bigger businesses in Georgetown. And the family pursuit of education for their children led these ultimately into the professions of law, medicine, public administration and, significantly, secondary school-teaching as well.

Perhaps the rise of the people, whom the haughty language of the early English records often referred to collectively as "John Chinaman," in their Colony that ultimately gained its independence in 1966, cannot be more pointedly illustrated than by the political choice in that same year of Mr. Arthur Chung, an ethnic Chinese and Magistrate, as the first President of an independent Guyana. Moreover that choice was at once heartily approved by the two major confronting Afric and Indic communities and endorsed by England's Queen as Head of the Commonwealth, whose only South American Member would now have as its first Head of State a judiciary descendant of the quondam "John Chinaman."

The title of Dr. Sue-A-Quan's book, ***Cane Reapers***, is perhaps well chosen both to emphasize the humble beginnings of the Chinese population in what today is Guyana, and to attract a readership for whom the socio-historical record of a relatively tiny ethnic group in a relatively insignificant third-world country (with a confusing name, too) may not at first seem so exciting. Indeed the total number of 13,541 arrivals recorded in the 26 years of actual immigration (1853 to 1879) is today drastically diminished, the official 1990 census showing a total of 1,251 (721m + 530f) out of a national population at that date of 701,704. This fact in itself, against the background of greatly increased respect and success of that particular ethnic group, should stimulate human interest — what has caused this near disappearance? One reason is the endemic shortage of Chinese women, which Dr. Sue-A-Quan explains, but the diminution stimulates much wider inquiry in the context of today's Guyana and the Western world. For the Guyanese Chinese have certainly not gone back to the human challenges of China. Dr. Sue-A-Quan, for example, lives and publishes his book from Vancouver in Canada.

For my own part, and the major basis of my recommendation of Dr. Sue-A-Quan's work to the reading public, there is a fourfold interest, stimulated by his scholarly plan of presentation.

First is the fascinating ethno-biography of a diaspora. Trev Sue-A-Quan, inspired by having in hand the actual contract of indenture of his great-grandfather S*oo A-cheong*, precisely dated according to both the Chinese and English calendars (11th December, 1873), explores the rationale for migration and describes in revealing detail the social history, heritage and contribution of a people of one race to Guyana's development. That it is his own race in a diaspora situation is very pertinent. The value of identity is that it authentic-cates, strengthens and reassures. All members of the Sino-Western diaspora should find, not mere interest, but personal value in the narrative Sue-A-Quan has made available to us all. Its potential, small a work though it be when contrasted with Alex Haley's emotive venture in **Roots**, might — just might

— enable some of us in the vast range of the Afro-Western diaspora to realize how much is lost in ignoring or despising one's ethno-biography, seeing how much respect is gained when others define theirs, as Dr. Sue-A-Quan has done so well, detailing good and bad alike.

Second comes my enlightenment by the unusual: the shock that the Chinese national supremacist self-image suffered from the European "barbarians" whose horrific contempt could incinerate eighty square miles of their Summer Palace, and force on "The Middle Kingdom" massively humiliating treaties; the utterly crazy social history of the Taiping Rebellion; etc.

Third, as a student of language myself, is the academic fascination of the romanization of Chinese names. The author could not be expected to expand on the problems of the *pinyin* spelling, about which he tells us something, but it is quite clear that many Chinese names changed several times even after romanization; and he only peeps at the manifold complications in his list in Chapter 10. Some Chinese also appear deliberately to have changed their names to safeguard their families back home in consequence of the threatening vengeance after the Taiping rebellion. The morphology of Chinese names, differing in Guyana, Trinidad, Surinam and further still, in the original homeland, while being essentially identical, looks like a matter for both linguistic and family-clan study that may well be now beyond scholarly reach.

My fourth definite (but perhaps not really my last) interest in what Dr. Sue-A-Quan's work reveals is an insight into why Britain's meek and ceremonial return to Chinese rule of the island of Hong Kong, which was of no commercial and only nominal geographic value when a British warship seized it in 1842, was so "sweet" to China's pride in 1997.

Cane Reapers is small enough a book to encourage reading in today's busy world, but its great value lies in easy reading in which a factual, scholarly and historical narrative of a people whose peaceful and hard-working character is sorely missed in the country they have largely left and which could have benefited so much from just such citizens today.

Richard Allsopp, Ph.D., Dip.Ed.
Former Acting Principal, Queen's College, Georgetown, Guyana.
Reader in Linguistics and English Language, University of the West Indies, Cave Hill, Barbados.
Director, Caribbean Lexicography Project - UWI, Cave Hill, Barbados.

INTRODUCTION

There are two kinds of historical writing on the Chinese in the West Indies. One is primarily concerned with the broad development of the larger society, and seeks to integrate the Chinese experience into the larger picture with varying degrees of comprehensiveness and complexity. The other is an old trend, increasing over the past ten years: the writing of the history of the Chinese in the English-speaking Caribbean by members of that community itself. The best examples of the former trend can be found in the works of K.O. Laurence, Brian Moore, and Donald Wood. Trev Sue-A-Quan's book, CANE REAPERS, belongs to the second trend. Starting over the past ten years with Marlene Kwok Crawford, and followed in quick succession by Margery Kirkpatrick, Laura Hall and Walton Look Lai, members of the Chinese community have been demonstrating their interest in their roots and publishing interesting new materials. Not all of these writers are trained historians, but the depth of their insights have come from intimate first hand knowledge of the community as well as meticulous historical and family research. They have in the process contributed to furthering knowledge about this small community in this small region of the Western Hemisphere (and world).

Each writer has brought special strengths to his/her research. The most obvious strengths of Trev Sue-A-Quan's research has been his thorough examination of a primary source relatively neglected to date, the records of the British Guiana newspaper, the ROYAL GAZETTE, during the relevant years. The text comes alive with the names of many hitherto forgotten immigrants with their multitude of problems and experiences under the indenture system. The detailed commentaries on the arrival of the individual immigrant ships also make this source a mine of information. Equally important has been the author's knowledge of mainland Chinese history and culture, which has enriched the insights not only into the global aspects of the Chinese nineteenth century migrations, but also into micro-processes like the evolution of West Indian Chinese names. Chapter Ten, NAME CALLING, was for me one of the most entertaining and insightful sections of this research.

CANE REAPERS is a valuable addition to the new literature on Caribbean Chinese communities, and should find its place on all library bookshelves which are interested in this topic.

Walton Look Lai, History Department, University of the West Indies, St. Augustine, Trinidad & Tobago

Cane Reapers is the result of many years of careful research by Trev Sue-A-Quan. In the first third of the book the author narrates the complex historical conditions leading to the migration of the Chinese to Guyana from their homes in Southern China. This was one of many migrations by Chinese but it is one that has had little attention in the past, often being subsumed into the larger and more infamous migration to Cuba. At the time however, the issue of migration to the British West Indies was one that engaged the attention of British and Chinese diplomats and politicians at the highest levels. The majority of the book focuses on the fortunes of the Chinese in their newfound homeland in Guyana, from the indentureship of the first generation to the assimilation of later generations into the Creole middle class. The author makes extensive use of contemporary accounts of the Chinese that appeared in newspapers of the day and which are reproduced here for the first time. The last chapter on Chinese Guyanese surnames shows the way that changing names reflect changing identities.

Cane Reapers will be of interest to scholars interested in the Chinese Diaspora, the Caribbean and issues of migration. Students of Guyanese social history will find it illuminates a fascinating corner of their history that has had little attention up to now. Finally, those Guyanese of Chinese descent will find much to interest, horrify and amuse them in the story of how their ancestors came to Guyana and how they fared once they got there.

Laura J. Hall, Ph.D.
Adjunct Lecturer in American Studies
University of California, Berkeley

CONTENTS

Foreword iii

Introduction vi

Preface xi

Chapter 1 Labour's Love Lost 1
☯ The end of slavery ☯ New immigrants ☯ Massa day done ☯ Trying to stay in the black ☯ Orientals from the East ☯ Orientals from the West

Chapter 2 China and the Barbarians 13
☯ 1834 for a start ☯ The opium trade ☯ The Napier fiasco ☯ Clampdown on opium ☯ Commissioner Lin takes charge ☯ Igniting the powder keg ☯ Expedition to Peiho ☯ The Ch'uan-Pi Convention ☯ Treaty of Nanking ☯ Postwar period ☯ Open Canton ☯ Treaty of Tientsin ☯ Taku repulse ☯ Conventions of Peking ☯ Taiping rebellion

Chapter 3 Chinese Take-Out 41
☯ Coming and going ☯ Coolies to go ☯ Crimping methods ☯ Initial experiences ☯ All at sea ☯ Death and disaster ☯ Cuba and Peru ☯ Regulating the coolie trade ☯ Convention on emigration ☯ Coolie trade at Macao

Chapter 4 Demerara Bound 69
☯ Visions in the hot sun ☯ First immigrants ☯ White's third encounter ☯ Second wave ☯ Pursuing Chinese women ☯ First ladies ☯ Emigration increases ☯ The season of 1861-62 ☯ Hincks becomes governor ☯ Revival 1864-66 ☯ Convention agreements ☯ Arrival of the Corona ☯ Free immigration ☯ The last shipment

Chapter 5 Working on the Plantation 123
☯ Making an impression ☯ Adjusting to local conditions ☯ Recruitment and distribution ☯ Odd men out ☯ Taking out the driver ☯ Work habits ☯ Slow boat to China

Chapter 6 A Walk in the Dark 143
☯ A word of caution ☯ Plantains ☯ Other dishes
☯ Murder ☯ Class conflict ☯ Mulling the motive ☯ Suicide
☯ Robbery ☯ Cream collar crime ☯ Opium ☯ Targets
☯ Innocents ☯ Going to court ☯ Respected citizens

Chapter 7 Becoming Creole 173
☯ The new environment ☯ Thought for food ☯ Health
☯ Family considerations ☯ Causes of death ☯ Recreation
☯ Opium and gambling ☯ In the eyes of the beholder
☯ Social interactions ☯ Christian influences ☯ Church building

Chapter 8 The Shepherd and Hopetown 209
☯ O. Tye Kim arrives ☯ A Chinese settlement proposed
☯ A town for Hope ☯ Flight of the shepherd ☯ Hopetown carries on ☯ The decline of Hopetown

Chapter 9 Going Further Afield 227
☯ Becoming free ☯ Sugar technologists ☯ Travels to Trinidad ☯ Sauntering to Surinam ☯ Sailing to St. Lucia
☯ The settlers ☯ Getting down to business ☯ Growing in Georgetown ☯ Blooming in Berbice ☯ Country shops
☯ Property purchases ☯ The second generation
☯ Gaining a higher education

Chapter 10 Name Calling 263
☯ Chinese characters ☯ Translation troubles ☯ Dash it all ☯ What-A-Name ☯ Anglicized names ☯ Lineages
☯ Name list ☯ Going international

Appendix 321

Bibliography 333

Illustrations on pages 112-122 and 296-320

PREFACE

For those of Chinese descent who have connections with Guyana through birth or ancestry, the story of our forefathers is generally believed to have the fabled beginning "Once upon a time . . ." and the usual ending ". . . and they lived happily ever after." It can be argued that this fairy-tale description is valid to some extent since our ancestors did indeed emigrate once upon a time from China to become field labourers in a distant land; in more recent times their descendants have, for the most part, become successful and prosperous and are skilled and talented people making valuable contributions in many countries all over the world. However, as with all stories, the part in the middle has many twists and turns and it is the nature of these painful and gainful experiences that is described here.

The presentation makes use of extensive quotes from published articles and news stories because it is felt that the language and flavor of the writings of those times are capable of conveying more fully the sense of the period as well as the prevailing attitudes and sentiments. As far as language is concerned the original documents contain words which are now considered in bad taste or outdated, including "Chinaman," the colonial name "British Guiana," and the old spelling "Peking." No attempt has been made to update these terms or to change them into phrases that are more politically correct today. It did not take much searching to find that these old stories have all the elements of a modern day movie script — crime, sex, racism, class conflict, bigotry, and religious bias, while spiced with violence, bad language, and nudity. However, the objective is not to present a sensational story but rather to take a realistic view of what actually took place, thereby gaining a better appreciation for what has been achieved over the generations.

How did this documentation all come about? Initially it began out of curiosity of my own family history, catalyzed by a copy of contract of indenture belonging to my great-grandfather dated

1873. The search was supposed to be one that would tie up the loose ends of a simple tale. It soon became evident that the story was much more complicated than it appeared at first glance. The contract of indenture itself aroused curiosity about the reasons why my great-grandfather left China, the nature of the selection process for emigrants, the voyage across the ocean, and the conditions encountered in a foreign environment. As answers were sought and understanding gained it was realized that there would be other descendants like myself who are unaware of this history and that they too might be interested in knowing about it.

The search has included an examination of books, periodicals, newspapers and letters. Some of these were microfilm copies of old documents, which were not in particularly good condition. There were missing issues, or the pages were torn, mutilated, or folded, so that sections could not be completely photographed, or were out of focus. Quotes from these articles have been clarified using editorial comments shown by square brackets [ ]. Many quotations have been taken from the *Royal Gazette*, the paper which generally reflected the views of the governing body of British Guiana. The editorials and commentaries in the *Gazette* naturally contained an upper-class slant representative of the plantation owners and colonial administrators with a preference for law and order, proper behavior, Christian ethics, formalities and protocol. There were more reports about promenade band concerts, fancy dress balls, newly published books and cricket matches than about the changing status of the immigrant Chinese. Even so, the articles and coverage of day-to-day activities provided a sufficient range of opinions to extract an overall perspective of the way events unfolded for the Chinese in British Guiana. At times the *Royal Gazette* took editorial swipes at other local newspapers — the *Colonist*, which spoke for the conservative and traditional estate owners, and the *Creole* which pressed for the needs of the labouring class and former slaves.

There are others who have written about the subject of Chinese immigration to British Guiana. The first was Cecil Clementi, who was Government Secretary for the colony and whose book *The Chinese in British Guiana*, published in 1915, goes into the details of the political manouvering and administrative efforts made to obtain Chinese labourers. His book is out of print but fortunately I was able to borrow a practically untouched copy lying dormant in the Beijing Library. Sometime after World War I a booklet was published by Frederick O. Low, magistrate, town councilor and second generation Chinese descendant, in which the Christian Chinese settlement in Hopetown, Demerara, is featured. In more recent times, Marlene Crawford, née Kwok, compiled a number of articles for her book *Scenes from the History of the Chinese in Guyana*, published in 1989, briefly describing the history of Chinese immigration and the associations that grew out of the need for later generations to pray, play and stay together as a viable community, along with highlight profiles of some individuals. Margery Kirkpatrick, née Ting-A-Kee, in her 1993 book *From the Middle Kingdom to the New World* presents a collection of stories about the experiences of some families and the influences of their Chinese ancestry upon their adaptation to Western society. Also in that year a study of Chinese and Indian migrants to the British West Indies was made by Walton Look Lai in *Indentured Labor, Caribbean Sugar*, focusing on the immigrants from India and China and their relationship to the sugar-based economy. In 1995, Laura Hall, in her dissertation for degree of Ph.D., discussed the role of religion on the Chinese community and the relatively smooth transition the immigrants had into becoming a welcomed part of the Creole society. A second book has been published by Walton Look Lai in 1998 entitled *The Chinese in the West Indies* which has many of the official documents and formal discussions of Chinese emigration to the Caribbean area. Various scholars of the Chinese diaspora have debated from a cultural or sociological point of view that the Chinese in Guyana are either different or similar to Overseas Chinese who have gone to other countries. All of these writings have been useful and help to present a meaningful perspective of the Chinese from Guyana.

In addition to the resource materials just described, I have been greatly assisted by Andrea Lee (née Lam) who spent many hours compiling family trees and gleaning information from the Public Records Office in London as well as from the archival records in Georgetown, Guyana. Information was also provided by Judy Fung in Florida who has developed an large genealogical database for her extended family, and Laura Hall in California whose research for her thesis has uncovered many useful documents concerning the immigrants from China as well as her own family history. There are many others with whom I have spoken or exchanged correspondence concerning family relationships. They themselves have gathered input from several others and the collected wealth of information has greatly enriched my understanding. The efforts of all these contributors are gratefully acknowledged. Even though they are not mentioned individually by name I hope that they can see themselves and their ancestors speaking through the words on these pages and share in the satisfaction that their story is being told.

Finally, the process of harvesting cane is correctly called "cutting cane" and the title chosen for the book, *Cane Reapers*, is a misnomer in the strictest sense. However, although the Chinese labourers were procured specifically to work with cane they did much more than the cutting. They planted roots for an immigrant society that would flourish in the new soil. The immense toil and hardship that our forefathers endured have produced the benefits that their descendants now reap.

Preface to the Second Edition

The first printing of *Cane Reapers* in 1999 has been favorably received by many people, from casual readers to scholars of Chinese studies. This response has prompted me to consider a second printing. In the intervening time, many archival records and family histories have been found or been made available to me. The newly acquired documentation has helped to clarify some uncertainties that were presented in the first edition, particularly in the origin and background of some families and their surnames. This second edition represents an upgrade of the historical information as well as an amplification of the knowledge currently available about the Chinese who immigrated to Guyana.

Preface to the Third Edition

In the third edition of *Cane Reapers* some additional accounts regarding family ancestries and biographies have been added.

CHAPTER 1

LABOUR'S LOVE LOST

THE END OF SLAVERY

In early 1853 three ships arrived in British Guiana carrying 647 Chinese passengers. This marked the beginning of an immigration program that came about not from the initiative of the Chinese but from changes that affected the European powers. The Europeans, particularly the British, had the latest military hardware and superior navies while China was weak and unable to resist their imperial incursions. They gained a foothold in China that grew into an established presence, and the Chinese people were drawn into the picture as unwitting participants in the affairs of the powerful foreigners.

The prevailing condition that affected the European nations was the aftereffects of the abolition of slavery. At the beginning of the nineteenth century, slavery had been an integral part of the economy of the European colonial powers for more than three centuries. Britain was a major player in the capture, transportation, trading, and utilization of slaves taken from West Africa to colonies in America and the West Indies. As with any profit-making venture, the operators of the slave trade used whatever means possible to maximize their financial returns. The transportation ships were modified so that every square foot of deck area was filled with slaves shackled shoulder to shoulder and head to foot in the holds of the vessels. The inhumane treatment and the inevitable high death rate were the most evident aspects of the slave trade and became the focus of a growing protest movement among religious and humanist groups in Europe and America, beginning in the last quarter of the 18th century. The protesters had an uphill battle because the mercantile interests did not welcome any curtailment to their profitable business. Furthermore these were the times when the merchant class and business entrepreneurs were gaining more and more clout in the political decisions of their respective nations.

It took a generation of persistence before the abolitionists were victorious in persuading the British government to pass a bill in 1807 to end the trading and transportation of slaves. It was following this that the realization surfaced that some thought should be given to obtaining an alternative source of manual labourers for the sugar plantations in the colonies. A committee of the House of Commons was "appointed to consider of the practicability and expediency of supplying our West Indian Colonies with free labourers from the East." On 12 June 1811 it reported:

> 1) that the Chinese Emigrants have uniformly conducted themselves with the greatest propriety and order, and have been peculiarly instrumental in promoting the improvement of those countries to which they have emigrated;
>
> 2) that such emigration, however, is contrary to the laws of China; although its existence to a great extent seems to imply that those laws are not strictly enforced.

The findings of the committee were not taken up at the time since the resident labourers in Britain's colonies were still a captive population in ample numbers. Besides, the monopoly held by the sugar barons in the West Indies did not generate much sympathy in the evolving economic climate of freer trade so that their concerns about a potential labour problem were not given much attention. In fact, attempts were made to obtain sugar from other places, including India, to challenge the West Indian sugar monopoly.

The labour situation took on a completely different complexion when slavery was finally abolished in the British West Indies in 1834. However, this did not take the form of an absolute declaration of freedom. In response to demands from the sugar plantation owners the British parliament granted compensation amounting to several million pounds sterling to slave owners in the colonies as well as a six-year transition period during which time the slaves would become apprentices to taking on the responsibilities of freedom while remaining bound to the tasks they were doing for hundreds of years. In effect the newly freed slaves would no longer be the property of the plantation owners but were still obligated to labour for them with the authority of the legal system to enforce their continued service. The apprenticeship period came to a premature end because of the reaction of both the former slaves and from public opinion in Britain when news reached the home country that the apprentices were still being ill-treated, just the same as before.

> It was to the slaves a happy day, that first day of August, 1834, and they everywhere evinced their gladness in song and dance, and in thanksgiving and prayer.
>
> But although they were no longer slaves, they were apprenticed labourers and subject to regular work. This they could not and would not understand. Everywhere complaints were heard of the unwillingness of the apprentices to perform their appointed work.
>
> In the county of Essequebo the alleged grievance of the apprentices took the form of open revolt. . . .
>
> It devolved upon Doctor McTurk to propose — against an almost overwhelming opposition, and for which, as well as for other substantial services to the Government of the Colony, he was deservedly knighted — that the termination of the non-praedial apprenticeship in 1838 should likewise end the praedial apprenticeship service, so that at that date slavery should be extinct in the colony of British Guiana.
>
> [*A Guianese Log Book*, excerpted in *Royal Gazette*, 28 Sep 1878]

New Immigrants

The labourers celebrated their complete freedom in 1838 by leaving the sugar estates in droves. They set up homes on the uncultivated fringes of the estates and soon villages sprang up on unused or abandoned land along the coastline as well as in the interior and on defunct estates, which were bought by collective pooling of funds. The resulting loss of manpower forced the plantation owners to make serious efforts to seek other sources of labour. Initially they looked towards acquiring surplus people from other colonies, for example, the Bahamas. These, however, were much too few in number to meet the demand. A shipload of labourers from India, who were termed "Coolies," was brought over in 1838 through a private venture, becoming the first arrivals from Asia. This source abruptly dried up when, in 1839, the British colonial administrators in India banned any further recruitment of their subjects following reports of alleged abuse. Several attempts were also made to recruit African immigrants on a contractual basis, but they failed to attract sufficient numbers

— a mere 32 traveled on the first boat chartered in 1843 and by 1845 a total of only 2,128 Africans had been induced to freely immigrate which resulted in an exorbitant drain on the coffers of British Guiana. All the while, the need for large numbers of plantation labourers became more urgent.

With this changed situation, great expectations were held by the planters in British Guiana that their call for more field workers would be heeded, but the Home Government was cautious to rush into any new scheme which might bear any similarities to the slave trade. In any case the lords in London, far removed from the scene, were undoubtedly puzzled why the plantation owners could not get the existing freedmen to work. The reality was that the vast majority of former slaves wanted to have nothing more to do with plantation labour and, because of the fertility of the land together with an abundance of fish and fruit, there was a sufficiency for their basic needs. Indeed, their withholding of labour represented a defiance of the authority and control that the estate proprietors previously held for so many generations. The planters had little alternative but to seek out workers from other lands. When famine struck the Portuguese island of Madeira in the early 1840s many of the inhabitants there accepted the offer to go to British Guiana to work as indentured labourers on the plantations. In subsequent years several thousand Portuguese from Madeira followed along, and they became a significant segment of the colony's population in terms of numbers and economic effect. But the main area of focus for labour recruitment became Asia, particularly India and, to a lesser extent, China. The Asian labourers amounted to several hundred thousand people.

The demand for additional manpower remained great over the years, caused on the one hand by a growing market for sugar and on the other hand by a significant attrition rate among the newer arrivals. In early 1864 the *Royal Gazette* fired off a gritty response to an accusation made in the *West Indian*, a Barbadian newspaper, which claimed that the climate of Barbados would have caused immigrants to fare much better than they did in British Guiana. Statistics indicated that 110,921 immigrants had arrived in British Guiana since 1835 but, according to the census of 1861, the total population was only 148,026. The editorial in the *Royal Gazette* provided an insight into the history and problems of immigration:

In what may be called the infancy of Immigration a miserable set of people were imported. The wretched Coolies were on the whole scarecrows, refusing, with few exceptions, to work and living either on alms or on the garbage and carrion collected from the streets and trenches. These people died of course, and would have died in Barbados as rapidly as here. There was no choice in their selection in India, and the consequence was that so long as the applicant were the human form, he was, forsooth, shipped off as an Immigrant for field labour in British Guiana. The arrangements on Ship board were also at that date far from being what they are in the present day, and therefore the people — such of them as deserved the name of labourers — were not landed in the same good condition as at present. The early Portuguese also were from their constitution and habits unfit for work as agricultural labourers here or elsewhere. Most of them, scantily clad, poorly fed — for they studied economy after their own fashion — and careless about their sleeping accommodations or pure air, suffered here as they would have suffered in any country than their own, and died in large numbers, not from any unhealthiness of the climate but from constitutional defects and neglect of the means requisite to promote their comforts, or even to preserve life.

It must not be forgotten that in respect to Immigration generally, the disproportion between the sexes is very great, particularly as regards Chinese, and that neither Chinese nor Coolies, except in very rare instances, ever mate with the other races in the Colony. As a necessary consequence the surplus males die out without progeny, and there cannot possibly be on the whole any material increase in the number of immigrants, exclusive of the consideration that a large proportion of infants and children die off. So also, as the List of Immigrants set down as having arrived here a great many are boys and girls, some perhaps only a few days old, and others only a few years, in calculating the number of immigrants these infants and children cannot fairly be taken into account.

Next, among the people brought here, even at the present day, notwithstanding the precautions taken to procure good labourers, many are persons who will not work, who will nurse a sore in order to have an excuse for shirking labour of any description, and who eventually die off through their own neglect. In addition to which, cases of a peculiar disease are rife among the immigrants, and especially the Coolies. Surely the death of an immigrant under such circumstances cannot possibly be ascribed to the unhealthiness of the climate, and these are drawbacks which the *West Indian* ignores. [*Royal Gazette*, 26 Jan 1864]

MASSA DAY DONE

Despite the great need for labourers, the resident population of former slaves could not be induced to work on the plantations. Two decades after the end of servitude the freedmen still had little interest in doing field labour on a regular basis. The situation was noted by Anthony Trollope in his book *The West Indies and the Spanish Main.* During a visit to British Guiana in 1859 he observed that the colony had a great potential for developing the sugar industry, if only there were sufficient manpower to work the cane fields. He directed some criticism at the Anti-Slavery Society in Britain for opposing the growing practice of introducing indentured labourers from Asia, which it was claimed would only lead to another form of slavery. Furthermore, the Anti-Slavery Society argued that the freed slaves needed some measure of protection from competition. Trollope commented:

> As it at present is, the competition having been established, and being now in existence to a certain small extent, these happy negro gentlemen will not work on average more than three days a week, nor for above six hours a day. I saw a gang of twelve negro girls in a cane-piece, lying idle on the ground, waiting to commence their week's labour. It was Tuesday morning. On the Monday they had of course not come near the field. On the morning of my visit they were lying with their hoes beside them, meditating whether or no they would measure out their work. The planter was with me, and they instantly attacked him. 'No, massa; we no workey; money no nuff,' said one. 'Four bits pay! no pay at all!' said another. 'Five bits, massa, and we gin morrow 'arly.' It is hardly necessary to say that the gentleman refused to bargain with them. 'They'll measure their work tomorrow,' said he; 'on Thursday they will begin, and on Friday they will finish for the week.' 'But will they not look elsewhere for other work?' I asked. 'Of course they will,' he said; 'occupy a whole day in looking for it; but others cannot pay better than I do, and the end will be as I tell you.' Poor young ladies! It will be cruel to subject them to the evil of competition in their labour.

In June 1861 William Lobschied, a missionary in China, whose role in recruiting several Chinese to emigrate is described in greater detail in a later chapter, visited British Guiana to gain first hand knowledge of the local conditions and the treatment the Chinese were receiving. He wrote a lengthy report to the governor in which he observed:

> Though the efforts of the Christians in this Country to raise the African and to place him on a level with the Europeans, have not been without fruit; they have not been able to inspire him with that spirit of emulation, which is so prominent a feature in the character of the Chinaman. . . . The Creole Laborer does at present nothing for the development of their immense resources of the Colony, and the heavy duty on the importation of provisions, necessarily falls much heavily on those who can least bear it. . . . The Creole laborer who offers his services whenever his inclinations prompt him, and who lives upon a few plantains and fish which he catches at his door, is not in the least affected by the location and being able to work on his own terms; he can within a few days, earn sufficient to respond to the calls of his fondness for a little display of gay dresser.

TRYING TO STAY IN THE BLACK

This scenario of inability to obtain sufficient workers from among the local residents persisted for many decades. Some sugar estates went insolvent and the remaining plantation owners racked their brains to find immigrants at a low cost so as to stay in the black. In 1860 the first batch of Chinese women were introduced, raising hope among the estate owners that they could establish a stable base of Chinese immigrant families. However, this development was not greeted with open arms by some people. In a letter to the editor of the *Royal Gazette*, dated 30 March 1860, it was suggested that a better labourer could be found in the United States:

> WANTED, A LEADER
>
> That the Colony is in want of immigrants there is no doubt; but the question of vital importance to the future interests is, What class of immigrants would attend most to its advancement? Will the thousands of Chinese who may be imported to our shores be of the same benefit as a similar or even lesser number of Africans? We think not and base our opinion on the following reasons:-
>
> Firstly, they are a nature that will not associate with the African or other nation, and although they have, by the requirements of the contract under which they arrive, to remain a certain time in the Colony, will, in most cases, be forced to return to their native land immediately after

> expiration of that time. Secondly, while here, they do not in any way improve the business of the Colony, save with their immediate service to the planter. . . . Now, in our opinion, the class of immigrants that are present suitable to our requirements are some of the thousands of African negroes who are at present in a state of starvation in the United States wandering about in search of a shelter to their heads. All our readers must be acquainted with the recent Harpers' Ferry Difficulties, better known as "The John Brown Insurrection," and they are doubtless aware that those difficulties have resulted in the expulsion of upwards of 200,000 negroes from the Southern States. . . .
>
> Now, what we propose is, that the Government should import some of those negroes, and ascertain whether or not they should be found more beneficial to the Colony, than the class of immigrants now arriving. We believe they would. They are used to hard work under the lash of a severe taskmaster in the Southern States, where the heat is as intense as it is here, and consequently would be found to work well on a plantation where the labor is similar to that they have been accustomed to. Again, they are of a nature that would spend more of their earnings among the mercantile community and thus improve the general business of the City. They speak our language, and would not require such trouble to instill the customs of the country into their minds, as is usually required when instructing a Chinaman. . . .

In addition to the thought of obtaining former slaves from the United States, the suggestion was put forward of obtaining the same from other Caribbean countries:

> Within two or three days of us lies the Island of Barbados, where the population is superabundant; a lengthened drought has prevailed, the sugar-crop being over there is little work to be done and money is scarce, while provisions are dear. . . . The passage money of a labourer from Barbados would not exceed $8 while a Chinaman costs $120; at this rate we can get 15 Barbadians for the same as we give for a single Celestial, and with this notable difference also, that while the latter requires to be inured to the climate, to be taught what he has to do, and is at times troublesome, the other is a dweller in a similar climate, is a ready-made cane planter, and has been always accustomed to laws very similar to those which prevail in this Colony. [*Royal Gazette*, 7 Aug 1860]

In response to the overtures from the plantation owners, a few thousand labourers migrated from Barbados to British Guiana. However, the dream of getting a flood of seasoned, hard-working,

English-speaking, culturally-adapted labourers from America was brought to a rude awakening by the sentiments held by the freed slaves:

> Happily to the credit of the Free States, it was found that scheme after scheme devised for this object was impracticable. The negro said, "No, Mr. Lincoln, this is my country; here I was born; my labour has contributed to its wealth; I have part in its misfortunes and I look forward to the time when I and my children shall share its prosperity; I decline to emigrate." [*Royal Gazette*, from *Daily News*, NY, 26 Dec 1863]

Orientals from the East

With the diminished prospect of attracting workers of African descent, the plantation owners had to rely primarily on the recruits from India. Being a British colony with an enormous population there were not many obstacles in obtaining large numbers of people and India became the source upon which the planters could always rely. Between 1838 and the end of the nineteenth century a total of 238,979 immigrants from India were introduced into British Guiana. The main concerns were whether they could be properly selected and would prove to be suitable agricultural workers. For these reasons the Chinese were regarded as the best of the bunch.

> If ever we are to be "developed" we certainly could not have better pioneers of commencing the process than the Chinese, nor is this idea of today. Mr. Henry Bolingbroke, who resided in the Colony for several years from 1799, and afterwards gave the world the benefit of his experiences in a quarto volume [Ed: "A voyage to the Demerary"], published in 1807, thus states his opinion on the subject. "Discoveries of what can be rendered useful, avail little without the human hands that are to turn the gifts of nature into a profit. The accounts given of the Chinese and the astonishing rapidity with which they have got up in Pulo Penang all parts of a complex and civilized society under British laws, and in a climate corresponding with that of Guyana, render it highly probable that Chinese colonists would form the most valuable accession to our present stock of labourers, which could be introduced. They have those habits of body which can bear the assertions of industry between the tropics, and they have those habits of artificial society which fit them for a variety of labours to which rude savages cannot be brought to attend. Above all,

they have a rational foresight and may be entrusted with the care of their own maintenance without danger of that ruinous improvidence, that careless alternation of intemperance and sloth that besets the African negro, when he is his own master. It is said that the Chinese will stay but never settle in a strange land, and that when they have earned a little money they go home to live upon it; but if they should not generally prove to be settlers, their labour will still have prepared fields and created houses for the use of their successors, and they will become the teachers of a multiplicity of those arts and habits which a long experience of hot climates has materialized among the Orientals. *Guyana is adapted to become the China of the West*, and may best be instructed by the nation which ought especially to be its mode."

These remarks appear to have been made almost in the spirit of prophecy, and are the words of one who evidently looked far ahead of the times in which he lived. [*Royal Gazette*, 2 Feb 1865]

ORIENTALS FROM THE WEST

It was because of opinions of this kind that the British Guiana plantation owners sought to pursue whatever opportunity they had to secure Chinese labourers from any source. In 1876 anti-Chinese feelings among the white population in California reached an extreme level that resulted in the introduction of laws restricting the introduction of more Chinese. The British Guiana Planters' Association held a meeting on the 29 May 1876 and passed the following resolution:

That this Association, being deeply impresses with the importance of Immigration as an element for securing the present and permanent prosperity of this colony, and having been informed of the difficulties that have lately arisen whereby the previous steady flow of Chinese into California is likely to be interrupted; and considering that there is hereby presented an opportunity for opening up a stream of Emigration from China to British Guiana, the effects of which may be of the utmost importance to the extension and well-doing of the colony in time to come, would respectfully suggest to your Excellency and Honorable Court, that the necessary communication be opened up with any European House of recognized stability who shall be prepared within six months to land in this colony a number of Chinese, not exceeding two thousand at a cost not exceeding £18 (eighteen pounds) per caput.

(Signed) Henry S. Bascom
Chairman. [*Royal Gazette*, 1 Jun 1876]

The planters were even prepared to dispatch a representative to California to see whether any disgruntled Chinese could be induced to emigrate to British Guiana, and to set up appropriate mechanisms for their deliverance. However, nothing came of this plan since the Chinese who were bent on emigrating to San Francisco, known in the Chinese language as Old Gold Mountain, could not be persuaded to change their dream and destination to undertake an agricultural existence in a little known country. Those already in America were similarly unimpressed by the prospects awaiting them on the plantations and preferred to see the hardships through in their own way.

A couple years later another opportunity arose when the Cuban government introduced some restrictive penalties. The Chinese there were being forced to re-sign for another term of indenture or be expelled. Knowing that most of the Chinese would have little means of gathering sufficient funds to escape the island the authorities in British Guiana began diplomatic overtures to try to obtain these Chinese at the estimated bargain price of £5 per person. Even if it "were £7 or £8, it would still be a very good deal under the cost of passage from China . . ." This venture also did not prove fruitful since the Cuban government most likely introduced appropriate measures to retain their Chinese labourers.

Because of these failures, the sugar barons could count on China as the only viable source of Chinese workers. By the time the era of immigration of Chinese indentured labourers ended in 1879 more than 13,000 Chinese had been transported to British Guiana from China and they became the nucleus of the Chinese community there.

The British interest in Chinese workers did not end there. In 1882 the suggestion was put forth that Chinese immigrants should be induced to go to Britain to work in sundry labour-intensive jobs. This resulted in British workers raising objections to the concept of a growing number of Chinese in their midst in England and prompted a representative for the West Indies, based in Britain, to lament that the West Indies was not being considered a desired destination by Chinese emigrants:

> John Chinaman is an interesting subject of public discussion in England at the present moment. Speculations are rife as to his value as a factor in our social system. As a merchant he is here already, competing with his European rivals. There is an exclusively Chinese firm in the City of London, keeping up the distinctive dress and all native characteristics. The Chinese clerks of this firm are such familiar objects in the streets that they attract no attention. A proposition has been made to introduce Chinese as artisans, labourers, and domestic servants, and the working men of England hold meetings to indignantly protest. Now, it is astonishing how many friends the Chinaman has in his country. The testimony to his good qualities comes from so many people as to be practically unanimous; and, curiously enough, it is not because of his vices that the working men fear his advent, but because of his virtues. He can work better and longer than they can; he can live more economically; he can be more civil and devoted to the interests of his employers. Therefore, shut him out! Now, all this discussion and interest ought to have an important bearing upon the question of introducing Chinese into the West India colonies. In Demerara they form an eminently practical and prosperous community. Even at the present time, and it seems strange if, excluded from the United States really by the political influence of the Irish vote, and from Australia by the fear of their competition in the labour market, and objected to by the working classes of England, they could not be induced to go to the West Indies, where they would be appreciated. . . . [*Royal Gazette*, 21 Oct 1882]

Clearly the British regarded the Chinese as valuable because of their ability to work hard, not in the heart of Britain, but in the remote colonies. This British fascination with the Chinese labourers had all along been the underlying motive behind the eagerness to procure Chinese to work on the sugar plantations. Once the motivation was in place, Britain was able to obtain the Chinese indentured labourers for British Guiana because of her position as the dominant superpower of the time.

CHAPTER 2

CHINA AND THE BARBARIANS

1834 FOR A START

In 1834 the 52-year-old emperor Tao Kuang of the Qing (Ch'ing) dynasty began the 13th year of his reign and it proved to be not a particularly lucky one for him. The Middle Kingdom, as China is termed in her own language, was considerably bothered by ever growing pressure from other nations clamoring for more trade and trading rights. For centuries the Chinese mandarins had regarded China to be the centre of civilization — cultured, organized and self-sufficient, with no need for any goods from abroad. Furthermore, merchants were regarded as belonging to the lowest level in the social order, beneath scholars, farmers, and workers, because the act of trading did not produce any new items of value and thus added nothing to the collective wealth of the nation. The foreigners were certainly living up to the title of "barbarians" and "foreign devils." These were the names the Chinese called them ever since Portuguese and Dutch seafaring pirates and adventurers first arrived in the 16th century and began pillaging the coastal villages, carrying off valuables and women and leaving death and destruction in their wake.

Trade was not regarded as a right but rather a privilege that could be denied by China if the barbarians did not display appropriate deference to the imperial throne. For many generations China exported tea, silk, chinaware, and spices and was paid in silver bullion. This caused a huge drain on the coffers of the foreign powers. But then the barbarians were able to find a product, which the Chinese began to consume in ever increasing amounts and which tipped the balance in favor of the foreigners, leaving China with a sharply escalating foreign trade deficit. That product was opium.

THE OPIUM TRADE

The opium trade evolved mainly from the initiative of the East India Company, a private British firm, which held a monopoly on the production and sale of opium in Bengal, India. The benefits of opium as a drug were long known in China but the foreigners introduced a novel use, which was to put it in a pipe and smoke it for pleasure. Opium addiction caused such harm to the people that, as early as 1799, China had issued an imperial decree prohibiting its importation. However, the incentive of profit was much more powerful than the penalties of prohibition.

The mode of operation of the East India Company was to grant charters or licences to locally-based British or Parsee merchants who operated private trading ships which were classified as "Country ships" rather than "Company ships." The honorable company could thereby claim that the shipment of opium was not a company policy. Initially, the captain and officers of the trading ships were allowed to use about 15% of the cargo allotment for personal goods. This allotment was used up in transporting opium and it grew considerably over the years until the amount of contraband greatly exceeded the trade in legal goods.

A trading procedure evolved which provided convenience for the many participants in the drug operations. The trading ships would first head for the opium depots moored at Lintin Island at the mouth of the Pearl River. These were out-of-service and worn-out merchant vessels and warships, which were resurrected by the barbarian traders and transformed into floating warehouses. By 1834 there were five such opium depots lying within easy reach of Canton, the only city in China permitted to engage in foreign trade. The traders would unload the opium chests at Lintin and then proceed to Canton to engage in authorized trade. Located 20 miles north-east of Macao, the hulks at Lintin were conveniently within range of the foreigners' gunboats prowling off the China coast, thus providing safety from any challenge by the Chinese authorities. The chests, each weighing about 160 pounds and containing 40 balls of opium pressed into spheres the size of tennis balls, were conveyed to Canton by "fast crabs" or "scrambling dragons." Heavily armed and propelled by up to 50 oarsmen, these vessels were able to outrun the patrolling mandarin junks.

There was a formalized procedure for conducting business transactions with foreigners. Peking gave the authority for Hongs, or commercial trading firms, to act as the sole intermediaries in conducting trade with foreigners, and was handsomely rewarded with tributes amounting to some 200,000 taels, or £55,000. The hong merchants were involved in a high-risk operation. Some of them went bankrupt, but there were others who were able to accumulate enormous wealth, such being the case with Pankhequa, Mowqua, and Howqua.[1]

The hong merchants conduced trade through "factories" or agencies which were warehouse-like buildings occupying a 21-acre riverfront site (rented from the hong merchants) located just outside the walls of Canton. The American, Belgian, British, Danish, Dutch, French, Spanish, Swedish, and other miscellaneous factories were commonly called the "Barbarian Houses." The trading season lasted about four months, from October to January, to take advantage of the monsoon winds, and the foreign ships were required to leave Canton immediately after their cargoes were loaded. However, the payment of an appropriate consideration to the "proper persons" could always gain an extension allowing the foreigners to remain in Canton after the trading season. Such bribery was only too common in China and was the key to clearing the official barriers that prohibited opium importation. The hong merchants took care of the Hoppo (customs superintendent), customs examiners and local officials, all of whom profited handsomely from the opium trade. Customs services were also provided by entrepreneurs who, after remitting appropriate business fees and customs duties to the court in Peking, were left with ample room for dealings under the tea-table. By 1834 some 20,000 chests of opium were entering China annually, and about a third was handled by one British firm — Jardine, Matheson and Company.

William Jardine began his opium trading operations in 1816 when he was 32 years of age and in 1828 he formed a partnership with another Scotsman, James Matheson, who was 12 years younger. By 1834 Jardine, Matheson owned a fleet of trading clippers as well as one of the five trans-shipment vessels at Lintin. Jardine was convinced that his own moral integrity was beyond reproach when both the "House of Lords and Commons

1 The suffix "qua" originates from "kuan" meaning official, a title which was allowed by the imperial court in acknowledgement of the contributions received.

with all the bench of bishops at their back" were not taking any action to curb opium trading. He furthermore defended the role of the opium traders by proclaiming that:

> It is the Chinese Government, it is the Chinese officers who smuggle, and who connive at and encourage smuggling; not we: and then look at the East India Company — why, the father of all smuggling and smugglers is the East India Company.

In April 1834, the charter of the East India Company expired and the British government assumed control for trade with China. By this time tea drinking had become a national trait in the British Isles and the government derived a tenth of its revenues from the tax on tea. Furthermore, the opium growers in India were paying hard cash to buy cotton fabrics, produced in mills powered by steam engines of the industrial revolution. The British government saw few other feasible options but to continue with opium trading in order to maintain the national economy and a favorable trade balance. A profitable trading triangle flourished, in which finished goods were shipped from Britain to India, opium from India to China, and tea and spices to Britain, with the British merchants reaping the greatest benefits. In autumn 1834 Britain passed the Free Trade Act, which broke the monopolies of the large companies and permitted individual merchants to trade at will. As a result, British shipping in the Pearl River leading to Canton increased sharply.

THE NAPIER FIASCO

In mid-1834 Britain's Chief Superintendent of Trade, Lord Napier, was sent to China with the intent to establish formal trading relations on an equal basis. He arrived in Macao on 15 July during the off-trading period bearing a letter from Lord Palmerston, the British Foreign Secretary, for delivery to the Chinese viceroy at Canton. Instead of following standard protocol and exercising patience, as advised by the merchants and local Chinese authorities, he insisted in executing his instructions to the letter. He failed to apply for a "Red Permit," the pass granting permission to sail upriver to Canton. His movements were duly noted in the daily report of the Hoppo:

> In examining, we perceived during the night of the 18th of the present moon [24 July], about midnight, the arrival of a barbarian ship's boat at Canton, bringing four English devils, who went into the English factories to reside. After having searched and examined, we could find no permit or pass; and having heard by report, that there is at present a Ship of War of the said nation anchored in the outer sea, but not having been able to learn for what purpose, we think that such coming as this is manifestly a clandestine stealing into Canton. . . .

Lord Napier sent his secretary to hand over the letter at the city gate but this broke with the normal practice of making a submission through the hong merchants and awaiting the mandate of the emperor. The fact of the matter was that established bureaucratic procedures and formalities were simply not followed. The Chinese viceroy ordered Napier to leave Canton and imposed a partial blockade on trade. Napier not only remained, but tried to appeal directly to the local Cantonese. He gave instructions for notices to be posted which lamented the fate of "the thousands of industrious Chinese who must suffer ruin and discomfort through the perversity of their government." Viceroy Lu K'un was definitely not amused and countered with some straight language:

> We do not know how such a barbarian dog can have the audacity to call himself an Eye (an official). It is a capital offence to incite the people against their rulers, and we would be justified in obtaining a mandate for his decapitation.

On 2 September, the viceroy tightened the screws:

> The Barbarian Eye . . . is indeed stupid, blinded, ignorant . . . there can be no quiet while he remains here. I therefore formally close the trade until he goes.

Lord Napier, a retired naval officer who had seen action at the Battle of Trafalgar, was not to be cowed by this not too subtle eviction notice. He now ordered the two available frigates, HMS *Imogene* and HMS *Andromache,* to sail to Canton. Foreign warships were strictly prohibited from going that far upriver. To be on the safe side, Napier gave instructions that, if fired upon, the frigates were to return fire. On 7 September as the frigates approached the Bogue, a narrowing of the river some 40 miles from Canton, the batteries on the protecting forts opened fire.

However, their cannons were fixed on solid masonry cradles and were unable to inflict great damage on the moving targets. The frigates, mounting 46 swiveling guns between them, pounded away at the forts until they were silenced. The British ships then tied up at Whampoa, the Canton dock facilities 10 miles down the river from the city proper, being too heavy to reach the site of the Factories.

Viceroy Lu K'un cut off all supplies to the Factories, had heavy chains drawn across the river, and threatened to launch fire-rafts against the wooden frigates, which were loaded with gunpowder and ammunition. The British were prisoners. Meanwhile, the merchants were by this time disenchanted with the Superintendent of Trade, and began to wonder why a free trade needed superintending. Some of the opium dealers, led by Lancelot Dent, who was Jardine, Matheson's chief competitor, expressed their discontent and tried to petition the Hoppo to resume trading. Lord Napier thought he could deal with just about anything the Chinese could throw at him, but he was wounded by what he felt was a betrayal by his countrymen. Viceroy Lu proceeded to rub salt into the wound by declaring that he would let normal trading activities resume once Napier and his warships removed themselves from the scene.

The tense situation came to a conclusion when Lord Napier was advised by his doctor to return to Macao for medical treatment. The viceroy seized on the opportunity to teach the barbarian an unforgettable lesson. His lordship must first give an order for his warships to depart before he would be issued a red permit to leave for Macao. Furthermore, he would have to be escorted in a Chinese boat, courtesy of the viceroy. No other way. So, surrounded by a boisterous crowd who banged gongs, clashed cymbals and fired off firecrackers and muskets, the sick peer was conveyed to Macao under military escort. With extended stops at intermediate posts, the 88-mile trip took almost a week, and at each stopover the cacophony created by the over-zealous Chinese caused his condition to worsen. From his sickbed in Macao, he asked that the ringing of church bells be stopped since the pealing was too much for him to take. The Portuguese complied with his request on 11 October, and that night he died in silence.

The failure of the Napier mission was the result of cultural misconceptions and misunderstandings. Imperial China still regarded foreign countries as tributary nations and uncivilized, little realizing that it had already become a significant part of the international trading market through these very barbarians. The Chinese could not conceive that an official would be assigned to such a trivial matter as trade.

They were expecting a taipan — a head merchant, or chief executive officer — and not someone demanding to be treated as an Eye. China had not encountered so unreasonable a nation as the British who flouted court regulations, refused to kowtow and offered trash as tributes (telescopes, globes, etc.) The Napier fiasco now deceived them into thinking that insistence on conformity to their traditional methods had been the key to success.

As for the foreigners, they saw much to gain if China's population and huge market potential could be successfully exploited. Merchants had attained the pinnacle of respect in Western society, and their word had much political clout. They could not understand how China could reject the material and monetary rewards brought by trade, and be so downright picky about bureaucratic niceties. What they were seeking was to establish an intercourse between officials of each nation on the basis of equality so as to facilitate trade. Britain had not encountered so unreasonable a nation as the Chinese in all their years of building a British Empire on which the sun never set.

It was as if China and Britain were playing at trade as if it were a game of checkers using imperial rules. China's approach to the game was "you play by imperial rules or you don't play at all," whereas Britain's was "you play by imperial rules or I'll smash your face." The further problem was that for China, "imperial" was interpreted as "meeting the needs of the emperor;" for Britain it meant "meeting the needs of the Empire."

CLAMPDOWN ON OPIUM

Trade at Canton resumed in accordance with old Chinese procedures. Britain dispatched Captain Charles Elliot as the new Superintendent of Trade in June 1836. Elliot had previously been appointed Protector of Slaves in British Guiana at a time when slave trading was abolished but slavery in the colonies was still practiced. His devotion to duty caused him to be greatly disliked by the plantation owners. His duty was now to see that British trading practices become a matter of policy in China. As a matter of practical course, Elliot realized that confrontation would not be productive and that acceptance of the Chinese ways would at least allow trade to continue. As a result he appeared to the Chinese to be a decent chap who had apparently learned from his predecessor's errors.

The Chinese government was still determined to get rid of the opium problem and in 1837 adopted a hard-line approach of complete suppression. The Chinese officials did not have the military capability to budge the hulks at Lintin, now numbering 25, and instead went after the Chinese-owned opium carriers, destroying practically all of them. However, the cunning barbarians quickly took their place using faster and heavily armed boats flying the British and American flags.

COMMISSIONER LIN TAKES CHARGE

On 10 March 1839 Commissioner Lin Tse-hsu arrived in Canton to take up his new appointment. A new imperial edict was proclaimed which called for severe punishment of everyone involved in the opium trade under which even foreigners were liable to be beheaded. Lin charged the hong merchants with conniving in the opium trade and declared that all the opium in the depot ships had to be surrendered. The foreigners held a tactical meeting and decided to offer up 1,036 chests of opium. Commissioner Lin responded by ordering that trading be terminated immediately, all Chinese servants and workers withdrawn, and the whole trading area blockaded. The Factories became a prison for the 350 or so foreigners.

Elliot ruled out any attempt at armed rescue, which could easily have resulted in the massacre of the foreigners at Canton. In light of the sharp drop in opium prices, oversupply of opium stocks, and threat of losing the tea trade, he ordered that all the opium that British traders had on hand be turned over to him. He vouched responsibility on behalf of the government, giving a guarantee that the traders would be indemnified later. With such assurance of compensation, the merchants were only too pleased to turn over the opium, which had been piling up unsold on the warehouse ships. In fact, they were even generous enough to offer up chests that they knew were soon to arrive. By Elliot's decree the opium became the property of the British government. Matheson wrote in separate letters that "the Chinese have fallen to the snare of rendering themselves directly liable to the Crown," and, "to a close observer, it would seem the whole of Elliot's career were expressly designed to lead on the Chinese to commit themselves, and produce a collision."

A total of 21,306 chests of opium were turned over. Lin had the opium dumped into specially dug trenches to which were added lime, salt and water. Lin composed a prayer to the God of the Sea, advising all marine creatures to seek refuge when the fetid, noxious sludge was discharged into the ocean.

Having completely destroyed all the opium he could obtain, Commissioner Lin issued a follow-up decree requiring all captains to sign a bond declaring that no opium was on board, with the penalty of death and the seizure of goods for violation of the bond. Elliot claimed that the bond was "incompatible with the laws of England," and the British traders supported him. Rather than accept, they all packed up and left for Macao on 24 May 1839. The tea drinkers in Britain now became indebted to the American shippers who managed to pick up the slack created by the absence of British vessels. The American captains were only too pleased to help out in this trying situation since, in true enterprising fashion, they were able to add service charges which made the cost of shipping tea for the 50-mile jaunt between Whampoa and Lintin even greater than it formerly was for shipping it across the ocean to the Boston tea parties.

Elliot considered running British trade for the time being out of Macao, but he had no war ships to safeguard his actions. Commissioner Lin was now left with the problems of duties lost for not using Whampoa as well as inability to control opium trading in Macao. He decided to flush the British out of there as well. Then on 7 June, a privately owned merchantman, *Cambridge* (1,080 tons), sailed into Macao. Her captain, James Douglas, was in Singapore when he learnt of Commissioner Lin's unique trench warfare. Going on a hunch as to the changing needs of the time, he disposed of his cargo of opium at a loss and loaded up with several high-powered cannons. Together with her normal complement of six 18-pound cannons, the *Cambridge* was a floating fortress and Elliot seized the opportunity to boost the British armed presence by renting *Cambridge* for eight months at a fee of £14,000. The presence of the *Cambridge* alone was sufficient to keep Admiral Kuan's war junks from interfering with the trans-shipment of goods from the American ships, which were rocking in sympathy and rolling in dough. Admiral Kuan watched their movements from a nearby anchorage.

IGNITING THE POWDER KEG

Commissioner Lin cut off supplies and food to the British and directed the governor of Macao to expel the British. Lin then assembled 2,000 troops at Hsiang Shan, 40 miles north of Macao. The governor was caught in a dilemma and the threat to the Portuguese presence in Macao was obvious. The Chinese had never conceded that Macao was a Portuguese colony, only that is was under Portuguese occupation. Rumors were in the air about a possible attack and the governor of Macao, not wanting to upset his own boat, sent a confidential message to warn the British that the Chinese were coming to arrest all British subjects. The committee appointed to look after the Brits in Macao made the decision to evacuate Macao. On 26 August 1839, British subjects embarked on all available vessels and headed for a small, barely inhabited island on the other side of the river mouth, which was known by the name "Hong Kong."

By September, Elliott was buoyed by the arrival of HMS *Volage* (28 guns) and HMS *Hyacinth* (18) and he terminated his agreement with Captain James Douglas for the protection provided by the *Cambridge.* The captain was peeved to end up with only £2,100 for two and a half months of service, and proceeded to strip the guns from *Cambridge,* selling them off to the British authorities. The ship was then sold to the American firm of Delano for £10,700, renamed *Chesapeake* and resold early in the new year to Commissioner Lin. The Chinese now possessed one fighting ship of the barbarian kind.

So far Commissioner Lin was victorious in every encounter with the barbarians. He still wanted to promote legitimate trade and when Captain Warner of the *Thomas Coutts,* deciding that Elliot had no authority to impose restrictions, signed Lin's anti-opium bond on 15 October, the commissioner invited the idle ships at Hong Kong to follow suit. He issued an ultimatum to those that did not comply to leave the China Sea within three days or else face destruction. Elliot himself faced the double trouble of an impending Chinese attack and the possibility of more traders capitulating to Lin's terms. On 3 November 1839 about 29 war junks dropped anchor within 500 yards from the HMS *Volage* and *Hyacinth.* The action was precipitated by the *Royal Saxon*, which had accepted Lin's bond and was sailing to Canton. Captain H. Smith fired a shot across her bow to stop her, whereupon the Chinese intervened on the *Royal Saxon*'s behalf. Smith then gave the signal to attack. In the ensuing Battle of Ch'uan-pi, which lasted for three quarters of an hour, one junk was blown up outright, three sunk and several damaged seriously. The Sino-British Opium War had broken out.

Commissioner Lin wrote twice to Queen Victoria (who had ascended to the throne in mid-1837) to seek her intercession. His second letter stated:

> There appear among the crowd of barbarians both good persons and bad, unevenly. Consequently, there are those who smuggle opium to seduce the Chinese people and so cause the spread of the poison to all provinces. . . . The wealth of China is used to profit the barbarians. . . . I have heard that the smoking of opium is very strictly forbidden by your country.[2] . . . Why do you let it be passed on to the harm of other countries? Suppose there were people from another country who carried opium for sale to England and seduced your people into buying and smoking it; certainly your honourable ruler would deeply hate it and be bitterly aroused. . . . Naturally you would not wish to give unto others what you yourself do not want.

The letter was carried by Captain Warner of the *Thomas Coutts* in January 1840, but the Foreign Office refused to recognize Warner. The fact of the matter was that established bureaucratic procedures and formalities were simply not followed. In any case, the pleas of Commissioner Lin would have gone unheeded because it had become a matter of self-interest for Britain to maintain the opium business to generate tax revenues and to uphold her position as a superpower in trade and military prowess.

---

2 Lin was misinformed on this point. Opium use was not illegal in Britain, but the British knew better than to let opium addiction take hold.

EXPEDITION TO PEIHO

In preparation for the next encounter, Commissioner Lin fortified Canton and blocked the river with huge chains. He assembled a fleet of about sixty war junks, and obtained two hundred modern cannons bought from abroad. The recently purchased *Chesapeake* was moored in the Pearl River to reinforce a blockade of rafts and sunken stone barges, which protected the approaches to Canton. *Chesapeake* was armed with thirty-four English-made guns bought in Singapore. Lin then waited.

In June 1840 Rear Admiral George Elliot (a cousin of Trade Superintendent Captain Charles Elliot) arrived with sixteen warships carrying 540 guns and troop carriers with 3,600 Scottish, Irish and Indian soldiers. The British viewed the impending war as one of reprisal which was necessary to defend trading rights, uphold national honor, and atone for the unjust treatment incurred by British subjects and property in China. From the Chinese viewpoint, they were merely implementing the edict to eliminate the evils of opium.

Captain Elliot's orders from Whitehall were to use only sufficient forces to blockade Canton and to sail north to present British grievances to the emperor. These orders were remarkably similar to the recommendations in the "paper of hints" that William Jardine had offered to Palmerston. It was felt that the score should be settled with the Chinese government and not the Chinese people in the South who welcomed the opium trade and may even hold resentful feelings towards the Manchu rulers. On their journey north the Elliots blockaded Amoy after their attempt to deliver a letter addressed to the emperor from Palmerston was rebuffed. They then took Tinghai on Chusan Island, near the mouth of the Yangtze River, leaving the main body of troops in occupation. There, the opium traders, following in the wake of the British armada, offered their goods at the wonderfully low introductory price of $100 a chest. The expeditionary force reached Peiho (the river leading to Peking) on 29 August 1840. At Taku, the letter was at last accepted by Ch'i-shan (Kishen), governor-general of Chihli[3] province.

---

3 Chihli's main cities included Peking. Boundaries have since been redrawn and what was Chihli is now part of Hebei Province.

THE CH'UAN-PI CONVENTION

Governor-general Ch'i-shan, who was responsible for the defense of Peking, stalled for time to find a way to appease the barbarians. He interpreted Palmerston's letter to be basically a list of grievances suffered by the British after Commissioner Lin had taken office. Ch'i-shan was able to persuade the emperor that the sole cause of the English anger was Lin himself, and that they were seeking his dismissal. Ch'i-shan's forte was to employ conciliatory tactics to soothe the barbarians into submission. Using courtesy, respect and abundant flattery he explained to the British that the emperor had decided to dispatch a high official to Canton to learn the truth and engage in a dialogue. Encouraged by the prospect of a negotiated settlement and having concerns about being able to sustain any substantial military operations with the approach of winter the Elliots departed for Canton on 15 September 1840. Without firing a shot Ch'i-shan had rid north China of the barbarian presence. The emperor was indeed impressed with the way Ch'i-shan resolved this difficulty, and dismissed Commissioner Lin Tse-hsu in disgrace for being unable to eliminate the opium traffic and for stirring up trouble with the barbarians. Lin was exiled to Sinkiang (Xinjiang) in the remote regions of northwest China and Ch'i-shan appointed the new Imperial Commissioner.

In December 1840 Captain Elliot and Commissioner Ch'i-shan commenced negotiations in Canton. Elliot started off with three major demands, one of which, the cession of Hong Kong, was a condition that Ch'i-shan could not accept since he knew very well that the imperial court would not approve the carving up of China. He stalled for time and negotiations were broken off several times. Elliot grew impatient and, on 7 January 1841 attacked the forts at Ch'uan-pi, near the Bogue. After a softening-up bombardment by the naval guns, the assault party went in, slaughtering some 600 Chinese troops in the process. On 20 January 1841 Elliot forced Ch'i-shan to agree to draft the "Ch'uan-pi Convention," by which (1) Hong Kong would be ceded to Britain and the Chusan Islands returned to China; (2) an indemnity of $6 million would be paid for the confiscated opium; (3) direct, equal intercourse between the officials of the two countries would be established; and (4) Canton reopened to trade within ten days of the Chinese New Year.

Elliot felt that the acquisition of Hong Kong would provide distinct trading advantages for Britain, and he gave the opinion that there was "not a nobler Harbor, nor a more valuable position, in every point of view, in the Queen's Possessions." On 23 January he wrote another letter, advising that "Hong Kong, my Lord, will soon be one of the most important possessions of the British Crown. Of that result I am well convinced."

The reaction of the British government, however, was not what the man-on-the-spot expected. Palmerston was displeased with the negotiated terms. On 21 April 1841 he spared no mercy in delivering his reprimand to Elliot:

> You have disobeyed and neglected your Instructions; you have deliberately abstained from employing as you might have done, the Force placed at your disposal, and you have without sufficient necessity accepted Terms which fell far short of those which you were instructed to obtain. . . . Throughout the whole course of your proceedings, you seemed to have considered that my instructions were waste paper . . . and that you were at full liberty to deal with the interests of your country according to your own fancy. . . . [You have accepted] a sum much smaller than the amount due. . . . You have agreed to evacuate the [Chusan] Island immediately. . . .You have obtained the cession of Hong Kong, a barren island with hardly a house upon it; and even this cession as it is called, seems to me, [without the Emperor's signature] . . . to be a permission to us to make a settlement there, upon the same footing on which the Portuguese have an establishment at Macao.

Ch'i-shan and Captain Elliot, in the meanwhile, continued to bravely act out their roles on the public stage, unaware of the manner that they were destined to be cast aside. When Ch'i-shan, in his usual style, displayed reluctance about keeping his side of the bargain, Elliot summoned his armed forces to do some more arm-twisting. On 25 February British troops launched an attack on another group of forts on the Pearl River. The British forces advanced far enough upriver to encounter the Chinese vessel *Cheaspeake* and the barbarian broadsides proved too much for the Chinese defenses. A boarding party entered the *Cheaspeake* and reported that the "decks resembled a slaughter house." The ravaged ship was then finished off by a rocket aimed at her powder magazine. The explosion was heard 30 miles away.

TREATY OF NANKING

Colonel Sir Henry Pottinger was appointed the new plenipotentiary to China and arrived in Macao on 9 August 1841 with a fleet of 14 ships (including two iron-hulls) and 2,500 men. Palmerston's intent was to direct the thrust against the seat of government in Peking rather than get bogged down in Canton. Pottinger followed instructions to the letter, setting out on 21 August 1841. He bypassed Canton and proceeded north, capturing Amoy, Tinghai and Ningpo in the space of two months. In Spring 1842 reinforcements arrived from India to bring his troop strength to 10,000. Peking mobilized provincial troops to push back the barbarians but the charging masses were decimated in minutes when the British artillery let loose with their recent inventions — canister and grape. The British then took Woosung and Shanghai in June with only minimal resistance.

Pottinger took the 74-gun battleship *Cornwallis* and four other supporting ships up the Yangtze River. Reaching Nanking, the British planned an assault on the morning of 15 August 1842. However, some three hours before the opening bombardment, the Chinese delivered a communication to the *Cornwallis* announcing that the emperor was willing to enter into peace talks. On 29 August 1842 the Treaty of Nanking was signed aboard the *Cornwallis*. The main points were as follows:

1. Hong Kong was to be ceded to Britain in perpetuity.
2. Canton, Foochow, Ningpo, Shanghai and Nanking were to become open trading ports.
3. British consulates could be established in the treaty ports.
4. China would pay an indemnity of $21 million for Britain's opium losses and war expenses.
5. The Chinese monopolistic merchant system, the Cohong, was to be abolished.
6. A fixed tariff rate was to be established on imports and exports. (The Chinese refused to have opium included in this category, or to let opium trading be legalized).
7. Equality would be established between Chinese and British officials of corresponding rank.

The fruits of England's victory (or otherwise termed the spoils of war) were soon shared by other nations, taking advantage of

China's weakness. The Americans secured similar treaty port rights in July 1844, and, later that year, the French gained the additional right of introducing Roman Catholicism. Similar privileges were then extended to Protestants by a decree in 1845. The Belgians gained the right to trade in 1845, and in 1847 Sweden and Norway signed comparable treaties. In 1851 the long ongoing trade between Russia and China was brought under further regulation by the signing of a convention. These treaties which were forced upon China at gunpoint and which encroached on China's sovereign rights were called "unequal treaties" by China.

POSTWAR PERIOD

The signatory to the first treaties with the West, Ch'i-ying (Keying), was acknowledged as an expert on barbarian affairs and on 6 April 1843 was made Imperial Commissioner. Ch'i-ying engaged in social intercourse with the British and developed friendly relations with Pottinger. This style of personal diplomacy was purposely intended to disarm the foreigners' suspicions, and to gain their confidence and trust. Such ingratiating behavior with the former enemy was resented by the imperial court and in November 1844 Ch'i-ying felt it necessary to justify his actions in a memorial to Peking. He explained that to attempt to make the barbarians conform to established Chinese traditions and customs was to beg for needless trouble:

> We have to curb them by skillful methods. There are times when it is possible to have them follow our directions but not let them understand the reasons. Sometimes we expose everything so that they will not be suspicious, whereupon we can dissipate their rebellious restlessness. Sometimes we have given them receptions and entertainment, after which they have had a feeling of appreciation. . . .
>
> The barbarians are born and grow up outside the frontiers of China, so that there many things in the institutional system of the Celestial Dynasty with which they are not fully acquainted. Moreover, they are constantly making arbitrary interpretation of things, and it is difficult to enlighten them by means of reason . . .
>
> The customs of the various Western countries cannot be regulated according to the ceremonies of the Middle Kingdom. If we should

> abruptly rebuke them, it would be no way of shattering their stupidity and may give rise to their suspicion and dislike. . . .
>
> With this type of people from outside the bounds of civilization, who are blind and unawakened in styles of address and forms of ceremony, . . . there would be no way to bring them to their senses, but also it would immediately cause friction. Truly it would be of no advantage in the essential business of subduing and conciliating them. To fight with them over empty names and get no substantial result would not be so good as to pass over these small matters and achieve our larger scheme.

Pottinger himself was also prone to utilizing double-faced tactics. In response to instructions from the new Tory government in London to deny protection to those who would engage in "illegal speculations," Pottinger faithfully issued a proclamation to that effect for Hong Kong. However, Matheson shed more light on the actual situation:

> The Plenipotentiary had published a most fiery Edict against smuggling, but I believe it is like the Chinese Edicts, meaning nothing, and only intended for the Saints in England. Sir Henry never means to act upon it, and no doubt privately considers it a good joke. At any rate, he allows the drug to be landed and stored in Hong Kong.

The seemingly friendly relations between Ch'i-ying and Pottinger resulted in relatively cordial trading practices in the post-war period. The atmosphere changed significantly when Pottinger retired in the spring of 1844 and was succeeded by John Davis, a former employee of the East India Company, who had been Lord Napier's second superintendent of trade in 1834, the time of the Napier fiasco. Davis made disparaging remarks about the "Chinese ability to comprehend the observance of good faith on the part of the strongest." To him, Ch'i-ying's style of diplomacy was "tiresome" and "childish," and he became so indifferent that Ch'i-ying abandoned his personal approach in 1846.

Open Canton

The biggest hurdle arising from the Treaty of Nanking was how to implement the British right of entry to Canton city. The Cantonese adamantly refused to allow the barbarians into their city, restricting them to only the Factory district. The Cantonese raised the point that although the city was now open to trade with foreigners, the treaty text was not clear on whether foreigners were to be allowed *within* the city. The other four treaty ports had raised no objections to the British entering their walled cities. In fact the foreigners found the standards of sanitation and housing in Shanghai to be so repulsive that they retreated and chose instead to establish their own settlements outside the city walls. But at Canton the British kept insisting on gaining access. Sensing that the "Canton City question" would eventually lead to open conflict, Ch'i-ying tendered his resignation to Peking, pleading old age and infirmity. In March 1848, Hsu Huang-chin was appointed Imperial Commissioner, and Yeh Ming-ch'en became governor of Kwangtung Province. These two officials were uncompromising in their relations with the foreigners and secretly co-operated in encouraging anti-foreign feelings among the people of Canton. British subjects became the victims of numerous attacks, insults, and stoning. To further inflame the situation, Emperor Tao Kuang died in 1850 and was succeeded by his son Hsien Feng, twenty-one years of age, whose stance on foreign policy was even more unyielding. Relations between China and Britain deteriorated.

TREATY OF TIENTSIN

Palmerston, now prime minister, sent Lord Elgin, a former governor-general of British North America (now Canada) as plenipotentiary and head of an expedition to China. The British contingent this time was boosted by French forces, the French capitalizing on the murder in February 1856 of a missionary in Kwangsi Province, which was not yet open to foreigners. The Americans and Russians also joined the allied cause but they sent representatives rather than troops in a "peaceful demonstration." On 12 December 1857 Baron Gros and Lord Elgin issued ultimatums for Yeh to start direct negotiations and for payment of indemnities (with the French demands calling for punishment of the missionary's murder). Yeh defiantly held his ground. On 28 December, after the ultimatums ran out, the Allied ships started a bombardment of Canton followed by an assault. The Chinese surrendered two days later and on 5 January 1858

Consul Parkes led a search party into Yeh's yamen. The viceroy was captured and imprisoned on board the HMS *Inflexible*. He was then shipped off to Calcutta where he died a year later. An Allied commission was set up to govern the city, with Parkes presiding, while the daily routines were handled by the Manchu governor, Po-kuei. This regime remained in power for three years until resolved in a treaty in 1860. It was during this period that significant changes came about in procurement of Chinese emigrants going to British colonies in the West Indies.

Following instructions from London, Lord Elgin took the Allied forces north and reached the Gulf of Peichili off Tientsin city in mid-April 1858. They advanced swiftly and captured the Taku Forts (at the mouth of the Peiho) and Tientsin when the defenders fled en masse. The imperial court hurriedly dispatched Kuei-liang, the 73-year old grand secretary, and Hua-sha-na, the 52-year old president of the Board of Civil Office, to negotiate with Elgin and Gros at Tientsin.

The Treaty of Tientsin was signed with the Britain delegation on 26 June 1858 and with the French on the following day. The treaty had 56 clauses. In summary, British warships were to be allowed into all Chinese ports; diplomatic representatives were to be exchanged on the basis of equality; British subjects could travel to the interior; and missionaries, both Catholic and Protestant, were granted freedom of movement in all of China. The Treaty also provided for the opening of ten more ports to trade, the payment of indemnities of 4 million taels to Britain and 2 million taels to France, and the legalization of trade in opium.

The terms of the agreement called for a follow-up conference in Shanghai a few months later to get an agreement on tariff rates and then an exchange of the ratified treaty within a year. At the tariff conference in Shanghai in October, the negotiators set a tax rate for the legal importation of opium at 30 taels per picul, amounting to about 7 to 8 percent of the average value.

Taku Repulse

On 1 March 1859 Frederick Bruce, younger brother of Lord Elgin, was appointed Minister Plenipotentiary. Elgin suggested that the presence of a substantial squadron would be a good way to "show the flag" and make an suitable impression on Peking, since backing out of commitments was "by no means novel in Chinese diplomacy." The British admiral was thus ordered to accompany Bruce with "an imposing naval force."

Bruce and the French plenipotentiary, M. de Bourboulon, arrived in Shanghai in May to hold preliminary meetings with the Chinese commissioners. The two Chinese negotiators of the Treaty of Tientsin began to put forward their best arguments that Shanghai was a much more preferable site for exchange of the final agreements. However, the Chinese side gave in when the Allied ministers remained unyielding. Unknown to the Chinese, Bruce was under orders to reject "any ceremony, or form of reception," which might "be construed into an admission of inferiority on the part of Her Majesty in regard to the Emperor of China."

On 20 June 1859 the allied warships made their rendezvous fifteen miles off the mouth of the Peiho. The British contingent consisted of nineteen vessels mounting 154 guns and carrying 2,068 men. Overall command of the allied forces was given to the British commander-in-chief, Rear-Admiral James Hope. Admiral Hope dispatched some small vessels to reconnoiter the river entrance. It became very obvious that the Taku forts, destroyed in the 1858 campaign, had been rebuilt and fortified. The scouting groups soon discovered three massive sets of barriers laid out across the river. On 25 June the Chinese sent junks to the Allies' rendezvous point bearing a message that arrangements were made for a reception at Peitang harbor, some 10 miles north of Taku — a message that had not been transmitted by the commissioners at the Shanghai meeting. The Chinese at the same time warned the Allies that any advance up the Peiho would be resisted.

The message came too late. Admiral Hope had already given the command to force a passage. Iron piles in the first barrier were removed and the admiral's vessel was just reaching the second barrier when a barrage of intense shelling came raining down upon the little gunboat, severely wounding the admiral. Only nine of a crew of forty came out unscathed. Throughout the afternoon the naval squadron engaged the enemy but the rebuilt earthen fortifications were able to withstand the pounding from shell and round shot. As evening approached the British launched one desperate attack. The marines began an assault across the oozing mud bank. Some 150 men, inching through the treacherous quagmire, reached the second defensive ditch; fifty were able to struggle the three hundred yards to the fortress walls where they were repulsed. In his summary report a few days later, Admiral Hope informed the Admiralty that the assault force was sufficient to capture the place, had the enemy behaved in their traditional manner. Altogether the British lost 426 killed, 345 wounded, four ships sunk and two badly damaged.

Conventions of Peking

The British cabinet condemned Bruce for his actions, but did not recall him. The Secretary of War summarized the prevailing sentiment when he told the Commons bluntly that if Admiral Hope had been able to demolish the forts, Bruce's decisions would not have been questioned. Nevertheless, the defeat was so damaging to British prestige that it called for retribution. The French position was that France was already at war with China.

In March 1860, Lord Elgin was placed in charge of another expedition. The British assembled a force of 13,000 troops under Elgin's brother-in-law, General Sir Hope Grant. The French contributed 7,000 led by General de Montauban. Early in March, the Allies sent an ultimatum via Shanghai to the imperial government demanding an apology for the Peiho clash, payment of an indemnity, and of course, ratification of the Tientsin Treaty. The deadline for the ultimatum was thirty days. Peking responded:

> If Mr. Bruce will come north without vessels and with but a moderate retinue, and will wait at Peitang to exchange the treaties, China will not take him to task for what has gone by. But if he be resolved to bring up a number of war vessels, and if he persist in proceeding by way of Taku, this will show that his true purpose is not the exchange of treaties.

The British considered this to be an ambiguously negative reply. Peking, it seemed, was ready to ratify the treaty, but on its own terms. The expedition headed north and reached Peitang on 30 July. By 12 August the Allies marched south-west so as to outflank the Taku forts. It appeared that the Chinese were anticipating a frontal attack from the sea as part of decent military etiquette. The Chinese were not prepared for this kind of flanking movement and the Allies found that their path to the forts was undefended. On 21 August the North Taku Fort was taken and on the following day, following the submission of the South Forts, gunboat crews removed all the obstacles to Tang-ku and Tientsin.

The Allied leaders were received amicably by the Tientsin elders on 25 August and shortly after by the emperor's Imperial Commissioners, including Hua-sha-na, Kuei-liang and the famous diplomat Ch'i-ying, signatory to the first treaties with the West. Ch'i-ying, after his retirement in 1848, was demoted in disgrace when Emperor Hsien Feng ascended to the throne in 1850. In 1858, when problems with the barbarians resurfaced, his clever diplomacy was remembered and he was summoned to apply his soothing formula once more. His appearance made the Allies become concerned, suspecting that some trick lay afoot. Elgin dispatched two young assistants, Horatio Lay and Thomas Wade (who developed a widely-accepted romanization method for the Chinese language) to deal with Ch'i-ying. When Ch'i-ying called for gentle restraint and assumed his old manner of effusing personal charm and lavishing praise for the English gentlemen they seized on the opportunity to teach the diplomat an unforgettable lesson. Lay dramatically produced a document – Ch'i-ying's own memorial of 1844. The document had fallen into British hands when Canton was bombarded and Viceroy Yeh captured. Now, Lay asked that the memorial be read aloud and the situation was a total embarrassment for Ch'i-ying. The Englishmen departed, rejoicing at their coup. The humiliated Ch'i-ying took leave of the group and for this unauthorized departure he was apprehended and conveyed to Peking in chains, where he was tried and condemned to death by self-strangulation, a punishment regarded as less shameful than decapitation.

The Chinese delegates were anxious to remove any threat of an Allied advance on Peking. On 2 September the Imperial Commissioners accepted all the conditions of the March ultimatum, but when asked to append their signatures, they called for time to consult with Peking. It was then that Harry Parkes, former consul at Canton, and Thomas Wade discovered that the credentials of the Chinese emissaries allowed them to hold discussions with the Allies but did not empower them to sign a binding agreement. Elgin was definitely not amused and called off the talks. On 8 September he ordered preparations for a march to Peking.

On the evening of 6 October French troops entered the Summer Palace, called Yuan Ming Yuan, on the north-western outskirts of the city. For the next two days there was wanton looting of the palace by French and British troops and later each ally was forthright in ascribing the worst of the plundering excesses to the other ally. The booty was incredibly valuable, rich in the materials used and in the craftsmanship involved. There were jades, cloisonné, silver and gold figures, porcelain, bronzes, furs, silks, jewels, works of art, worth many millions of dollars. The choicest spoils were shipped away to adorn the palaces of Queen Victoria and Emperor Napoleon III. Among the treasures found in the palace were some small unusual dogs, which were bred to resemble the Chinese traditional lion. Five of them were taken to Britain, and one of them, appropriately named "Lootie," was given to Queen Victoria. This became the first encounter that Westerners had with this breed of dog — the Pekingese.

On 13 October Peking surrendered to save the city from further destruction. However, the Allies found that there was no court to deal with since the emperor had fled to Jehol[4] in Manchuria. To exact punishment Elgin decided to burn the celebrated Summer Palace, which was already partially looted. The French expressed disapproval of this "destruction for destruction's sake" but Lord Elgin had made up his mind. He later gave his rationale: "It was the Emperor's favorite residence, and its destruction could not fail to be a blow to his pride as well as to his feelings."

The Summer Palace was a huge complex spread over eighty square miles, with more than 200 buildings. It was pillaged and methodically burnt by the allied troops. The enormous conflagration was started on 18 October, and for two days Yuan Ming Yuan continued to burn. Prince Kung, the emperor's brother, was terrified by the destruction of the Summer Palace and, to avoid total destruction, he sent a declaration of unconditional surrender. On 24 October 1860 Lord Elgin dictated the terms of the Convention of Peking, which granted Britain the right to diplomatic representation in the Chinese capital. The convention also provided for: (1) an indemnity of 8 million taels each to Britain and France, to cover the costs of the expedition, (2) permission for Chinese subjects to emigrate

4 Presently called Chengde (pinyin), about 150 miles north-east of Peking.

at will as contract labourers or otherwise, and (3) the opening of Tientsin to foreign trade and residence. In addition Britain acquired Kowloon to become a part of Hong Kong while France secured the right for Catholic missionaries to own properties in the interior of China. With the peace settlement secured, the allies, including diplomats, left Peking on 9 November 1860. The long-sought treaty was yet another one forced on the Chinese at gunpoint. This time it resulted in an effective peace between Britain and China, which held for forty years.

One significant consequence of the intimidation felt by China was the concession in November 1860 to another foreign power. Without a shot being fired the Russian ambassador, General Nikolai Ignatiev, was able to gain some 400,000 square miles of territory, more than the size of France and Germany combined, thereby realizing the long-held hope of having an ice-free harbour to provide access to the Pacific Ocean. A new naval base was set up and the city renamed Vladivostok, meaning "Rule the East."

TAIPING REBELLION

While the conflicts with the barbarians were bad enough, there was an even bigger problem threatening the dynasty — the Taipings. The Taiping Rebellion centered around one man, Hung Hsiu-ch'uan,[5] who was born to a farmer's family on 1 January 1814 in a small village populated by Hakka clans some 30 miles from Canton. The Hakkas, meaning "guest people" were originally residents of Central China who had migrated to Kwangtung and Kwangsi provinces at different periods but particularly during the Southern Sung period (1127-1278) when the dynasty moved south in an attempt to escape the barbarian threat of Genghis Khan and the Mongols. They were not welcomed by the local Kwangtung residents (who were called Punti, meaning "original inhabitants"), and they settled mainly in the less fertile mountain regions of the province. There was little integration between the lowlanders and highlanders and this situation was aggravated by different dialects, habits and mode of life. By the middle of the 19th century, a new cause of friction was introduced: many Hakkas took up Christianity, while the natives persisted in their worship of idols and traditional gods. The Hakka attacked

5 Hong Xiuquan (pinyin).

the natives for their superstition, and the natives despised the Hakka for accepting a foreign faith. Without deep social ties in the local region, the Hakka were generally more independent, daring, and prone to take action than were the natives.

The young Hung Hsiu-ch'uan displayed great potential in scholastic learning but he failed the civil service exams on three occasions in 1828, 1836 and 1837. After failing for the third time, Hung became very distressed and fell seriously ill. He went into a delirium during which he had various visions of the Heavenly Mother, a venerable bearded old man, a middle-aged man whom he addressed as Elder Brother, and Confucius confessing his failure to explain the Truth clearly in his Classics. He suffered with these bouts of delirium and visions for a period of forty days before recovering.

For the next six years Hung served as a village school teacher. In 1843 he took the examinations for the fourth time, and again he failed. This occurred just when there was the build up of popular resentment over the "Canton City question." Hung felt some sympathy with this display of "nationalism" and, coupled with his disgust with the existing system, which promised slim hope for success, he felt a compelling urge to start a nationalistic-racial revolution aimed at overthrowing the Manchu dynasty.

One day Hung was visited by a cousin, Li Ching-fang, who borrowed some Christian tracts which Hung had acquired from a missionary seven years earlier and now were lying idly on the shelf. Li was struck with their unusual content and urged Hung to read them. Hung did so, and came to the sincere belief that the tracts held the meaning to the strange visions he had six years previously: the old man was God the Father, the middle-aged man was Jesus the Elder Brother, which meant that Hung himself was the younger son of God and the brother of Jesus. Overcome with joy at this revelation, Hung and Li baptized themselves, pledged that they would abstain from the worship of idols and vowed to honor His Commandments. Conversion of Hung's kindred and villagers to the faith soon followed, and among the early converts was Feng Yun-shan, another frustrated scholar.

The new converts interpreted the "Heavenly Kingdom" as being China, and "God's selected people" to mean Hung himself and his fellow Chinese. They then proceeded to destroy idols in the temples and remove Confucian tablets from the schools, which resulted in their dismissal as teachers in 1844. They broadened their preaching to the neighboring province of Kwangsi where Feng organized an Association of God Worshipers. They attacked opium smoking, gambling, and drinking, and emphasized the egalitarian idea that all people were a family of brothers and sisters.

By 1847 the Association of God Worshipers had more than 3,000 converts among the miners, charcoal workers, and poor peasants, the majority being Hakkas. As the movement grew, those with a better education and of greater wealth also became believers. By the spring of 1850 there were 10,000 followers and on 11 January 1851, the God Worshipers made a formal declaration of revolution from their Kwangsi headquarters, proclaiming the "Heavenly Kingdom of Great Peace" or Taiping Tian Guo (in pinyin spelling). Led by Hung who assumed the title "Heavenly King," five others were named as kings — the East, South, West and North kings, and the Assistant King.

The Taipings headed northward and lost the South and West kings to enemy fire when they displayed themselves in colorful royal attire. On 20 March 1853 the Taiping forces took Nanking and proclaimed it the Heavenly Capital. A serious strategic error was made when the Taipings launched simultaneous military expeditions on two fronts, to the north to challenge Peking and to the west to expand their territory. The defeats during these campaigns left the Taiping forces considerably weakened.

Another major factor contributing to the eventual collapse of the Taiping rebellion was the intense internecine struggle between the kings. The East King tried to usurp power but his plot was discovered and he was murdered by the Chihli King, acting in collaboration with the North King. Following this, the North and Chihli kings themselves hatched a plot to overthrow the Heavenly King. Their attempted coup failed and they were beheaded. When the Assistant King tried to restore a situation of normalcy the relatives of the Heavenly King became suspicious that he too would try to seize power. The Assistant King decided to take his supporters and army away from Nanking. A few years later the Assistant King was captured by imperial troops and put to death by "slicing."

The leadership void left by the fratricidal struggle was unexpectedly filled when Hung Jen-kan arrived in Nanking by a circuitous route and presented himself at the palace of his cousin the Heavenly King on 22 April 1859. Within a few weeks the overjoyed Heavenly King granted him the status of Shield King. Hung Jen-kan drew up a plan for an Eastern Expedition to take Soochow, Ch'ang-chou and Shanghai, where the foreigners were well established.

From the outbreak of the Taiping rebellion, the foreign powers had adopted an official policy of neutrality. However, Western neutrality was based on the well-being of their own commercial interests, and the protection and expansion of those interests also fell within the barbarians' policy of neutrality. Over the years, the British had been able to extract ever greater concessions from the Manchus in Peking and believed that there were distinct advantages in preserving the status quo. From information gathered through emissaries, correspondents and observers, the British concluded that the Taipings were too weak and incapable of toppling the Ch'ing dynasty. But a major consideration was their trading privileges, and one grave matter of concern was that the Taipings prohibited the use of opium. The British had already managed to coerce Peking into legalizing opium trading and were in no mood to see this concession abrogated by a change in government. The Taiping cause was doomed to failure when the British tacitly cast their lot with the imperial government.

The threat of attack from the Taipings sent the foreign enclave in Shanghai scrambling to assemble a defensive force to protect its interests. With the initiative and financial support of rich Chinese merchants a motley force of deserting sailors and rowdies was assembled under the command of Frederick Ward, an ambitious American adventurer. After an initial defeat Ward dismissed the drunken lot and recruited Filipinos and, later on, local Chinese. The discipline, surprise tactics and modern arms of the irregular force brought success after success against the Taipings and resulted in it being called the "Ever-Victorious Army." Ward was killed in action in September 1862 and the Ever-Victorious Army was taken over by Charles G. Gordon, later to become General Gordon of Khartoum. Although the force was small compared to the numbers of imperial troops it nevertheless was an important factor in suppressing the Taiping rebellion, especially by capturing several strategic cities and forts thereby cutting off the support network for the Taipings and reducing the territory under their control.

In early April 1864 the Heavenly King became ill and on 1 June 1864 fifty-one year old Hung Hsiu-ch'uan, founder of the Taiping Revolutionary Movement, died. Remnants of the Taiping armies continued to fight on in other districts but eventually the losses from battle and from attrition took their toll. The Taiping Revolutionary Movement had lasted for just over fifteen years since the zealous uprising began in January 1851. It had claimed some twenty million lives.

The enormous disruption caused by the Taiping Rebellion affected the people mainly in southern and central China. Since Hakkas constituted the core group of the dissidents, they became primary targets for revenge by the imperial forces. Once the name of a rebel was known it was not unusual for the vengeful soldiers to seek out the village where those with the same surname prevailed so as to attempt to exterminate all of that clan. This resulted in the dispersal of many families fleeing persecution. Among them was the son of Hung Jen-kan who took refuge in Hong Kong and later sailed with his family aboard an emigrant ship bound for British Guiana in 1879.

CHAPTER 3

CHINESE TAKE-OUT

COMING AND GOING

Not long after the founding of the Qing (Ch'ing) dynasty in 1644, the new Manchu rulers enacted statutes, which made emigration illegal, since they feared the possibility of rebellion by Chinese returning from afar. This policy was aimed particularly at preventing Koxinga,[1] a famous general who had regained Taiwan from the Dutch, from mounting an attempt to restore the Ming dynasty. Any Chinese found to have returned from abroad could be sentenced to death, and a similar penalty was applicable to those found guilty of assisting such returnees. Because of the extensive coastline the policy was difficult to enforce although extreme measures were tried, including the evacuation for a period of time of everyone who lived within a few miles of the coast. As the years went by the fear of returning Chinese diminished and since it was impractical to effectively enforce the law in the numerous coastal villages and towns Chinese began taking to the sea in increasing number. Many made up their minds to go abroad to escape the deprivations brought on by famine and feud, particularly those in the southern part of China. In time a system evolved to facilitate illegal emigration which operated through headmen, who were essentially brokers who organized the migrants, collected the money and arranged for passage abroad by junk. In this fashion, the population of Chinese in the Philippines, Malacca, Java and Sumatra grew significantly over the years; there they engaged in farming, trade and commerce.

The prohibition on emigration was still on the books in the nineteenth century when the Western powers were stepping up their effort to gain increased trading rights. By this time though, the restrictive law could hardly be enforced because of the weakness and corruption of the government and local officials. When open trading ports were conceded to the Western powers

1 Zheng Cheng-gong (pinyin), 1624-1662.

by force of arms, the Chinese authorities became powerless to stem the flow of people going abroad. Eventually several ports were being used for embarkation, including Singapore which became an assembly and trans-shipment centre. The departure of emigrants on a large scale was facilitated and encouraged by the foreigners who held a totally different view of emigration.

Britain had, in 1807, passed a bill against slave trading, and slavery in all British colonies was abolished in 1834. The United States prohibited the importation of African slaves in 1808, and slaves already landed there became officially emancipated in 1863. In 1848, France also abolished slavery in its West Indian colonies. Spain and Portugal were not as willing to abandon slavery so soon and delayed until the mid-seventies. The abolition of slavery represented a challenge since the demand for cheap labour to work the land in the colonies of the European powers did not diminish and substitutes for the freed slaves had to be found. With a large population of impoverished Chinese to call upon, the western powers realized that China was an excellent source of the sought-after manpower, and that source was exploited to the fullest means possible. The coolie trade was on in earnest.

COOLIES TO GO

The term "coolie" is believed to originate from the name of an aboriginal group in western India, *koli* or *kulo*, or else from the Tamil word *kuli*, and, following the colonization of India, became a term in the English language. India was the initial source of emigrant labourers and after China became a recruiting ground for emigrants the term became generally used in Asia as well as in Britain in reference to the whole class of people who did menial labour. Thus the British administrators of the emigration drive in China drew up documents, which referred to their charges as "coolies." Nevertheless, it is interesting to note that in British Guiana the word "coolie" was a specific designation for people originating from India and those arriving from China were called Chinese or Chinamen. As a consequence the term "coolie" has a different connotation depending on the location where it is used. In this chapter, which describes the recruitment of workers primarily from the British perspective, the word "coolie" refers to emigrant labourers in general, whether from India or China.

Trade in coolies was initially carried out by captains of trading ships who offered their vessels on charter to the colonial authorities, merchants or plantation owners. Later, coolie brokers, mainly European merchants well established in the treaty ports, became the leading force in handling Chinese emigrants in the fifties, sixties and seventies. For them the Chinese emigrants became just another export commodity. A third avenue of processing emigrants was formalized, starting in 1852, when the colonial powers appointed on-the-spot emigration agents in an effort to better regulate the traffic in coolies and to minimize the atrocities that were becoming associated with the coolie trade.

The emigrants belonged to two basic categories, either "free labourers" or "contract labourers." The former group comprised those who could pay their own way and willingly went abroad. The vast majority of those travelling to California and Australia belonged to this group. However, only a limited number of them could afford the fare, such as prosperous merchants and those who had property or assets that they could sell to raise money for the passage. Most of the free emigrants made the journey only after borrowing money from relatives, friends or creditors. The great demand for assisted passage naturally created a bustling market for the "credit-ticket" method for overseas travel in which brokers and shippers would first provide the fare and be repaid by monthly installments once the emigrant became established in the new land. This "travel now, pay later" opportunity was conveniently provided by the creditors at a 25 to 50 percent mark-up above the normal fare. In some locations, such as San Francisco, the emigrants were required, upon arrival, to join established associations or clubs based on their native place of origin. These clubs provided social and cultural services and an avenue for the immigrants to be associated with their own kinsfolk while they adjusted to the new surroundings. In addition, the clubs worked closely with the shipping companies and provided debt collection services, which were considered by the Chinese to be a method of effective management more so than a mechanism for coercion. Although the credit-ticket system was not a formal contractual agreement, it was in effect a virtual contract because of the obligation to repay the debt. The only "free" aspect about it was that the emigrants voluntarily went abroad and could chose their own work upon arrival.

By contrast, contract labourers signed on before leaving China to a specific term of work, wage rate and destination, and their passage was paid for by the country to which they were to be shipped. For example, emigrants to New South Wales in Australia in 1848 were bound for five years and received two and a half dollars per month plus rations. A term of contract for Cuba in 1852 was eight years with wages of three dollars a month. Although the contracts were intended as a declaration of mutual agreement there were numerous abuses. There are accounts of contracts being ripped up by the captains once the ships left Chinese waters. In other cases contracts were substituted aboard ship by more demanding and already pre-signed contracts with the coolie being given no option but to accept the new "agreement" and name. Contracts were sometimes sold to third parties once the emigrants arrived at their destination. Emigrants to Cuba and Peru, in particular, were often sold into slavery. Many promises were undoubtedly made to the prospective emigrants but it could hardly be expected that every European recruiter was meticulous about explaining the contractual obligations. Questions were raised about the conduct of one English gentleman in particular — Mr. Tait, whose business enterprise in Amoy, Messrs. Tait and Company, managed to become the largest procurer of coolies for several European countries because of the fact that he was, at the same time, the resident consul for Spain, Holland and Portugal.

CRIMPING METHODS

While the plantation owners or their colonial governments were willing and able to provide the transportation for the coolies, recruitment of labourers functioned only with the help of hired Chinese brokers, sub-agents or runners, who were better known as "crimps." The crimps would go to nearby villages to distribute appropriate advertisement and enticement either by word of mouth or through printed leaflets describing promising future prospects and attractive employment conditions. They worked on a commission basis, being rewarded according to the number of persons delivered to the receiving stations. Such payment by head count, coupled with the incentive that the ships' captains would be paid in proportion to the number of emigrants embarked, rapidly transformed the coolie trade into a corrupt and inhuman practice driven by profit and greed. The Chinese began to call it the "pig trade" and the receiving stations, known variously as "sheds" in Amoy, "eating houses" in Swatow, "depots" or "warehouses" in Hong Kong, "barracoons" in Macao, and "guesthouses" in Singapore, were commonly referred to as "pig pens."

The techniques used by the crimps to obtain sufficient numbers of people for emigration varied from subtle inducement to outright kidnapping. Food, lodging, clothes, money, and sexual favors were among the common things offered by the crimps to prospective candidates. Men were invited to a place to enjoy a good meal or to have a comfortable rest or induced to go to the private quarters of female escorts and there they were drugged and sold to crimps. Those who liked to gamble, a traditional form of amusement among the Chinese, were given a few dollars as starting stakes by the crimps. If the gambler won, the winnings would be shared with the crimp; if he lost, his freedom was also lost and he would find himself in the "pig pen." Deception was the trademark of the crimps. Claiming to be representatives of foreign firms, they would offer attractive employment opportunities or recruitment into the armed services. Crimps would take their boats into coastal channels and invite impoverished natives on board to receive charitable donations. The innocent victims would then be pushed below and the hatches fastened. In some cases the labourers were purchased, being either slaves or servants, or else losers in clan fights. When these methods of procurement failed to produce sufficient candidates, the crimps turned to grabbing them wherever convenient. Working in small groups the crimps would simply overpower the victim in a secluded place, small village, quiet street, or remote waterway. Even fishing boats were intercepted and their operators taken away. Between 1859 and 1860, when the business of Chinese emigration flourished in the Canton area, the crimps had been actively kidnapping all along the Pearl River delta.

Once the prospective emigrant entered the barracoon, it was virtually certain that he would end up on a ship going abroad. If he wanted to buy back his freedom he would first have to find a way to pay a levy to the crimp (for all the trouble and lost commissions) as well as the cost of maintenance in the depot during his detention. These charges amounted normally to between $25 and $30. Without paying the compensation the emigrant was not permitted to leave. At a time when one dollar was a considerable sum, the money needed to gain freedom amounted to an insurmountable barrier from the moment the prospective emigrant was taken through the doors of the depot. The barracoons typically had only two doors, one serving as the welcoming entrance and the other leading to the emigrant ship. This arrangement was justified by the argument that other doors would merely provide the opportunity for insincere candidates to use the depot to get a free meal before escaping. Even so, some did escape, slipping through the hole of the primitive toilet into the excrement and mud of the riverbank.

The reception in the barracoon was of course intended to ensure that the procured subjects took the next step, which was to board the ship as a consenting emigrant. The practices of the welcoming group were described to an investigating committee by a Chinese man who was set free after an inspection raid on one of the emigrant ships:

> Before sending the men, all are mustered in the large room (or compound), and the keeper cries out that those who are willing to go are to take one side and those not willing the other. Then the unwilling ones are flogged into acquiescence; I was so flogged myself. There were men of family and men of literary pretensions among the captives. These were most reluctant to go and were most flogged. . . . On one occasion there were four or five of the most reluctant flogged until nearly dead, and then put into a sick room and fed on congee for weeks. One of them escaped or was purposely sent away, and he it was that told my family where I was. Others in their despair, committed suicide with opium, and others hung themselves.

The last remaining opportunity for a persistently reluctant Chinese to protest was when he was taken aboard the emigrant ship. John E. Ward, the American minister based in Hong Kong, visited Canton in January 1860 and became enlightened about the effective methods employed to persuade the coolie to emigrate at this stage. He wrote to U.S. Secretary of State Cass:

> The horrors of this coolie traffic, as conducted at Whampoa, cannot within the limits of a despatch be properly described. The usual mode of operating seems to be to charter at once three or four vessels and send

them to Whampoa, having first arranged the order in which they are to leave for Canton.

When a Chinaman has been kidnapped or stolen, he is taken to the first vessel and asked if he wishes to emigrate. Should he answer in the negative, the captain, with great apparent honesty, declares he cannot receive him. His captors then leave the ship with him, and he is held in the water, or tied up by the thumbs, or cold water is trickled down his back, or some other torture inflicted, until he consents to go, when he is taken to the next ship, and the same question repeated, "Are you willing to emigrate?" If his reluctance to become an exile is still unsubdued, he is again returned to his captors, and this process repeated until a consent is wrung from him, when he is received as one of the "willing emigrants." When the consul visits the ships to examine into their condition, they are questioned under the painful recollection of what they had already suffered, and what they must still endure if a ready assent to emigrate is not given.

Initial Experiences

The first foreign ship to engage in the contract emigration trade was a French vessel, which sailed from Amoy bound for the Isle of Bourbon (Reunion Island) in 1845. The clever French adventurer had speculated on obtaining the coolies cheaper in the country of origin than from the Straits of Malacca. Two years later the British vessel *Duke of Argyle* took some 800 men to Cuba and a year after that the first dispatch of Chinese contract labourers arrived in Australia. Chinese labourers were first shipped to Peru in 1849 after a law was passed there to entice new "colonists." In the late 1840s, many departed by the credit-ticket system to join the gold rushes in California and Australia. Emigration of Chinese to the British West Indies began in 1852.

Amoy was the first port of activity in the coolie trade. Emigration from this port was already a fairly common practice for Chinese leaving by junk for nearby destinations in south-east Asia, the trips being organized by fellow Chinese. However, the pace increased markedly when the foreign ships began their trade in human cargo. Two British firms, Tait and Company and Syme, Muir and Company, were the main procurers of contract labourers. The governor of Hong Kong, Sir John

Bowring, described in August 1852 a part of the procedure that he witnessed at Amoy:

> Hundreds of them are gathered together in barracoons, stripped naked, and stamped or painted with the letter C (Cuba), P (Peru), or S (Sandwich Islands[2]) on their breasts.

The vast majority of Chinese labourers shipped at Amoy were kidnapped by fraud and force, seduced by false representation, and otherwise conveyed aboard emigrant ships against their wishes. The increasing number of cases of irregular recruitment brought about a popular outcry and in 1852 posters were put up throughout the city warning citizens to beware of the "pig stealers." Eventually, Amoy residents became outraged by the continuing abuses and began to threaten the Chinese crimps with violence, whereupon the foreigners put forward the claim that, as their employees, the crimps (or, more politely, brokers) were entitled to extra-territorial protection. In November 1852 a crimp employed by Syme, Muir and Company was seized by an angry crowd. The Chinese authorities then arrested him and confined him in a guardhouse. On 21 November Mr. Syme came in person and forcibly released him from the lock-up. Later that day the Chinese guards retaliated by attacking two Englishmen who happened to be strolling by and on the following day a crowd of Amoy citizens marched on the foreign quarter, shouting violent threats. When the anger of the mob rose to a menacing level the British decided to bring ashore a force from HMS *Salamander* to protect the foreigners. The crowd, however, was not intimidated and pushed the British soldiers back. The soldiers then fired into the mob, killing and wounding several Chinese. The British carried out an investigation, which conceded that the broker in British employ was indeed involved in kidnapping, this in itself being a crime. Furthermore he was forcibly liberated by a British firm, which was breaking Chinese law prohibiting emigration. Even so, it was concluded that there was no violation of *British* national law and Mr. Syme was slapped with a fine of two hundred dollars. The uprising by the Amoy city folk had a long term effect since, from then on, the coolie trade at Amoy went into decline.

When the coolie trade began, the permitted allotment of passengers aboard a British ship was one person for every two

2 Now known as the Hawaiian Islands.

tons of registered ship weight and a surface area of ten square feet per person — a space such as five feet in length and two feet in width. These guidelines were ignored in many instances. The *Duke of Argyle* sailed in March 1847 with an equivalent of nine square feet per person and a loading ratio of one and a half tons per passenger. Non-British ships were even less inclined to follow such guidelines about space requirements. The overcrowded conditions and corresponding deaths and health problems became so unacceptable that they eventually led to the passing of the British Passenger Act in 1852 which increased the allowable space to 12 square feet per person. Once again, these regulations applied only to British ships, and the enterprising captains could very easily change the ship's registration and fly the flag of another nation for convenience.

All at Sea

Once on board, the emigrants faced a journey of several months in severely cramped quarters. Sailing times were considerably affected by the season, with north-westerly winds speeding up the trip in the monsoon months of October to March. In 1856 the travel times posted in Hong Kong were 20, 65 and 147 days to reach Singapore, the Cape of Good Hope and the West Indies, respectively, during the monsoon season. These lengthened to 60, 85 and 168 days, respectively, in the summer months. Travel in the opposite direction via the Pacific Ocean was shorter when there were no monsoon head-winds. The time to reach California was posted at 100 days between October to March, and 75 days from April to September.

The shippers initially provided a minimal amount of clothing (maybe one suit and perhaps a pair of shoes and a bamboo hat) for the emigrants, but this was by no means a universal practice. In some cases emigrants from Amoy arrived at their destination naked to the waist, wearing only trousers. Between 1852 and 1854 Chinese labourers from Amoy and Macao received two suits of clothes from the contractors, but the cost of these suits, valued at two-and-a-half dollars, was deducted as an advance from their salary. Only after 1867 were suits provided free of charge.

Regarding sustenance, the governor of Hong Kong, Samuel

George Bonham, in 1853, issued a dietary scale for a Chinese passenger on board emigrant ships as follows:

Rice	1 ½ lbs. per day
Salt pork	½ lb. "
Lard, salted fat, fresh fat, or oil	½ oz. "
Tobacco	½ oz. "
Salt	1 oz. per week
Pepper	1 oz. "
Vinegar	½ oz. "

> Three weeks supply of biscuits is to be place on board, to be issued at the rate of two lbs. a day only when the weather is too bad for cooking, or when required by the surgeon. Peas or beans may be substituted for rice, and opium for tobacco, to the extent and in the proportion to be fixed, by the surgeon. Half issues to be made to children under ten years of age. The issues in accordance with this scale are to be made daily, the first issue to be made on the day of embarkation.

In 1855, revisions to the dietary scale were made, giving the choices of either 2/3 pork and 1/3 fish, or else 1/3 pork, 1/3 beef and 1/3 fish rather than the prevailing standard of salted pork, but with no increase in the amount of the daily allowance of these meats. In addition, half a pound per day of salted vegetables or pickles was allotted. These requirements applied only to British ships cleared by the British consuls in treaty ports. Non-British ships were not so supervised.

Two meals were served each day, at nine o'clock and four o'clock, the food being cooked in a galley on the upper deck. The cooks would go down below with rice and other food in large platters, each containing food for ten. Water rations varied depending on each ship and port of embarkation, ranging from ¾ gallon per day to 12 gallons per week. The amount of water actually given to the emigrants remained at the discretion of the captain. Some accounts tell of a pint a day being rationed out and of emigrants having to thrust dollars through the gratings of the hatches in exchange for cups of water.

During the voyage the labourers were all confined below deck. On the *Don Juan* two of the three hatches were kept locked, and the other watched by several guards; only the privileged persons such as corporals (supervisors), cooks, and barbers, all of whom were selected from among the Chinese labourers, could go up on deck, but the cooks and barbers were not permitted to remain above at night. The labourers were allowed on deck only when they were sick or needed to go to the opium smoking room, and in these instances they would come up only in small parties.

The emigrants in the hold spent their time gambling or playing musical instruments. The most popular games were dominoes and cards; fantan was also played, although prohibited on some ships. They played music using cymbals, drums, gongs, trumpets, two-string fiddles, tambourines, and wind instruments resembling clarinets and flutes. These instruments were prepared and distributed to the labourers by the emigration agent or the captain of the ship in order to soothe the restless hordes during their journey.

Death and Disaster

The main causes of death on board the emigrant ships were sickness, suicide, being shot during a mutiny, drowning following a shipwreck, fire, and accidents; by far the largest number of fatalities was due to sickness. Between 1847 and July 1866 the mortality rate on Chinese emigrant ships was 13.2%. Of 85,800 embarked, 74,591 landed, and 11,209 died during the voyage. Counting only the ships that did arrive at their destination, five ships had fatalities in excess of 40%, the highest being on *Lady Montague*, which sailed from Hong Kong in February 1850 and suffered 300 deaths out of 450 embarked (66% mortality). By contrast, British convict ships sailing to Australia had a mortality rate under 5% and Indian coolies transported to the West Indies on fifty-nine ships in 1872 and 1873 had a 4.3% mortality rate. One consideration in the higher death rate on Chinese emigrant ships was that the shipments of convicts and Indian coolies were under British government care, while the conveyance of Chinese labourers was mainly in the hands of businessmen.

After comparing case histories, three surgeons on board separate emigrant ships agreed that the diseases prevailing among the Chinese emigrants might be traced to intestinal worms, opium, and tuberculosis. The ordinary symptoms of intestinal worms were those of irritable fever and nausea. Vomiting, diarrhoea and dysentery were also a common result of the presence of worms. Illness resulting from the consumption of unclean food and water was frequent since the meat and vegetables, although excessively salted, did not remain wholesome over an extended time and became putrid. The lack of proper nutrition also gave rise to scurvy. The emigrants who managed to survive the arduous journey invariably suffered from malnutrition. Only in 1871, after 25 years of experience in the coolie trade, was it reported that hospital facilities were erected on the deck of an emigrant ship.

It was undoubtedly a traumatic experience for the young men who were kidnapped to suddenly find themselves severed from family and friends and destined to be transported to some barbarian country. The emigrants who lost all hope resorted to suicide, mainly by hurling themselves into the sea. This ultimate form of protest was also used in response to cruel punishment such as whippings and beatings. Suicide could be controlled only by strict confinement to the holds below deck.

The Chinese labourers frequently revolted and attempted to seize the ships. Usually the action took place after the ship had been only a few days at sea when a sufficient number of emigrants came to realize their common plight and the vessel was still close enough to home to attempt a return. There were at least forty-two emigrant ships from Chinese ports that experienced mutinies between 1850 and 1872. Of these, thirteen ships were captured or deserted by Chinese emigrants, and six were destroyed by fire. More than half of these 42 ships sailed under British or French flags and 35 of them were bound for Cuba or Peru. This was no coincidence, since the vast majority of coolies headed for Cuba and Peru were forcibly taken on board. The Chinese used two general methods in attempting mutinies: first, attacking the captain and officers, and, failing in that, setting fire to the ship. On six of 42 ships the crews were able to remain in control after their captains or officers were killed or wounded. On ten other ships the Chinese seized control. Nine ships were set ablaze after failed revolts, and of these the fires were put out on four ships while the remaining ships were destroyed.

The suppression of a mutiny on a Chinese emigrant ship was always followed by punishment of the mutineers, using such means as flogging, kicking, cutting off or tying their pigtails to the iron barricades or gratings, and clamping irons to their legs. In order to establish their authority and prevent trouble, it was not unusual for the captain or the officers to arbitrarily punish Chinese labourers even though they had not violated any regulations. Those who actually committed offences received brutal whippings, after which their wounds would be doused with vinegar and salt.

Cuba and Peru

In July 1860, twenty-six years after Britain had abolished slavery, the British government admonished Spain for continuing to support the African slave trade, and expressed the hope that a more merciful alternative might be found in the Chinese coolie trade. In practice, there was little difference since the Chinese coolies who were taken to Spanish-American colonies were sold into virtual slavery. From the beginning, the treatment of Chinese in Cuba was no better than that meted out to African slaves, as witnessed from the following advertisement which appeared in a Havana newspaper in 1847:

> FOR SALE: A Chinese girl with two daughters, one of 12-13 years and the other of 5-6, useful for whatever you may desire. Also one mule. . . .

Following numerous reports of cruelty and exploitation of Chinese labourers over the years in Cuba, the emperor of China finally agreed to dispatch a commission of inquiry to make an investigation between March and May 1874. The commission collected 1,176 depositions and received 85 petitions supported by 1,665 signatures. The commission made a summary based on the testimonials of the Chinese coolies:

> On landing, four or five foreigners on horseback, armed with whips, led us like a herd of cattle to the barracoon . . . [where we were] treated like pigs and dogs. . . . After a detention at the quarantine station our queues were cut and we awaited in the men-market the inspection of a buyer, and the settlement of the price. . . . We were divided into three classes — 1st, 2nd and 3rd, and were forced to remove all our clothes, so that our persons might be examined . . . in the manner practiced when oxen or horses are being bought.
>
> Ninety percent are disposed of to the sugar plantations. There the owners rely upon the administrator . . . and the administrator who forces the Chinese to work 20 hours out of the 24 is a man of capacity, . . . but he

> may strike, or flog, or chain us, as his fancy suggests him. If we complain of sickness we are beaten and starved; and if we work slowly dogs are urged after us. . . . Those of us who are employed on farms or coffee estates, in sugar warehouses and brick-kilns, on railways and in baker, cigar, shoe, hat and other shops are . . . ill-treated, flogged, confined in stocks and in jail, and tortured in every way as on the plantations. . . . We are fed worse than dogs, and are called upon to perform labour for which an ox or a horse would not possess sufficient strength . . . and it is impossible to reckon all those who have died from ill treatment. . . . The overseers rode about with cowhide whips and pistols, striking all, good or bad indifferently, inflicting blows on those at a distance with whips, and striking with sticks those within reach. Ribs were broken and spitting of blood was produced, . . . and suicide was of constant occurrence. . . . No count can be made of the numbers of those who have thrown themselves into wells [or sugar cauldrons], cut their throats, hanged themselves, and swallowed opium.
>
> We get up at 3 A.M., and labour until noon; at 1 P.M., we resume work until 7 P.M., when we rest half an hour and are allowed a ration of maize, after which work is continued up to midnight. . . . Our master also continually urged the negroes to beat us; he used to say, "If one were killed, two others could be bought." . . . I did not dare complain to the authorities, because such a course only resulted in being chained and flogged with even greater severity.

Of those signing the petition, eighty percent said that they were kidnapped or decoyed. Fractured and maimed limbs, blindness, heads full of sores, teeth knocked out, ears mutilated, skin and flesh lacerated were noted by the commissioners as visible proofs of the cruelty endured. On the termination of the contracts, the employers, in most cases, insisted on renewal of engagements, which sometimes extended to more than ten years. If the Chinese coolie refused he was taken away in chains to a depot and forced to work on road repairs without compensation, suffering exactly the same fate as convicted criminals.

Peru was already an independent nation when coolies from China were first brought there, but the treatment they received in this former Spanish colony was no better than experienced in Cuba. Cheap labour was needed to work the guano beds and mineral ore mines, and in cochineal, sugar and cotton plantations. Later on, more manpower was needed for national construction projects such as canals, harbors and railways.

Regarding the work in the guano beds under conditions of stifling tropical heat and humidity, a contemporary writer noted:

> No hell has ever been conceived by the Hebrew, the Irish, the Italian, or even the Scotch mind for appeasing the anger and satisfying the vengeance of their awful gods, that can be equalled in the fierceness of its heat, the horror of its stink, and the damnation of those compelled to labor there, to a deposit of Peruvian guano when being shovelled into ships.

The United States consul wrote in 1870:

> Those employed on the Guano Islands have a daily task to perform of 100 wheelbarrow loads of guano, should they fail to get that amount, . . . their task had to be completed on Sunday. They are indifferently fed and clothed, and as a consequence become sick, but are not admitted to the hospital while they retain enough strength to stand. . . . Many of them too weak to stand are compelled to work on their knees picking the small stones out of the guano, and when their hands become sore from the constant use of the wheelbarrow it is strapped to their shoulders. . . . Life to the Chinaman under such circumstances possesses no attractive features, and death . . . is welcomed by him as his deliverance from the miseries of his lot in life.

Plantation owners made good use of the racial prejudice that existed, particularly the contemptuous attitude held by the Africans, native Indians and those of mixed blood for the Chinese. The Black Christians could always be counted on to take the side of the master against the Yellow Heathen. One account of punishment in Peru related that "two dozen lashes made them breathless, and, when released after thirty-nine lashes, they seemed slowly to stagger over, reeled and fell, and were carried off to the hospital — in most cases, if they recovered, committing suicide."

As late as 1874 the Chinese were still regarded as property. In October of that year the *Anti-Slavery Reporter* noted:

> According to the *Commercio* of Lima, some time ago there was a sale at the Hacienda de Talambo, consisting of 37 Mules, 30 Yokes of Oxen, 40 Asses, 100 Mares, 600 Sheep, and 123 Chinese Coolies.

Between 1849 and 1874, an estimated 90,000 Chinese "colonists" were introduced to Peru and some eighty percent were obtained by deception.

REGULATING THE COOLIE TRADE

After the abolition of slavery in 1834, Britain, although very interested in securing cheap labour, could no longer follow the methods used for African slaves in an official capacity. Thus, in general, the Chinese taken to British colonies were considerably better treated than those sent to Spanish territories. By 1850 the coolie trade to other countries was well established and British ships played a significant role in providing transportation to non-English speaking countries, although they had to take the precaution of operating from non-treaty ports. Officially, the British government hoped to have some regulation of the coolie trade but the reality of the situation, much like the opium trade, saw the British authorities in China fighting a losing battle against the profit that could be reaped by the coolie merchants. Thus, diplomatic and consular personnel were instructed to neither assist nor interfere with those Chinese who were willing "to risk the penalty attached to the transgression of the law [against emigration]." The Americans, noting that the procurement and treatment of the coolies bore a remarkable similarity to the African slave trade, became advocates for the abolition of coolie trading. However, the U.S. representatives in China found themselves in the dilemma of seeing fellow Americans, in their larger vessels, become the major carriers of Chinese coolies. Without any directions from Washington to curtail the trade, the American ministers in China realized that their nation's prestige was threatened.

When John Bowring became governor of Hong Kong, he recommended changes to the existing regulations and on 30 June 1855 the Chinese Passenger Act was introduced into the House of Commons. The act was applicable to all British ships as well as foreign ships departing from a British port with "more than twenty Asiatics on a voyage of more than three days duration." Emigration agents were required to carry out inspections to ensure that every ship obeyed the regulations and that every Chinese on board was emigrating voluntarily. In spite of the new act there were violations. In March 1856, the emigration officer at Hong Kong determined that only about 81 of the 298 passengers on board the *John Calvin*, bound for Havana, were willing emigrants. Nevertheless, he did not insist that the remainder be set free, nor did he prevent the ship from sailing with all on board.

Britain felt that real emigration control could be achieved only with cooperation from the Chinese government. When Lord Elgin was dispatched with an expeditionary force in 1857 he was instructed to pursue the matter with Chinese officials. Lord Elgin raised the subject during the course of negotiating the Treaty of Tientsin, but he decided not to press further since the Chinese might use it to delay settlement of more important issues. After the forceful resolution of the "Open Canton" question by the British and the capture and exile of Viceroy Yeh in January 1858, a joint administration of the city by British, French and Manchu commissioners was established. Harry Parkes, the British commissioner, essentially became the chief administrator of Canton. It was during this allied occupation of Canton that practical attempts were introduced to control the excesses of the coolie trade. In the spring of 1859 the British Consul, Rutherford Alcock, reported:

> The acts of violence and fraud connected with the coolie trade at this port have lately reached such a pitch of atrocity that a general feeling of alarm spread through the population, accompanied by the degree of excitement and popular indignation which rendered it no longer possible or safe for any authority interested in the peace of the place to remain inactive. . . . The intolerable extent and character of the evil has thus tended to work its own cure. When no man could leave his house, even in public thoroughfares and open day, without a danger of being hustled, under false pretences of debt or delinquency, and carried off a prisoner in the hands of crimps, to be sold to the purveyors of coolies at so much a head, and carried off to sea, never again to be heard of, the whole population of the city and adjoining districts were roused to a sense of common peril.

A system of regulated emigration at Canton was introduced through the initiative of two British men, Harry Parkes and John Gardiner Austin, Immigration Agent General of British Guiana. The Chinese officials were also eager to eliminate the oppressive methods of procuring emigrants. Although emigration was still illegal, the governor-general for Kwangtung and Kwangsi, Lao Ch'ung-kuang, was cooperative since kidnapping was a significant threat to the citizenry and, in the Chinese view, by far the most unacceptable part of the coolie trade. In any case, if Peking were to raise questions, the Chinese officials in Canton could always resort to a plea that they were coerced by the barbarians. On 6 April 1859 the Chinese merchants submitted petitions and the district magistrates thereupon drew up a proclamation laying out the conditions for acceptable emigration:

> If, after the date of this Proclamation, foreigners continue to hire people or engage labourers for service in foreign countries, let all those who are disposed to go be careful to ascertain whether the offers made them are bona fide, and that they are not exposing themselves to the kidnappers' designs; let them arrive at a distinct understanding as to the rate of remuneration, the period for which they are to be engaged, the place to which they are to proceed, and whether they will be able, when absent, to communicate with or remit money to their families or friends; and let a special contract, containing all these conditions, be then drawn up, which can be recorded in proof of the agreement. When both parties have given their consent to those conditions, there is then no objection to your going with the foreigner.

On 28 October 1859 a proclamation containing five articles of regulation, endorsed by the governor-general, was issued confirming the right to emigrate and describing the conditions under which emigration was permitted. On 10 November a licence was issued to Mr. Austin, and an emigration house soliciting labourers for work in the British West Indies was established under the joint control of Mr. Theophilus Sampson, the local British agent, and a Chinese deputy magistrate.

The British officials soon came to realize that regulation at one port, just as in the case of the opium trade, had little effect on the activities at other ports. Furthermore, after only one month, the old coolie trade resumed right at their doorsteps at Whampoa, the port district serving Canton. Receiving ships were moored off the Whampoa docks where they continued to buy coolies. By merely changing their anchorage they effectively evaded any attempts to regulate them, since the traders knew that they were just beyond the reach of the allied troops whose protection of the people did not extend beyond Canton city itself.

Governor-general Lao devised a plan to attack the bases outside Canton by forcing the foreigners, through their governments, to conduct all recruitment through Canton. On 1 November he dispatched a fleet of war junks to the Whampoa anchorage. Forty-one kidnapped coolies were set free and thirty-six kidnappers seized, of whom eighteen were beheaded. On 8 December more kidnapped coolies were freed from Hong Kong receiving stations and fifteen brokers beheaded, and their heads displayed on poles at Whampoa. Despite these efforts, Lao realized that he had to have the support of the foreign powers other than England and France for his policy to be effective. In November he sent a circular to the foreign consuls to inform them that the regulations covered all emigration and to request that the consuls not permit their countrymen to obtain coolies except from the licensed emigration houses at Canton.

CONVENTION ON EMIGRATION

Both Chinese and European officials were eager to obtain an improved system of regulation for the coolie trade, but each side was restricted by existing legal stipulations. The break came in the autumn of 1860 when Lord Elgin and his expeditionary force marched on Peking, eventually leading to the destruction of Yuan Ming Yuan, the old Summer Palace, and the signing of the Peking Conventions. Article V of the British Convention of Peking read, in part:

> Chinese choosing to take service in British colonies or other parts beyond the sea are at perfect liberty to enter into engagements with British subjects for that purpose, and to ship themselves and their families on board any British vessel at any of the open ports of China.

The British convention resolved the problem of securing cheap labour for the West Indies without the need for kidnapping and deception, at least in theory. Spain and Peru did not obtain treaty rights for Chinese emigration and they continued in procuring kidnapped coolies, particularly through Macao. In the autumn of 1864 the Chinese recognized the shortcomings of having disparate treaties and the emperor approved a recommendation that the governor-general be instructed to confer with the foreign countries and devise mutually satisfactory emigration regulations. This initiated a process that resulted two years later in a comprehensive agreement intended to protect Chinese emigrants from exploitation at home and abroad.

The *Convention to Regulate the Engagement of Chinese Emigrants by British and French Subjects* was signed in Peking on 5 March 1866 by Sir Rutherford Alcock, British minister in China, M. Henri de Bellonet, French chargé d'affaires in China, and Prince Kung, head of the Tsungli Yamen (Foreign Office). This convention, consisting of twenty-two articles, stipulated that emigrants be over 20 years of age and be registered in the presence of the emigration agent and an inspector appointed by the Chinese government. A contract stating the destination, length of employment, working conditions and benefits was to be drawn up for each emigrant. Four days after registration, the contract had to be read to the emigrant in the presence of the Chinese inspector, and the emigrant asked if he agreed to it. If he responded in the affirmative, he was then required to sign the contract. When the ship arrived at her destination, the captain had to hand over the duplicate of the list of emigrants to the local authorities. Opposite the name of each emigrant, note had to be made of deaths, births, and diseases during the voyage, as well as the location where he was to be employed. This document was to be sent to the British consul at the port of embarkation, and there to delivered to the Chinese authorities. The distribution of the emigrants must be such that husbands would not be separated from wives, nor parents from children under the age of fifteen.

When the text of the convention reached their respective capitals, both British and French governments declined to ratify the convention. The French and Spanish objected mainly to the term of indenture while the British were unhappy about the need to pay return passages. After long deliberation, the British, French, and Spanish governments in April 1868 agreed on a set of twenty-two modifications to the convention but they were rejected by the Chinese government in June 1868. All attempts at resolving the stalemate failed.

This impasse was a source of frustration to the plantation owners in British Guiana and various methods were thought up to again obtain emigrants from China.

London 27th Feb., 1869

My Dear Sir, — A despatch has been lately received from Sir Rutherford Alcock, in which he informs Her Majesty's Government that his most earnest representations to the Chinese Ministers in Pekin with regard to emigration have been unavailing. Notwithstanding the decision of the English and French cabinets to reject the convention, the Chinese government has positively refused to allow emigration to the West Indies under the regulations previously existing. But they have, nevertheless, expressed some disposition to permit emigration to be resumed without the condition of providing for a back passage, if the contract for service under indenture shall be limited to five years. As we have never proposed anything else, we consider this suggestion as a mere pretext to save the dignity of the Chinese Ministers appearing to make any concession by stating it as something now imposed by them. If we can accomplish our purpose by humouring them in their design, we shall proceed by humbly acquiescing. Mr. Commissioner Murdoch has accordingly recommended the Foreign Office to reply that Her Majesty's Government will readily accept the proposal of the Chinese Government as being very reasonable, and authorize Sir R. Alcock to have the arrangement concluded with the least possible delay.

I have at the same time been again considering with Mr. Murdoch the desirability of establishing our West Indian agency at Hong Kong, where our operations could be conducted independently of the Chinese Government, and without any chance of intervention. The agricultural people of the adjacent province of Quantung could easily leave there for embarkation under the direct inspection of the British functionaries, and render emigration to the British Colonies still more distinct than it has been from all other emigration from China. Mr. Murdoch has written to the Governor of Hong Kong, with whom he is acquainted, requesting to be honoured with his opinion on this subject in order to discover whether he would cordially afford his support and co-operation.

It will be well to communicate with your friends in Demerara, and to ascertain their views with regard to these possible arrangements.

Yours, very truly,
(Signed) A. MACGREGOR

The Chairman of the West Indian Association, Glasgow.

[*Royal Gazette*, 30 Mar 1869]

This letter, sent to Mr. Booker, a plantation owner in British Guiana and member of the Combined Court, is most revealing of the self-interest of the parties concerned and both the above-board and underhand tactics that they were willing to employ. It is very true that saving face was a most important consideration for the Chinese. However, the Chinese had been presented with proposals for periods of indenture of five years from the British, seven years from the French and up to ten years from the Spanish. That the Chinese chose to go for the least demanding term of five years was only natural. The fact that this coincided with the British request was a fortunate occurrence, which made a convenient common ground for the British and Chinese to come to agreement. Despite this apparent opening in the diplomatic stalemate the chairman of the West Indian Association was prepared to set up an alternate plan, attempting to use the British colonial status of Hong Kong as a protected base to induce potential emigrants from Guangdong province.

The Chinese position was that the convention of 1866, agreed to by the negotiating ministers, should be the basis of Chinese government policy toward emigration. China held to this view until the law was eventually changed in 1893. The effect of the 1866 convention not being ratified was that legal emigration from the treaty-ports came to a halt but it still continued unabated from Macao through kidnapping. In 1871 Spain proposed a five-year term of indenture after which the labourer could accept $50 towards a return passage to China or else sign on for another five-year term with a $25 bonus. On this basis Spain was permitted to resume the procurement of coolies through Canton. It constantly baffled the British how $50 could be anywhere near enough to enable a Chinese emigrant to get back to China, but it seems that the Spanish were operating large ships plying back and forth between Cuba and China. Nevertheless, Britain came into compliance in 1872, as far as China was concerned, when it also agreed to the payment of $50 in lieu of return passage money, and thereby gained permission to re-open its Emigration Office at Canton in late 1872.

Even though some agreement was reached in the way emigration should be conducted there were still many crimps who were procuring emigrants for those nations that were not a party to the agreement. In November 1866 notices were posted in Canton warning the citizenry of the dangers of falling prey to the crimps:

> There is no greater calamity in life than separation — no greater cruelty than changing men into brutes, yet both are involved in the present Pig selling. [The Pig sellers] entice, deceive, entrap or forcibly kidnap men, everywhere spreading nets which constantly lead to the loss of numberless young men and youths causing wives to become widows, and cutting off the heir of family descent. From the Creation to the present

time there has never been such a monstrous curse. The Kidnapped men are sold to Foreigners and embarked for different countries. During the voyage four or five tenths of them die and are buried in the fishes' bellies, and the remainder are sold to be slaves: these are chemically treated and made black like devils and are kept at severe labour, cultivating barren ground. All their lives until they die, they are as horses, bullocks or other beasts of burden. A sailor of a ship saw all this with his eyes, and returning home face to face told it very distinctly to his relatives. The hearts of the hearers were wounded, the eyes of the beholders shed tears. Now it is said the kidnappers have received from the Foreigners, three million dollars for the purchase of one hundred thousand Pigs — thus kidnappers are spread about in every village, Hamlet, Market and Town for the purpose of enticing beguiling Men to Hong Kong and Macao; they pretend to have things for sale in a ship and thus induce men to embark, or they say that labourers are wanted in a certain place, or they pretend to buy things and require men to take their purchases to a ship, or they buy small boats and pretend to take passengers, or in retired places they actually kidnap men.

By a hundred devices they are bound to deceive enough to supply one hundred thousand men to the Foreigners and fill their avaricious pockets. Assuredly Gods and Men are indignant at these villains. Last month seven kidnappers were caught in Canton and were promptly beheaded, and three who were caught in Heung-Shau were killed by the Kelung torture. Now let the Elders of every village offer large rewards and establish severe regulations for the capture of Pigsellers that they may be handed over to the Officers and be thoroughly exterminated, thus exhibiting boundless virtue. Let the young and inexperienced be very careful in their goings out and comings in, and let the Elders strenuously warn the younger ones. Moreover spread this abroad and let every one be informed, and every place be on the guard. Perhaps young men may by these means be preserved from destruction. This is a very important matter so do not pass carelessly over this urgent notice.

Yesterday, a friend arrived at Hong Kong from Shanghai and said he had seen a man and woman beheaded there. On asking the reason he was told that they had been employed by a large [foreign] ship to which had beguiled 394 men, or but 6 short of the full number 400, then [in order to make up for the deficiency] representing that a companion had died, they bought a coffin, and thus induced grave-diggers and friends to go to the ship, where they were immediately forced below. One man however jumped into the water, made good his escape and ran to lay complaint before the magistrate who immediately searched the ship and liberated the three hundred and ninety odd men. The man and woman kidnappers were then beheaded to the joy of all. [*Royal Gazette*, 23 Mar 1867]

Coolie Trade at Macao

While progress was slowly being made at the negotiating table between Chinese, British and French diplomatic representatives, the one European power that failed to participate was Portugal. The Portuguese-occupied territory of Macao was a special case in the coolie trade, having a long history in the kidnapping of Chinese subjects. In 1573, sixteen years after the Portuguese were allowed to trade at Macao, the Chinese erected a wall across the narrow isthmus between the peninsula and the mainland to isolate the barbarians and prevent kidnapping. Three centuries later, in 1849, when China became preoccupied with resisting the British barbarians, the Portuguese seized the opportunity to expel the Chinese customs officials, stopped paying rent, and unilaterally declared Macao under the sole jurisdiction of Portugal. From 1853 to 1868 the main export item from Macao was coolies bound for Cuba and Peru.

Since Macao by itself could not provide sufficient quantities of coolies, the crimps spread out into neighboring areas, employing any subterfuge to fill their quotas. The pay upon delivery of the coolies to the barracoons was initially about three dollars but later rose to eight to ten dollars per head. Competition in the coolie trade as well as the desire for greater profit resulted in overcrowding on the ships since the captains were paid seventy to a hundred dollars per head for the number boarded, not for the number delivered.

From time to time the Chinese authorities protested to the Portuguese authorities about manner in which the coolie trade was being conducted, but to no avail. During the early 1860s the abuses had become so offensive that the Chinese decided to take action. They focused their attention on preventing kidnapping in areas under their own control, and strove to reach a suitable arrangement with the treaty powers to regulate emigration. Not being a treaty nation, Portugal was immune to these efforts and Macao proved to be a safe haven for the crimps. The tightening of the prohibitions against kidnapping failed to deter the crimps, and while some of the treaty powers sympathized with China or declined to recruit labourers from Macao, two very important exceptions were Spain and Peru. The Chinese government by itself was unable to eliminate the rampant kidnapping, with its energies already committed to struggling to contain the opium trade, controlling the barbarians and fighting the Taipings. The ineffectiveness of efforts to suppress the coolie trade was reflected in the number of barracoons in Macao, which increased from some three dozen in 1866 to three hundred in 1872.

A series of incidents eventually brought a halt to the coolie trade in Macao. By 1868 the British and French were working on details for resolving the 1866 convention on emigration. America had just gone through a costly civil war to free its own slaves and the U.S. Senate passed a resolution on 16 January 1867 declaring that it was the duty of the government to "prevent the further introduction of coolies in this hemisphere, or the adjacent islands." With such changes in official policy by the major powers Portugal became the odd man out.

In late 1870 the *Delores Ugarte*, flying the Salvadoran flag like many others in the trade, left Macao with 608 coolies headed for Callao, the port serving Lima, the capital of Peru. Arriving at Honolulu, the captain requested permission to land his passengers to give them a breath of fresh air. The Honolulu *Commercial Advertiser* reported on the condition of the coolies:

> In consequence of a disposition to mutiny which had manifest itself among the coolies before leaving port, they for the first three weeks of the voyage were not allowed upon deck, but were stowed away between decks in four rows, a space of only 16 inches wide being allotted to each individual. At the end of this term of imprisonment the coolies were allowed to come up on deck in gangs of 50 for one hour's exercise in the course of the day. Sentries fully armed kept watch and guard over the wretched creatures, lest in a moment of desperation they should turn upon their gaolers. On one occasion a scuffle did take place between the crew and the coolies exercising, which resulted in eighteen of the latter jumping overboard. . . . Twenty-five died [of disease] before the vessel reached Honolulu. The condition of the ship on arriving at that port is spoken of as indescribable. The mate himself confessed that the stench from the main hatch was so overpowering that it was impossible to hold one's head over it "one minute without vomiting." Forty-three of those too ill to proceed were landed at Honolulu, where, by the exertions of a kindly resident, they were permanently detained. Their plight was

> most pitiable. Twelve were in the last stages of decay — some with ship-fever and others with diarrhea; two were rendered blind for life by ulcers which had formed in the corners of their eyes, and all were in a dreadfully emaciated condition.

When the *Delores Ugarte* finally reached Callao it had lost 270 of its 608 coolies — an attrition rate of 44%. The following Spring the *Delores Ugarte* was again in Macao ready to take on another boatload of coolies. The American consul in Hong Kong wrote Governor De Souza on 21 April 1871 asking him to prevent the ship from repeating the horrors of her previous sailing. The ship was then permitted to change its name to *Don Juan* and to become registered to Peru. On 4 May the *Don Juan* left Macao with 665 coolies. Two days later a fire erupted in the hold containing the coolies. The captain took appropriate action: "To save his own and his crew's lives, he battened down the hatches on the passengers, and took to the boats." Six hundred Chinese died.

Another incident brought Japan into the picture. The *Maria Luz* was under the command of a Peruvian naval lieutenant, Captain Ricardo Heriero, an experienced captain with six coolie shipments from Macao to his record. The ship left Macao in late May 1872, and within a few days there were several attempts at mutiny, three suicides, and three other deaths from illness. The ship then lost the masts in a storm and was forced to head for Yokohama harbor for repairs. On 13 July an exhausted coolie was pulled from the water and taken aboard the British ship *Iron Duke*. He told of being maltreated and begged to be kept in protective custody. The coolie was turned over to the British chargé d'affaires, R.S. Watson, and then to the Japanese authorities. On 3 August Watson reported to the Japanese minister of foreign affairs that he suspected that maltreatment was being practiced within the jurisdiction of the Japanese authorities. Inquiries were conducted on board the ship and sufficient evidence gathered to warrant a full-scale court hearing before the governor of Kanagawa. On 22 August all 230 coolies were taken ashore and interrogated. Every one of the coolies testified that he had been unwillingly detained on board the *Maria Luz*. Governor Oye Tak on 26 August found the captain guilty of abusing and restraining the passengers. Captain Heriero himself admitted this and also acknowledged severing the queues of three coolies. A punishment of one hundred lashes was customary, but the governor, in view of the delay and inconvenience caused by the inquiry, pardoned the captain. On 30 August Captain Heriero wrote the governor to request that the coolies be returned to the ship so that it could set sail. The governor promptly replied that none of the coolies wanted to return and the Japanese government could not compel them to do so. Chinese officials from Shanghai then arrived to arrange for the return of the freed coolies to China.

The mutual involvement of the nationals of various countries in the coolie trade became evident with the *Fatchoy*. Originally a British steamer named *Vixen,* the ship was sold in April 1872 to a German firm based in Hong Kong, which changed its registry so as to fly the Spanish flag. Before proceeding to Macao, iron gratings were installed on the hatches and below deck. The captain, first, second, and third mates were German; the chief engineer was an American; and the remaining crew were English, Scottish, and Irish. The *Fatchoy* left Macao on 26 August with 1,005 coolies aboard. Four days later the coolies attacked the guards, but the mutiny was checked when the mate and second mate fired into the crowd, wounding three. A number of coolies were then tied by their queues to the barricades and gratings and about 150 were put in irons. The American engineer described that on the following morning the prisoners were brought on deck, placed across rice bags and then "unmercifully flogged and beaten by two men keeping time with their whips or sticks. In a short time the deck was covered with blood. As each coolie was flogged, he was washed with salt and water and sent below." There were three mutinies and one arson attempt by the time the ship arrived in Havana.

Even before the *Fatchoy* incident, the Hong Kong government had been aware that the colony was playing a significant role in the Macao coolie trade. Coolie ships were invariably fitted in the port of Hong Kong or provisions sent to Macao in steamers or junks. Public opinion in Hong Kong and the world was turning against the coolie trade. Three ordinances were passed in Hong Kong in 1873, which strengthened the regulations on the coolie trade and, more importantly, denied coolie ships access to Hong Kong.

The Chinese authorities were also taking active steps to cut off the supply of coolies. Governor-general Jui-lin repeatedly ordered the arrest and punishment of those involved in kidnapping. He commissioned two war junks to intercept clandestine shipments of coolies. Inspections were made of the steamers plying daily from Whampoa to Hong Kong and Macao. On one such inspection, the steamer *Spark* was caught carrying 110 potential emigrants. They were released and 20 crimps taken for trial before Chinese magistrates. By autumn of 1872, a wholesale roundup of crimps was conducted. The reduction in supply of coolies forced Portuguese entrepreneurs to mount raiding sorties in districts west of Macao. When Jui-lin learnt of this he dispatched Brigadier General Fan Kan-t'ing by steamship to the area. Several foreign ships and sailors were apprehended and numerous Chinese set free.

On 4 September 1873 the Macao correspondent for the *Hong Kong Times* wrote that "many private barracoons have been closed, and the two or three that remained have their gates wide-opened — a sure sign that no birds are in them." The reason for the lull was Jui-lin's blockade of Macao harbor itself. All ships coming to the harbor were boarded, inspected, and forced to undertake a guarantee of non-involvement in the coolie trade.

Macao was now isolated, condemned by the West and deprived of coolies by the Chinese actions. On 27 December 1873 following instructions from Lisbon, Januario proclaimed that Chinese emigration as "hitherto carried on in the port of Macao" must end within three months. However, Governor Januario introduced regulations modeled after the Hong Kong ordinances establishing "free emigration" from Macao. He then granted licences to the former barracoons under the names of "inns" or "hotels." Jui-lin promptly dispatched a colonel to inform Januario that if emigration were to be resumed, regardless of whatever name used, Chinese troops would be sent to destroy the barracoons and arrest the perpetrators. Januario then wrote to tell Jui-lin that he had been misled and the barracoons would not be reopened. The combined efforts of the nations opposed to the coolie trade finally brought the Macao trade to a close.

CHAPTER 4

DEMERARA BOUND

VISIONS IN THE HOT SUN

Although a British parliamentary committee had expressed interest in 1811 in obtaining Chinese immigrants, no firm action was taken until slavery was completely abolished in British Guiana and the demand for plantation labourers had become urgent. It was under these circumstances that, in May 1843, a proprietor from British Guiana made a tour of Asia, particularly Singapore, Malacca and Penang, and observed some 100,000 Chinese immigrants working there. He wrote a public letter to the West India Committee, the body based in Britain, which represented the region's business interests:

> At Prince of Wales, Isle Penang, there are 2,000 acres of land cultivated exclusively by them; and during the heat of the day, I have seen them cutting canes, digging canals, carrying canes, etc., and I can state, without hesitation going through all the work as well as the best picked men (Creoles) would do. The climate is much the same as in British Guiana. The men are strong and powerful and from infancy accustomed to toil; industrious and eager to acquire money. I have seen all classes of coolies and the different tribes of Asia; but nowhere have I seen a people who would suit us and our purposes better.

He also estimated that the cost for landing Chinese immigrants in British Guiana would be £10 to £12 per head. Lord Stanley, Secretary of State for the Colonies, agreed with the sentiment that the Chinese could become valuable immigrants and issued licences effective from 3 November 1843 to 1 January 1844 allowing 2,150 Chinese labourers from the British settlements in the Straits of Malacca to be introduced into British Guiana. But before any practical measures could be taken to obtain Chinese labourers, the governor-general of India acceded to Lord Stanley's request to allow Indian contract emigration under government control. As a result almost 800 immigrants arrived from Calcutta and Madras in 1845. With the cost of transportation being lower for the Indian labourers the urgency for securing Chinese emigrants abated. Then, in 1846, some 6,000 Portuguese arrived in British Guiana within a short period, fleeing from a terrible famine in the island of Madeira, located even closer to the colony than India. In the same year the quota of Indians from Calcutta leapt to 1,373 and from Madras to 2,455. In addition, there was some success in attracting a few thousand labourers from Africa and the West Indian islands. Over the next few years the ready availability of immigrants from India and Madeira was able to satisfy the needs of the plantation owners. However, the new arrivals suffered from a mortality rate of some 10%, and concerns were raised about their suitability to plantation work. When the colony's financial affairs collapsed due to a dispute about local policy, immigration from India was suspended from 1848 to 1851.

First Immigrants

In September, 1850, James T. White, emigration agent for British Guiana based in Calcutta, made his first trip to China, an investigative tour on behalf of both Demerara county and the neighboring colony of Trinidad. He came to the conclusion that the Chinese would make excellent immigrants who would be even "superior to the Bengalese." Mr. White estimated that the cost per head for Chinese emigrants would be about £15, slightly higher that the £13 required for emigrants from India.

On 2 September 1851 George Booker, a sugar plantation owner in British Guiana, informed the government that he was willing to dispatch the *Lord Elgin,* 351 tons, to bring Chinese immigrants, provided that, on the way out, it took 146 Indians who wanted to return to Madras. This plan was approved and *Lord Elgin* departed from Georgetown on 6 October but by the time it arrived in the Far East, James White had already returned to England.

In August 1851 the Court of Policy in British Guiana, the administrative body for the colony's affairs, approved and budgeted a bounty of $100 for each Chinese immigrant delivered. Concerns were expressed in Britain that Messrs. Hyde, Hodge and Company, operating in Hong Kong, was prepared to cash in on the bounty by taking the initiative in dispatching two shiploads of Chinese emigrants. The West India

Committee, based in Britain, decided that some supervision of the recruitment operations would be appropriate and appointed James White as Government Emigration Agent at Hong Kong with a salary of £1,000 per year. White reached Hong Kong for his second mission to China on 10 October 1852 only to find that the first two emigrant ships, *Lord Elgin* and *Glentanner,* had already left for Demerara and that a third was expected to leave the following month.

The *Lord Elgin* had taken on 115 adult men and 39 boys at Amoy and departed on 23 July 1852. The voyage to Singapore took 62 days during which time 4 Chinese died. Then on 24 October the ship sprang a leak, which allowed seawater to enter the hold. The rice stored there began to ferment and generate clouds of steam and poisonous hydrogen sulphide, which made the people sick. By the time the ship arrived at the Cape of Good Hope there were 45 more deaths to report. *Lord Elgin* finally reached its destination on 17 January 1853 after a journey totaling 177 days, with 69 fewer Chinese that it started with, a mortality rate of 44.8%. The ship's round trip journey from Georgetown brought back fewer passengers than had departed on it and the effort sustained a loss of £1,500. It was a disastrous venture to all concerned.

The *Glentanner* was chartered by Hyde, Hodge & Co. and left Amoy on 1 September with 305 Chinese, arriving in Georgetown 5 days before the *Lord Elgin.* There were fifty-one deaths during the journey or shortly after arrival, for a mortality rate of 16.7%. There would have been a greater number of deaths had the journey been prolonged. It was found that the *Glentanner* was unsuited to serve as an immigrant ship because of bad ventilation and inadequate deck space.

James White found out that Hyde, Hodge & Co. was preparing its second shipment of Chinese labourers on the *Samuel Boddington* and that Tait & Co. at Amoy was being sub-contracted to recruit the labourers. White felt that because of its past scandals concerning the procurement of coolies for Cuba and other Spanish colonies Tait & Co. was not a suitable agency to be involved in gathering emigrants for the British West Indies, but he had no authority to intervene in the private venture. Traveling to Amoy, he reproached the company for the inferior quality of the emigrants being collected, particularly the number of boys who were being passed off as adults. Embarkation began on 10 November, the day after White returned to Hong Kong, and continued until 23 November. The surgeon-in-charge then examined the emigrants and pronounced that only 202 of the 352 were fit for travel. It was precisely at this moment that the Amoy citizens were rioting on shore against the widespread practice of "pig stealing." Tait & Co. then informed the captain that he could either sail with everyone on board, since all were acceptable as far as the company was concerned, or else he could go with a short load and bear the loss from the resulting reduced bounties. Money proved to be the deciding factor — the captain took off with all 352 emigrants, and in fact there was an added profit margin since, according to the regulations, the ship was permitted to legally carry 335 passengers. The ship sailed on 25 November 1852 and arrived in Demerara on 4 March 1853 after a crossing lasting only 98 days. During the journey the Chinese staged a mutiny and came close to taking over the ship. Of the 352 that set out, 41 emigrants died and 11 were lost overboard — a mortality rate of 14.7% — and 29 had to be hospitalized immediately upon arrival. When the governor of British Guiana realized that the bounties had become merely an incentive for stacking the ships with bodies, he introduced an ordinance rescinding the bounty payment and this amendment was passed by the Court of Policy on 1 August 1853.

WHITE'S THIRD ENCOUNTER

In April 1853, White reported having difficulty in finding ships to take emigrants to the British West Indies since there was more profit to be made carrying willing passengers to the gold rushes in California and Australia. In addition, the accounts of mutiny and murder on the coolie ships headed for Spanish territories made the captains uneasy about taking on emigrants. This prompted White to suggest that the procurement of labourers would be better accomplished under government control rather than leaving the business to private entrepreneurs.

James White had spent quite some time investigating the nature of the Chinese people and reported to Sir Henry Barkly, the governor of British Guiana:

> The peculiar character of the Chinese will render the management of them, on their first arrival, . . . a matter of some difficulty before they get

> accustomed to their new locations. To all appearance they are perfectly impassive, cold and hard as a rock, yet they are fond of music, such as it is, and of theatrical shows and amusements, and at their sing-song exhibitions I have seen hundreds, if not thousands of them, convulsed from ear to ear with roars of laughter. They have an unexhaustible fund of obstinacy, and yet they are always willing to do anything that is required of them provided it be clearly explained to them and that they are allowed to do it in their own way. On their first arrival they must be kept cheerful and managed with kindness and a consideration for their feelings and habits. Yet indulgence will spoil them, for they are extremely cunning, and will profit by the least opening to obtain an advantage. Possessed of strong animal passions, I am afraid they may become sullen and discontented unless they should form connections with the negro women, but if this difficulty can be overcome, they will be found cheerful, contented, and industrious.

White left for England on 11 April 1853 and his proposal to adopt a government-regulated system was accepted in September. He was re-appointed Emigration Agent for the West Indies in China with the task of procuring 1,500 Chinese labourers and 200 to 300 young females (preferably with families), along with the guideline that each boatload should include a musician or two. His third mission to China, however, was a complete flop. He was unable to charter a single vessel to take emigrants to Demerara. As for obtaining females, he wrote on 10 December 1853:

> If the Government will authorize me to advance money for this purpose, I have no doubt of success. Girls of respectable connexion may be obtained for about $40, of 10 to 15 years of age; and I propose to pay this amount to a few of the more respectable emigrants, and leave them to make their own arrangements on condition of their marrying the women before the departure of the vessel. When favourable accounts are brought from the West Indies by returned Chinese emigrants, it may become unnecessary to resort to this method to procure women and children; but until that takes place, if my information be correct, there is no probability of obtaining women without purchase; for such is the universal custom of the country.

Facing the prospect of failure with no ship to call upon, White resorted to making an arrangement with the notorious Tait & Co. in Amoy asking that if any suitable vessel were found to take emigrants it should go to Nanao for their embarkation. Nothing came of this attempt although it greatly alarmed the British Foreign Office since Nanao was off-limits, not being a treaty port. Equally disturbing was the notion of paying money to procure young Chinese girls. Lord Clarendon expressed his opinion to the Duke of Newcastle, Secretary of State, that the scheme appeared "to afford an opening for the greatest abuses, and in fact to set on foot a trade little different from the Slave Trade."

In the meantime the new governor of British Guiana, P.E. Wodehouse, became concerned about the cost of importing Chinese. Because of the competition for suitable ships the cost of sending emigrants from China had risen to £25 per passenger as compared to £15 for Indian emigrants. He further felt that to pay an additional $40 for women was unjustifiable, economically speaking.

The Combined Court, consisting of the Court of Policy and a number of elected representatives from among the estate owners, sided with the governor's position and on 8 May 1854 resolved that it was "expedient for the present to put a stop to the introduction of Chinese immigrants into the Colony." The Court also resolved that Mr. White's employment be terminated as soon as possible. James T. White left Hong Kong in June 1854 after failing to recruit a single Chinese emigrant for British Guiana during his three missions to China.

SECOND WAVE

Despite the questionable nature of the way they were procured, the initial batch of Chinese to British Guiana proved to be good workers in their new environment and won praise from the plantation owners. Over the next few years the proprietors were therefore eager to obtain further shipments of Chinese. In October 1855 Governor Wodehouse advised the Colonial Office that the planters were desirous of securing more Chinese immigrants but this request was declined since relations between Britain and China at the time were tense because of the unresolved issue of allowing foreigners into Canton. The British authorities were far more interested in gaining access to Canton and did not want to raise the subject of emigration with their Chinese counterparts. Eventually, on 3 December 1856,

Governor Wodehouse asked the British government to approve immigration by private enterprise. The governor himself, having reviewed the returns from the plantations, made an about face and wrote that the Chinese "are the most valuable labourers, giving no trouble, and doing any sort of work required of them without question." However, the proposal did not find favor in London because of the anticipated difficulty of procuring female immigrants. Meanwhile, the situation was changing in China — the Taiping rebellion was in full swing, causing great disruption to the Chinese people in several provinces, and Britain and China were again engaged in armed conflict. Britain thus became less sensitive to Peking's feelings on the matter of transgressing China's prohibition on emigration.

The Combined Court took advantage of this change in Anglo-Chinese relations to pass a resolution on 15 May 1857 calling for the introduction of Chinese immigrants by private enterprise. After some wrangling about details, Lord Stanley gave consent for a one-year period. John Gardiner Austin, Immigration Agent General of British Guiana was dispatched as the colony's agent in China with the particular task of obtaining a suitable proportion of females. He arrived in China in early 1859.

The West India Committee anticipated approval for the private venture and in June 1858 sent Thomas Gerard, who had spent some time in China and spoke one of the dialects, as their agent to recruit up to 2,990 Chinese labourers, including 1,470 women, if possible, for British Guiana and Trinidad. Gerard commenced operations before Austin could reach China and on 8 December 1858 dispatched the *Royal George* with a shipment of Chinese bound for Demerara. Gerard expressed a concern about the immigrant ship losing precious time in having to go back to Hong Kong from Macao in order to get final clearance for the voyage. He tried to use the logic of expediency, convenience and financial savings to have his vessel depart directly from Macao and avoid an inspection at Hong Kong. Although Gerard, as a private agent, was operating beyond the direct control of the British authorities, the governor of Hong Kong denied his request. Thomas Gerard reluctantly abided by this decision.

Despite the inspection at Hong Kong, there were some irregularities concerning the *Royal George* which later came to light. As measured by an Emigration Commissioner in Liverpool, the space for passengers was 3,370 square feet, corresponding to a full legal complement of 280½ emigrants. By taking account of some upper deck area, the Government Marine Surveyor at Hong Kong managed to show an available space of 3,521 square feet, thereby allowing 293 passengers. Even so, the ship carried 300 Chinese! Gerard provided the explanation that the additional 7 Chinese were cooks who were accounted for as part of the crew. He was indeed cooking the books and added that the chefs so happened to be selected from among those willing to stay on in British Guiana, thereby saving the colony the expense of having to ship them back to China. As a further cost saving measure, Gerard decided to use up the old employment contract forms printed up several years before by James White, even though some stipulations were outdated or changed by law.

Gerard was indeed a man of action. He pressed on with his task and sent the *General Wyndham* with 461 emigrants. Gerard's work was of the same standard as in the dispatch of the *Royal George* since there were 15 more passengers than the legal limit, all of the excess number again being cooks carried on the crew's books.

Of the 761 Chinese on the two vessels contracted by Gerard, there was not a single female. It was then learnt that they had all been taken from the barracoons at Macao. J. G. Austin decided to pay a visit to the Macao barracoons in spring of 1859. In a letter dated 8 March 1859 he wrote that by chance he was at one of these establishments when some "miserable-looking wretches" arrived. What caught his attention was

> the speedy secrecy with which their reception was attended, the smallest possible portion of the gate, looking out on a small private pier in the inner harbour of Macao, being opened hastily and closed as speedily, whilst the men were hurried upstairs in charge of a Chinaman, who appeared so especially anxious to avoid scrutiny, or so heartily ashamed of what he was doing

that Austin's initial impression was that he was a fugitive from justice attempting to escape by emigrating. Austin described one of the barracoons as "a grim-looking, thick-walled heavily barred and well-guarded edifice." He was courteously received by the owner of three of the largest establishments and noted:

> These depots were all that could be desired as regarded space, order and cleanliness, and every means were apparently being adopted to

> render the coolies satisfied with their position; but the lofty walls and clusters of guards in every direction told but too truly that the buildings were but well conducted gaols and the inmates but hopeless prisoners, shut out from all communication with friends, and with the heavy hand of fate upon them for the future.

The Colonial Office, the emigration commissioners and the government of British Guiana all commented adversely on the way Gerard had conducted the venture. After returning to England in July 1859, Gerard was informed that his employment as emigration agent would not be renewed. The West India Committee indicated that they would not carry on the experiment in the next season.

The voyage of the *Royal George* took 111 days and suffered a significantly high casualty rate. Governor Wodehouse then faced the embarrassing situation of having to draw up new contracts to replace the illegal pieces of paper that Gerard had utilized.

> On the 29th March the *Royal George* arrived here from Hong Kong with 251 Chinese immigrants, after a passage of 112 days. We regret to say that 49 deaths occurred on board, and it is very strange that all of these but two were from dropsy. A Medical Board was, as his Excellency tells us, ordered to inquire into the circumstances of the case and, it appears, that the mortality is attributed to the small size of the vessel, difficult ventilation, and a too abundant supply of food during the voyage. One may readily admit that a want of proper ventilation, and the crowded state of the vessel, might affect the health of the passengers, but it is scarcely credible that an abundant supply of provisions should have a fatal result, and the presumption is that there was some latent and unexplained cause for the mortality. The survivors, generally speaking, are a fine set of people, healthy, clean, and robust, and if they be industrious as those who have preceded them, they will prove a very valuable accession to the labouring population of the colony. The error appears, in this instance, to have been with the Agent in Hong Kong, who chartered for the purpose, not only a slow sailer, but one whose accommodations were insufficient for the number of immigrants put on board. [*Royal Gazette*, 9 Apr 1859]

The *General Wyndham* reached Georgetown on 13 May 1859 after a passage of 84 days with the loss of 11 lives. Five more died in Georgetown Hospital within ten days of landing while 16 others were detained in hospital for a longer period. On arrival the vessel was inspected by the Immigration Agent-General, James Crosby, who reported that the immigrants "were almost all in the best health and spirits . . . a very fine body of strong, healthy, active, young men." As before, the contracts had to be changed and the Court of Policy passed an ordinance on 24 August 1859 updating the contracts of all immigrants arriving in 1859 so as to conform with current laws.

PURSUING CHINESE WOMEN

In early February 1859, even before the arrival of this second wave of Chinese, the colony's administrative body debated and passed an ordinance aimed specifically at encouraging the immigration of Chinese women. Among the provisions included the capability of enforcing a quota system for female Chinese by empowering the governor of British Guiana with authority to withhold payment to a passenger ship not having a reasonable proportion of female emigrants. As an incentive, a sum of fifty dollars was also set aside to be paid towards the passage of each female Chinese immigrant. Finally, "no Chinese female shall be compelled to labour on the plantation to which she may be allotted. . . . " These intentions were idealistic, if not bureaucratic, and the *Royal Gazette* quickly noted that this issue of female immigration would be a difficult one to come to terms with in practice.

> In the course of conversation which took place in the Court of Policy, it was understood that the women introduced must be in proportion to the men. This is the rock upon which, we fear, the scheme of Immigration from China will split, and, notwithstanding the expectations of Mr. GERARD, there is much reason to believe that the number of immigrants will fall short of what we could do with. Chinese labourers, from all we have been able to learn, are exceedingly useful, and no exertions should be spared to procure as many of them as can possibly be obtained.
>
> [*Royal Gazette*, 8 Feb 1859]

The new arrivals from China were making a sufficiently favorable impression that the Court of Policy made a commitment to introduce many more on a continuing basis. In May 1859 the Court passed resolutions requesting that the British government undertake responsibility for the procurement of Chinese labourers, with a reasonable number of the emigrants being females. In August 1859 the Duke of Newcastle instructed Mr. Austin to secure 2,200 male emigrants for the current season. In practice some 1,500 male Chinese were procured. With regard to females, the Duke of Newcastle had stated:

> I am of the opinion that a minimum of 10 per cent be required for the present season and that as to future years the same proportion must be required as in the case of Coolie emigrants, namely for the season of 1860-1, and 1861-2, not less than one female to three males and for subsequent years not less than one female to two males.
>
> [*Royal Gazette*, 10 Nov 1859]

The difficulty in obtaining women emigrants became quickly recognized in a society where it was uncommon for females to accompany their partners to distant places. On 16 July 1859 Mr. Murdoch at the Emigration Office in Hong Kong expressed these concerns to London as well as his reservation about maintaining control over the situation if mixed company was going to be permitted on board ship:

> The points which would have to be decided by his Grace are:-
>
> *First* — The proportion of women. Upon this point it is difficult to offer any opinion. The number, in the first instance, cannot be otherwise than small, not probably, exceeding 10 or 15 per cent. It would, perhaps, be better to leave the exact proportion to be settled by Mr. Austin, with the approval of Mr. Bruce, with the clear understanding, that unless there is a prospect of obtaining a fair proportion in future years, the emigration cannot be continued. Another question which also arises, whether the women should be sent in the same ships with the men, and if so, what precautions are to be taken against fighting and disturbance on their account. This, however, is a question which can only be settled on the spot, and by those acquainted with the Chinese character.
>
> [*Royal Gazette*, 10 Nov 1859]

J. Gardiner Austin was left in sole charge as emigration agent in China. He drew up proposals for recruiting Chinese labourers including the opening of a depot in Hong Kong, free passage for emigrants to the West Indies, a contract agreement for agricultural work for a period of 5 years, wages of $4 per month, and a premium of $20 if a wife were taken along (or $40 for a family with two or more children). He tried to enlist the help of Reverend William Lobschied, a medical missionary who had been resident in China for several years. In a letter to Mr.

Austin dated 18 February 1859 Mr. Lobschied gave the opinion that the proposals were most liberal. He also indicated that he would be pleased to assist and be able to effectively control the recruitment process:

> I have communicated the nature of your mission to people connected with me, and from the adjacent districts on the mainland, and I have the pleasure of holding out the prospect to you of getting at least 5,000 married families who would embark here at Hong Kong. But great care should be taken not to put affairs into the hands of the Chinese Government because that would most decidedly use its influence to check the female emigration. This is the more necessary since the districts from Hong Kong to the north, and north east to the provinces of Fukien, are the only places in China where females have no small feet, and where the people are most willing to emigrate to foreign lands.
>
> [*Royal Gazette*, 6 Aug 1859]

Rev. Lobschied tried to impress on Mr. Austin the benefits that could be gained from publicizing the conditions that the prospective emigrants would encounter, and stressed the importance of keeping people of different clans separated. He also urged that the sailors should not touch the Chinese women in a joking fashion since the gesture could be interpreted to be insulting or offensive to the dignity of the women.

Austin was caught in a dilemma — those who were very poor, but who could arguably be persuaded to emigrate, were unsuited to field labour and liable to complain while those who were experienced in agriculture did not have the inclination to go abroad. Added to this, there were rumors spread wildly among the locals that those who were taken away from China were transformed into opium and that the interest in females was merely to gratify the lust of the debased foreigners. The only way to persuade suitable emigrants would be through careful explanation. But this approach also had its own dilemma. The literati were by and large opposed to the concept of emigration, particularly since the Confucian practices of ancestor worship would cease with the departure of the emigrant, thereby constituting a breach of filial duty. If some of the scholars were persuaded to speak in favor of it through appropriate remuneration the peasants were capable of sensing that their words were coming from the mouth and not from the heart. For these reasons Austin felt that he had to place greater dependence on missionaries such as Rev. Lobschied. In this regard the missionary influence was important in being able to persuade prospective emigrants to go to British Guiana since the converts to Christianity were willing to accept the guidance of their spiritual leader.

First Ladies

Assistance then came from an unexpected quarter — the governor-general of Kwangtung and Kwangsi provinces. British and French troops forces had forcefully taken Canton in January 1858 and a joint Euro/Chinese administrative body was established to govern the city. The kidnapping of Chinese by crimps had reached such an intolerable level that any effort to curtail their activities was welcomed. Emigration had become a fact of life and proclamations were put forth by Chinese district magistrates as well as by Harry Parkes, head of the joint administration of Canton, denouncing the activities of the kidnappers while offering a regulated system of emigration. The governor-general added his influence on 9 April 1859:

> I also myself proclaim these measures to the poorer classes in all places for their information. Let it be known by you all that those who desire of their own will to go abroad and seek employment in foreign lands should proceed themselves to the emigration houses and there make a clear report, when the Chinese officer and the emigration agent will carefully examine the applicants and thus ascertain whether they are indeed voluntary emigrants, and not victims to the crafty designs of the kidnappers. This having been clearly proved, they may then negotiate together the terms of service of their future destination and record these in a formal contract.

On 27 October 1859 Austin opened a depot for emigrants in Hong Kong, a modest place consisting of a few bamboo sheds. In November a similar depot was opened in Canton under the direction of Theophilus Sampson, who was previously cashier and chief clerk for the Allied Commissioners. On 24 December 1859 Austin dispatched his first batch on the *Whirlwind* consisting of 304 men, 56 women, 7 boys (less than 15 years of age), and 4 girls (less than 13 years of age). The voyage took 78 days and the ship arrived in Georgetown without a single life lost. Thus did the first Chinese women-folk reach British Guiana, seven years after Chinese men were first introduced there. Five more ships from Hong Kong and Canton departed for Demerara in the 1859-60 season. A total of 1,563 men, 305 women, 53 boys, 26 girls and 17 infants embarked, and of these 1,549 men, 298 women, 53 boys, 26 girls and 18 infants landed in Georgetown.

The arrival of the first ship carrying Chinese women proved to be the event of note:

> The Ship *Whirlwind*, after a quick run of only 78 days, arrived yesterday from China with 377 Immigrants, of whom 56 are females. Not a single death occurred on the passage. On the vessel entering the river, His Excellency the Governor, Mrs. WODEHOUSE, the Honble. WILLIAM WALKER, and Mrs. WALKER, and other ladies and gentlemen went on board to look at the newcomers, who appeared in excellent health and spirits. As few persons have had an opportunity of seeing a Chinese female, the arrival of a batch of 56, necessarily excites considerable interest. The health of the immigrants can be partly ascribed to the cleanliness and excellent arrangements on board, but partly also, and perhaps chiefly, to care in selecting only such as were likely to answer, and were in fit condition to undertake the voyage.
>
> [*Royal Gazette*, 13 Mar 1860]

> The married folks occupied the afterpart of the vessel, and were separated from the single men by a screen; each couple had separate accommodation, so as to secure privacy, and at the same time the partitions dividing, what might be termed the berths, were scarcely five feet in height, in order not to check the circulation of air. The centre and fore-part of the ship were allotted to people from Hong Kong and Canton, the two being separated to prevent collision between them. About a dozen others occupied the long-boat the whole passage, as they were not on good terms with any of the Hong Kong or Canton immigrants, but, before leaving the ship, the feeling of mutual distrust seemed to have disappeared. . . . [*Royal Gazette*, 23 Mar 1860]

Mr. Crosby, Immigration Agent General, went aboard the ship when it arrived and reported the immigrants to be

> a very fine body of people and apparently of a very much superior class of persons to any of those who have been hitherto introduced into the Colony.

The departure from Hong Kong of the second ship *Dora* was also an event with some fanfare. The *Hong Kong Register* reported that "a grand *dejeuner* was given by Mr. Austin, on board the

Dora to celebrate the intended despatch of the vessel to the West Indies." The guests included none less than the governor, His Excellency Sir Hercules Robinson, and Lady Robinson as well as the Lord Bishop of Victoria and other dignitaries.

The Ship *Dora* arrived this afternoon from Hong Kong, 84 days out, with 385 immigrants, of whom 113 are females. There were 387 shipped; of these two adults and an infant died, and one woman committed suicide by jumping overboard, but two births took place during the passage. The people are said to be, like the first batch, cheerful and healthy.

[*Royal Gazette*, 3 Apr 1860]

The Ship *Red Riding Hood* from China came in yesterday with 311 immigrants. She took on 314 at Hong Kong but one woman died in child-birth, one man committed suicide by jumping overboard, and another fell overboard and was drowned, so that no deaths occurred on the passage from disease of any kind. . . .

Twelve days after the *Red Riding Hood* sailed a conspiracy or disturbance of some kind broke out among the people, and two of the leaders were seized and put into chains. These proved to be one a pirate and the other a robber — something of the same, only the one was a sea and the other a land pirate. During the rest of the passage the greatest vigilance was exercised on board; the crew were kept on the alert, and the guns on the quarterdeck were trained forward. No further disposition, however, to turbulence or disorder was evinced, and during the latter end of the voyage the people were quiet and peaceable. On board the *Whirlwind* — and possibly the *Dora* also — great precautions were taken to prevent in the first instance, and, if need were, to suppress, anything like an outbreak among the people, and although nothing of the kind occurred, at the close of the voyage a considerable degree of uneasiness was felt by many of them, because they were not fully convinced that their destination was Demerary and not Havanah, but the word "Demerara" on the Light Ship dispelled any lingering doubts of the truth.

There is one point connected with the arrival of these Celestials to which we would invite attention. . . . There may be, and probably are, among the late arrivals, people who have no idea in the world of agricultural labour, but have been accustomed to pursuits of a very different character, and to put such as these to dig a trench or plough a field might be bad policy, unless they understood fully beforehand what would be expected from them, as their representations might have the effect of deterring many others from emigrating to this colony. Where no express understanding exists on the subject, it would be advisable to indenture all such people to those carrying on the trade or occupation to which they have become accustomed. Among every batch of immigrants, come they whence they may, there will be the black sheep of the flock, who will never be satisfied under any circumstances, but it would be the most polite course to let such of the immigrants as have been taught particular trades or professions, follow them out, under such regulation as may best meet the circumstances of the case.

[*Royal Gazette*, 10 Apr 1860]

The Ship *Norwood*, BRISTOW, master, arrived this morning from Hong Kong after, according to the telegraph, an unusually long passage of 133 days, with 316 immigrants; 14 died on the passage, from, it is said, the excessive use of opium. [*Royal Gazette*, 24 Jul 1860]

The *Norwood* was the last ship of the 1860 season and the Chinese, for the most part, were regarded as desirable plantation labourers. The government realized that it had no control over the quality of the immigrants but that at least some measures had to be taken to reduce the obstacles and disparities encountered by the new arrivals.

"An Ordinance to amend certain of the regulations related to Immigrants to this colony." Although general in title it refers chiefly to Chinese immigrants, and its leading features are — 1st. That every contract shall secure to the immigrant the same rate of wages as paid to the unindentured labourer, — or otherwise $4 per month, with sufficient food, on condition that he shall work seven and a half hours per day, except Sundays and holidays. 2nd. That every immigrant shall have, gratis, suitable lodging, and, while sick, sufficient medicines, nourishment, medical attendance, and hospital accommodations. 3rd. That one dollar per month shall be deducted from the immigrant's wages, for advances made in China, and such portion of his wages as he may assign to any party in China. 4th. That every immigrant may terminate his contract at the end of each year, on payment, for each unexpired year of the term of the contract, of a sum equal to one-fifth of the amount of the passage money; and also that the immigrant may change his employer at the end of the third or fourth year of his contract. 5th. Every immigrant who may contract in China for wages at $4 per month, may, after notice to the Stipendary Magistrate, exchange such contract for the rate of wages paid to unindentured labourers. By section 5, every Chinese female immigrant shall be required to reside on the estate on which her husband or father is indentured, but shall not be called upon to labour, except with her own consent. . . . [*Royal Gazette*, 7 Aug 1860]

The novelty of Chinese women landing in British Guiana in 1860 was celebrated, in a fashion, when the following poem was recited at a Christmas Extravaganza held on Christmas Eve of that year for the colony's elite.

This year first saw *Celestial* women on
Our shores — not *Heavenly* — because there are none.
But in earnest, three hundred Celestials
Who are much smaller than Terrestrials.
These tiny creatures of the Heavenly kind
Came some on the *Dora*, some ex the *Whirlwind*,
Some ex *Minerva*, some ex *Red Riding Hood*:
Ambrosia, surely, was not their only food.

[*Royal Gazette*, 25 Dec 1860]

Emigration Increases

To meet an increased demand for 2,500 Chinese emigrants for the 1860-61 season, Austin set up a branch agency at a farmhouse in Hang-tsai, about 50 miles from Hong Kong in December 1860. In fact Austin was able to exceed expectations by dispatching 2,854 male adults during the season. Reverend William Lobschied, who was instrumental in getting many of the Chinese to emigrate, decided that on his journey home to recover from a bout of illness he would make a detour to Demerara. One week before the *Mystery* arrived in Georgetown he took the time to tell the governor of British Guiana his observations of his fellow passengers.

May 29th 1861

Sir

China is a place where, with the exception of the pure Caucasian race, the best immigrant in the World can be obtained; but there are also men living in the outskirts of large cities who have not their equal in misery. There are lepers, broken down or frightfully diseased victims of vice, or men that have been so long in a starving condition, that their health is undermined, and to whom wholesome food is poison. If any person collect these men, he can easily load a ship, but the losses to the Government would be so enormous that hardly more than one third of the emigrants would be landed in a condition suited to the Colony.

The collectors of such men have hitherto been Portuguese, who sold them for the Cuban Market. Hence the immense losses on the Coolie ships, which sometimes amounted to about 35 per cent. The British immigration had put an affected ban against fraudulent acts of Chinese Agents by enlisting the interest of men who were able to communicate with the migrants without the medium of an interpreter. Hence crimps kept at a distance and some afraid of showing themselves in Hong Kong. But I had hardly proceeded to Canton, when a Portuguese arrived with a lot of men who would under the new regulation, have been rejected by the Cuban Agent, and whom he gives out as their speaking a dialect different from that of Canton, Hong Kong and their vicinities. He represents them as men being in a starving condition occasioned by intestine war and other miseries, as anxious to emigrate, but only as a body, they being unwilling to leave one of their number behind or to go to the Portuguese, as I learnt from Mr. Austin.

The truth is that the Portuguese parceled up the men in Macao and adjacent cities, where they were lying about in the streets by thousands, looked upon by the people as outcasts, most of them frightfully diseased and emaciated from habitual vice of opium smoking. Unable to procure the poison any longer, the Portuguese had acquainted them with a new channel of getting money, but instructed them to pretend to be unable to understand the local dialect. If they did not, and were consequently refused, he would not release them but keep them as hostages until they should have discharged their obligation towards him. The Crimp went even further and declared it to be their unanimous resolution to go together, and if one be refused, all would not go.

Mr. Austin yielding to this piece of important fraud, passed all the men, though with the conviction that he was doing wrong. He saw the money paid by him to the poor wretches to go into the bag belonging to the Portuguese; he tried, as he told me, to interfere, but gave it up after the men, from an impulse of dread of the omnipotent Portuguese paid over the money to him again. The poor wretches proceeded then on board the ship, and the Portuguese left with at least $600 for miserable, rotten men, 'hardly able to walk.'

Upon arriving on board the ship I was shocked at the sight of these men, though the extent of misery presented itself only after our departure from Hong Kong. At least two thirds of the men on board were opium smokers; but it being cold and the deck always occupied by the crew — in the discharge of their duty, I did not like to force everybody on deck until we should have set sail. Then after our departure from Hong Kong I tried to get the men on deck, I could hardly believe my eyes, for

I fancied myself in the most disgusting outskirt of a large Chinese town with scenes of misery around me which defy description.

Men teeming with vermin, full of sores about them, emaciated so as to consist of nothing but bone and skin, scaly and spotted all over from former diseases, three in four full of itch in its most loathsome state, dirty as if they had never seen water, and dull from opium smoking, some of them so weak that they would cry like children when being called to me and wash themselves.

I need hardly add that I regretted having undertaken a duty so desperate and hopeless, being sure that every gale would demand its victims from a crowd that had grown old at the age of from 25-35, ruined their digestive organs, who could not breathe without the poisonous drug, and were too weak to withstand a single day's starvation from sea-sickness. Ninety of these men had paid from $15-$18 each to the Portuguese and a crimp of the name of Nung from Sinning, they had no money left for purchasing any refreshment. Hence many of them had sold their clothing and were now lying there in the miserable rags in which they had first presented themselves; yea one of them had not even a pair of trousers and, could hardly be got to move, which alone disclosed the shocking state he was in.

Seeing the scanty supply of opium which they had been able to secure for the few dollars left them from the $20 advances, nearly exhausted, two of them tried to commit suicide immediately after we had set sail, thus could only be prevented from trying the same by the assurance from me that if their opium be really short, and there be no means of saving their lives, they should apply to me and I would see what I could do for them. The second evening after our departure from Hong Kong, I was called down to see a man who, I was told, was in a dying state. Upon coming down I found a man, a mere skeleton, lying before the stair case, his trousers pulled off, and his quilt wrapped around him as a mapp would be around a helpless baby. His body was in such a state that I could hardly get a person who would touch him, and remove him to a small room set apart for the reception of such as required to be removed from the rest of the emigrants. The slight motion of the ship had been the means of bringing to light his inability to walk up stairs, for once removed to the room, which was close to the water closet, he lived apparently a happy being, smoked his opium, his tobacco, and enjoyed a very good appetite, though so lean and weak that he could scarcely move his legs. We hoped to be able to bring him alive to Demerara, when the very rough weather at the Cape of Good Hope terminated his life. Sixteen of the deaths are of the same class, whose money had gone to the crimps, whose clothing were sold for a song, and who after all, not only died before reaching the place of their destination, but a number of the same class as do arrive, will be good for no work, but will have to go to the Hospital merely to die. Two of the rest here on board are lepers. They were a burden to themselves and to those around them.

The rest, who are bona fide emigrants from the Country, are in general in a very good state of health, and will prove to be useful Colonists. Their treatment here on board has been very kind, and they have enjoyed liberties such as are very seldom accorded to Europeans.

[*Public Records Office*, Colonial File CO 111]

The quality of the emigrants became the subject of another voyager, Dr. T.A. Chaldecott, the surgeon superintendent on board the *Whirlwind*. He wrote to London on 13 August 1861:

There is of course no doubt that a bona fide immigration of respectable families is very much to be desired, but it would in my opinion be far better to give up the idea entirely rather than introduce into the Colony such specimens of the sex as many of those ones aboard the "Whirlwind" were.

I think I am justified in stating that most of the women on board the "Whirlwind" were only married to their so called husbands immediately before the sailing of the ship, and that the men were tempted to bring them by the twenty dollars advance allowed for them in China.

Now it has been considered that out of this sum a certain amount has to be paid for the woman and yet there must be surplus sufficient to tempt the cupidity of the immigrants. It will be seen, therefore that the amount paid for the wife must be so small that she must necessarily belong to the lowest and the most miserable class.

As a consequence of this we had on board the "Whirlwind" two notorious prostitutes, four idiots, one helpless cripple, one hunch back, one deaf and dumb and several much disfigured by scars.

Several of the men told me that they had never received any advance for the wives; that the only reason they were married was that they were told by some of Mr. Austin's Chinese employees that they would not be received as emigrants unless they took wives with them and that these employees found wives for them and took the $20 advance for payments.

. . . I would suggest therefore that the amount given as advance to women and children should be paid on arrival at Demerara instead of at Hong Kong.

A great temptation to Chinese Employees would thus be done away with and cases of kidnapping (to which women and children are particularly exposed) would be much less likely to occur.

With respect to opium smoking. Unless some precautions are adopted I fear that the Colony will be overrun by a number of Opium smokers of the worst class. Among the lower classes those who are confirmed Opium smokers are often reduced to such extreme distress as would make them most anxious to Emigrate if there was a chance of their being able to continue the practice during the voyage and after their arrival in the Colony. These men will never make really able bodied labourers though of course some work may be got out of them if they are judiciously managed. It will be found too, I think, that, independently of their Opium smoking, these men are not of the class most eligible as Immigrants, for most of them will turn out and have been Artisans, Mandarin Officials, Tailors, petty shop keepers, cooks, schoolmasters, and who have fallen from their station in life by indulgence in the vice and have never been used to hard labor.

Opium smoking is at present allowed without limit in the depot at Hong Kong and on board the ship, and the consequence is that the men spend the greatest part of their advance in laying in store of the drug and give themselves up to a regular debauch as long as it lasts for which the entire leisure they enjoy affords a good opportunity.

The knowledge of this opportunity and the power of obtaining a supply of the drug which the advance gives them will tempt more and more of these men to emigrate and in my opinion the increased mortality which has occurred among Chinese Immigrants during the past season is thus partly accounted for. It will scarcely be wrong to attribute the greater part of the deaths reported as from diarrhoea and dysentery to the sudden abstinence from the drug on the voyage after their stock has been exhausted. . . .

The Chinese in Demerara.

. . . I heard only one complaint from the Chinese on the Estates but this was a serious one, and I am afraid that there would be some difficulty in removing it. I refer to the high price they have to pay for provisions, and more especially for their staple food — rice — for which they had to pay from five to six times more than they did in China. Now this must I should think be owing in a great part to the greed of the retail dealers from who they have to purchase it, and it might be possible perhaps for the Planter to buy this article wholesale and that one of the Overseers should sell it to the Coolies at cost price. The ships which bring Coolies from China generally have a good deal of spare tonnage and the Captains would doubtless be glad to fill up with rice on Government account at a low [cost] of freight.

From what I could learn, the Chinese complain very bitterly of the price of rice and it would be most desirable if possible to reduce it.

It is hoped that in time they will grow rice themselves as the Country is so well adapted for it, and also that they will breed their own pigs, ducks and poultry. . . . [*Public Records Office*, Colonial File CO 111]

The observations by Rev. Lobschied and Dr. Chaldecott show that, despite all his good intentions, Mr. Austin was unable to obtain a sufficient number of suitable emigrants and counted on the bodies that the unscrupulous crimps supplied in order to fill the quota. In addition, a number of the women who were accepted as being married were in fact bonded to their spouses only by monetary incentive.

Besides the two ships about which these first-hand reports were given, there were eight others during 1861 — *Sebastopol, Red Riding Hood, Claramont, Saldanha, Chapman, Montmorency, Sea Park,* and *Lancashire Witch.*

The Ship Montmorency, after a passage of 105 days from Hong Kong, arrived here on the afternoon of the 27th instant, assigned to Messrs. Jones and Garnett, with 281 Immigrants of whom 17 were females — a fine, contented batch of people. Seven deaths took place on board and one birth. One of the deaths, as we are informed, was from natural causes, and by others from excessive indulgence in the use of opium. The Captain says that he has been in the habit of carrying English, Irish and Scotch to Australia and that he has much more trouble with them than with this last set of immigrants, who were so peaceable and well disposed that he had no occasion to erect a barricade as usual, and they were permitted to walk about the quarter-deck.

[*Royal Gazette*, 29 Jun 1861]

We are glad to say that the *Lancashire Witch* arrived yesterday, after the unusually long passage of 131 days. She took in 461 immigrants and one birth occurred on board, but she lost 29 people during the voyage. Of these, 24 died, chiefly from diarrhoea, and 5 were missing, supposed to have been drowned either from suicide, or through accident; the last death took place three days ago. Of the 433 persons brought here 26 are females. [*Royal Gazette*, 6 Aug 1861]

The Season of 1861-62

The 1861-62 season started well with the rapid filling of the first two ships, which departed from Canton and Hong Kong. The situation suddenly changed when German missionaries began industriously circulating some adverse letters written by some of the Chinese in British Guiana who had been sent by Rev. Lobschied. This greatly affected the recruiting efforts at Hang-tsai and Austin quickly opened stations at Tat-hao-p'u (near the coast of Guangdong Province), Swatow and Amoy. During this third season under J. G. Austin's administration seven ships took 2,139 men, 504 women, 32 boys, 11 girls and 4 infants, for a total of 2,690. During the voyage 54 men, 46 women, one boy and one girl died while four births were recorded.

By the Spring of 1862 some negative opinions about the Chinese as cane field workers were beginning to emerge in British Guiana. Even so the Immigration Agent-General, James Crosby, continued to present to the government his usual glowing report about the new arrivals:

> Tuesday 4th March 1862
>
> I have the honor to report for the information of His Excellency the Governor, the arrival on Saturday, the 15th February last at 6 am of the Immigrant Ship the 'Agra' 714 tons NNM with Chinese Immigrants from Canton, Philip de St Croix Sgt Comande and Tsoi-a-fai, a Chinese Medical Practitioner as Surgeon Superintendent.
>
> The Agra left Canton on Tuesday 26th November last, and the mouth of the River on the Thursday following, touched at the Cape of Good Hope on Tuesday the 14th January last, took in fresh provisions, water, and vegetables, left the next day, and arrived here - after a voyage of eighty days. The ship was in admirable order. Clean and well ventilated, the provisions were good, and the water pure and wholesome. The appearance of the Immigrants was highly satisfactory. They were clean, cheerful, orderly, in excellent health, and a very fine body of people, and there appeared scarcely a man above the age of Forty years, and three fourths of the whole varied from eighteen to Thirty years of age. The women were also more cleanly and respectable in their appearance than any I have hitherto seen come to the Colony. On first going on board I did not consider they much exceeded in appearance many other bodies of Immigrants introduced into the Colony, but after a careful muster and the observation I made in the course of their distribution, I feel convinced

they are on the whole, the finest body of Chinese Immigrants hitherto introduced into the Colony. . . .

It is the first time any ship has come from China to this Colony with Immigrants without having on board a European Medical Officer as Surgeon Superintendent, and it is almost impossible any voyage could have been more successful or satisfactory. Mr. Tsoi-a-fai appears a very respectable intelligent person, and Ko-wan-Ki the only Interpreter on board, being also a very active intelligent man.

[*Public Records Office*, Colonial File CO 111]

Among the seven ships of the 1861-62 season the *Earl of Windsor* had an unusually high complement of female emigrants, which was said to have had a restraining influence on any tendency towards fighting among the passengers. In fact, violence was apparently not really on the minds of some of the passengers who made use of the 104 long days at sea to become more intimate with each other.

The Ship *Earl of Windsor*, of 738 tons, DICK Commander, arrived today from Hong Kong, after a passage of 98 days, with the following Immigrants, 174 males, 123 females and 7 children, giving a total of 304. Twenty-three deaths occurred during the passage; one man was missed, and it was supposed that he had jumped overboard. There are two remarkable features in this case; one the very high per centage of mortality — which we have not yet heard accounted for, — and the other, the large proportion of females to males, as compared with former arrivals. [*Royal Gazette*, 18 Mar 1862]

The Commission of Enquiry in the case of the *Earl of Windsor* have sent in their report, but we have not received any accurate information as to the results. It is said that the charge of promiscuous intercourse between the sexes was correct in the main, although the Captain and Officers endeavoured to guard against the evil, but that the other charges preferred by the Doctor — whatever those may be — were not substantiated, and that consequently, the passage money has been paid.

[*Royal Gazette*, 12 Apr 1862]

In contrast, the *Persia*, the fourth ship of the same season, was apparently a floating battlefield and Mr. Chapman, the Surgeon Superintendent, resorted to physical confinement, denial of food, and even caning, which was done by the captain himself to prevent any revenge being targeted at the crew. At the end of the voyage accusations were made against the captain and at a subsequent inquiry he explained that passengers embarked at four places — Hong Kong, Canton, Swatow and Amoy — and even before the vessel left Chinese shores there were bad feelings between the people from the different areas who spoke mutually incomprehensive dialects and who bore an inherent dislike each for the other. Many clashes took place between the factions. The Surgeon Superintendent could do little

> when 500 Chinese were fighting all over her, on deck, in the 'tween decks; yells and noises sufficient to stun you; billets of firewood, choppers, chopping-blocks, holystones, boards, iron bars, knives, etc., flying about, and glass bottles breaking in all directions.

The surgeon's testimony was confirmed by several of the crew as well as the interpreter. Despite the ruckus, only six deaths occurred among the 531 passengers and James Crosby was again able to issue his upbeat report of another fine batch upon the ship's arrival at Georgetown.

At the end of the 1861-62 season Mr. Austin's health failed and he returned to England on 15 April 1862. All in all his three seasons as Emigration Agent were successful in filling most of the demand set by the colonies and in obtaining a significant proportion of female emigrants. Furthermore, he was able to do so at a cost of between $57 and $64 per person, much lower than the $70 a head allowed by the Combined Court.

HINCKS BECOMES GOVERNOR

In January 1862 a new governor of British Guiana took office, and he almost immediately began to dismantle the system for bringing Chinese immigrants. Governor F. Hincks wrote to the Duke of Newcastle on 3 February 1862:

> I am firmly persuaded that there is an ample supply of labour in the Colony at present, the best evidence of which is that some estates will have to remove unindentured African and other labourers from their houses to make room for the immigrants about to arrive during the present season.

Four days later he sent another letter stating that some planters who had requested immigrants were now insolvent and that there was a surplus of labourers resulting in unemployment. Later in the month it was determined that only 270 new immigrants were being sought by planters. The Court of Policy held several meetings on the matter but came to an impasse when a motion to cut off immigration failed to be seconded. Some members then spoke out on the value of the Chinese labourers and the merits of having an ongoing supply. Governor Hincks expressed surprise that, if the Chinese were so satisfactory, why were there so few applications for labourers from China compared to those from Calcutta. The answer was that it was well known that the demand for Indian labourers could not be met and so the plantation owners would invariably request a number exceeding their actual needs. With the Chinese labourers, however, the quotas were being filled so there was no need to ask for any excess.

The governor then raised some questions about Austin's incidental expenses in China such as for fishponds, flower beds, champagne and gifts. Austin later replied that these were necessary to make the emigration depot more presentable from the damage incurred by a British bombardment of the area and for expressing cordiality to the appropriate Chinese authorities. On closer examination Austin's administration had incurred a total of $120, $125 and $139 per person for the three seasons, including all overheads, wages and passages. By contrast, the private operations by Gerard in 1859 had cost $144 per capita.

In the meantime, the Court of Policy, after much debate, had increased the immigration requirement to 905 labourers. This number was too small to maintain depots at Swatow, Amoy and Hang-tsai, and they were closed. Theophilus Sampson was asked to take over as Emigration Agent and he chartered the *Ganges*, which sailed with 293 men, 100 women, 12 boys, 4 girls and 4 infants on 4 April 1863. Sampson was unable to secure another suitable vessel so the *Ganges* was the only ship carrying immigrants to British Guiana for the 1862-63 season. In August 1863 Sampson was instructed to dispose of the land and buildings at Swatow. They were sold off for $345, whereas their original cost of purchase had been $4,000.

In 1863 the Chinese on some plantations were reported to be uncooperative and this adversely affected local opinion of the Chinese as immigrant labourers. In a letter to the Duke of Newcastle on 7 October 1863 Governor Hincks pointed out that "it will give more satisfaction to the planters to pay a larger amount per caput for really good labourers than to have the ships filled with the dregs of the Canton population."

For the 1863-64 season Governor Hincks informed Sampson that only 450 to 500 immigrants were to be recruited. This quota was quickly filled by the *Zouave* which sailed with 337 men, 157 women, 15 boys, 3 girls and 5 infants on 19 December 1963. The cost per person was $121.70, or £29. 8s. 9d.

Theo Sampson observed that one of the difficulties in getting Chinese who fit the desired criteria as plantation labourers in British Guiana was that such people did not exist. In China the farmers were more like gardeners than agriculturists. When the rice crop was sown it would be done by all, including women and children. The fields would then be left basically unattended until harvest time. At that time relatives and friends living and working in the towns would take to the fields to help in gathering in the harvest, after which they would head back to resume their town occupations. The threshing would be done at leisure by experienced hands. This cycle would be repeated for a second crop and then the fields left fallow until it was time to resume the first annual sowing. In fact, it was the women who did most of the field work while the men took the produce to market. Thus the Chinese were seen to be more adept at prolonged labour rather that intense labour.

REVIVAL 1864-66

Sampson recommended that operations would run more efficiently if there were less fluctuations in demand and if a minimum of about 2,000 emigrants per year were dispatched. Governor Hincks asked Governor Keate of Trinidad whether he would make a commitment to take 750 immigrants. Trinidad responded positively and British Guiana undertook to accept the other 1,250 beginning in the 1864-65 season. By the time the season was in full swing, Sampson received a communication saying that the British Guiana requirement had been increased to 1,500, i.e. exclusive of women and children. The first ship was the *Brechin Castle* which sailed from Canton on 18 October 1864. Four other ships followed for a total of 1,290 men, 416 women, 56 boys, 2 girls and 4 infants dispatched.

Mr. Sampson remarked that it was difficult to commission ships to take emigrants for three reasons, 1) the ship required a large outlay for provisions and fittings; 2) emigrants were more trouble than cargo; and 3) the risk of death and desertion of the emigrants was borne by the ship. A ship could make about 26% more profit taking cotton to England than transporting emigrants to Demerara, both journeys being of comparable duration. The problem was compounded by the uncertainty of whether there would be any outgoing cargo to take on at British Guiana. The ships were thus willing to embark emigrants only if there was an over-abundance of shipping capacity waiting around at the Chinese ports.

There was one notable exception to this — the *Red Riding Hood* made voyages with emigrants in three successive years, 1860, 1861 and 1862. However this vessel was chartered in England and not only stocked up with provisions before departure (rather than purchase supplies at Hong Kong) but also took on a full cargo of Demerara sugar destined for England. One other ship, the *Whirlwind*, undertook to engage in a charter on two occasions, in 1860 and 1861. On the second journey this vessel was provided with wood and water as part of the charter agreement so as to alleviate costs. The *Agra*, which had taken emigrants in 1861 was in Hong Kong harbour in 1863 but the ship's agents told Sampson that they wanted nothing to do with emigrants since the previous experience was "ruinous."

The 1865-66 season proved to be a difficult one because of Franco-Cuban competition. French ships were involved in transporting Chinese to Cuba at very attractive terms. On 13 March 1863 Sampson reported:

> The French-Cuban House, a few doors from my own, certainly was opened on the 4th instant without the recognition of the Chinese authorities, and a determination thus evinced to carry their point against all obstacles, and at the present moment there is not that accord which it is desirable to see in emigration matters. The Franco-Cuban prospectus was also published in Chinese on the 4th instant. . . . Nearly the whole of it (in Chinese) is copied word for word, with certain additions and suppressions necessitated by the altered circumstances, from parts of Mr. Austin's prospectus of 5th November, 1859.

The atmosphere was soured by this competition and Sampson found that the better quality emigrants were being induced by greater monetary rewards to register with the Franco-Cuban House. Sampson eventually had to request that he be allowed to increase his advance to $20 for each emigrant and to take emigrants from Swatow and Amoy, if needed. To complicate matters further, the Emigration Commissioners were unable to get satisfactory tenders in response to their advertisements for ships.

The first ship of the season, *Pride of the Ganges,* encountered trouble while lying at Whampoa, the port district of Canton, because of the difference in advance paid to some men. The mutinous situation was settled by paying all equally at the high rate of $15. The ship departed on 8 December 1865 with 240 men, 44 women and 9 children. A couple of days later the cooks complained that the rice was bad, but nothing was done about it. The following day a mutiny broke out and the captain and purser were thrown overboard. The Chinese seized control and forced the first mate to sail to Hainan Island, where they disembarked, taking the provisions and rice. The mate then set sail for Hong Kong and arrived there on 31 December. The incident was attributed to ineffective measures to control the original trouble-makers as well as to discontent about the poor quality of the rice. The British had no naval vessels on hand to send to Hainan Island and the Chinese customs steamer dispatched to find the mutineers broke down. Thus nothing was done to bring the mutineers to justice.

Later in the season, the *Jeddo* sailed from Amoy on 18 March 1866 with 480 emigrants, of whom only 3 were women. On 27 March, five emigrants who were enlisted to join in a mutiny informed the crew that even before leaving Amoy a plot to murder all the Europeans had been hatched. The captain had the ringleaders seized, flogged and put in irons. On 16 April, when some ten miles off land in the Straits of Sunda, a fire was reported in the fore hold. About 30 Chinese rushed forth and attempted to take possession of a lifeboat. The mate and some of the crew jumped into the lifeboat to prevent its seizure. One of the blocks supporting the lifeboat then gave way causing the mate, two crew members and almost of all the Chinese in the lifeboat to be hurled into the sea and killed. Meanwhile the fire raged out of control and the captain ran the ship ashore to save as many lives as possible. When a count was taken, no less than 161 Chinese had died.

Despite these disasters, Sampson was able to meet the request for 625 male labourers with two ships, one of them being the *Pride of the Ganges* which reloaded and departed from Whampoa on 31 March 1866. The total number embarked was 798, comprising 747 men, 33 women, 16 boys and 2 girls. Amoy proved to be a difficult place for procuring female emigrants and permission was granted for Sampson to close the depot there.

CONVENTION AGREEMENTS

Emigration of Chinese to British Guiana came to a halt for the next eight years although Britain was still eager to obtain labourers and had forced China to agree to allow emigration in the 1860 Treaty of Peking. Attempts to come to a diplomatic agreement about the terms of indenture took many years, as described in the previous chapter. Eventually, in January 1873, an understanding was reached between the British and the Chinese governor-general at Canton and Theo Sampson again got into action.

> Mr. Sampson to Mr. Walcott
>
> Canton, 25th February, 1873
>
> Sir, — I have the honor to inform you that after a delay arising form the New Year Holidays I formally opened the Emigration House on the 14th inst., at the same time causing the fact to be known by the posting of notices in and around Canton, as well as advertising in the Chinese newspapers published in Hong Kong.
>
> My best hopes were centred in the influence of certain Emigrants who had returned from British Guiana, and who had been recommended by the Governor of the Colony as likely to prove useful in the collection of other Emigrants. Accordingly I wrote to one of them, Chun-kum-Po by name, and desired him to come to Canton to arrange matters. I then had a long discussion with him, the result of which was for present purposes a natural decision that the season was too far advanced to attempt operations in his part of the country.
>
> In the meantime the house has been opened, but I had refrained from chartering a ship, wishing first to test my powers of filling her.
>
> The result so far has been very unsatisfactory, but a very few men — and they are not of a very desirable class — evincing a willingness to emigrate, and not one family. I do not think that during that ten days, during which I have been offering to receive emigrants, I can boast of a score of men willing to go. Had I had a ship on the berth I think it

possible I would have filled her in about five months, but I believe with males only — a result than no emigrants at all would I have no doubt be deemed less unsatisfactory.

Theo Sampson to Stephen Walcott

Canton, 4th March 1873

Sir, — In continuation of my letter of 25th February I have the honor to report that I am now closing the agency for the season. . .

Since the opening of the house I have registered the names of 193 single men, of whom, probably 40 or 50 have really a wish to emigrate. These men are mostly from the streets of Canton, but my selection from this class of people have hitherto given fair satisfaction, and would doubtless do so again. The number is small but would probably be larger if there were a ship on the berth, nevertheless it would take a long time to fill a ship with them, were it desirable to do so.

The position of affairs has led me to close the house; but independently of these, my real reason for doing so, there is not — or a few days ago there was not — a suitable ship in Hong Kong open to charter. . . .

The return of immigrants during last year, and the prospect that more will return year by year, may be considered as rendering the future more hopeful. But the source from which the women were mostly obtained in previous years is now dried up: in plain language, the feuds which rendered large numbers of women destitute widows are at an end; and future family emigration must, I think, consist of bona fide families influenced to emigrate by the reports of those who have returned. It is not likely that this class of people will be numerous, and my chief hopes rest on the influence of those who returned last year. They assure me, or rather they express an opinion, that one or two hundred families will be willing to go to the West Indies from their part of the country next year. This number, if obtained, supplemented by some well selected men from Canton and its immediate neighbourhood, would represent two small ships or one large one. . . .

I have, &c.

THEO. SAMPSON [*Royal Gazette*, 8 May 1873]

The situation that Sampson referred to as a source of female emigrants was the Taiping Rebellion, which had produced many widows, displaced persons and refugees. Later on that year, as the emigration season of 1873-74 approached, Sampson enlisted the help of Ch'an Kun-po. He was one of 29 Chinese who had returned to China from British Guiana in 1870 and 1871. A number of them were granted a free passage to India by Governor Scott with the onward passage to China being paid by the returnees themselves. Since many of them had expressed a willingness to return to British Guiana after visiting family and friends the governor had arranged for free passage between Calcutta and Georgetown on the return journey. Ch'an began disseminating information in a Hakka district and by September Sampson reported that recruitment was progressing well.

> Canton, 25th September, 1873
>
> Sir, — I have the honor to inform you that the collection of emigrants appears to be progressing favourably, there being upward of two hundred in my depot, the bulk of whom I believe intend to emigrate.
>
> In the absence of a ship I have not yet publicly open my office to all applicants, nor have I taken any steps to publish generally the re-opening of the establishment. All that are now in the depot have come in consequence of the representations of the people who have returned from the West Indies.
>
> Suitable tonnage, I regret to say, is very scarce, I have accepted the Corona, now at Shangai at £16.
>
> The vessel is 1200 tons register, and is larger than I could have wished, and the rate is high; but if I had refused her I shall probably have had to wait two, or three months for one, and the cost of feeding the emigrants at the depot in the meantime would perhaps have almost equalled the excess in the rate of passage money. [*Royal Gazette*, 6 Dec 1873]

A month later Sampson reported on the problems he was having with crimps:

> Canton 28 October 1873
>
> Some crimps who entered my depot, either in the guise of emigrants or under the pretence of visiting or looking for friends, beguiled off eleven raw country lads of about twenty years of age; some were told that the ship (my ship) had arrived and were invited to go to see her; others were invited to a feast at an eating house, to an opium pipe, or to a brothel; some were probably persuaded that they would get more money in Macao, or lucrative employment in some neighboring place. Amongst the inducements sometimes offered and which prevents the victim giving a full explanation of the reason that he was so easily fooled, is the assurance that at Macao he can get eight dollars, and afterwards he can refuse to emigrate, whereupon the Macao Authorities will send him back to Canton. "I've done it often," adds the crimp, "and if you will give me two of the eight dollars I'll go down with you and put you up to the ropes."

> By some such means the eleven men were induced to accompany the crimps, and were lodged in a shop which professed to be that of a stone cutter, preparatory to being taken off to "see the ship" or to the Macao passenger boat. The facility with which raw countrymen may be deceived by glib-tongued city folks may perhaps be compared to the position of an English farm labourer of fifty years ago, being for the first time in his life removed from his native village and placed in the busiest part of London.
>
> Two of the eleven, however, after getting a good meal, and one of them accepting the loan of a good jacket to hide his rags, made an excuse for returning to the depot, with the understanding that the crimps were to come and fetch them at dusk. They told no one of what had occurred until about 4 p.m. When the other men were missed and enquiries were made, they made statements of which the above is the substance, though some of the particulars were not elicited until later in the evening.
>
> A watch was set for the expected return of the crimps, and at dusk three made their appearance; two remained outside while one entered. No sooner had he done so than a number of emigrants attacked him, and would probably have seriously injured him if he had not been released by my men and locked up. The other two of course decamped.
>
> It was too late to go to the stone-cutter's shop that night; it was visited next morning, but the birds had flown, and no tidings of their whereabouts could be learned.
>
> In course of time the Chinese officials took charge of the prisoner, and promised to make enquiries about the stone-cutter's shop; and there the matter now rests.

Sampson was able to send off the *Corona* on 23 December 1873 with 314 indentured men, 40 women and 34 children. Among the passengers on this ship was the author's great-grandfather, Soo A-cheong, who was accompanied by his wife and son. The contract of indenture signed by him and Theo Sampson, with the details of the terms of engagement, is shown in the Appendix.

Arrival of the Corona

Mr. Sampson felt that he had exercised due care to ensure that all the emigrants on the *Corona* were fit for the anticipated work in British Guiana and that they understood the commitments they were undertaking. He later commented that Guangdong was a hopeless place to recruit emigrants and, as an example, "the Corona sailed with 108 short of her complement. Extraordinary efforts might secure 600 yearly but the outlay would far exceed the proportionate value in the people." He felt that the shortfall was attributable in part to the low market price of rice locally and the prevailing climate of peace and prosperity.

> The Ship Corona, 1199 tons, Captain Bate, arrived from Whampoa, after a passage of 71 days, with a cargo of 600 tons of rice and 368 Chinese immigrants. Only one death occurred on the voyage, and that about six weeks ago. There are about 40 females on board. The re-opening of Chinese Immigration has been signalised by one of the shortest and most successful voyages on record.
>
> [*Royal Gazette*, 24 Feb 1874]

The *Corona* had to wait at the Light Ship for a few days of quarantine and the Immigration Agent General, James Crosby, made preparations for allocation of the immigrants. It was not a straightforward task since there were applications for 2,590 adult labourers from the estates, 1,365 in Demerara, 750 in Essequebo and 475 in Berbice. The immigrants were eventually distributed to 48 estates, the largest number, 17 males and 6 females, going to Lusignan, while Bel Air took one male.

The immigrants on the *Corona* disembarked in Georgetown on 1 March 1874 and very soon became involved in the local scene, although not without some controversy. The *Royal Gazette* reported:

> Since the arrival of the *Corona* the immigrants she brought have been promenading the city with all the airs and eagerness of a body of Cooke's tourists visiting some celebrated continental city for the first time; they have travelled over it from end to end and have climbed to the top of some of its highest buildings the better to enjoy the scenery; they have pried into the stores, the churches, the Public Buildings; they have patronized the cabs to a liberal extent, as many as 10 of them airing themselves in one vehicle at the same time. . . . Amongst the lot there is scarcely a man who has the appearance — not of being an agricultural labourer — but of being a likely person to be converted into one, . . . They look 'of the town,' and are more at home in it than they will be with a cutlass or shovel in their hands on an estate. . . . To persons like them, evidently used to town life and no other, country life and country work must be thoroughly distasteful, and we inhabitants of Georgetown

may look forward with every confidence to having our city population increased by the influx of the *Corona*'s immigrants who will prefer the chance of living on their wits in town to steady hard work on an estate.

. . . It would be better to have no Chinese at all than to have such as are only qualified to increase the least desirable class of our varied population. [*Royal Gazette*, 5 Mar 1874]

There seems to be some difference of opinion amongst the local press regarding the merits, as agricultural labourers, of the Chinese brought on the *Corona,* one journal holding that they are altogether unsuited for country work, and another describing them as men of "superior intelligence" certain to prove of valuable service on a plantation; but whatever their qualifications for estates' work may be, one thing is daily becoming more apparent and that is, that their "superior intelligence" renders their presence in the city rather oppressive than agreeable, and the sooner they are sent off to their respective destinations the better. The freedom with which these men of "superior intelligence", as soon as they landed, roamed over the city, prying into stores, offices, public institutions, and (sometimes) private houses, took the city by surprise; the newcomers walked about with a patronizing air and examined the various objects that met their attention with a nonchalance amounting in some cases to positive impertinence. For a day or two the novelty of the sight amused the inhabitants, the kindness however with which the immigrants were treated was mistaken by them for inference to themselves as persons of consequence, and they were thus encouraged to take still greater liberties, as for instance helping themselves to whatever they found eatable, in some of the private dwellings they entered. Their love of good living has led them to an appropriation of Government property, that, though it may create a smile amongst those who enjoy practical jokes, is a very serious matter, especially for gentlemen who have the honour of invitations to dinner at Government House. At the back of the Immigration Depot is a fish pond which is, or rather *was,* stocked with excellent fish, kept principally for the supply of Government House table; a preserve of this tempting kind did not long escape the notice of these Chinese of "superior intelligence," and by the simple act of opening the sluice door and draining off the water, the Chinese to the number of upwards of 200, were enabled to wade in and enjoy the fun of catching fine fat lively fish — an enjoyment all the keener that it was provoking an appetite which these same fish were soon to appease. The Immigration Agent General, we understand, has not quite recovered from the shock which the news of the robbery gave him, and he has hardly ceased "blessing his soul" yet, but *cui bono,* these pious "ejaculations" won't restore the fish. Men like these fish-catchers, are not likely to wait long for any delicacy that their estates or its neighbourhood can provide, their superior intelligence will soon discover the secret of living well without the necessity of working much. If the various managers to whom they are about to be consigned would keep a special record of the labour performed by the *Corona*'s people, a short sketch of their principal escapades, and the dates of their desertions from the estate, these joint records, a year hence, would form an interesting document to students of the great Labour question and, incidentally, to the general public.

The Immigration Agent General has given Proprietors and Attornies due warning that the Immigrants will be ready for delivery on Wednesday the 11th instant (tomorrow) and that in the event of their not being taken away on this day they will be boarded at the expense of the estates. Considering the worry and anxiety the Chinese have caused the staff of the Immigration office already, it is to be hoped Managers will not neglect sending tomorrow for their lots of "superior intelligence," otherwise the country may have to deplore the untimely and premature death of at least one nimble, energetic, and highly respected, Official thorough the Herculean labour thrown on his shoulders of conducting a *table d'hote* for two or three hundred fastidious Chinese. Perhaps the daily expense of boarding these people who have given proof of their superior taste in the food line, may induce our country friends to carry them off early, and thus the possible calamity which we have hinted at, will be averted.

A contemporary last night says that the Chinese celebrated their arrival in the Colony with a Ball. This, we are authorized to state, is slightly incorrect. They celebrated their safe arrival with a series of theatrical entertainments given in the evenings under the portico of the Immigration Office, to which the public were made welcome, and many availed themselves of the privilege. Our contemporary's mistake may have arisen from an ondit afloat that the public intended to repay the kind and flattering attention of the Chinese with a Ball.

[*Royal Gazette*, 10 Mar 1874]

A number of events took place in 1873-74 that resulted once again in the interruption of the just-resumed flow of immigrants from China. Unfavorable weather in 1873 disrupted sugar producing operations and this sent some planters into insolvency. The price of sugar on the world market fell thereby affecting the profitability of the plantation owners while the cost of bringing immigrants from Asia had increased. These factors caused a severe cutback in the need for immigrant labourers. The situation was compounded by the passing of a local ordinance resulting in the contributions from the colony's coffers to the Immigration Fund being reduced from one-third to one-sixth of total costs. Then the Secretary of State for the Colonies expressed displeasure at all the expenses incurred over the past eight years for keeping the Emigration House at Canton open — eight years during which not a single emigrant was procured. On 31 October 1874 the governor wrote back that the colony had decided to close the Canton agency although the *Corona* immigrants were well received.

FREE IMMIGRATION

The various problems associated with recruiting suitable agricultural workers, the difficulty of obtaining ships, the fluctuating needs in British Guiana and, above all, the cost of introducing Chinese immigrants created an environment in which the thought of attracting Chinese emigrants on a free basis, i.e. without contracts of indenture, began to be considered. Such a possibility was suggested by Mr. Firth, the Emigration Agent in India, who made an investigative tour of China, and filed his lengthy report in 1875.

At the meeting of the Court of Policy on 28 April 1876, Mr. William Russell presented a letter from his friend, which described the current "condition of the Chinese in California, and particularly to the fact that Americans and Irish members of the society there were getting up in arms against the Chinese. The writer of the letter suggested that this was a fitting time for us in Demerara to make some effort to turn the stream of Chinese immigration from California to this place. . . ." Mr. William Russell thought this was an excellent idea and felt that the Chinese who were going to be excluded from landing in California would have a great future in British Guiana. As an example of how one group of people have succeeded, he made reference to the Portuguese who had arrived as agricultural workers and were now much better off, or words to that effect. His exact words, however, did not go over very well with one person who retorted:

The chief object in writing these lines to you is to call attention to the reference made by Mr. Russell to the Portuguese in his speech in the Court of Policy yesterday.

He stated; — "That the Portuguese who came here ignorant and needy were now rolling in their carriages; and seeing what the Portuguese, ignorant as they were, had done" etc., etc. In making these remarks he showed very bad taste. Is it so long ago since he was a man of straw? And are there not many of his countrymen who came here as poor and as ignorant as any of the Portuguese? We have hundreds of Englishmen and Scotchmen who, raw as raw can be, have made their way to the front of this community, and yet would Mr. Russell dare throw this at their teeth in a public assembly?

The Portuguese have done wonders for this country as well as for themselves. You have among them, like among all nations good and bad — clever, stupid, ignorant, and the reverse. When Mr. Russell points to those Portuguese rolling in carriages he must not forget the number is limited and his remarks may hurt the feelings of the few, but there are many more not Portuguese, who can ill afford it and still sport many horses, &c., and who came here with little in the shape of clothing. . .

Yours obediently,

DIANA [*Royal Gazette*, 29 Apr 1876]

While Diana did not find Mr. Russell's presentation to be a shining example of political correctness, the speech aroused some local reaction, voiced by an alleged Chinese supporter who did not mince his words:

Sir, — Me likee Mistel Lussell too muchee. He say Potugee ridee in calidge, no walkee a dam like a 'Cotchman. Potugee come dis land — he not bling one bit, self. 'Cotchman come, he bling too muchee money. Potugee no readee no ritee; Potugee flooree too bad. 'Cotchman no flooree. 'Cotchman good good man; he no lidee in calidge like dam Potugee. Mistel Lussell, he 'Cotchman, he good man. He likee Chinaman, say Chinaman good man, no tief, no lidee in calidge, no do noting 't all 't all; keep um shop and sell 'um too much cheap. 'Cotchman good man; Mistel Lussell good man; Chinaman good man; Mistel Lussell and Chinaman mattes — all two good men, no lidee in calidge like dam Potugee. Me likee Mistel Lussell too muchee; me go bling um Black man and Potugee fowl. Evly time me to takee fowl, me give Mr. Lussell some. Goodbye; me go lookee for fowl-bag now, now. Me go ridee on house post; — "'Cotchman good man, Chinaman good man — all two no ridee calidge dam Potugee ridee calidge."

Ching A Fung
Charlestown Nut Store, April 29th 1876.[1]
[*Royal Gazette*, 29 Apr 1876]

Lengthy debates occurred among the government officials in June 1876 with regard to free immigration of Chinese. The reporter for the *Royal Gazette* recorded that at the Combined Court:

Mr. Russell moved the following resolution:-

Resolved, — That if it shall appear expedient to the Governor and the Court of Policy to establish free emigration, without contract, from China, and if such emigration shall be sanctioned by Her Majesty's Government, this Court will be prepared to provide the necessary funds for conducting such free emigration, and establishing steam communication between China and this colony.

. . . Mr. McCalman . . . hoped that they would be able to induce many of those immigrants so highly recommended by Mr. Firth to come, and if the selection were wisely made, very few of labourers would be found either in the gaols or in the hospitals.

Mr. Smith thought it was very considerate in the last speaker to couple Chinese immigration and gaols together, and he was afraid that several members of the Court would agree with him that one would follow closely on the heels of the other. . . . He admitted that there were difficulties in getting the Chinese brought under indenture; it was necessary to take them free or not at all; but he would confine it to the Chinese, and not make it applicable to coolie or other immigration. He considered that the stay and backbone of the Colony was coolie immigration. . . . Entertaining these views he considered it his duty to vote against the resolution.

. . . Mr. Garnett said he . . . did not expect that the people that they would get from China would be better than those that came on the Corona. They had 125 of whom 26 per cent. only were agricultural labourers. He had a list of the trades of the others, and for the information of the Court he would read it. There were pedlars, hucksters, barbers, confectioner, domestic servants, money changer, druggist, opium seller, rice cleaner, actor, boatman, silk weaver, mason, painter, shop-keeper, tailor, sailors, tobacconist, gardeners, tea makers, pack maker, mat makers, stick maker, dyer, weaver, eating home keeper, cake maker, jet maker, schoolmasters, clothes maker, distiller, stone cutter, and six of no trade at all. When

1 This letter was evidently written by an English-speaking person as a satirical response to Diana's outrage regarding the sentiments expressed by William Russell about the Portuguese while he was trying to urge the immigration of more Chinese.

these people come here they would not go on sugar estates if they could get profitable employment elsewhere; but they would become general consumers. They would consume a good many fowls belonging to the inhabitants (a laugh) — they would consume other things and would contribute largely to the taxation of the country. . . . Yet he saw a number of the very men he had named, amongst them the cake maker and the actor, working in the buildings. They had been there only a very few weeks and yet they were doing the work as well as if they had been brought up to it all their lives. . . .

Mr. Russell said he would be sorry if it were to go out from the Court that the Chinese were so intimately connected with gaols as had been represented by his hon. friend opposite (Mr. Smith). He defied anyone to show from the proceedings in the courts of justice that the Chinese were habitual gaol-birds. He held that the Chinese on the contrary were a good example to the other classes in the country. . . . He would recommend to his hon. friend to read Mr. Heyworth Dean's new book "The White Conquest," which showed that John Chinaman was mentally and physically the equal of the Europeans. He could undersell the Europeans in his own particular trade, and the aptitude with which he took up any new business was wonderful. . . . The hon. member mentioned a case in which a Chinaman coming from Essequebo by the steamer, sat down to breakfast and drank his beer like an Englishman, and even took his glass of wine with one of the passengers hob-a-nobbing in true style. With regard to the population question, the hon. member pointed out that with the first importation of Chinese there came no women whatever, and altogether there were only 10 per cent., which would more than account for the difference pointed out by the hon. member opposite. In the Chinese quarter at Leonora he knew there were chubby Chinese children, and he had never known of an instance of a dead Chinese child.

. . . Mr. Smith having left the room, the resolution was passed unanimously. [*Royal Gazette*, 17 Jun 1876]

Chinese arriving of their own free will was, in fact, already an ongoing practice but only on an individual basis. A few came from countries in the region from as early as 1853 while others who had left the colony after completing their service later returned. However, the total number was very small in comparison to those who came on the immigrant ships. In the Immigration Agent-General's annual report for 1877, James Crosby reported:

There were 64 Indians and 49 Chinese who paid their own passages and were consequently not subject to compulsory service under indenture.

> These latter are described in the records of the Immigration Office as "Casuals." [*Royal Gazette*, 5 Dec 1878]

In 1879 fourteen such Chinese casuals arrived from neighboring countries.

Much discussion took place about the manner in which free immigrants would be given employment and the cost of transporting them to British Guiana. To estimate the scope of interest in Chinese labourers the Governor sent a circular to the 113 sugar estates, and 96 of them sent in applications for labourers not under indenture. A proposal was thus put forth for procuring one or two shiploads of Chinese on an experimental basis with a bounty of $60 offered for each person arriving at Georgetown. Lord Carnarvon, Secretary of State for the Colonies, gave consent provided that the bounty did not exceed one third of the cost of introduction.

THE LAST SHIPMENT

In December 1878 thirty-one plantation owners put up a total of £8,647. 1s. 8d. to engage the *Dartmouth* to bring a boatload of Chinese from Canton. The emigrants were collected by Messrs. Turner and Company, merchants in Hong Kong, who, as agents of Messrs. Hyde, Hodge and Company, had been involved in recruitment for the first two ships ever to embark Chinese for British Guiana in 1852.

After the *Dartmouth* arrived at Georgetown some of the Chinese, including a group of 60 to 70 Christian converts, were about to disembark when others of their fellow passengers threatened to murder them. It was discovered that the latter had signed promissory notes in China for the $45 passage money to be repaid at $2.50 per month for 18 months and they would not leave the ship, or let others do so, unless they first had signed contractual agreements for work. James Crosby resolved the dilemma by inviting a representative party of some 30 people to go ashore to discuss the matter with the settled Chinese.

> The safe arrival of the Dartmouth after a remarkably rapid passage of 81 days from Hong Kong, with 500 Chinese immigrants (436 men, 47 women, and children) imported at the instance of certain members of the West Indian Committee, inaugurates what we sincerely hope will prove to be the immigration system of the future. . . . Taking them as a

lot, these new immigrants are just what they could be wished. Active, muscular, and healthy, most of them used to hard continuous labour in tilling the ground, they give the promise of turning out industrious and trustworthy labourers, such as are greatly required on the sugar estates. In the Hong Kong Agent's letter to Mr. Ferris Grant, he says the people belong to a peculiar race of Chinese called Hakka, celebrated for their industry and hardiness. As soon as the vessel entered the harbour yesterday afternoon, the immigrants exhibited the greatest impatience and anxiety to put their foot on land. Some of them were carried away by this feeling to such a pitch that they jumped over board to swim the short distance between the vessel and the land, and the ship's boats had to be lowered to their assistance. When this was reported to Mr. Crosby he at once sent a Chinese Interpreter on board to tranquilize the people and explain to them that they would not be detained on board a moment longer than would be necessary to make the arrangements between them and the estates on which they would be settled; and as soon as these arrangements were completed they would be able to come ashore and meet their countrymen. The people heard the Interpreter with every show of respect and at once consented to do as he had suggested. The Immigration Depot has been surrounded these two days with well-dressed Chinese waiting to receive their fellow countrymen and give them a welcome. Amongst the new arrivals are sixty-five Christians who expressed a desire to be located together on one estate, and this has been done as nearly as practicable under the system of allotment decided upon by the Planters' Committee which fixes 50 as the number to be sent to an estate, the fiftieth man being a headman or 'driver' who, it is anticipated, will be able to exert a powerful and salutary influence over the 49 people under his charge. The people, we may mention, will be under no legal obligation to work upon an estate.

. . . The collective cost of recruiting ($60 each woman, $40 each man); of provisions, &c., &c., during the voyage; of passage money (£6 10/ per adult); and of all the sundry expenses attending the shipment and transport of the Dartmouth's people, is about $55,000 or $110 each. From this is to be deducted the sum which the Government allows for every free able-bodied immigrant introduced into the colony, — a sum which in the case of the Chinaman may be regarded as a very good investment for the colony, John being a very liberal consumer of imported goods and consequently a large contributor to the general revenue. It is possible, — highly probable we should say — that the cost per caput for these free Chinese would be materially smaller if the system were once organised and fairly set going. What, however, first has to be settled is

> whether the new system is workable with profit, and only time can solve that question. That it may prove an unqualified success must be the wish of all who take an intelligent interest in the colony's welfare.
>
> [*Royal Gazette*, 13 Feb 1879]

The experiment with free Chinese immigrants produced mixed results. They were distributed to ten sugar plantations across the country in groups varying from 35 to 73 persons. A survey was made after 15 months and Plantation Great Diamond, to which a large batch of Christians were allotted, reported the retention rate of *Dartmouth* immigrants to be 89%. On four other estates more than half of the *Dartmouth* passengers were still on the same plantations. However, less than half stayed on the remaining five estates. Plantation Hampton Court in Essequebo county, which also took a large number of Christians, seemed to have drawn a bad lot who would not settle down to work and were constantly deserting so that only 8% still remained on the plantation after the same time interval. James Crosby reported that those who had left the estates were gaining an industrial livelihood. Thus he was able to give the evaluation that the immigrants were "as satisfactory as could well be expected." However, his optimistic evaluation was not supported by the plantation owners who felt that the experiment was not sufficiently profitable to warrant another attempt at procuring free Chinese immigrants.

The *Dartmouth* was thus the last ship sponsored by plantation owners to bring Chinese to British Guiana. Over the period from 1853 to 1879 a total of 13,541 Chinese had landed in the colony. In subsequent years there were a number of Chinese who immigrated but they traveled on their own initiative and at their own expense.

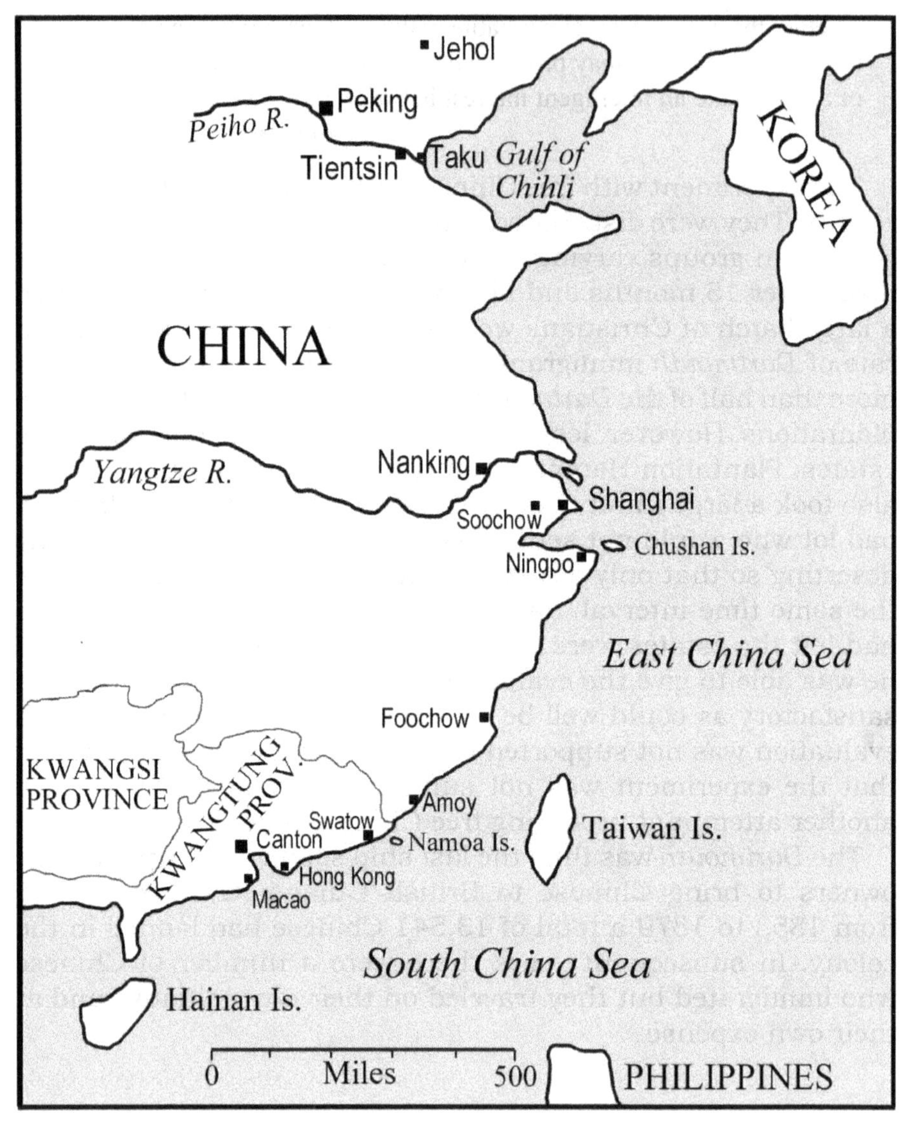

Sea Coast of China

Current names in pinyin spelling:
Kwangsi (Guangxi); Kwangtung (Guangdong); Peking (Beijing); Jehol (Chengde): Tientsin (Tianjin); Taku (Dagu); Nanking (Nanjing); Soochow (Suzhou); Foochow (Fuzhou); Amoy (Xiamen); Swatow (Shantou); Canton (Guangzhou); Hong Kong (Xiang Gang); Macau (Aomen); Gulf of Chihli (Bohai Sea).

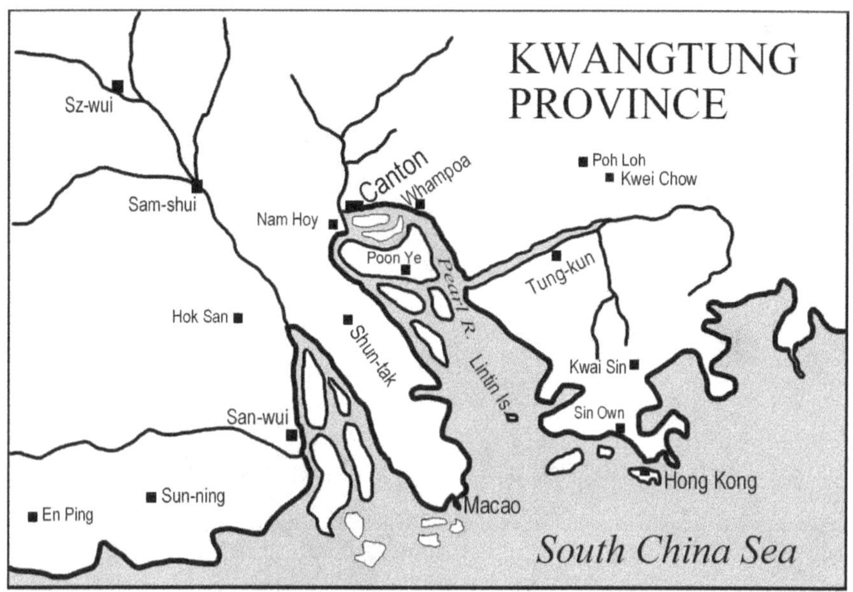

Pearl River Delta Region
Current names in pinyin spelling: Hok San (Heshan); Kwai Sin (Huiyang); Kwei Chow (Huizhou); Lintin (Lingding); Nam Hoy (Nanhai); Poh Loh (Boluo); Poon Ye (Panyu); Sam-shui (Sanshui); Shun-tak (Shunde); Sin Own (Xin An); Sun-ning (Taishan); Sz-wui (Sihui); Tung-kun (Dongguan); Whampoa (Huangpu).

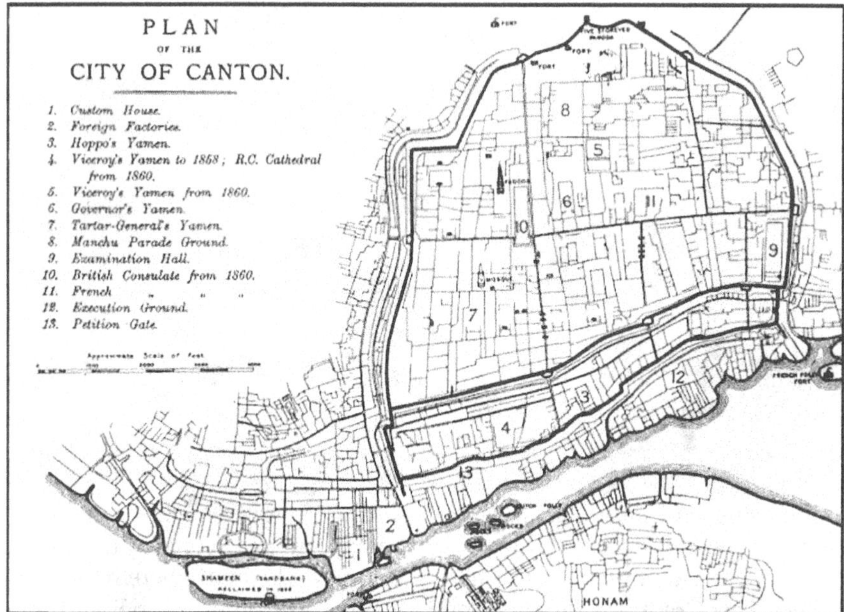

From H.B. Morse "The International Relations of the Chinese Empire."

Clippers were built for speed and preferred for the shipping of goods and opium by foreign merchants trading in China.

Opium ships at Lintin Island, painted by W.J. Huggins in 1824. On the right is a custom-designed vessel powered by sail and scores of oarsmen, used for carrying opium from Lintin to Canton. The boats were popularly called "Fast Crabs" or "Scrambling Dragons." The opium carriers were well armed to prevent undesired intrusion. *HSBC Holdings plc.*

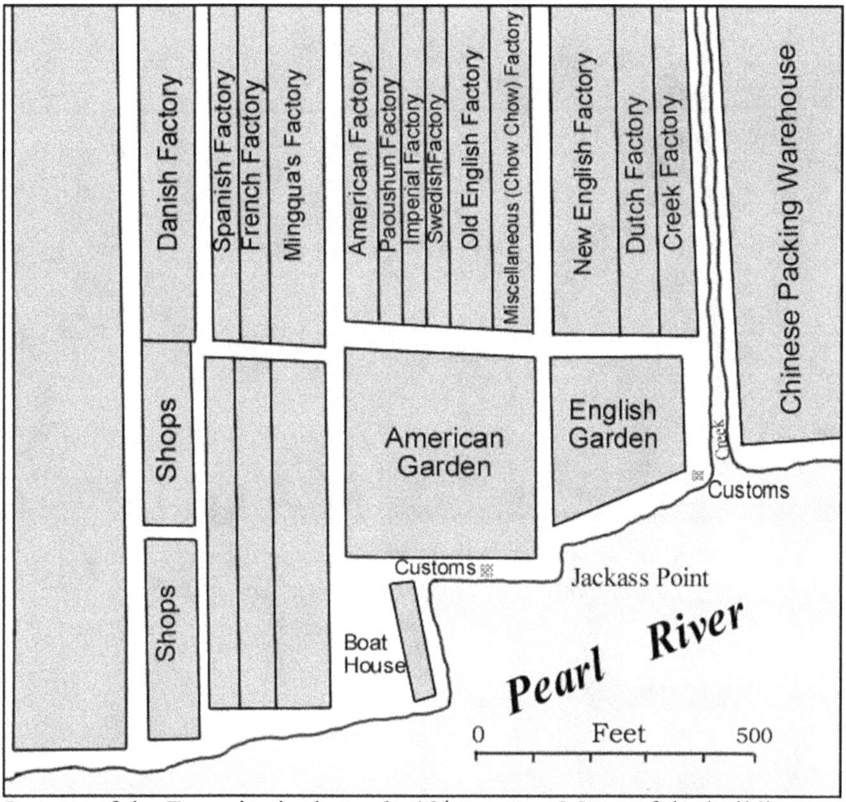

Layout of the Factories in the early 19th century. Many of the buildings were destroyed by a fire in 1822 and later rebuilt.

Chinese war junks. *Illustrated Times*, 2 May 1857.

Hong Kong as seen by a Western painter in the early 1840s.
Urban Council of Hong Kong, Museum of Art.

Hong Kong 15 years after its cession to Britain.
Illustrated Times. 20 February 1858.

In an attempt to get Canton to open up to foreigners, the British bombarded the city in October 1856. The Chinese retaliated by attacking the Factories on 14 December, as portrayed above. *Illustrated Times*, 21 March 1857.

The British response to the destruction of the Factories was the dispatch of an expeditionary force. France, aggrieved by the murder of a French missionary, sent naval support. The Allies gathered in the Gulf of Chihli in April 1858 and subdued the forts at Taku on 20 May 1858.

Illustrated Times 4 September 1858.

Lin Tse-hsu (L), 1785-1850, was sent to Canton as Commissioner in 1839 in charge of ridding China of the opium problem. He forced the foreigners to surrender their opium stocks which he then destroyed. This led to the Opium War with Britain and Lin's subsequent exile.

Hung Hsiu-ch'uan (R), 1814-1864, was a Hakka who believed he was the brother of Jesus Christ. He exalted himself to become Heavenly King of the Taiping Heavenly Kingdom, but he failed to overthrow the Ch'ing dynasty and some 20 million people were killed. A few Hung clan members managed to escape to British Guiana.

Illustrated Times, 16 October 1858

Baron Jean Baptiste Louis Gros (above), 1793-1870, was in command of a joint Anglo-French military expedition in 1860. The Allies sought retribution for China's failure to ratify the Treaty of Tientsin and to make amends for the defeat suffered in 1859 when attacking the Taku forts.

Elgin to Emperor. "Come knuckle down! No cheating this time!" *Punch*, 4 Nov 1860.

James Bruce (R), the 8th Earl of Elgin, 1811-1863, headed the British contingent. The Allied attack on Peking ended with the sacking of the Yuan Ming Yuan. The resulting Treaty of Peking permitted Chinese subjects to emigrate at will as contract labourers or otherwise.

Yuan Ming Yuan (the former Summer palace) was built in the 18th century in the north-western suburb of Peking. The massive complex (80 square miles) featured a small section with Renaissance-style architecture designed by the Italian missionary painter Castiglione. In October 1860 Yuan Ming Yuan was plundered by British and French troops and then burnt in a conflagration that lasted three days. *Bibliotheque Nationale de France*, Paris.

Yuan Ming Yuan, meaning Garden of Perfect Splendour, was known as the Garden of Gardens to the Chinese and referred to as the Versailles of China. Ruins of the Western-style section remain the most visible feature of Yuan Ming Yuan today since the Allies were pressed for time and could not set sufficient explosives to level all of the marble and stone structures. Xiaoli and David Sue-A-Quan, wife and son of the author, stand in the foreground (1996). *TrevSue-A-Quan.*

Marketplace in Canton.
Illustrated Times. 20 February 1858.

Street cooks at Canton.
Illustrated Times. 17 April 1858.

PUBLIC NOTICE.

By Austin, Special agent of the British Government for the regulating and encouragement of Emigration from China to the British West Indies.

Some difficulties having arisen from the imperfect understanding of the clauses of the Public Notices, heretofore issued by me, I have judged it expedient to set forth fully again, for the information of all, the condition of emigrants in the British West Indies, and the terms on which I am authorised by the British Government to engage Emigrants for service therein.

There is no slavery wherever the British Flag flies.

The law is the same to rich and poor. All Religions are tolerated and protected, and the Queen of England has appointed Special Magistrates in Her West Indian Colonies, to look after and protect the strangers, who go there to seek their fortunes.

All Chinese may therefore go without fear to the British West Indies.

The climate is very much like that of Southern China.

The cultivation is chiefly that of Sugar cane.

The wages offered during five years service under contract, are in accordance with the current price of labor in the West Indies, and vary from 2 shillings to 4 shillings per day, according to the industry and ability of the emigrant. House, garden ground, and medical attendance, are supplied free of charge.

Any laborer entering into a contract for five years, and desiring to cancel it at the end of the first year, and work where he pleases, can do so on repayment of four fifths of the passage money from China to the West Indies, estimated at $75. At the end of the second year he can cancel it on repayment of three fifths, and so on, one fifth being deducted for every year's service.

Special means of remitting money, and of corresponding with relatives gratuitously, will be afforded.

A free passage is offered, and clothing for the voyage.

This public notice was prepared by J. Gardiner Austin during his term as Immigration Agent in Canton (1859-1862). It was translated into Chinese and distributed around the city and the surrounding villages.

Public Records Office, Colonial Office File CO111.

Western impressions of Chinese common folk were not always flattering. Shown on the left are Chinese coolies who did the hauling and transportation of goods and sedan chairs in Hong Kong. On the right the distinction between single and married women is drawn. The former wear their hair "in a long tail just like the men do." Married women have their hair "turned up in form much resembling a rudder." *Illustrated Times*, 2 January 1858.

Chinese coolies destined for Cuba were kept in barracoons in Macao. This depot was formerly a factory and "the windows were strongly secured with iron bars; the doors were lined with sheet iron." 250 Chinese "burst open their prison door by united pressure" and escaped. *Illustrated Times*, 27 June 1857.

CHAPTER 5

WORKING ON THE PLANTATION

MAKING AN IMPRESSION

All of the 85 surviving immigrants on the *Lord Elgin* in 1853, who constituted the first shipload of Chinese immigrants, were assigned to Plantation Blankenburg, West Coast Demerara. Those from the two remaining boats landing that year were distributed to other estates on the West Coast and along the Demerara River. After a mere two months on the sugar cane plantations the Chinese labourers received several favorable assessments, as described in Cecil Clementi's book, *The Chinese in British Guiana*:

> I am willing to take 50 or 100 more Chinese on the terms I got the last, or if any planter may be dissatisfied with his batch I will be glad to take them over, with the consent of the representative of this property.
>
> [B. Trotman, manager, Pln. Blankenburg]

> . . . a very useful class of people, exceedingly apt and intelligent and very willing, quite equal to any coolies we are now receiving.
>
> [Stephen R. Butts, manager, Pln. La Jalousie]

> The Chinese on this estate are some of my best labourers; for strength and endurance they are equal to the Africans. . . . The people are happy and contented and cheerful, and I am well satisfied with them; I have advised Mr. Bascom to make application for a hundred more, and sincerely hope we can get them. . . . Three or four of the men keep a night school, and are teaching the boys to write and sing; I often go to their house in the evening and they always appear glad to see me, and ask many questions about their work; I think I have done my people justice in speaking of them in a flattering manner.
>
> [Griffin H. Bascom, manager, Pln. Windsor Forest]

> My opinion of the Chinese is, that in course of time they will be very good and useful labourers: but the heavy wet season coming on so shortly after their arrival has been greatly against them, giving them fevers and ague, which they are very much troubled with at present.

> . . . There is another and very serious drawback to their doing well, which is that there is no one among them that can talk a word of English, consequently we can only communicate with another by signs.
> [Alex. M. Bethune, manager, Pln. Stewartville]

> I find the Chinese labourers allotted to this estate a tractable and useful people. I may mention that since the rainy season set in, they are not earning much money, yet they are not idle for a day, unless in case of sickness, of which I cannot complain.
> [M. Vaughn, manager, Pln. Hague]

The reports from a few other estates were not as glowing, primarily because the newly arrived Chinese were suffering from the effects of the long voyage or from various illnesses brought about by the local climate.

Among the 647 Chinese immigrants who arrived in 1853 there were only three who had previously been exposed to a foreign language to any extent. Aboard the *Glentanner* was a man who had previously resided in Sydney where he acquired a limited knowledge of English. Another fellow on the same ship had gained a few French words from Mauritius. One of the boys who arrived on the *Samuel Boddington* knew a few words of English. In light of this the rapid adjustment of the Chinese labourers to the work on the plantation was regarded as delightfully surprising. This contributed to the favourable evaluation that the British Guiana government sent to London which praised the "actual usefulness and ultimately greater value" of the Chinese immigrants.

The *Royal Gazette* also expressed a good opinion of the Chinese labourers:

> Numbers of them have been brought here, and that their importation has proved a benefit is clear, from the fact that we are now trying to get as many of them as we can. They are not only intelligent and healthy, but are very industrious, and live far better than any other class of immigrants; and if they are not so saving as others, it is to be accounted for by their propensity to gambling. This is a moral evil and does not affect their good qualities as labourers; in fact they are on the whole, as we have been told by their employers, and particularly by one who has had about 300 of them under his orders, superior to the Coolies, Portuguese, or Africans. If with the crude efforts heretofore made, by which, so we may suppose, only the worst of them have been sent here, they have proved so efficient, it is but fair to conclude that when females

> are introduced with males, and with a zealous agent to superintend their immigration, we will have a very valuable addition to our labouring population. [*Royal Gazette*, 12 Feb 1859]

A comparable praiseworthy evaluation was given about the almost one thousand Chinese labourers who landed in Trinidad in 1853. This gave support to the sentiment that more Chinese should be brought for the island plantations:

> In our last we alluded to the admirable report of Mr. MITCHELL, the Agent-General of Immigration in Trinidad. He states that at first, owing to the want of competent interpreters, misunderstandings which took place on the subject of work were not settled without difficulty, but afterwards the Chinese were looked upon as a valuable class of labourers, and those employers who had succeeded with them in the first instance, preferred them to all others. Some people maintained that they were insubordinate, too fond of working their own grounds when they should be otherwise employed, and apt to abscond without any reasonable cause, but those who disliked them most as indentured servants, had been glad to secure their services as day labourers, and his own impression was that, under masters qualified to manage them, they were the best agriculturists hitherto imported. This is good testimony in their favor, and is conformed by the experience which we have had of them in this colony. The last batch imported here, were, as we had at the time took occasion to remark, a fine body of men, superior to those first introduced, and if they answer to their appearance, it will be a strong argument in favour of the prosecution of immigration from China.
>
> [*Royal Gazette*, 16 Apr 1859]

ADJUSTING TO LOCAL CONDITIONS

Despite the declared interest in securing more Chinese, immigration from China stopped for reasons described earlier and it resumed six years later in 1859 when two shiploads arrived through private auspices. In the following year the first womenfolk and families landed in British Guiana. During the interval between 1853 and 1859 local conditions had changed with respect to the wages and terms of employment and the government had to introduce ordinances to update the situation. In 1860 an ordinance was passed to standardize policies and procedures governing new immigrants. The amendments were designed chiefly for the Chinese who signed on in China to a certain set of contractual obligations but found themselves at some disadvantage when compared to the prevailing wage levels or benefits available to other labourers in British Guiana who were not indentured.

Although the indentured labourer was now able to choose to fulfill the contract or to buy his way out, the decision was not always a simple one.

> His Excellency stated that the Chinese had sent to their friends and relatives a full statement of their condition and future prospects, and that while some were pleased at being permitted to take task-work, instead of the four dollars per month and their food, in terms of the arrangement entered into in China, others disapproved of this, on the ground that when sick they got no pay. Many also had complained of having been obliged in the dry season to make use of trench water. In some instances a little management may be required, in explaining matters to the Immigrants. Intelligent as they are, there cannot be much difficulty in making them understand that if they prefer being on the same footing as other labourers, as regards wages, they have no right to expect wages without work, and that as they can always find employment if they please, they must be satisfied, when sick, to get medical attendance and medicine gratis — a privilege which the chance labourer who works only by the day does not enjoy. It is surely no small benefit that, so long as health lasts, they can always rely on having work supplied to them at a remunerative rate, and that when sickness assails them, they have the best of Hospital accommodation and of medical advice, free of charge. If they but represent facts to their friends, on this score, many a Chinaman will come to these shores, where he can always rely on permanent and remunerative employment, who would otherwise remain a starveling in his own country. [*Royal Gazette*, 4 Apr 1861]

Amendments were made to the 1860 Ordinance in later years and by the mid 1870s the immigrant was able to terminate his contract with three months' notice, or on even shorter notice if mutually agreed between the indentured person and the estate manager. In 1880 a list of 84 immigrants was published naming those who had arrived on the *Corona* and who had not completed their five-year contract of indenture and therefore "not entitled to the sum of Fifty dollars." Among them were Ho-a-shing and Kwan-a-yu, aged 31 and 27, respectively, who checked out from Cove and John estate in May 1874, which meant that they put in a minimum of contractual work, if any. Soo-a-cheong, indentured to La Grange, worked for only a year and it may have been because of his advanced age of 61 years that his contract was ended prematurely. Curiously enough, Yong-a-yee, who would have been 23 years of age, terminated his contract with Lusignan when there was only a month or so remaining.

The majority of the Chinese immigrants served out their obligation of indenture even though many were not skilled in field labour before leaving China. A traveler in British Guiana penned this account for readers in England:

> Riding one Sunday afternoon on the railway, extending now from Georgetown some twenty miles towards Berbice, I was pleased at meeting three Chinese, who got in at the Beterverwagting station; they had each got a piece of fresh sugar cane, five or six feet long. These men had been a year in Demerara and pronounced it a "No. 1 fine country." On another occasion I met with those who complained that their money did not go so far as in China. Possibly the selection of emigrants made in China has not always been so judicious. Generally speaking, the Hakas make better immigrants than the Puntis, as a Norfolk or Dorsetshire labour would be preferred in the Far West to a Spitalfields weaver or Manchester spinner. One planter complained to me of the batch allotted to him ex *Sebastopol*, said he had got nine peddlers, eight barbers, one umbrella maker, one professional gambler, but not one agricultural labourer!
>
> [*Royal Gazette*, 24 Oct 1861]

One location to which a number of Chinese families were allocated was Plantation Skeldon in Berbice, and on 25 June 1862 Mr. J. Ross, the plantation owner, gave his evaluation:

> The manager of Skeldon writes:- "I find the Chinese invaluable for field labour and have since found that they are equally useful in the buildings." On the two estates that I am personally connected with we have nearly 200 and 100 respectively, and the mortality on both has been extremely small, much less so than it would have been in a corresponding number of Indian emigrants. As far as I am concerned myself, and as far as my experience goes, I definitely prefer the Chinese to any class of immigrants I have previously had on the estates.

Recruitment and Distribution

As the favorable reports of the Chinese as labourers spread throughout the country the plantation owners in different regions began to express interest in acquiring Chinese immigrants. The allocation of Chinese to the various plantations was handled by the Immigration Office, based on input from the plantations. Even before the arrival of the immigrant ships the process for distributing the labour force was set in motion. Early in the year the plantation owners were asked to submit their wish list to the Immigration Agent-General stating the number of labourers required. The number requested by any one estate varied from 15 to 50 and was generally an overestimate to allow for any shortfall in recruitment. The Immigration Office compiled the numbers and forwarded the tally to the government for approval or amendment. The final numbers were then transmitted by letter to the Emigration Agent based in Canton in time for the opening of the emigration season later in the same year. In several years the Emigration Agent was unable to get as many emigrants as requested by the planters and proceeded to ship as many as could be obtained before the arrival of the monsoon brought the season to a close.

On arrival at Georgetown the immigrant ship would lie at anchor near the light-ship located at the entrance to the Demerara river. The intent was to wait for a few days as a period of quarantine before the passengers were allowed on shore, even though the ship had already been traveling in isolation for many weeks. Only those requiring immediate medical attention were removed to the hospital. During the waiting time the Immigration Office would take a count of the able-bodied men and begin negotiations with the estates' agents to distribute them to the various plantations as best that the numbers and circumstances would allow. Within a few days of landing the immigrants were on their way to their assigned estates. The table on the following page shows the distribution of the passengers on the *Ganges* in 1863, which is fairly typical.

ODD MEN OUT

Even though the general opinion of the Chinese immigrants was positive there were instances as early as in 1860 where it became evident that some of the Chinese did not really care about raising cane.

Allotments of Immigrants:
Ganges, 839 tons ar 29 Jun from Canton.

	M	W	B	G	I	Total
Anna Catherina	19	6				25
Better Hope	35	15	1	2	2	54
De Kinderen	15	5	3			23
Farm River	15	5		1		21
Haarlem	20	4	1			25
Houston	21	5	1			27
Leonora	19	6				25
Peter's Hall	23	7	1			31
Success, E.C.	15	4	1			20
Windsor Forest	15	5				20
La Belle Alliance	20	5				25
Athion	15	6				23
Hope & Experiment	15	4	1			20
Skeldon	20	7	1	1		29
Smythfield	15	5	1			21
	284	89	11	4	1	389
In Colonial Hosp		1				1
In Alms House			1			1
Died in Col Hosp	2	2			1	5
	286	92	12	4	2	396

[*Royal Gazette*, 19 Jan 1864]

It is, we believe, the fact that, on more than one estate, some of the Chinese immigrants have proved rather troublesome; but at other places they have behaved well, and appear to have made up their minds to work. It is but natural that, among the large numbers introduced, there should be some few unruly ones who set a bad example to the others, and some may also exhibit dissatisfaction, not from their being any positive ground for it, but from misapprehension of the truth, and consequent distrust. Our belief, however, is that after a time they will learn their real position and that, being intelligent and industrious, they will settle down quietly into their proper places, and prove a good addition to our population. One requisite to effect this desirable object is proper management, and fair dealings at all times. In the extract from the Report of Mr. ALCOCK, . . . it is stated that the Chinese, although hasty in temper, are on the whole good humoured and patient; that they can get through a good deal of work, but cannot bear to be kept very closely to it, or to be driven forwards at a faster pace than is habitual to them, and that rather than be fretted they would give up in the best situation. This Extract Report ought to be in the hands of every manager and overseer, and should be carefully explained to every headman.

It was stated to us the other day that, about ten days ago, several of the Chinese located on an estate not far from town, having, as they supposed, cause for dissatisfaction, left the estate and came into town. They were met at the bridge of plantation *La Penitance* and stopped by some mounted Police, who were afterwards reinforced by two or three others on foot. Some water, at the request of the Chinese was sent out to them by a gentleman in the neighbourhood, but the bucket was knocked off the bearer's head by a policeman, and another policeman beat one of the strangers on the head with his staff, and, as we have been since informed by an intelligent Chinaman who was present, drew blood. The same party told us that others of his countrymen had been struck by the Police. Such conduct is exceedingly reprehensible, and, if permitted to pass unpunished, might be productive of serious consequences. Could we have ascertained the number of the principal actor, we would have preferred a direct charge against him, but, from the data given, the truth may be ascertained by the Police authorities, — the most likely persons to shirk the enquiry. The fact is that policemen are too fond of using their staves upon the heads and arms of prisoners, without any necessity for such violence . . . [*Royal Gazette*, 12 May 1860]

Three or four years ago, we saw a number of these people employed on the West Coast, and they were said to be the best laborers on the estate, doing their work cheerfully and well. The chief complaint against them was that they did not seem to understand the difference between *meum* and *tuum* very clearly, and therefore made no scruple about helping themselves freely to the provisions grown by the black people. This characteristic, however, did not lessen their value as laborers, a man's capability for work and his propensity for thieving being two distinct qualities. We have heard some managers say that they would on no account ask for Chinese immigrants, and others again are quite content to take them. In some places they do well, but in others they give a great deal of trouble, and some of them refuse working altogether. The only feasible explanation of this is that the people who have been brought here are not all agricultural laborers. Many of them, we know, complain of having been deceived, and say that in their own country they were not accustomed to work in the field. We fear that, in the anxiety to procure a

> sufficient number of emigrants from China, the emissaries of our Agent have misled the people and that numbers of tradesmen and others have been induced to leave the country under the impression that they would be allowed to follow their own occupations, or else that the prospect of remuneration has been represented in colours far too flattering. . . .
>
> We have said that in some places the Chinese are doing better than others. About ten days ago a gentleman informed us that at first he had had trouble with those located on the estate of which he is the manager, but that latterly they were going on very well; and another mentioned that those he had charge of, when they found their contract wages reduced, from sick days or other causes, to a mere pittance, had applied for task work, and were earning forty cents each per day. As a proof that the task was not very heavy, one man who did not go to the field until breakfast time finished his work by 5 o'clock, P.M. Forty cents per task will give for the six days ten shillings, and this is not a bad allowance for a Coolie or a Chinese, who are not accustomed to expensive living and who besides have free residence, medicines and medical attention.
>
> [*Royal Gazette*, 31 Jul 1860]

For those able-bodied men who decided not to go along with the wishes of the estate managers, there were basically only three options. The first was to buy their way out of the contract. This required a considerable sum compared to the monthly earnings of only $4 before discretionary spending. The discontented person could resort to three methods to accumulate such funds — beg, borrow or steal — or else try his luck at gambling. The second option available to the reluctant labourers was to give up on the whole thing altogether by committing suicide. There was a significant number of suicides over the years although it is hard to know how many were prompted by the work situation or by personal difficulties. The third option was to abscond from the estate. This was by far the most appealing option and from time to time long lists of people were published in the newspapers under the headings "absent from work" or "desertion." Their cases gained even more publicity after formal charges were laid.

> Chan-a-Choo and five other Chinese indentured to pln Versailles were charged with refusing to attend at the time and place fixed to perform certain work allotted to them. [*Royal Gazette*, 27 Oct 1870]

A Chinese was charged with deserting from pln. Peter's Hall. [Sentenced to one month imprisonment with hard labour.]

[*Royal Gazette*, 20 Apr 1871]

A Chinaman named Chang-a-Fook was indicted for wounding another named Lung-a-chung on the same estate, on the 6th July last. The prosecutor is an immigrant indentured to pln *Anna Catherina*. On the 6th July he went to pln *Stewartville* to buy fowls, and saw the prisoner there. He knew that the prisoner was a deserter from *Anna Catherina*, and he advised him to return to the estate, and set about his work. The prisoner said he had nothing to do with him, and that he was not going to return to the estate. The prosecutor said that as he (prosecutor) was a driver on the estate, he had a great deal to do with him, and that he had better go back with him to the manager. The prisoner said that he would not go, and made a blow at him with his fist, upon which the prosecutor raised his stick, but did not strike him. The prisoner then ran into his house, which was near by, and took up a knife . . . The jury, after a short consultation found the prisoner *Guilty* of unlawful wounding. Mr. Justice King . . . sentenced him to be imprisoned and kept to hard labour for nine months.

[*Royal Gazette*, 25 Nov 1871]

A number of those who took leave without permission headed to Georgetown to hang out in the emerging Chinatown area.

To-day the police made a clearance from Charlestown of a host of runaway immigrants, mostly Chinese, who have, of late, made that district their headquarters, whence they issue to gain daily or nightly bread at the expense of the inhabitants of the city. The men were taken in a gang to the Immigration Office to be identified, if possible, and sent back to the places of their indenture. From the appearance of some of them it struck us as probable that their employers would be anxious not to get them back but to get them to perpetuate their absence. However, there were several strong looking men amongst them, who, doubtless, are marked "absent" on some planter's muster-roll. A visit to the gang may restore some missing hands to the various estates.

[*Royal Gazette*, 6 Jun 1872]

The penalty for absenteeism was 30 days imprisonment but this was not a great deterrent to those who were determined to get out of field labour. In some cases they accepted their punishment as if it were of little consequence — if they were caught and sent back to the estates they would again abscond. But there were others who took incarceration as the last straw.

> This morning, a Chinaman, named Chung-a-Poo was found dead, suspended by the neck in his cell, in Georgetown jail. The unfortunate creature committed suicide by attaching a piece of cord to the bars of the cell window, and kicking the bucket from under him when he had fastened the cord around his neck. The deceased (who was an indentured labourer) was undergoing a sentence of 30 days imprisonment and hard labour, for having absconded himself without leave, from the plantation upon which he was engaged — *Stewartville*, we understand.
>
> [*Royal Gazette*, 17 Mar 1864]

Taking out the Driver

Although there were quite a number of Chinese who were discontented enough to abscond from the estates they acted as individuals and there were no reported cases of wholesale uprising against the plantation owners or managers. It was the overseer or driver, equivalent to foreman or team leader, who took the brunt of the discontent.

> Chang-a-Ti [was charged] for beating an Overseer at pln. *Success*.
>
> [*Royal Gazette*, 23 Jul 1866]

> Yesterday an Overseer on Pln Ogle, Mr. Jamieson, was severely beaten by three Chinese. These men, no doubt, had been paid according to the work done, but they considered themselves underpaid, and avenged their imaginary grievance on the person of the innocent Overseer.
>
> [*Royal Gazette*, 15 Jun 1867]

> Tan-y-tim a Chinese labourer of pln. *Vrydslust* was brought up and charged with threatening to kill Mr. Crosley the overseer of the estate. It appeared from the evidence that the complainant found fault with the prisoner's work in the field, when the prisoner replied that it was well enough executed for eight bits, and the more so as the coolies were getting nine bits for the same amount of labour. The overseer simply denied that such was the case and advised the accused to complete his work in order that he might secure payment for it on Saturday. Upon such hearing this the Chinaman became very violent and declared that he would "*tang tang*" him and make him "*obtie*;" the meaning of which is that he would beat him to death. . . . The prisoner had tried to incite the other Chinese to riot. . . . Mr. Cather, [the estate manager], explained

what the coolies got nine bits for was nearly double what the Chinese had to do for eight bits. . . . [Tan-y-tim was sentenced to] two months hard labour. [*Royal Gazette*, 28 Apr 1870]

Yesterday the Chinese gang at *Schoon Oord* gave their driver, a black man named Cyrus, a good beating. If our information be correct, the driver reported to the Overseer that some of the work had not been properly performed, and on the Overseer leaving the field the people turned upon the driver. The man may have only been doing his duty in reporting bad work, but we think it is a great mistake to put a black man as driver over either Chinese or Coolie immigrants, as we know that the frequently leads to great dissatisfaction. It is well known that, whatever others may think of them, the Chinese think very highly of themselves, as being natives of a country which they consider the greatest and most enlightened on the face of the globe. This idea is not altogether destitute of foundation, as in some respects the Chinese excel the most civilized nations of Europe, and it is not surprising that such of them as are introduced here, although made to work as field labourers, should entertain strong objections to having a black man placed over them as driver. There is antipathy between the races, and, such being the case it is not to be wondered at that occasionally the parties come into collision. The Coolies form a very different class of people, and those who are brought here as labourers are much below the Chinese in many respects, but we know that even they are opposed to a black driver being put over them. [*Royal Gazette*, 20 Aug 1870]

One unconventional form of protest was noted in October 1875 when Yeo-chun-Ching was brought before the magistrate, charged by the estate manager with destroying a number of plants valued at one dollar. Yeo pleaded not guilty and in his defense said that the plants were too tall to be transplanted and so he cut off the roots. The magistrate was not convinced by this argument and Yeo was fined $1 plus costs of 72 cents, with the alternate of 14 days imprisonment with hard labour.

There were some estate owners who believed that the best way to get the labourers to work was to enforce strict compliance with the law. In particular this meant that the labourers should be required to complete the obligated hours of work and that absentees be captured and prosecuted to the fullest extent of the law. These sentiments were put forward in the *Colonist* which essentially represented the position of the plantation owners. The *Royal Gazette*, however, proposed a different approach.

The *Colonist*, on the 24th, coolly remarks that, "it is only by the strict enforcement of stringent laws that the planter can get out of his immigrants the amount of work which they are bound to give, and which he cannot do without." A good deal must depend on tact and the manner in which the people are treated. We must draw attention to the advertisement which appears in another column, brought to our office this day by Chinese who know nothing of the remarks of the *Colonist.* These people came forward voluntarily to thank Mr. Hutchinson of *Enmore* for his kindness to them. Such a tribute speaks volumes, and is honourable to the people themselves, as well as to the gentleman mentioned. We could instance other cases where the people have shewn themselves very sensible of kind treatment, and we would advise those who cry out as lustily against their labourers to try the same experiment. If it has succeeded so well in several cases, why should it not succeed in all? The question is one well worthy of consideration. [*Royal Gazette*, 30 Mar 1869]

ADVERTISEMENT

The CHINESE LABOURERS on Pln. *Enmore*, would have express their thanks to Mr. HUTCHINSON, for the kind manner in which he has treated them during the seven years and a half he has been Overseer on that Estate.

For that time, they have always been able to work under his Overseership with the greatest satisfaction and pleasure. March 30, 1869.

[*Royal Gazette*, 1 Apr 1869]

By 1875 the planters were facing a new problem in keeping their labouring hands. Many, especially the Indian immigrants who were continually landing in the colony, found it more to their liking to absent themselves from work and take the consequences. This situation became an increasing concern and a topic for debate, as described in this letter to the editor:

By their contracts, the immigrants are entitled to receive $4 per month besides their rations. No provision was, however, made for the stoppage of any portion of this amount for the absence from work, or detention in hospital. Allowing that they could be brought before the Magistrate under Ordinance 7 of 1873 for willful indolence, what is the result? They may be fined or imprisoned, but there is no indemnity to the Manager for the indolence complained of, as he has to pay the wages of the immigrant.

Very few of the Chinese introduced in the *Corona* are now working under their contracts; most of them having agreed to work by the day or by the task in the same way as other immigrants. The opening up of this question now has therefore been deemed advisable, principally for the purpose of directing attention to the necessity of a special Chinese Ordinance being framed in the event of the continuance of Immigration from China, unless there should be agreements so clear and comprehensive as to render any such Ordinance unnecessary.

[*Royal Gazette*, 9 Oct 1875]

WORK HABITS

The workday typically started in the early morning with the assembly and counting of the labourers. The estates conducted this in different ways, which led Government Secretary William Walker to comment in 1861:

The daily muster is a most essential element in the machinery of management of these people, and it is I fear at present in many instances either neglected altogether or but indifferently attended to. The rolls should invariably be called in some fixed place and before the commencement of work in the morning. I am aware that the law leaves the time and place altogether to the discretion of the managers; but if I am correctly informed, the very lax practice on some estates in this particular may render it advisable in the future consolidation of the Ordinances to introduce more stringent and definite provisions of its proper observance.

Every immigrant not present in the morning muster should be immediately sought out and dealt with as circumstances may require. *All* should be inspected with special reference to their state of health; the first appearance of sores noted; if chigo bites occasion them, spirits of turpentine should be applied two or three times a week after the feet have been washed; if *bête-rouge* occasion the irritation, rags or strips of leather dipped in oil should be worn around the legs. If unfortunately notwithstanding such precautions sores should become so severe as to require hospital treatment, the diet should be liberal and nutritious, for as an impoverished state of the blood is favourable to the development or enlargement of ulcers, a return to strength and health can only be secured by appropriate nourishment. Attention to these and similar matters, though it may be irksome and disagreeable, will nevertheless be probably found as conducive to the interest of the employer in a pecuniary sense as it is essential to the comfort and well being of the immigrants.

It was not unusual for the Chinese to apply the work habits to which they were accustomed in China to the field work in British Guiana. In some instances they would start work at the crack of dawn, even before roll call was taken, and work until 10 or 11 o'clock. They would then take a break in the middle of the day for a siesta and relief from the blazing sun. Work would be resumed later at about 3 o'clock in the afternoon to complete the tasks at hand. Initially this practice was regarded with some suspicion as a way of shirking work. However, since much of the work was allocated on a task by task basis the daily and weekly assignments were invariably completed on time and eventually this work style became acceptable to the estate managers

An unusual sighting was reported at a suburban estate of Georgetown, which, on the surface, exposed a great deal about the habits of some of the Chinese labourers. The observer went to the press to describe the bare facts:

> A gentleman informs us that, on going up the East Coast at an early hour a few mornings ago, he saw a number of male Chinese Immigrants working in a fields at Plantation *Kitty* stark naked. The field is one which immediately adjoins the village, and as the men were working on what is called the head bed, they were exposed to the gaze not only of the villagers but of every persons who passed along the public road. It was at that hour of the morning when ladies and gentlemen take an airing in their wagons, and women and girls pass from the country to town and from town to country with their wares for sale. It cannot be said that this was a chance occurrence, and without the knowledge of those who might have checked it, for on the day referred to there was an Overseer within 50 roods of the place, and a respectable villager, who reprobated the indecent exhibition, spoke of it to our informant as an occurrence that was by no means unusual among the Chinese on the *Kitty*. It may be a question of whether the field labourer suffers less from heat when in a state of nudity than when clothed, but there can be no doubt about the impropriety of any set of immigrants being allowed to work without a vestige of clothing, even when engaged at a distance from any public path or from the buildings of an estate. Common decency should be observed at all times and under all circumstances. Were any member or believer in the Anti-Slavery Society to witness such an exhibition as that referred to, he would at once set it down as an indisputable fact either that the

immigrants in this colony were forced to toil without clothing under the scorching sun, or that they were so poorly paid for their labour as to be unable to procure even a decent covering for their persons. It would be a capital text for those pseudo-philanthropists to expatiate upon, and it is wrong to give them any opening for their calumnies against the colony or the planter. Morality and good policy require that every immigrant should be decently clothed, however humble and plain his garments, and we feel assured that the proprietor of Pln. *Bel Air* has not been aware of the Chinese labourers attached to that estate being at work without clothing, and that, so far as lies in his power, he will put a stop to the practice on future. [*Royal Gazette*, 13 Apr 1867]

SLOW BOAT TO CHINA

Those who completed their contract of indenture were offered the option of renewing for another term or a sum of $50, which was intended to be a partial payment toward a return passage to China. Only a minority of the total Chinese immigrant population elected to return to China, traveling mainly on the ships chartered specially to take "return Indian immigrants" to India. According to Mr. Crosby, the Immigration Agent-General, the returning Chinese were persons who were over-qualified for agricultural work, such as doctors.

The Commission of Enquiry sat at 11 o'clock this morning of Mr. Crosby was resumed. About 8,000 Chinese had come to the Colony, and there were about 6,000 now in it. . . . With reference to a question put to him yesterday, whether any Chinese had returned to China, he now recollected that some came here in immigrant ships in the capacity of doctors, evidently with the intention of residing here, probably thinking, as might have been represented to them, that they could practice here; but that was not asserted by any one of them. They remained in the depot for some time, when, becoming a burden on the Colony . . . he was instructed to get rid of them by one means or other. Small sums of money were given to them to "set up" with, and land was offered them; but not being agriculturists, they did not find it worth their while to accept it. Chinese have no legal or moral claim upon the colony for a return passage to their country. . . . [*Royal Gazette*, 6 Sep 1870]

In September 1871 the *Wellesley* was chartered to take immigrants on a return voyage to India. There were 219 men,

96 women, 40 boys, 22 girls and 17 infants registered to go back to India. In addition there were some Chinese passengers,

> 4 men, 4 women, 1 boy and 3 girls, 2 male and 1 female infants: 15 souls, equal to 10 statute adults. These all paid their passage to Calcutta, and remitted money to the Agent there to secure passages hence to Canton; besides depositing with the Agent-General a considerable sum for remittance to China. [*Royal Gazette*, 23 September 1871]

> In our last Review we mentioned the departure of the Ship *Wellesley* with Return-Immigrants for India and China, and we subjoin a return of the money taken with them.

Calcutta People	50,016.89
Madras "	120.0
	50,136.89
Chinese	3,200.0
	53,336.89

[*Royal Gazette*, 7 Oct 1871]

Several more Chinese decided to make the journey back to China in the following year.

> The Governor said he saw that there were some Chinese now asking for back passage. In the report of the Immigration-Agent General he observed that there was a family of seventeen and another of thirty making for a back passage, to Calcutta, and stating their willingness to pay their passage on to China. [*Royal Gazette*, 13 Feb 1872]

> The fine clipper ship *Rohilla* chartered by Government to take coolies entitled to a return passage, back to Calcutta . . . received on board the following people:-

	M	W	B	G	Inf		
East Indians	257	79	31	23	16	-	406
Chinese	21	22	6	6	3	-	58
							464

[*Royal Gazette*, 24 Oct 1872]

The experiences aboard this ship were recorded by one of the Chinese passengers:

> The following letter from one of the Chinese who sailed from here on the *Rohille* may be of some service to any of his countrymen who are thinking of returning to their native land. The writer was by occupation, an Interpreter here.

"Garden Reach, Calcutta

15th Feby 1873

My dear Friend — I embarked on board the ship *Rohille* on the 18th October 1872. Tugg out to the light ship by a steamer on the 19th; the morning and evening [meals were for] each person half a loaf of pan bread and a table spoon full of sugar, and the following afternoon each person 1 tin cup can and 1 tin plate, these our meals was provided for our voyage to Calcutta on Sunday the 20th October 1872.

We thought it was impossible to take the Coolies' vituals, therefore we went to the Doctor and told him the Chinese were unable to eat the Coolies food we ask him for a loan of three Chinese [dollars] thus our supply was successful. [On] Monday Fish and Rice, Tuesday [they] serve mutton, Wednesday morning biscuit, afternoon Rice and fish, Thursday flour and pork, . . . Saturday fish, Sunday Fresh mutton, this is our weekly food. The same afternoon the Doctor and Captain came round and take away every box and trunk and put them below, fearing the ship will roll to and fro, on the 28th we see nothing but large Fish floating on top of the Blue water, she sail all the directions of the compass. On 1st November one Girl Birth for Chinsee, the 21st day about 1 o'clock we meet an Rocky Island nam *Rocas*, we was told many ships been wreck, the 19th December she fetch the *Cape of Good Hope* it was very cold. She anchor for two days *meself* and *Chinsee*, 2 Coolies, Doctor, and Captain went ashore, it is a very pretty place, Demerara is nothing to compare with it, food is very cheap, mutton 6 cts per lbs, 1 penny for two lobster, she set sail on the 22nd, and on the 13th January 1873 we passed an island named New Amsterdam, then the weather is hot and miserable again, on the 12th February, 1873 she arrived at the light ship of Calcutta, 2 o'clock she was tugg by a steam boat, the river is very crocket with muddy water, however we got to Calcutta 13th at 2 o'clock and all landed safe and well at 4 o'clock, we lodged at the depot. The next day Mr. Firth give us a letter to Apear and Co., and engaged our passage to China for 40 rupees, tween deck accommodation, on the 20th Feby, 1873, to find food ourself, Ship find fire and water.

Dear Friend, I beg to mention to you, if any of our friend who wish to return to China they must provide sufficient food and warmth clothing for their voyage.

Joseph you must have a copy of this letter and send to Mr. Griffiths, my best regard to you and families and my parents beg to join the same thanks be to God Almighty for we are all well, I hope you are in the same health, it is of no use writing any more, when I reach Hong-Kong I shall have more time to study letter to you all, my time is so unexhausted I couldn't spare one moment to be lost, the parrot is catch a few words nicely.

Yours ever faithfully,
JOHN WONGAH-CHUN

P.S. — I trust will tell William, Cashew and all enquiring Friends and let them know that we all reach safely and well at Calcutta, that foods are very cheap, for example, 2 shillings is one rupees, and 1 ditto is 16 anna, and 1 anna is 4 pisas.

1 lb. of beef or pork is 4 pisas.

1 drum head cabbage 4 pisas.

1 pisas for one egg.

Calcutta is about more of less fifty times Demerara.

I hope you are getting on nicely with your situation, and how business stands with William and Cashew nicely I hope to say.

J.W.C. [*Royal Gazette*, 19 Jun 1873]

There was another Chinese passenger on this ship who had made an impact while he was in British Guiana and whose presence was sorely missed.

The sailing of a Coolie Ship with acclimatised immigrants from our shores is generally made the occasion for an expression of regret at losing so many good people just at the time when they have become of real value to the colony; and managers are heard lamenting over the departure of some favorite driver or handy workman whose service he thought it hard to lose; we question however if any immigrant of the many hundred who have gone before him, have ever created a greater sensation by his leave-taking than has one — a venerable old person — who just sailed in the *Rohille*.

This old man whose later movements have closely interested some of our colonists, is a native of China, and was pretty well known amongst us as the "Chinese Doctor." He opened a Village shop a year ago and acquired a reputation for fair dealing, which was the mean of getting him credit from several houses in town. To the surprise of his creditors, they discovered this week, that the suave and amiable doctor with his family had taken passage in the *Rohille* and was already over the bar. Sorry to lose him in this abrupt way, they secured the services of a Marshall to go out to the *Rohille*, which was lying at anchor beyond the Light Ship; the Marshall went and returned this morning without the doctor, for on reaching the vessel the captain told the Marshall what the officer should have known before, that he would only get himself in trouble by arresting any one so far out from the shore. We believe, however, the doctor has sent in a promise that he will come back again. In the meantime, those who have occasion to lament his sudden departure may learn by heart the following lines:-

"Which is why I remark,
  And my language is plain
That for ways that are dark
  And for tricks that are vain
The heathen Chinee is peculiar
Which the same I am free to maintain."

[*Royal Gazette*, 11 Oct 1873]

This poem was an extract from a much longer one entitled "The Heathen Chinee" first published in the United States in 1870 at a time when sentiments against the Chinese, especially in California, were becoming vicious. The title of the poem quickly became a catch phrase to be used against the Chinese whenever any of their practices or customs were regarded as unacceptable in the eyes of those wielding influence or power. The escape of the wily doctor must indeed have raised questions about the moral integrity of Chinese scholars, not to mention those who were not intellectuals.

In later years the Chinese returned in small batches on the ships bound for India, seemingly without controversy.

The *Ailsa* return Coolie ship for Calcutta embarked her living freight this afternoon as follows :- 314 men, 88 women, 19 boys, 26 girls, 16 infants: in all 457 souls equal to 419½ adults. Amongst these there are the following Chinese, 12 men, 9 women, 1 boy, 4 girls, 11 infants; 27 in all. [*Royal Gazette*, 13 Dec 1873]

The ship *Rohilla*, from London, Geo. Hutchinson, Esq., Commander, chartered to convey to Calcutta the return Indian immigrants this year, came to her moorings in the harbour off Kingston Stelling, on Sunday evening. The immigrants who were classified thus:-

M	W	B	G	Inf	Total	Adults
			INDIANS			
245	116	41	40	10	461	401½
			CHINESE			
17	8	3	3	00	31	28

were embarked after being inspected on Tuesday afternoon. . . The Chinese paid their own passage. [*Royal Gazette*, 7 Sep 1876]

CHAPTER 6

A WALK IN THE DARK

A WORD OF CAUTION

The reader is forewarned that the content of this chapter can be disturbing to some people. It contains graphic descriptions of socially unacceptable behavior on the part of the Chinese immigrants and reader discretion is advised. It should be remembered that the labouring classes, regardless of race or origin, were not the sort of people that would be the talk of the town when it came to social gatherings, sporting events, concerts, or fancy dress balls (although Chinese, Indian and other cultural groups were depicted by the revelers in costume). On the contrary, the news pertaining to the immigrant labourers that ended up in print were usually of a negative nature. However, by examining more closely the nature of anti-social activities of the immigrants and the circumstances of their participation a better understanding can be gained of their lives and of the times.

As explained in earlier chapters the Chinese immigrants to British Guiana were not a homogeneous group, having come from diverse regions, speaking mutually unintelligible dialects, being of a wide range of ages, having varied skills and holding different beliefs. It is therefore not surprising to find that they reacted to their new situation in a non-uniform manner. Several of them had been picked up off the streets and had already become social outcasts in their native land. Others emigrated to seek an escape from miserable circumstances, war and oppression. It could hardly be expected that their transport to British Guiana would have changed their behavior and outlook on life. When some of the Chinese immigrants began to give trouble and become involved in criminal activity it was not considered to be unusual. Although the anti-social acts were by no means the exclusive domain of Chinese, the numbers of offences were excessive in proportion to their relatively small population.

PLANTAINS

As part of the contract of indenture, the plantation owners were required to provide adequate food and shelter to their hired hands. The interpretation of what was adequate seems to differ since a significant amount of crime perpetrated by newly arrived Chinese was related to satisfying basic food needs. William Des Voeux, a magistrate from 1863 to 1869, witnessed the plight of the indentured immigrants, and wrote to the Secretary of State for the Colonies:

> I have strong reason for believing that on some Estates the food at least provided in Hospitals, in all but the severer cases, is of a wretched description, and that this fact is well known to the medical men, who dare not make complaint.

Rice, which was the preferred staple for the Chinese, was an imported item in those days and it would seem that the supply was not enough to satisfy the need or else the price too expensive. In the colony the main target became plantains, which were grown in cultivated plots, called plantain walks, typically situated adjacent to the sugar plantations. In the dark of night the plantation walks became a tempting place for those with a taste for ripe plantains.

> From the first introduction of Chinese into this Colony, it has been found that the lower classes of them are notorious thieves, and up to the present day they have no scruple in plundering the provision grounds of others. In many instances they have been known to go around with cutlasses affixed to long sticks, and with other weapons, and to drive away with threats the owner of the provisions which they were about to carry off. For some time the plantain walks on Plantation Klein Pouderoyen have been so systematically plundered, that those who farmed them laid a trap for the thieves, and on the 23rd ult., four Chinese were fired at, two of whom were killed, and the other two wounded. The latter say that the assassins were Portuguese, and this is more than probable, as most of the land is farmed by them. . . . [*Royal Gazette*, 8 Mar 1862]

> There have been several Chinese killed and wounded when engaged in their nocturnal deprecations on the lands of the Farmers, but this seems to make no proper impression upon these determined and hardened thieves. It was only the other day that an Inquest was held on the body of a Chinaman who had been killed when out on a plundering excursion,

and during the following night some of his countrymen managed to carry off about a hundred bunches of Plantains from a provision ground. Two Chinamen were catted last Tuesday morning at Jones Town, and this is, perhaps, the only punishment calculated to have a beneficial effect on checking the thieving propensities of these people.

[*Royal Gazette*, 18 Apr 1863]

The incidents of plantain stealing became so numerous and distressing that the government formally authorized the use of whipping as a punishment for stealing plantains. An ordinance was passed which provided for a jail term with hard labour as well as a maximum of thirty-nine lashes. At the same time other solutions were proposed, including curfews and supervision.

Yesterday morning a Chinaman at Peter's Hall who had been found guilty of stealing plantains, received thirty-nine lashes with the cat-o'-nine-tails. This is the first case of flogging under the new Ordinance we have heard of, and we trust it will be followed with the most salutary effects, in the shape of deterring others of his countrymen from similar crimes. [*Royal Gazette*, 13 Jun 1865]

In their own country, we are told that there people are accustomed to pay almost implicit obedience to the head men of the Village or little community in which they live; who, indeed, in some places, are held responsible for the good conduct of all under their immediate rule, and probably it would not be very difficult to introduce on the Estates in this country, a somewhat similar system of paternal government to the extent, at all events, of enabling the head man to check the wanderings of their countrymen after sunset. It would probably cost the pay of a patrol or two in the neighbourhood of the cottages occupied by the Chinese, and even if the expense fell on the Colony it would not be ill spent in putting a stop to what is becoming a serious and alarming evil. The Chinese are a cunning race, and in the way of crime are 'Up" to a thing or two of which Europeans have no idea. In their case we nay fairly adopt the motto *fas est ab hoste doceri*, and employ them against themselves, on the principle of "set a thief to catch a thief."

[*Royal Gazette*, 11 Nov 1865]

His Excellency hinted at making the whole mass of Immigrants on an estate responsible for acts which could be proved to have been committed by a considerable number of them. What overwhelming objection is there to this plan? It would obviously interest a large number of the Immigrants on the side of order; and there is no better judge of his

> own interest than a Chinaman nor a man more obedient to law, if he is but made to feel it. Why not prevent his having weapons of offense at all, and why not take from him at night, that terrible cutlass, in which Mr. Clementson could perceive nothing more formidable than a harmless instrument of peaceful labour? In this way, coupled with some more stringent supervision at after-hours by his superiors, these Chinese gangs in all probability would be broken up. In Hong Kong, where there are over 80,000 Chinamen, to a very few hundreds of Europeans and Americans, no Chinaman is allowed to be out after 8 o'clock, *without a pass*. Any one meeting a Chinaman after that hour, may demand his pass, and if he cannot produce one, may hand him over to the first policeman he meets. No objection is ever made to this by the Chinamen, though their numbers do so preponderate. [*Guiana Times*, 21 Nov 1865]

The concept of having a head-man and trying to institute the type of discipline or accountability that existed in the villages of China was just too impractical. The authority of the village leader and the elders in China came from the members of the community knowing each other, with many being related by blood or through marriage. Acts that would be considered unacceptable would be a reflection not only on the individual but also on family honor. Such a dynamic did not exist among the motley collection of Chinese immigrants on the plantations of British Guiana. As for imposing a curfew in the vast countryside, the idea was unenforceable without a substantial policing force, especially when the curfew breakers would be carrying with them their plantain-reaping implement — the cutlass.

The plantain plundering expeditions still continued regardless of the threat of the whip. In fact there are accounts where the Chinese were taking their blows stoically while others were reported to be wilting after a couple dozen lashes. In one case, Cho-a-King found himself at the mercy of vigilantes who were only too happy to take the law in their own hands.

> Cho-a-King was flogged for stealing plantains at Canal No. 1. He pleaded guilty but was so severely beaten. On the Chinaman being examined he was found to be covered with bruises from neck to foot, and was so stiff from the punishment he had received, that he could hardly walk. Considering the severe beating the man had already received the Magistrate felt justified in discharging him.
>
> [*Royal Gazette*, 2 Mar 1866]

> Yk-A-Kow, Chin-A-Ping and Tan-A-Hok were given 39 lashes each for plantain stealing. Hamlet, the executioner urged that he be allowed to inflict the flagellations, arguing that as his normal course of work was the most disagreeable in the colony, "it was only proper that when any remunerative business of a respectable and pleasant kind, bearing upon criminal reform, was to be done, it should also fall to his lot. Amongst the latter class of job was ranked naturally enough by Mr. Hamlet, the flogging of a few celestials for plantain stealing."
>
> [*The Colonist*, 12 Sep 1866]

Two years after the introduction of flogging the authorities felt that they had broken the back of plantain stealing, metaphorically speaking.

> It has been reported that two nights ago a Chinaman who was stealing plantains at the *Sisters*' Estate near Plantation *Wales* was shot dead. Occurrences of this kind are rare now a days compared to what they were a couple of years ago, and this we ascribe to the wholesome dread which most people entertain for the cat-o'-nine-tails.
>
> [*Royal Gazette*, 16 Apr 1867]

The reduction in numbers of plantain raids was more likely caused not by fear of the whip but by waning interest in this type of activity. In the dark the plantain walks had become a virtual shooting gallery. Besides, the stolen goods were bulky and disposing of them was not an easy task. Because of their heavy losses the owners of the provision grounds were also reluctant to expose their plantains for easy picking, deciding instead to patrol them heavily or else to abandon the land altogether.

> Three Portuguese were, on Thursday, committed by Mr. Plummer for trial, at the next session of the Supreme Court, on a charge of having murdered a Chinaman, who was caught stealing plantains at *Versailles* about ten days ago. We are informed that since that murder the thefts of the Chinese have been more frequent and daring. The Portuguese on the West Bank near town have lost upwards of 50 bunches of plantains, exclusive of those stolen from farms at Canal No. 1. The constant losses to which they are exposed have induced Portuguese to give up about thirty acres of plantain-land, and more is likely to be given up. Several private premises have during the week been invaded, and goats, provisions, house utensils and other property carried off. At *Goed Fortuin* two Chinese, neither of whom owns a farm, sold 20 bunches of

> plantains to the labourers on the public road at low prices.
> [*Royal Gazette*, 13 Mar 1869]

OTHER DISHES

Plantains by themselves were much too plain to create suitably appetizing dishes and there was a spate of activity coveting the four-legged and winged stocks.

> Kong-a-Soi, a Chinaman, was convicted of stealing a goat, and sentenced to imprisonment with hard labour for two years.
> [*Royal Gazette*, 16 Nov 1861]

> Lo-a-lung, killing a pig with intent to steal, 20 August 1863. [12 months with hard labour.] [*Royal Gazette*, 3 Sep 1863]

The *Royal Gazette* carried a commentary deploring the apparent disregard for law and order by some of the citizenry and cited a case where a girl of about 12 or 13 years of age was sent to court for stealing ice from an even younger boy. The editorial continued:

> But, perhaps, the most incurable kleptomaniacs in the Colony are the Chinese, who prowl about at all hours of the night clearing out the hen roosts, so that poultry promises to become a mere tradition in this country, like the DODO and APTERYX in their native habitats.
> [*Royal Gazette*, 19 Nov 1864]

> On the 25th ultimo, a Chinaman and three or four black men were arrested on a charge of having stolen and killed a young bull at plantation *Potosi* on the West Bank of the River. The skin was cut into four pieces, each of which contained a portion of the carcass. We have of late mentioned the frequency of robberies and thefts across the River, but this is the worst which has come to our notice.
> [*Royal Gazette*, 1 Apr 1869]

> Yesterday two policemen and two constables proceeded to Pln. *Zeelugt* to arrest a Chinaman who had been making free with his neighbour's feathered stock. The Chinaman objected to leave his comfortable house for the hardship of a lock-up, and his natural objection to an unquestionably disagreeable change of quarters, found sympathy with his celestial brethren, who rose like one man and drove the police and constables from the estate. The policeman escaped with a fright; but one

of the constables, probably not so swift of foot as the rest, got amongst the heathen and was badly beaten. [*Royal Gazette*, 19 Aug 1873]

Where's the beef?

The Carrion-crows proved the other day successful detective officers where the Police had failed. A cow disappeared from plantation *Leonora* last week, and nothing could be heard of its whereabouts, when a few days afterwards the attention of the neighbourhood was drawn to a cane-piece by the immense number of Carrion-crows alighting in it, and a searching which, a considerable part of the carcase of the missing animal was discovered. The Chinese who are great adepts at thieving rarely if ever carry their plunder to their houses, and in this case the culprits who were Chinese, had adopted their usual method of disposing of their booty altogether forgetting the fact that, in case of any sort of flesh the Carrion-crow would be sure to find it out. The interpreter in the estate, who had purchased some of the beef from the thieves, gave evidence against them which drew down upon him the ire of his fellow countrymen, and it has been found necessary since to protect him from the effects of their rage. Three of them were tried at the Hague Police Station, and sent to the Supreme Court. Three others supposed to be implicated have absconded from the estate. [*Royal Gazette*, 5 Nov 1964]

The clever Chinese indeed knew how to put the curious off the scent while enjoying their plunder hidden away in the cane-fields. In the following case the Chinese perpetrator managed to elude his captors by putting on the scent when he sought refuge in an outhouse.

During the night of Thursday last six or seven Chinese entered a yard at *Pouderoyen*, where pigs and poultry were kept, and where there are a number of rooms hired out to various parties. These people being aroused by the barking of dogs gave chase to the thieves, one of whom took shelter under a certain back building, where he was discovered, but on his emerging from his delectable place of concealment he was in such an excessively odorous condition that his pursuers ran away from him instead of affecting his capture. . . . [*Royal Gazette*, 13 Apr 1869]

MURDER

The other sphere of anti-social activity, which caused great consternation among the colony's administrators, was the numerous cases of murder involving Chinese. There were of course instances where the assailant was Chinese and the victim of another race, as well as vice versa, but the most disturbing incidents were the much more frequent cases of Chinese killing other Chinese. A similar phenomenon was taking place among the immigrants from India, particularly with the murder of their wives. The press presented an opinion for the difference between the two Asian peoples.

> Although the Chinese are worse off than these Coolies in respect to disparity in the number between the sexes, we do not hear of their murdering their wives or reputed wives, and he [the editor of the *Berbice Gazette*] comments on the reasons we assigned for that fact, namely the fidelity of the Chinese female, and the practice by the males of an abominable act. [*Royal Gazette*, 18 Dec 1862]

The newspapers were alluding to a circumstance where, with the dire shortage of women, the males had to comfort themselves with brotherly love. The situation was summarized for readers in Britain as follows:

> The Chinese being great thieves — that is, such of them as are brought here as immigrants — in the course of their depredations are either the assailants or the assailed; and among the Coolies the disproportion between the sexes leads many to murders or attempts to murder. It might be supposed that the disproportion being greater in the case of the Chinese than in that of the Coolies the same sad result might be expected, but the experience has shown that while, as a rule, the Chinese females are chaste, the same cannot be said for the Coolie women.
> [*Royal Gazette*, 23 Jul 1863]

The observation of a lower incidence of wife murder among the Chinese did not mean all Chinese women were chaste, although, most likely, all chased. On occasion, unfaithfulness was indeed the motive for murder, but in the main the people involved in the fatal disputes were men.

> A Chinese watchman was brutally murdered on Sunday or Monday last, aback of plantation *Blankenburg*, on the West Coast. Our informant stated that it was suspected that he had been killed by one of his own countrymen, to get possession of his money.
> [*Royal Gazette*, 21 Apr 1859]

> A Chinese labourer on his return from work missed $30, and charged a countryman, who had remained at home, with having committed the

theft. A dispute arose, which was terminated by the loser of the money stabbing the other so fatally as to cause death. Our informant adds that the guilty party admitted the fact, and stated that he had killed the man because he would not work but steal. [*Royal Gazette*, 1 Dec 1863]

Ho-Lem-He, a Chinese labourer, indentured on plantation Belmont, Mahaica, was charged with the murder of Chan-Chee, his wife on the 27th May last. . . . [He] in her absence possessed himself of her entire store of rice and salt fish and devoured a greater part of it. The woman seems to have cared more for her provisions than her husband, and in consequence of these depredations of his a violent quarrel forthwith burst out between the two — which came to a struggle. . . . At 9 that night Ho-Sing, another Chinese living in the adjoining room, was awoke by the sounds of a struggle and blows in the next chamber, and getting up and going in with several other Chinamen, he found the woman dead upon the floor, her nose broken in, a severe concussion on the temple, and black and blue marks and swellings about the neck; a heavy stick or pole 4 or 5 feet long also on the floor; and the prisoner composedly seated down before a pan containing some of his favorite rice.

[*Royal Gazette*, 2 Feb 1864]

On the 22nd ult., two Chinese men on pln *Cane Grove*, had a dispute about a trifling sum of money when one of them called Chan Tuk Ming with a sheath knife stabbed the other Chun-a-Yeung on the right side piercing the liver. [*Royal Gazette*, 8 Nov 1864]

A most attrocious murder was committed at Pln De Kinderen, on the West Coast, on Saturday night. . . . It appears that three Chinamen had agreed with another Chinaman that he should steal a sheep belonging to Mr. J.B. TROTMAN, and sell to them the mutton at 20 cents per lb. After he had stolen and killed the sheep they refused to pay him and told him to take it to the manager and he would give $5 for the carcase. The man who stole the sheep got vexed and stabbed the three Chinese, one of whom died shortly after from the wounds, and the other two lie in the De Kinderen Hospital in a very precarious state.

[*Royal Gazette*, 26 Jul 1865]

On the 1st instant, another of those brutal murders which unhappily at present so frequently occur among the Chinese race in this colony, was perpetrated at Pln Blankenburg West Coast. It appears that a Chinese woman named Wong Shee who had resided with a man named Kong-a-Thoi at plantation Windsor Forest until April 1865, when she, not being apprenticed, took into her head to leave, and cohabit with the driver at

Blankenburg Estate. Matters remained in that state until last Tuesday when Kong-a-Thoi took the opportunity of going over to Blankenburg to see his faithless spouse. When he reached the room where Wong-Shee resided, he found the door ajar, and on peeping in, discovered her lying on a bed. He at once rushed upon her and with a large knife, stabbed her in not less than fourteen parts of the body. The unfortunate woman cried out to a man who was in the adjoining room, but before he could come to her assistance she had been fatally wounded.

[*Royal Gazette*, 8 May 1866]

Yesterday a Chinese immigrant named Chum-Kow, indentured to plantation *Malgre Tout*, was murdered by a countryman under indenture to the same estate. . . . The deceased had had $21 in cash and sundry goods stolen from him, mainly, one pair black silk trousers of the value of $6; three pieces ordinary clothing worth about $1.20 each, and four of five other belonging to his wife, the total loss being about $35. . . . Having got a clue to the identity of the thief and the course he had taken, he followed him as far as *Schoon-Oord*. There he found that the silk trousers had been sold to a certain individual, and he at once got a warrant and had that party arrested. Yesterday morning when standing at his door, talking to a friend, *Lum-a-sing* came up and said to him, "why did you put my friend in the Station House for stealing your things? You did not see him." Deceased was about to make some reply when *Lum-a-sing* stabbed him with a long knife in the breast, the weapon, it is said, passing through his shoulder. The poor man ran to a distance of about a hundred yards from his house and then fell down and died. So far as we can learn, the murderer was not the thief, but was annoyed at the arrest of his friend the receiver of the stolen goods.

[*Royal Gazette*, 15 Apr 1869]

Lum-a-sing, when arrested is said to have remarked — "Suppose man dead, they hang me, story done." The Jury did not hesitate about finding the prisoner guilty of the murder. . . [*Royal Gazette*, 17 Apr 1869]

At about noon to-day a Coolie and a Chinaman, who were convicted of murder at the last session of the Supreme Criminal Court, were executed within the Georgetown Gaol. . . . The Chinaman was quiet; but seemed more or less alarmed, and repeatedly looked upwards as if inspecting the fatal noose. It is said that during the greater part of the past night he was or appeared to be praying, and just before being launched off he kissed the Cross presented to him by a Roman Catholic Priest.

[*Royal Gazette*, 19 Mar 1870]

Low-a-Chow, a Chinaman indentured to *Pln. Ruimveldt*, was indicted for the manslaughter of Wang-go-a, on the 4th February last. It appeared from the evidence that on the day in question the prisoner had a dispute with the overseer about his wages. He and the deceased had been working together, and when they went for their money he said that the amount offered him was not correct, while the deceased maintained that it was. The overseer divided the prisoner's money into small pieces, and reckoned it out to him, and he expressed himself satisfied. He and the deceased then had some words about the matter, and the deceased struck him. Upon that he struck the deceased a blow with his fists on the ribs. They then walked along the road together, and when they reached the megass logie the deceased fell down. The prisoner and another man helped him up, and he walked on a little further, but soon after he fell down into the trench. The prisoner and another Chinaman then carried him to the hospital. He was almost unconscious and in a state of collapse, and died very soon after. Dr. Scott, the medical attendant of the estate, made a *post mortem* examination of the body, and found the abdomen filled with blood, caused by a rupture of the spleen. The spleen he said was so much diseased, that a very slight blow would have been sufficient to cause a rupture.

The Jury *Acquitted* the prisoner. [*Royal Gazette*, 25 Apr 1871]

On Thursday afternoon last, in New Amsterdam, some Chinese were gambling, and one of them won $100. Exasperated at their losses, the others called on him to divide his winnings, and give each of them a portion. The request was refused, the winner was stabbed by one of them in the neck and side with a knife, and he died shortly after from the effects of these wounds. The assailant has been apprehended.

[*Royal Gazette*, 13 Nov 1875]

Beside these clashes which caused loss of life there were many others which ended in injury, giving rise to several court cases for assault, beating, injury with intent, cutting, wounding, maiming, occasioning bodily harm and the like. In one case the victim was not even human:

Tang-a-Tuck indicted for wounding a cow.

It appears that the prisoner is an indentured immigrant on Pln *Hope and Experiment*, where he kept a garden. Being annoyed at a cow entering and destroying the garden, he threw his cutlass at her and inflicted a wound, which was described as being three inches in depth and seven in length. In his defence he admitted inflicting the wound, but said it was accidental. The cow having come into the garden and destroyed what he had devoted many tedious hours to in accomplishing, he threw the cutlass at her, intending to drive it away, but unfortunately the sharp edge of the instrument inflicted the wound. The prisoner stated that the cow had since recovered.

The jury returned a verdict of guilty, but recommended the prisoner to mercy, owing to the great provocation he had received.

His Honor the Judge, in addressing the prisoner, said that, in consequence of the recommendation of the jury, he would be more lenient with him than he otherwise would have been. He was sentenced to six months' imprisonment with hard labour in the county gaol.

[*Royal Gazette*, 26 Oct 1864]

CLASS CONFLICT

On occasion the disputes between those who took the law into their own hands led to full-scale riots involving Chinese immigrants. One notable one took place in Essequebo county:

A serious riot occurred at plantation *Zeelandia*, Wakenaam on Saturday last, between two of the resident races. The Chinese had lately been guilty of theft on a somewhat extensive scale, and of a daring character not confining their deprecations to plantains and poultry. A few days ago a goat disappeared, and then a shop was broken into from which a large quantity of salt pork, rice and brandy were abstracted, the brandy, probably, for the purpose of barter as the Chinese in general do not indulge in spirituous liquor. Early next morning twelve bottles of brandy were found behind the buildings occupied by the Chinese, and pork and rice in their dwellings but there was not sufficient proof to fix the theft upon any individual. This led, however, to an important discovery which bears strongly on the subsequent riot. A Chinese hut, thatched with canes, and provided with cooking utensils, was found in a cane piece. A watch was set and an immigrant was captured when entering the hut. The case, we believe, is under investigation. The fact became known on the Thursday preceding the riot, and the Chinese found out that a black man was the informant. The man had drawn his wages on the afternoon of Saturday, at the pay table, and was on his way back when he was attacked, before he had got beyond the Hospital and within a stone's throw of the Overseers' quarters. A signal was given on a drum, and at once the whole Chinese gang turned out armed with cutlasses, shovels, bludgeons, bricks and bottles. The black people came up to support their countrymen and a fierce and general riot ensued.

Several times the Chinese were worsted, but they renewed the combat again and again, until they could no longer resist their opponents, when they were compelled to yield. Between a hundred and a hundred and fifty persons were engaged in the melée and it was fortunate that the Coolies were prevented from taking part in it, or the affair would have been of a still more serious character. As it was the Chinese suffered more than the black people, and a good many of them are in the Hospital; one with two arm bones broken, another with a fracture of the skull, and several with wounds more or less severe. Some of the rioters are in gaol awaiting an investigation of the case. [*Royal Gazette*, 28 May 1863]

The result of the enquiry into the riot which recently occurred at Plantation *Zeelandia* in Wakenaam has been that five of the Chinese who were ring leaders on the occasion have been sent on for trial at the next Session of the Supreme Criminal Court. Strange to say, no charge has been preferred by the Chinese against any of the black people who were engaged in the riot. This may arise from the impression on the part of the Chinese that as they were the aggressors any charge brought by them against their opponents would not be entertained, or they may be ignorant of the fact that they have the right of making such a charge. However this may be, we do not see why the Chinese alone should be punished for a breach of the law. It was natural that the countrymen of the party assailed should come to his assistance, but at the same time, by taking part in the affray and thereby causing a serious riot, in which some of the Chinese received serious injuries, they made themselves amenable to the law and ought not to escape punishment. This is desirable not only on the grounds of public justice, but to show the Chinese and other immigrants that they will not be made scapegoats of and that others who may have been implicated with themselves in any violation of the law will also share the punishment. Had the man who was attacked made his escape, and he probably could, there might have been no riot at all, but no doubt the feelings of race against race was too strong to permit of the attack being avoided, and it was therefore met in a manner which led to a most serious result, and nearly to the loss of lives.

[*Royal Gazette*, 2 Jun 1863]

Mulling the Motive

In the mid-1860s, when the population of Chinese in the colony reached its peak, the number of criminal cases also reached a maximum. It caused the authorities much concern to figure out the reason and a solution.

It is impossible to look over the Calendar of the Supreme Court without remarking the number of cases in which Immigrants are charged with Murder, Manslaughter, Cutting and Wounding, and such-like "irregularities." For the most part the Criminals are Coolies and Chinese, and the proportion of other races charged with similar offences is comparatively trifling.

It is worth considering, how much of this crime is due to *opportunity*, and whether it might not be possible, under altered circumstances, to preserve these men from the serious, too often fatal, consequences of their own want of self-restraint, and of their tempestuous and unbridled passions. The Chinaman is an apathetic being; at least he has not the fiery, excitable temperament of the Coolie, and we believe that the frequency of the cases in which Chinamen are brought up for the use of deadly weapons, is really due more to their familiarity with the weapon, and to a disregard of consequences, than to any settled intention to inflict a serious wound. With the Coolies it may be different — their passions are more gusty, more intense, and a paroxysm of rage may, and often does, carry them into the commission of the most tigerish ferocities. Not so with the Chinaman. . .

For the Chinaman, especially, we think much more might be done than ever has been done for him. Here he fills the gaols, and is the most troublesome and unmanageable part of our population. This is by no means generally the case with him. On the contrary, a Chinaman is naturally most tractable, and is never so happy and contented, as when he is earning money, and has at the same time some one who will take the complete management of him, so that he can rely upon this *some one* to think for him, and deal with him, just as a father does to a child. It seems presumptuous, and we hesitate to say it, but nevertheless, when we see the Chinaman so difficult of management, and turning out so unsatisfactorily as they do here, we cannot help thinking that there has been some flaw in their management to bring about the state of things which exists. It may be taken as an axiom, perhaps, that Chinamen cannot be prevented from gambling, — that is they find an opportunity, they will smoke opium, — and that they do not object to take what do not belong to them; very "difficult" vices, no doubt, and very suggestive ones, — but still, much may be done with them in these matters by management, provided always that this management is brought home to them, and is both personal and direct. Nothing has worked more satisfactorily than the appointment of *Chinese Protectors* in Australia. These gentlemen are Magistrates, who are charged with the whole arrangement of the

Chinamen, their "protection" and their coercion too, at times; but the Chinamen looked up to them, deferred to them, and brought their disputes to them for settlement. We believe that, *mutatis mutandis*, a similar arrangement would work wonders with the Chinamen in our Colony. [*Guiana Times*, 25 Nov 1865]

The press failed to attribute any blame on the immigrant recruitment process and poor quality of some of the people who found themselves in British Guiana. From the comments made by Rev. Lobschied, the dregs of the populace were being picked up off the streets in China to fill the immigrant ships. It is not surprising that a similar crime wave was also being noted in Trinidad causing the island's press to comment:

The coincidence is by no means remarkable, that at the very moment when the people of British Guiana are fretting about the lawlessness of their Chinese Immigrants, we should be doing precisely the same thing. [*Royal Gazette*, 8 Sep 1866]

SUICIDE

The transition to an alien land and culture was not likely to change those who were already good-for-nothing. At the same time the environment proved a great challenge to those who were willing to adapt. Of these there were some who did not adjust sufficiently well resulting in a number of suicides from discontent with their fate in the new land. They took their own lives mainly by hanging, drowning and overdosing themselves on opium.

A few days ago a Chinaman drowned himself at Plantation *Land of Plenty*, Essequebo. [*Royal Gazette*, 19 Jun 1860]

Two cases of suicide, committed by Chinese females, by means of opium, have occurred on the East Coast, within the last few days. [*Royal Gazette*, 18 Jun 1861]

The body of a Chinaman named Lam-a-Shing was found in a trench on the *Peter's Hall* Estate, yesterday morning, with his throat cut. An inquest was held the same day, when it appeared from the evidence that deceased had cut his throat and after doing so ran and threw himself into the trench. The jury returned a verdict of "committed suicide by cutting his throat." [*Royal Gazette*, 26 Sep 1864]

The Chinaman who hanged himself at Malgre Tout . . . was recently indentured to the Estate, . . . earned a fair wage, but was unfortunately a gambler. The week previous to his death he earned six shillings which he lost at the gambling table and had to borrow from one of his countrymen to buy rice. [*Royal Gazette*, 27 Nov 1865]

We mentioned in our column of the 6th instant, that two immigrants had been found dead, with ropes around their necks, in a cane field on Plantation *Hampton Court*, in the county of Essequebo. . . . It appears that one of the deceased LIN-SHEE, who is described as having been a large powerful woman, was on her first arrival in the Colony, wife of one SEE-A-SOON, but she was in the habit of beating him and he gladly transferred her to his friend Koo-a-Kop, whom she also led a sad life, beating him, and declaring he was unable to maintain her properly, and subsequently left his house for that of another man. On Monday, the 27th ultimo, the bodies of LIN-SHEE and KOO-A-KOP were found as described, and the question naturally arose whether considering their former connection, the female had been enticed into the cane piece, and there murdered by KOO-A-KOP, who afterwards strangled himself; but the Jury came to a contrary conclusion, and returned the verdict "that KOO-A-KOP died from apoplexy caused by strangulation, and that LIN-SHEE was willfully strangled, but apparently with her own consent by the said KOO-A-KOP who, thereafter, committed suicide by strangling himself. " [*Royal Gazette*, 14 Dec 1865]

A Chinese woman, residing at Haarlem, committed suicide on the night of Sunday last. The rash act, on the part of the deceased, it is said, was owing to her having been deserted by her reputed husband, who had gone to live with a Coolie woman. [*Royal Gazette*, 25 May 1876]

[At the inquest on his wife's death] Chan-a-Chow said that . . . on Monday morning last he opened the curtain of the deceased's bed and found her dead hanging by a piece of cord. Deceased was a sickly woman and was blind. [*Royal Gazette*, 16 Feb 1882]

A Chinaman hung himself this week at Pln La Grange, because his reputed wife ran away with all his money. [*Royal Gazette*, 29 Jul 1882]

A China woman died at La Jalousie on Tuesday last from an overdose of opium. It appears that she quarreled with her husband on Monday evening, and in his absence in Georgetown, where he had gone to buy goods, the parties owning four shops on estates, she dosed herself with opium and died from the effects. [*Royal Gazette*, 7 May 1885]

ROBBERY

It should be remembered that the majority of Chinese immigrants were law-abiding people who tried their best to adapt. At the same time it should be pointed out that adaptation was also a practice that the not-so-law-abiding were able to use to their advantage. With the ever-growing difficulties associated with plantain stealing, the Chinese anti-social elements began to turn to different forms of acquisition such as the taking of personal valuables and goods from individuals and shops.

> Yesterday morning, about one o'clock, a daring attempt was made by three Chinamen to break into a shop, near the High Bridge in this town belonging to a Portuguese gentleman. The owner, who lives on the premises, was aroused by the noise and raised the alarm; when the thieves made off at full speed and the Portuguese followed in hot pursuit. A most exciting chase then ensued. The latter, however, gained ground and seized one Chinese. The other attempted a rescue, but assistance coming up, they quickly decamped, leaving their companion in the iron grasp of the enraged shopman; who soon had him committed to the safe keeping of a station cell. We believe this is the third time that such an attempt has been made on the same shop, and we rejoice that a capture has been effected. The Chinamen are supposed to belong to *Providence* estate. [*Royal Gazette*, 16 Jul 1864]

> A robbery of 350 dollars had been committed on the Manager's house of plantation Skeldon on the 3rd instant. . . . Policeman Jackson, who succeeded in capturing three Chinesemen on whom suspicion had fallen in consequence of their appearing to have more money in their possession than could be well accounted for. He also succeeded in recovering 200 dollars, supposed to be part of the stolen money, and about twenty bags of rice, which the Chinamen had purchased in a store in town. It appears that one of the three was a servant in the Manager's house. . . . [*Royal Gazette*, 20 Jul 1864]

> Chansee and Ho-a-Hop [were] charged with breaking and entering the premises of one Jose Rodrigues, and stolen therefrom eighty-nine dollars in silver, and various other articles amounting in value to $117.94. [Chansee was found guilty and sentenced to seven years imprisonment, while Ho-a-Hop was acquitted.] [*Royal Gazette*, 17 Nov 1865]

> Tang-a-san, indicted for burglariously entering the dwelling-house of Lena L'Esperance on the 8th April last and stealing $5 in change and

sundry articles. [Sentenced to 5 years in prison.]
[*Royal Gazette*, 29 Jul 1869]

Coolies are very rarely found engaged in burglaries and larcenies, their operations being chiefly confined to stealing cows and goats, but their fellow immigrants the Chinese are noted for their daring and skill.
[*Royal Gazette*, 9 Sep 1869]

A clever dodge was tried with success, a day or two ago by a Chinaman in Charlestown. The ingenious celestial carried a large bag at a late hour into a Portuguese shop in the district, and telling the shopman that it was a bag of yams, begged to be allowed to leave it in the shop while he went about some business, The unsuspecting shopman gave his permission to leave his load, but the "artful dodger" did not return for it that night. The shop was shut up at the usual hour, and at about midnight, hearing a slight noise in the shop, the shop-keeper went down to see what was the matter, when, to his astonishment, he discovered that the bag which had been left in his keeping had contained — not yams, but a live Chinaman, who made himself scarce immediately on seeing him, carrying away with him all the money he had found in the shop, besides several packages of goods. He has not since been heard of.
[*Royal Gazette*, 25 Sep 1869]

Po-cho-an, a Chinaman, was indicted for burglariously breaking and entering the house of Akobar, a Coolie on the 1st February last, with intent to commit a felony. . . . Shortly after falling asleep, [Akobar] felt something hike a hand about his neck, and opening his eyes, he saw the prisoner trying to sever the strings which held a gold-piece round his neck. He jumped up and seized him, and another Coolie who was sleeping in the room with him at the time rose to his assistance. [Guilty.]
[*Royal Gazette*, 20 Apr 1871]

In-kit, a Chinaman was charged with stealing a silver soup ladle and two spoons, and other articles, the property of Isaac Wrong, on the 1st January. Mr. Wrong had left his house for a few moments and on returning found the prisoner held by his two dogs in the yard, one holding him by the hand and the other by his trousers. The silver was found in the trench. [In his defense In-kit said that] Mr. Wrong's cook had accidentally thrown it there with a pan of water. [12 months imprisonment]. [*Royal Gazette*, 30 Jan 1872]

A Chinaman broke into a coolie driver's house at Pln. *Ruimveldt* on Thursday night and stole some jewellery and other things. As he was making off, an alarm was raised, and he was pursued by some of the other coolies on the estate. One seized his pigtail, but the Chinaman cut off that appendage and left it in his pursuer's hand. Two coolies named Mootoo and Ramlall, seized the man and were both stabbed in the body. The Chinaman was at last knocked down and secured. [One of the men later died.] [*Royal Gazette*, 15 Sep 1877]

CREAM COLLAR CRIME

As the years went by and the immigrants became settled, there came yet another change in the form of criminal activity. It emerged among some of the Chinese who had made a reasonable start in securing an economic base. These represented the cream of the crop among the Chinese immigrants but some were a bit too eager to increase their rate of acquisition of wealth. The authorities were on the lookout for these corner-cutting practices.

In Chan-a-poo vs. Burrowes the conviction of the magistrate was quashed. Charged that he on the 21st December 1872, . . . [was] the occupier of certain business premises situated at Phoenix Village in Leguan, on which said business premises was then and there found one half gill measure, the same being unstamped, contrary to Ordinance No 13 anno 1851. The magistrate convicted the appellant and sentenced him to pay a fine of $10, with costs. [*Royal Gazette*, 10 May 1873]

Mr. Chan got a break when the judge of the Court of Review overturned the conviction saying that it was an offense to use unstamped weights and measures, but not an offense to be in possession of them. Some others were not so fortunate:

Chee-a-Kwee, a Chinese Shop Keeper of *Schoon ord* was fined $10 for having in his possession light weights.

[*Royal Gazette*, 23 May 1876]

Tung-foo Tuch was charged with . . . with having light weights in his shop on the 24th June last. . . He was sentenced to pay $20 and 72 cents costs. [*Royal Gazette*, 18 Jul 1882]

Lum-sung-hing was charged with selling a pint of porter without licence at Pln. Hope. [Fined $50 or two months in prison.]

[*Royal Gazette*, 9 Sep 1875]

At one spot on the West Coast of Berbice three cargoes have been landed within the past fortnight, and that too with only the most formal attempt at concealment. The gentleman who gives us this information says that one of the drivers met, the morning of one of these landings, three Chinese carrying toward the estate two small kegs of rum each holding about ten gallons, intending undoubtedly for sale, by retail, amongst the estate's labourers. The driver at once went in search of a constable to have the rum seized, but before he could get one, Chinese and rum had disappeared and the former did not make their appearance until some days afterwards when they made no attempt to deny having been in possession of smuggled spirits. [*Royal Gazette*, 29 Feb 1876]

The seizure of smuggled rum has been made by Mr. Shaw, overseer at *Leonora*, the contraband having been found in the possession of a family of Chinese. While Mr. Shaw was engaged near the water side, he noticed 8 Chinese landing from a small craft, and carrying 8 parafine oil tins and 2 demijohns. Suspecting that the packages contained rum, he stopped the party, inspected their luggage, and, finding his suspicions to be correct, seized the whole stock and forwarded it to the Commissary of the District. [*Royal Gazette*, 29 Apr 1876]

Harsue, a Chinaman was charged . . . with selling a pint of wine on Sunday the 16th instant. [*Royal Gazette*, 2 May 1976]

The charge is this case was because it was an offence to sell liquor on the Sabbath. The commissioner was also on the prowl for liquor that was in excess of the allowable limit or located in premises not licensed for the sale of spirits.

Wonn-Sam, a Chinese of Bagotville was charged with having one gallon of brandy on his business premises on 3rd March 1876. Fined $20. [*Royal Gazette*, 2 May 1876]

Hong-a-Yong, a Chinese shopkeeper [was charged] for exposing for sale rice, flour &c, wine and malt liquor, without being provided with the necessary licences. [Fined two dollars in each case and ordered to take out licences.] [*Royal Gazette*, 19 Mar 1880]

To the Editor.

It is not an uncommon thing to see Chinese vending spirits to an alarming extent on some of our sugar estates and in some of our villages on Sundays as well as week days; and the manner in which it is done is that a number of them come to town and procure each the quantity allowed by law to be carried by a single individual at one time. On their return home all is mixed and entrusted to one of their number for sale, who accounts to each of the others for his share of the outlay in the procuring of the rum as well as the profit therefrom. Opium dealing is conducted in the same manner, and at the same time, and the profit derived from both is sometimes astonishing. Neither Commissary nor Police will interfere, and therefore a profitable business is carried on. . .

Your obedient servant

A SPIRIT DEALER [*Royal Gazette*, 8 Jun 1880]

In the following story the author of a letter to the editor expressed some concern that some healthy cattle belonging to the estate of a deceased Chinese person were suddenly not the same healthy beasts when they were put up for sale:

> That the Heathen Chinee is peculiar, is a proposition, the truth of which is generally admitted, but the peculiarity of the Chinaman is not exclusive, it exists amongst the animals that belong to him, and from what I hear, there is a good deal of peculiarity in the eastern quarter of Berbice. A dead Chinaman's flock of cattle had to be sold to wind up his estate, but through their peculiar cussedness, the cattle the Chinaman possessed had quite altered in appearance by the time they came to be sold. Some prime fat oxen had become transmogrified into very lean and very old cows, — which was very hard on the gentleman intrusted with the sale of the cattle, for it might have been supposed he had had something to do with the transmogrification, especially as he was a cattle-breeder himself. The peculiarity of the occurrence shows how careful one ought to be in dealing with a Chinaman, or a Chinaman's cattle. [*Royal Gazette*, 13 Mar 1880]

OPIUM

The reports above suggest that the Chinese were taking to liquor with eagerness. However, their satisfaction came from the profit that was derived from the trading of the spirituous product rather than the imbibing of it. The greater affliction of the Chinese was addiction to opium, a problem which they brought with them from China. The sale and use of opium in British Guiana was permitted by law, although there were strict controls on the amounts and methods of distribution. A licensed opium merchant could obtain his supply only from a registered opium importer and a record of each transaction had to be kept. The ordinance regulating retail sales stipulated that "no dealer in opium or bhang shall sell or dispose of, within any one period of twenty four hours, to or for the use of any one person, any quantity of opium exceeding five grains." The interpretation of this ordinance became the subject of a court case when a licensed Chinese dealer took a certain quantity of the product for his own use and was charged.

> One day last month Mr. DARRELL visited CHUN-CHAI-CHIN's establishment, and on inspecting his record, discovered that though the defendant had never sold or disposed of within one period of twenty-four hours, to or for the use of any one person, any quantity of opium exceeding five grains, yet he had, on one occasion, taken half a pound for his own use which, with commendable honesty, he had entered in his book to "self" . . .
>
> The Magistrate . . . this morning gave judgment in favour of the defendant, remarking that he did not see very clearly how a person could "dispose of" to himself, an article which was already his own and which he had already purchased from another party and paid for. He thought that the meaning of the words "dispose of" must be decided by the word "sell" which preceded it. [*Royal Gazette*, 17 Jan 1865]

As might be expected from the addictive nature of the drug there were a number of cases where charges were laid for possession of opium illegally or in quantities in excess of the regulated amount.

> Chua Lee, shop keeper of Den Amstel was brought up . . . with having illegally in his possession on the 16th instant, 15 lbs of opium. Chua Lee pleaded guilty to the charge, and was fined $90.
>
> [*Royal Gazette*, 1 Jun 1866]

Trading in opium was legally permitted through to the twentieth century and a significant reason for this could be deduced from the large amount of revenue that the government obtained by way of taxes and duties.

> Duties received on imported opium $15,839.45 from 10,559 lbs @ $1.50/lb. [*Royal Gazette*, 2 Jun 1870]

TARGETS

The nature of these infringements of the law — involving the plying of liquor, the trading in opium or the selling of everyday goods — shows that a number of Chinese had become entrepreneurs and opened shops across the country. This change in status from their initial occupation as field labourers naturally placed them in an elevated status and economic position, especially compared to those who did not acquire shops and businesses. They thus became the targets of those involved in crime.

Tan-Ti-O was found guilty of larceny of $59 60 in paper money, the property of one Loy-a-Choy. [12 months imprisonment.]
[*Royal Gazette*, 4 Sep 1875]

James Taylor was charged with the Larceny of six cents in goods from the provision shop of a Chinese Man named Ah-sui-hee. The accused entered the shop of the defendant and after calling for some bread and sugar, which he devoured in the twinkling of an eye, he ran away. [Sentenced to 10 days with hard labour.]
[*Royal Gazette*, 23 Dec 1880]

Baboo, a coolieman, was charged by Wong-a-Shin, a Chinese, with having entered his provision shop with a stick and piece of wax attached to its end wherewith he extracted 8 cents from his drawer. . . . He was sentenced to one month's imprisonment with hard labour.
[*Royal Gazette*, 6 Jul 1882]

At nine o'clock this morning, a Chinaman, described as assistant shop-keeper at *Malgre Tout*, while on his way to town became suddenly unwell, and was compelled to sit down on the bridge of a rum shop in Pouderoyen village. His friends were sent for, and they conveyed him to the hospital of pln. *Versailles*, but before he reached there he died. When lying in an unconscious state on the bridge of the rum shop, some unfeeling monsters robbed the poor man of the money on his person. The thief has not yet been heard of. . . . [*Royal Gazette*, 13 Feb 1883]

The following is a contemporary tale about loaves and fishes:

William Francis, a stout ruffianly looking fellow, was on remand charged by a Chinese woman Yong-a-Chee, shopkeeper at Pln Schoon Ord with stealing 6 cents in bread and one tin of sardines valued 12 cents. The prisoner and another man went into the shop of the Complainant, and seeing Complainant alone called for the goods named, and on receiving them took to their heels. They were pursued and the prisoner was caught, the other having managed to escape. The prisoner was sentenced to thirty days' imprisonment, and at the expiration of that time to pay a fine of $20, or a further imprisonment of two months.
[*Royal Gazette*, 16 Jun 1883]

G. Europe was charged with having on the 9th Sept., extorted from the person of Thang-Fung-Khoy, a Chinese, the sum of $ 1 92. [Guilty.] [*Royal Gazette*, 15 Nov 1883]

John Payne, a boy, was charged by A-Sing, a Chinaman, with having on the 23rd instant stolen a quantity of nuts from his tray, valued 2 cents. Defendant was ordered to receive fifteen stripes with tamarind rods. [*Royal Gazette*, 21 Jan 1884]

James Porter, a black old man, was charged by Ton-a-Shaw, a Chinaman, with having stolen from him a skillet, valued at 88 cents, and a quantity of cooked rice, valued 8 cents, and two spoons, all to the value of $1 04, his property. Defendant was sent to jail for twenty-one days. [*Royal Gazette*, 28 Mar 1884]

John Atwell, Jeremiah Drakes and Augustus Newman, were indicted for having on the 5th April, feloniously stolen 2 barrels of mackerel from the shop of Chun-chi-Lung. [Guilty.] [*Royal Gazette*, 23 Jul 1885]

INNOCENTS

The apparent lack of respect for property and person that the Chinese had shown after their arrival in British Guiana soon created the conception that the Chinese were a bunch of gangsters. Indeed the number of criminal activities committed by Chinese immigrants was greatly in excess of their proportion in the population. Even though these anti-social acts were carried out by a few they still gave a bad name to the Chinese community as a whole. Inevitably innocent Chinese became singled out for accusation whenever a crime was perpetrated.

Two Coolies were employed as watchmen at a plantation walk aback of plantation *Nonpareil*, one of them living in a thatched hut or watchhouse, with his wife (or reputed wife) and a son about eight years of age. On Sunday morning about 3 o'clock one of the men made an appearance at the buildings of plantation *Nonpareil*, in a wretched condition, his skin being blistered and nearly peeled off from the effects of fire. He was taken to the hospital and afterwards made a statement to the following effect. On Saturday afternoon two Chinese came aback, and, in passing the watchhouse, one of them remarked in English that the plantains were good but that the watchhouse was not good and should be burned. At night he (the Coolie) with the others went to bed — the bed being on a sort of cockloft in the watchhouse — after having put out the lights and seen that everything was secure. About midnight or later he found himself amid flames which were scorching him, and breaking through them, he fell or jumped into the trench. On scrambling out of the trench he observed by the light of the fire the two Chinese whom he had seen in the afternoon, walking away from the hut, a distance about four roods. . . . The bodies of three Coolies found amid the ruins of the watchhouse were fearfully charred and their features and limbs more or less contorted, evincing the painful nature of their death. A bottle containing some rum was found in the ruins. The whole of the Chinese gang of plantation *Enterprise* were taken over to *Nonpareil* and passed in review before the watchman who had escaped from the fire and he identified or pretended to identify two of them as the parties who had passed the watchhouse on Saturday afternoon. They were thereupon arrested, but there was evidence to shew that they had slept in the same room with two of their companions, and had not left the room at any time during the night of Saturday, and yesterday when the Inquest was resumed they were liberated by Mr. J.D. FRASER, S.J.P. . . . The conclusion we come to is this, that the two watchmen, and perhaps the wife of one of them, had been drinking freely; that they had been careless in the use of their pipes, the cockloft being so near to the thatch of the roof, or had not been sufficiently careful in extinguishing their fire, and that when the watchhouse was in flames they were so overpowered either by the steep of intoxication, or by the smoke, that they could not effect their escape. . . . We must, therefore, look upon the melancholy death of the Coolies as attributable to accident, and not to the act of Chinese, who, however anxious to plunder a plantain walk, had no motive for taking the lives of four of their fellow-creatures. The Coolie who escaped half dead, died on Sunday . . . [*Royal Gazette*, 31 Dec 1861]

A Chinese beggar woman, was charged by "Indigo" 192, with having a fowl in her possession in Water-street, between 10 and 11 o'clock, last night, without, of course, being able to give a satisfactory account of either herself or her chicken. When the fact that the Chinese woman could not speak, the language of 192, and *vice versa*, it can be at once understood, why the curiosity of the latter functionary had not been satisfied. But 192 having no doubt, as much relish for tender fowl as for Newspaper notoriety, took the exiled child of Confucius to see his official residence in the Brick-dam,[1] where she was pressed to spend the night. Somehow, the edible parts of the chicken disappeared, meanwhile, for all that 192 could produce this morning, was both its legs tied together with a string. The prisoner was discharged. [*Royal Gazette*, 1 Jan 1866]

Irregular actions on the part of the police were noted from time to time and in one incident took the life of the Chinese

1 The police station.

victim:

James Richard, an ex-police officer, was indicted for the manslaughter of a Chinaman named Ng-a-kin.

The deceased was under remand in the lock-up at Vreed-en-hoop. The prisoner was a policeman on duty there and it appeared that he went into the lock-up, and because the Chinaman did not do something which he wished him to do, he stucked him kicked him. The man fell to the ground, and, according to the evidence, he never rose again. This policeman, who had abused his authority, seemed to have left the man groaning upon the ground, and very shortly after he died. There were several other prisoners in the lock-up at the time, and at the inquest it was discovered that death was caused by a rupture of the spleen. . . . The defense argued that it was probable that the spleen was diseased and it was suddenly ruptured by a violent fit of laughter or mental emotion of the most utmost kind.

The Attorney General . . . protested against the doctrine that prisoners in the lock-up were obliged to clean stables and to do the duty work of the police. The learned counsel for the prisoner might with equal soundness of reasoning contend that a violent fit of laughter would produce a black-eye. A verdict of guilty was returned. [*Royal Gazette*, 22 Jul 1869]

Attention has been recently drawn to the crusade carried on by the Police against the Chinese for the seizure of opium. The houses of these people are invaded without any warrant, and they themselves are stopped on the public street, and have any parcels they may be carrying searched to see if they contain opium. Such proceedings are quite improper, being an exercise of authority not warranted by law, and grossly unjust. If goods — such for instance as silver — be stolen there may be some excuse for examining bundles carried not only by the Chinese but also by other classes of people, but to do this in the hope of detecting opium, and pocketing a part of the proceeds in case of forfeiture is illegal and reprehensible — the more so, that there is nothing to shew that opium found in that way, in any quantity, could be declared forfeited. Looking at the Ordinance, No. 22 of 1861, there is not a word said as to what is to be done in the case where a man is found in possession of opium, nor is there any direct definition of the term "illegal possession."

[*Royal Gazette*, 27 Jul 1869]

[Advertisement] Georgetown, 9th December, 1872

TO THE EDITOR OF THE "GAZETTE."

Sir — May I kindly inform you that on the 18th July, a Policeman and Sergeant at Hyde Park, had taken all of my articles from me to the value of $48 84, when I went to the Inspector I had received no redress so that I can get my articles. The Sergeant also has taken a gold trinket value $5 64, (and cannot get either.) Mr. Editor, do you not think this a most shameful thing for Policeman in this colony to detain poor people goods in that way, and to be deprived in that *manner*. And also a Free Ticket.[2]

I am Sir,

Your obedt. Servant,

[X] his mark LEUNGLUN KONG

[*Royal Gazette*, 31 Dec 1872]

The Police are still continuing to molest, under the excuse that they are suspected of being indentured immigrants, certain old and well known Chinese who, for years past, have been residing in the city, making their living by working in fancy paper work or selling cheap luxuries for the poorer classes. In acting in the reprehensible fashion, the police are simply taking the opportunity afforded them by some judicious hasty order issued lately, of having some fun and frolic at the expense of these offenseless people. The police are no more justified in arresting or shoving along to the station-house one of these Chinese who have been located in town for years, and whose faces must be familiar to the inhabitants, than they would be in arresting and dragging to the station any citizen no matter how high in position. As a illustration of this kind of horse-play which is prevailing amongst certain members of the Force at the present moment, we mention an incident which occurred to-day near the station at the corner of Wellington and Church Streets. An old Chinaman was standing with his tray selling nuts, when a policeman came up to him, and demanded to see his 'ticket.' The Chinaman was confounded. He had no ticket with him. He had been selling in the streets of the city for years past and though he possessed a ticket which he kept at home he had never found it necessary to carry it about with him. The policeman would take no excuse, the Chinaman must follow him to the station; and as the sport was getting exciting another policeman came up to take part in it. These two rascals badgered the old man and pretended it to be necessary that he should go with them to the station, until they were tired of the fun, when they agreed to let him go *if he would give them some nuts*. The Chinaman gave them their handful of nuts with which they retired laughing at the success of their rascality. The state of things, if not checked immediately, will bring about for the free Chinese in this colony a reign of terror similar

---

2 Certificate of Freedom issued to those not under indenture.

to that which the low Irish and Americans at one time exercised over indentured Chinese immigrants in the Pacific States of America, and which, we believe, still exists to a certain extent. But, of course it will not be allowed to remain unchecked; for if the Police department do not show more discretion in their search for missing indentured immigrants, the Governor, we confidently believe, will very quickly bring the police to book. The fact of its being possible to collect in one day so large a number of Chinese as that which was marched off on Tuesday to the Immigration Office, to be identified, points to a gross neglect of duty highly discreditable to every one concerned with it. The law giving the police instructions regarding estates' deserters is not an Ordinance of yesterday. Since it came into operation, there has been time enough for the police to become acquainted with every free Chinese in the City and be able to spot a stranger as soon as he made his appearance. But the City Inspector or his men, or both, neglect the requirements of this particular law; they fall asleep over their duty, and after slumbering for month after month they awake like men with half their senses about them, and in their anxiety to show what clever fellows they are, go stumbling and blundering about, arresting quiet and orderly citizens simply because they happen to be of the same nationality as the men they (the police) are anxious to capture. This mode of procedure may be regarded by the police as a sign of their activity and zeal, but to others it had the look of incompetency, or negligence. It is all very good to say that the arrest of the free Chinese, if illegal, are made in the interests of the Planters; but that excuse wont bear investigating. We have already pointed out that if the police had been doing their duty every free Chinaman would have been known to them by this time; and not only would these illegal arrests have been unnecessary, the Planters would have benefited by having their missing labourers returned to them immediately after the fellows made their appearance in the city. [*Royal Gazette*, 26 Aug 1875]

GOING TO COURT

The number of crimes, particularly those in which Chinese were simultaneously both perpetrators and victims, would suggest that the Chinese immigrants did not realize that there was an alternative way to solving their conflicts besides taking matters into their own hands. The language barrier as well as a court system operating under unfamiliar legal codes did not leave the notion that their grievances could be successfully resolved. Nevertheless, after years of acclimatization to local circumstances, the Chinese came to realize that the courts were there to uphold the laws of the land and that legal recourse could be used to seek redress.

A Chinese shopkeeper, whose name was recorded as Low-a-tung-tu, was convicted of possession of opium and asked to pay a fine of $48 and costs. He appealed the conviction and the facts of the case were reviewed:

> [Low-a-tung-tu] kept a licenced provision shop at *De Willem*, on a search being made for rum being made at his shop and premises by the Inspector, a parcel containing 1½ lb. of opium was found underneath the house of the shop "hid away near one of the beams." . . . There was ground for suspicion, but not satisfactory evidence of knowledge to support the conviction. [*Royal Gazette*, 14 Dec 1872]

Low-a-tung-tu managed to gain the benefit of the doubt because the opium was lodged in a place that was open and possibly accessible by others. The authorities on the day of the search were on the lookout for contraband liquor and the same shopkeeper found himself convicted on another charge. His defense counsel claimed that:

> The man had been for some time in ill health, and had consulted the Surgeon-General about his case. The Surgeon-General in his evidence before the magistrate said that he could not recollect ordering him to take stimulants; but he recollected that the recommended him to live generously, and he also said that brandy would be good for him. . . . The brandy . . . was contained in a pint bottle, as one witness swore, as half full. [Fined $50 with costs.] [*Royal Gazette*, 4 Jan 1873]

Pun-a-Yung was sentenced to one month in prison with hard labour for the "larceny of thirteen feet of white pine lumber, value 39 cents, the property of Timothy Pile." Pun-a-Yung took the case to the Court of Review and received a nice Christmas present when the Judge declared:

> I reverse the magistrate's decision for the following reasons: — Firstly because in the charge and conviction the property is laid out to be the property of Timothy Pile, whereas in the evidence the board is sworn to be the property of Samuel Pile. Secondly, because the Complaint was made under Ordinance No. 20 of 1856, section 2, by which the magistrate was only authorized toward imprisonment with or without hard labour for thirty days. In awarding imprisonment with hard labour for a month there was excess of jurisdiction. [*Royal Gazette*, 21 Dec 1878]

A Chinese nut-seller who, yesterday, had four nuts taken from his tray, in mischief, by some one of the lads engaged in Messrs. Park and Cunninghame's store, went to a 'charge' writer, had a charge made out with the name of the offender left blank, and then found a policeman to put the charge in force. When the policeman and the nut-seller reached the store, it was shut, and the store lads had all left. The charge, however, was a convenient one — there was no name on it, and as it answered one person as well as another, the Chinaman asked the policeman to arrest Mr. Cunninghame (brother of the partner in the firm), who was in the act of stepping homewards; and this the obliging policeman did. It was not until Mr. Cunninghame had been paraded along the street, to the Station, and kept there for some time, that he was set at liberty.

To-day, the Chinaman obtained possession of a warrant with which he has been prowling around the streets, evidently determined to get value for the money it cost him. It is a grand thing to live in a land of freedom! [*Royal Gazette*, 27 May 1875]

Respected Citizens

Over the years as the Chinese became settled in their new land the number of crimes attributed to them became less and less in comparison to their population. The ones who had chosen the path of evil came to an evil end, or so it would appear since the general opinion of the Chinese community gradually changed from one of disgust to one of respect. This came about not only because of the reduced number of criminal infractions but also because the incidents were not as outrageous as before. By the mid-1880s the Chinese had established themselves in a significant way in the business field and large numbers of them had converted to Christianity. These factors contributed to their being regarded as respected settlers held in high esteem. The Chinese became welcomed and accepted in the community as contributors to the general well being of the country. From this time onward they gained the reputation as hard-working, law-abiding citizens, a reputation that carried on through subsequent generations with much pride.

CHAPTER 7

BECOMING CREOLE

THE NEW ENVIRONMENT

The Chinese immigrants found that it was no easy task to adjust to the environment in British Guiana. In the first place they were by no means a homogeneous group and not all arrived as voluntary immigrants. Those who found themselves in a strange land without their prior consent would not have represented prime candidates for assimilation. At the same time each immigrant was an individual with his own vision for the future and it is therefore not surprising to find that the Chinese responded in different ways to the new situation. The fact that they were assigned to estates all over the country meant that they became dispersed, with each cluster composed of small number of people compared to other workers on the same estate. This created a need for stronger bonding among their own countrymen for mutual support while at the same time putting greater pressure on them to adopt the prevailing customs and habits of the colony.

The second challenge the newly arrived Chinese had to deal with was the strange environment they faced which had novel features in just about every aspect of life. They encountered a completely different language, culture, customs, legal system, religion, festivals and holidays, people and food. As with any population of immigrants, the second and subsequent generations assimilated more readily to the prevailing lifestyle while the adult immigrants, for the most part, retained their customary ways throughout their lives, particularly in their style of dress.

> As I walked along [Water Street] I was struck by the busy scene around me, and the various types of humanity constantly flitting past me in every direction. At one moment it was the lithe and supple Bengali, with his quaint best suit of many colors, boots a furlong too long for his feet, and skin glistening with cocoanut oil; now it was the solemn

> yellow visaged Chinaman, with wide-flapping blue salampores jacket and pants, pig-tail trailing on the ground, and wide bamboo hat; . . .
> [*Dreamland Guiana or Notes from the Yarns of a Romancer*, reprinted in *Royal Gazette*, 17 Feb 1883]

The composition of the local population affected the way the Chinese related to the other inhabitants of the colony. The population was comprised of people from six main ethnic groups — Amerindians, Blacks, Chinese, Indians, Portuguese and Whites (non-Portuguese). While they worked on the plantations, the Chinese had minimal interaction with the Amerindians who, over the years, had become displaced from the fertile coastal areas and now lived in the interior parts of the country where they maintained their traditional culture and customs. Those of African descent were still enjoying their freedom from slavery and viewed the Asian immigrants, both Chinese and Indian, as their replacements in the tasks of menial field labour, looking upon them as having lower status in the society. This attitude was reinforced by the fact that the immigrant Asians were obliged to work in the plantations by contract while the Blacks were completely free.

The immigrants from India were by far the most populous group among the labourers on the plantations and they shared the same living conditions and work assignments as the Chinese. The Portuguese were among the early immigrant labourers who replaced the freed slaves and, after completing their indenture, became merchants and tradesmen so that by the time the Chinese arrived the Portuguese owned many shops and businesses in the cities and villages. Although they shared a similar skin complexion and features as other Europeans, the Portuguese were regarded as a separate ethnic group by virtue of the history of their introduction to the colony, their numbers and their social standing.

At the top of the social ladder were the Whites consisting mainly of the colonial administrators, plantation owners and landed gentry. Some of them were Dutch and French colonists who maintained their presence when Britain gained through war or political compromise the three counties, Berbice, Demerara and Essequebo, that together became British Guiana. The mainstay of the colony was sugar and the plantation owners were virtual lords of the land and the quantity of sugar produced in British

Guiana exceeded that of any other colony in the British Empire. The entire economic and administrative structures were based on maintaining the prosperity derived from sugar.

Anthony Trollope described the atmosphere prevailing in 1859 as follows:

> The men in Demerara are never angry, and the women are never cross. Life flows along on a perpetual stream of love, smiles, champagne, and small-talk. Everybody has enough of everything. The only persons who do not thrive are the doctors; and for them, as the country affords them so little to do, the local government no doubt provides liberal pensions.
>
> The form of government is a mild despotism, tempered by sugar. The Governor is the father of the people, and the Governor's wife the mother. The colony forms itself into a large family, which gathers itself together peaceably under parental wings. They have no noisy sessions of Parliament as in Jamaica, no money squabbles as in Barbados. A clean bill of health, a surplus in the colonial treasury, a rich soil, a thriving trade, and a happy people — these are the blessings which attend the fortunate man who has cast his lot on this prosperous shore.

In this piece, Trollope was of course referring to the life of people in the upper echelon who enjoyed the luxuries associated with their status. Imagine indulging in champagne rather than rum. The governor, appointed from London, did indeed influence the path that the colony followed, although in the matter of greatest concern, the fiscal well being of the colony, the plantation owners had a great stake and a great say. The ongoing governing body, the Court of Policy, consisted of the Governor, the Government Secretary, the Attorney General, the Auditor General, the Immigration Agent-General and five members elected from among the plantation owners. For major overall policy decisions and matters of significant economic concern the members of the Court of Policy were joined by six Financial Representatives who were plantation owners elected from different regions and they altogether formed the Combined Court. It was the Combined Court that set the policies for immigration, including affirming the number of people to be introduced and the budget for importing the labourers.

Thought for Food

One of the first considerations for the new immigrants in adjusting to the new land was adaptation to the local foods. For

Chinese originating from the southern part of China the staple food was rice. The plantations in British Guiana were primarily devoted to the cultivation of sugar cane and little consideration was given to growing rice for the increasing number of immigrants from India and China. Rice sometimes became available when it was left over from a voyage that brought immigrants. In the auction sale advertised below the disposal of the excess goods was being arranged at the same time as the allocation of the immigrants was in progress.

NEW AUCTION SALE
OF CHINESE STORES
By Order of
Messrs. Sandbatch, Parker & Co.,
At their stores, in Water Street, Charlestown
On Friday, the 6th instant
At ONE O'CLOCK, P.M.
THE Surplus Chinese Stores
Landed ex Ship "Corona"
Bates, Commander, from China,
Consisting of:-

Bags rice	Tierces BEEF
Tierces PORK	" FISH
Pickles	Salt'd Cabbage
Peas	Lot Firewood

AND A LOT OF
WATER CASKS
&c., &c.,
Jos. Jacobs, Auctioneer
3 March 1874

[*Royal Gazette*, 5 Mar 1874]

Rice had to be imported from other countries and this resulted in a market price in British Guiana that was considerably higher than that to which the immigrants were accustomed in their native lands. This eventually created an incentive for the planting of rice, firstly in small sized plots to satisfy individual family or community needs and later in larger fields when the profit margin was sufficient for rice to become a marketable commodity. In the early years the immigrants had to adjust to foods locally available, such as plantains, root vegetables and tropical fruits. With their innate curiosity for exploring any source of food the Chinese were able to adjust readily to the local fare although there were occasions when the experience was not agreeable:

> A Chinaman came to his death by eating frogs. He stewed two of these animals in rice, and made a hearty meal, but it was his last, a severe affection of the stomach and bowels having followed the indulgence. He was, we understand, suffering from disease of the heart, but the food taken no doubt brought the case to a crisis. This is not the only instance of the kind which has been reported to us. One of a precisely similar character occurred little more than a week ago on the Arabian Coast [Essequebo]. A Chinese woman stewed two greenish-colored frogs in rice, and although strongly advised not to eat the mess, she partook of it heartily and died in a few hours. Whether she too, like the man, was suffering from any disease at the time, we cannot say, but the effect in both instances was precisely the same. One would infer from the cases that frog-eating is customary among at least some portion of the Chinese, but whether the frogs of China differ from those of this Colony, or whether those used on the occasion referred to were not the proper kind, and others might have been found of a harmless character, we leave to those versed in the science of frogology to determine.
>
> [*Royal Gazette*, 30 Oct 1860]

Even after six years, the warnings about the effects of such a dietary choice had not spread sufficiently to protect Chinese and frog:

> An inquest was held on the 25th instant at plantation La Grange on the body of a Chinese named Chung-a-Kum, whose death [came] from the effects of eating a crapaud. . . . The medical evidence proved that the liver and stomach of the deceased had not been in a sound state at the time. [*Royal Gazette*, 31 Apr 1866]

Fortunately, such cases of terminal frog consumption were isolated ones and on the whole the Chinese immigrants maintained a nourishing diet and were able to enjoy a healthy lifestyle. In particular they used their plots of land allotted by the plantation managers to grow vegetables, an important component of their traditional diet. Government Secretary Walker emphasized the importance of these plots in an 1861 report:

> The allotment of suitable provision or garden grounds at no great distance from the dwellings is also a subject worthy of attention. . . . The Chinese apart from their proficiency in the mechanical arts

are remarkably skilful horticulturists, and to the industrious and well behaved the occasional donation of a few packets of seeds would be alike useful and gratifying.

Vegetables, some varieties brought from China, were carefully cultivated in these private plots and the harvest, though small, made a significant contribution to the diet and economic well-being of their owners. Many Chinese engaged themselves in garden cultivation and even achieved some recognition for their efforts. In 1871 a few Chinese growers participated in the biennial exhibition of local products ranging from the major crop, sugar, to manufactured items such as chocolate. The exhibition also featured livestock, farm produce and handicrafts, and in a few categories Chinese participants were able to garner prizes.

Class VIII Fruits, Vegetables, Flowers

A basket of eddoes	Yung-a-Fat	$0.72
Best sweet potatoes	Yung-a-Fat	2.00
Best assortment of squashes	Chung-a-Fat	3.00
Best lot of green gingers	Yung-a-Fat	3.00

Honourable Mentions -

Chau-che-chin	Fancywork of sea weed
Kim Chinaman	Flower stand
Yung-a-chow	Chinese pillow

[*Royal Gazette*, 4 Mar 1871]

An exhibition of local products was also held in early 1878 from which the prize-winning items were to be selected for display at the International Exhibition in Paris later in the year. There was great anticipation regarding the products from Chinese participants since there were special exhibition categories for traditional Chinese items such as fans, embroidery and other handicrafts.

The Indian Productions and Manufactures will contribute a very attractive feature of the exhibition, and a space is being screened off at the western end of the room within which a number of Aborigines will exhibit their method of making cassava bread, preparing their weapons of war and the chase, and other avocations of the noble savage. Nor will the Chinese be far behind, if at all. Already it is quite apparent that our friend John Chinaman intends to pocket a good many of the prizes in the Miscellaneous Department, besides those appropriated to the manufacturers characteristic of his own country.

[*Royal Gazette*, 12 Jan 1878]

The Chinese failed to live up to expectation, however, and either did not submit exhibits or else the quality of the displayed items was not deemed to be prize-worthy. Only Hyolack Chung came away with a prize of $10 for the best collection of wooden flower pots.

The 1881 British Guiana Exhibition was postponed to April 1882 and it was thrown open to products from other countries — Surinam, Cayenne, Trinidad, St. Lucia, St. Vincent, Grenada, Barbados, Dominica and Jamaica. A few days before the exhibition opened the *Royal Gazette* was made aware of a curious communication:

> A most extraordinary document in the shape of a telegram has been sent to us to-day, which our correspondent says was found in front of a store, and which runs as follows:-
>
> "From Wong-a-Shi
> Naturalist
> Georgetown
>
> To Inspector Stevenson
> Belfield
>
> me want wild black same koolie katch field Cove and John, got in Belfield jail, advortise Kronacle paper Friday last week, me want um for Exhibition Thursday tell um price one time me send money."
>
> In looking over the "Chronicle" of Friday last, we notice a paragraph in which allusion is made to an 'able bodied' man having been found concealed in the canefields, and as he was painted, to as having a "wild unsettled look," Wong-a-Shi must have, through ignorance we presume, taken him for a "wild beast" and thought him a good subject for the Exhibition. [*Royal Gazette*, 27 Apr 1882]

Health

The attention that the Chinese paid to their diet was reflected in their general good health and well being. In early 1865 an outbreak of cholera was recorded and appeals went out to all citizens imploring them to maintain careful sanitary practices. People were asked to pay attention to getting sufficient nourishment to ensure good health.

> We believe not only the Coolies, but also the Chinese — we speak of the well-to-do industrious immigrants on the estates — live better and more regularly than the Creole. The Chinese are great consumers

of animal food and nothing can be sleeker or healthier looking than one of this race, who has not impaired his appetite by opium eating. The worst liver among our labouring population is the Portuguese at his first outset in life, and we fear his frugality so praiseworthy when exercised to a certain extent is frequently carried so far as seriously to affect his health. [*Royal Gazette*, 19 Jan 1865]

The Chinese succumb most frequently to diarrhea, dysentery and to those diseases vaguely termed "other afflictions of the respiratory organs." Phthisis [consumption] carries away a few, but does not appear to do so, so often as it does amongst the negroes and East Indian Coolies. They are fond of the good things of life, and like nothing better than to enjoy them, when in a position to do so, which by-the-way, is not at all seldom. I have seen them shovels in their hands, and cigars in their mouths driving in a cab at 7 o'clock in the morning to the estates on which they proposed working for the day. In the evening the cab was in waiting to drive them home. While the East Indian or negro may be met at any hour of the day or night reeling along the road in a state of gross intoxication, nothing is more uncommon than to meet a Chinaman in this condition. If he gets drunk, he prefers to do it at home.

. . . The diet of the labouring population is, except in the case of the Chinese, usually miserably same and poor. It consists chiefly of fish, rice, and plantains, varied now and again by fresh-fish (often of indifferent quality), salt beef, pork, and certain kinds of fruit. Vegetables could be grown cheaply and easily, but are not much cultivated.

Report by Alexander Gordon, M.B., C.M., L.R.C.S.E., Medical Officer, Queenstown District, and Surgeon to H.M. County Gaol, Essequebo. [*Royal Gazette*, 15 Feb 1876]

As far as the mental stability of the Chinese is concerned, a report by the doctor at the Berbice Lunatic Asylum provides a glimpse of the status of those confined there.

Notes on Lunacy in British Guiana. By James S. Donald, M.B., Edin., Resident Surgeon, Lunatic Asylum, Berbice.

In the year mentioned [1871] the ratio of lunatics to population (1,000) was 2.49 [in England and Wales], while in this colony it was only .91. Among Creoles of the West Indies the ratio was .41, Coolies .82, Portuguese, principally from Madeira, 1.00, and Chinese 1.59. . . . Among the Chinese inmates I have been struck with the frequency of epilepsy and epileptic mania, and have been equally puzzled to account for it. It is particularly more noticeable in females, the attacks being in some cases periodic and generally very violent. It has been suggested

> that opium-eating might account for it, but were this the case it would be met with more commonly among Coolies, who are also addicted to the use of this drug. As a rule the characteristic stolidity and impassiveness of the Chinese is little altered during mental aberration. The cheerless, unhappy expression of countenance gives the patient the appearance of one suffering from profound melancholia, and totally indifferent to anything around him. The number of Chinese now in the system is too small to warrant my giving any decided opinion as to what may be considered the more prominent features and nature of their mental disease. They are generally quiet, docile patients, very amenable to treatment, and, except in the epileptic, violent symptoms are rare.

It is interesting that the doctor found that the people in British Guiana were less than half as mad as the British in their own home country. A closer examination of the figures shows that the incidence of mental disorder increases as the population among the different racial groups decreases. In other words, the Creoles, being the most numerous and also the longest term residents, had the lowest incidence of lunacy while the Chinese, being the smallest group and the most recent to arrive, were almost four times as likely to have crazy people. This would suggest that the doctor did not have a truly representative population sample and furthermore the different racial groups did not have comparable histories at the time of his survey. For example, in February 1882 there were no Chinese among the 357 inmates, which might seem to indicate that the Chinese were the sanest of the whole lot. However, in the following month two Chinese were admitted. Although a small number, this change caused a significant increase in the overall statistic when taken in proportion to the limited Chinese population.

Besides those in the Lunatic Asylum there were other Chinese deemed to be mentally incompetent, otherwise termed imbeciles, who were not similarly confined but who were unable to secure employment. They joined those who were disabled because of accident or illness and, rejected by the estates, wandered the streets begging for handouts.

> For sometime past the streets have been infested with beggars — Creole, Coolie, and Chinese. Wherever one goes there they are to be met with. On the street we meet the Coolie with his "Salaam-ho! Sahib" his long bow and his beggar's mallet. At the corners of the streets and elsewhere, we find the black man with his "Massa, massa, please for

half-a-bitt." Stuck up at almost every store-door we come across some wretched object, in the shape of a Chinaman, with his Chow-Chow and other outlandish language. [*Royal Gazette*, 2 Sep 1865]

Twenty paupers named respectively Collychur~, Chow-ah-kie, Yep-tehe, Sum-poo, Woung-yeung-ho, Lai-chung-fook, . . . and Tchien-che were brought up on remand of a charge of wandering abroad on the public streets in Georgetown and begging alms on the 16th instant. . . . Chow-ah-ke is indentured to Wales. Yahpah-che is reported unable to work. . . . Wing-yang-ho is also reported by the surgeon as being unable to work. Tcheung-chee [a female] is reported by the doctor to be apparently an imbecile. [*Royal Gazette*, 21 Sep 1876]

Family Considerations

For the healthy, able-bodied labourer who had made up his mind to settle down nothing would have been better than to have a wife and family. However this was very difficult because of the very high ratio of males to females and the great reluctance by the majority of men to engage in inter-racial unions. A similar phenomenon had already been recognized among the immigrants from India. The situation was a source of serious problems and prompted the Court of Policy to draw up a bill to address some of the effects.

It has been matter for serious observation that, in the great majority of cases where a murder is committed among Coolie immigrants, the unfortunate victim is either a wife or mistress. A number of females are always introduced in every shipment, but, to use a common expression, the supply is not equal to the demand, and hence it arises that, as the Coolies will not, except in rare instances, marry or even cohabit with any of the black population, jealousies prevail among these people to a very considerable extent, the seduction of a wife or mistress being a matter of common occurrence. Apart from this consideration, there are other points in which the matter may be viewed. It is difficult to arrive at a knowledge of what constitutes a legal marriage among Coolie immigrants, and ignorance on this point must lead, among other evils, to a frequent breach of the law of succession in the event of death, and to marital rights being at least questioned if not wholly ignored. To meet the difficulty as far as can be effected by legislation a Bill was introduced, on the 8th instant, to regulate the celebration of marriages among Heathen immigrants . . . [*Royal Gazette*, 25 Feb 1860]

The Bill was termed "An Ordinance to Provide for the Celebration and Registration of the Marriages of Heathen Immigrants." Among its provisions,

> The Immigration Agent-General shall keep two Registers . . . the first of which shall be termed the "Register of Married Heathen Immigrants introduced into the Colony," and the other shall be termed the "Register of Marriages of Heathen Immigrants celebrated in the Colony."
>
> [*Royal Gazette*, 15 Mar 1860]

The ordinance came into effect four days before the first Chinese female immigrants arrived in British Guiana. It served to put marriages among the heathen on a comparable footing as Christian marriages, in terms of legal recognition, common ownership of property, and the rights and obligations of the family. Four years later came the realization that the reluctance to enter into inter-racial marriage would affect the growth of population.

> It must not be forgotten that in respect to Immigration generally, the disproportion between the sexes is very great, particularly as regards Chinese, and that neither Chinese nor Coolies, except in very rare instances, ever mate with the other races in the Colony. As a necessary consequence the surplus males die out without progeny, and there cannot possibly be on the whole any material increase in the number of immigrants, exclusive of the consideration that a large proportion of infants and children die off. [*Royal Gazette*, 26 Jan 1864]

By 1873 there were just 585 born to Chinese families and only a half of the original immigrant population remained:

> The Chinese are industrious, intelligent and quiet; they live well and dress well and are more likely to settle permanently in this colony than any other class of immigrants. . . . Between the years 1851 and 1866, 12,531 Chinese arrived in the colony, of whom 6295, including 585 children born here, remained at the date of the last census. . . .
>
> [*Royal Gazette*, 1 May 1973]

In his annual report for 1877 the Immigration Agent-General reported that the mortality rate among indentured Indian immigrants was 802 out of 22,711, or 35.31 per 1000, whereas the comparable rate for Chinese indentured labourers was considerably less — 23 in 879, or 23.49 per 1000. This statistic is not unusual considering that only the *Corona*, which landed 388 immigrants in 1874, had arrived from China in the past eleven years, whereas the flow of immigrants from India was continuous. By the time of the 1877 survey, those under indenture consisted of seasoned and healthy Chinese field workers and they would naturally compare favorably with the recently arrived labourers from India just beginning their service of indenture. In contrast, the mortality rate among Chinese not under indenture in that same year was 77 out of 2,467 or 31.21 per 1000, somewhat higher than their Indian counterparts who recorded 768 deaths out of 26,000, or 29.53 per 1000. This statistic is also not unusual since the Chinese immigrants who were free of indenture had arrived between the years 1853 and 1866 and, on average, were an aging group of people compared with the Indian immigrants who had been coming annually and thus being restocked in large numbers.

The statistics for births in 1877 are very revealing, with the Indian immigrants having 21.61 births per 1000 but the Chinese population saw only 5.80 per 1000. This was the direct result of the disproportionately high ratio of men to women among the Chinese, with the vast majority of the men not having spouses and families. A decline in the Chinese population was inevitable.

In the census of 1881 there were 252,186 inhabitants in the colony, of whom 149,639 were locally born. Among the Chinese, 454 males and 387 females were born in British Guiana out of a total population of 5,232 of Chinese ancestry. There were 13,541 people who immigrated from China between 1853 and 1879 and the census reveals that by 1881 less than half of them remained.

CAUSES OF DEATH

As described in a previous chapter, a significant number of Chinese died as a result of criminal activity, either as victims of murder or else as convicted murders sentenced to hanging. Among the law-abiding immigrants, the causes of death within the Chinese community were not much different to those affecting other residents. Disease and accidents were primary reasons for early death.

> . . . Some Chinese were returning from work on an estate on the East Coast, at one o'clock, P.M., with their hoes on their shoulders, during

a thunderstorm, when one of them suddenly dropped and rolled into a trench. On medical assistance being called in, it was at once ascertained that he had been killed by lightning. . . . Such accidents are very rife in this Colony. . . . [*Royal Gazette*, 23 Oct 1860]

Leung-a-tshe . . . fell into a furnace when the brickwork collapsed. [*Royal Gazette*, 9 Aug 1870]

Coroner's Inquest on the body of Chun Sing, a Chinese shop-keeper, resident in Essequebo.

Verdict — Chun Sing was drowned by the capsising of the sloop *Henrietta*; further, they are of the opinion that the capsising was caused by the very culpable carelessness of the people in charge of the *Trafalgar*, these not altering the latter's course till a collision had taken place. [*Royal Gazette*, 1 Apr 1875]

Chow-a-Yee died after *Victory* ran over his batteau. [*Royal Gazette*, 31 Aug 1875]

A Chinese labourer on Pln Schoon Ord died yesterday afternoon from the kick of a mule. [*Royal Gazette*, 14 Mar 1878]

[An] inquest [was held] into the death of Li-a-quee which occurred in the colonial hospital on the 22nd inst. [He had been] run over by a mule cart [and died of blood poisoning]. [*Royal Gazette*, 1 May 1879]

The procedures in place for the delivery of health care apparently were instrumental in the death of a Chinese woman. The woman, who was suffering with a severe cough and fever, was taken to the hospital at Providence estate but was refused treatment. When she was brought back later it was too late to save her life. At the inquest Chan-a-Cheung testified:

I live at Providence, deceased was my wife [Wong Shee]. . . . On Monday at about 10 a.m., I saw Dr. Carney at the Providence hospital, and I asked him to look after the deceased and give her some medicine. The doctor said "If you are a free man you must pay me a dollar. If you have not got a dollar, you must send her to the Colonial Hospital."

Henry Edward Bullock, the estate manager, testified that Chan-a-Cheung did indeed work on his estate but was not under indenture. He added:

It is my practice to receive any immigrant, whether free or indentured, who complains of sickness, into the estate's hospital, any people so received are fed and supplied with medicine at the cost of the estate.

Dr. Carney then gave his version of events, saying that he first asked the dispenser whether the deceased worked on the estate, to which the dispenser responded “No, she grows provisions and sells them in the New Amsterdam market.” Some question was also raised about whether her companion was really her husband. Dr. Carney then confirmed that he informed Chan-a-Cheung that without paying the fee of one dollar the patient would have to go to the Colonial Hospital. After her death, he examined the body and found that she had died from pneumonia or solidification of the lungs. The *Royal Gazette* editorialized that this incident was highly deplorable and the death was probably preventable and should not have occurred in light of the manager’s statement that any immigrant, indentured or free, would be given medical treatment.

Reprints of two woodcut illustrations originally presented in the book *The Coolie. His Rights and Wrongs*, written by Edward Jenkins, are shown at the end of Chapter 10. Jenkins explained that the woodcuts were based on drawings made by an immigrant who was schoolmaster in China. Without knowledge of the intent of the original artist it is difficult to accurately interpret the events portrayed although Jenkins, with his sympathy squarely on the side of the unfortunate labourer, did not spare his own commentary. In the first illustration which is believed to depict hospital conditions Jenkins claims that the cooks at the cauldron are brewing chicken soup but with the chicken roaming free outside the pot. The written notice is also said to be the “diet-list” written in Chinese, Indian and English.

The second woodcut is said to depict the house of an estate manager who, together with his attorney, are figuratively fattening themselves off the blood of the Indian and Chinese labourers. The scrawny labourers are literally bound which Jenkins interprets as a reflection of their sentiment regarding indenture. The Chinese person being pursued by a rural constable is said to be attempting to escape from bondage, while the free Indian is happily able to herd several head of cattle.

Although these woodcuts are evidently portrayals of unpleasant circumstances experienced by the indentured labourers it is hard to give an accurate and unbiased interpretation of each detail and it is left for readers to see what they would in these artistic renditions.

RECREATION

With regard to organized recreational activities the government was aware that the Chinese New Year was a festival of great significance to the Chinese and allowed them five days of holiday.

> An official notice from the Immigration Department, draws attention to the fact that the Chinese holidays will commence on the 10th and terminate on the 15th of next month, and a request is made to Managers, Magistrates and others to afford all possible facilities to indentured labourers in the enjoyment of relaxation and pleasure, and it is quite right that the people whom we import here from China and India should have theirs. How the Chinese manage to amuse themselves we know not, but we have never yet heard of any disorderly conduct on their part on any festive occasion, and in this respect they stand in favorable light as compared with the Coolies, who go to work on a large scale and sometimes disturb the public peace, even to the extent of the loss of life. . . . [*Royal Gazette*, 19 Jan 1869]

> The Chinese inhabitants of the city have been celebrating their New Year last week, after the fashion of their countrymen at home. For a succession of nights they marched through the principal streets in procession, dressed in costume, bearing aloft immense bright coloured paper lanterns of various clever devices, but mostly fish-shaped, and beating gongs and tom-toms. They were followed by a large crowd of the unwashed, who we have no doubt would gladly have had some horse-play at the expense of the celestials, if a number of policemen, wisely furnished by the Brick dam authorities, had not accompanied the procession to maintain order. In the Charlestown district of the city, where the Chinese most do congregate, the New Year festivities were held with much feasting, fuddling, and gambling, but though the people were very hilarious and very noisy there was no single instance of conduct requiring the interference of the police.
> [*Royal Gazette*, 24 Feb 1880]

Besides the festivities associated with Chinese New Year the immigrants were treated on occasion to a party, courtesy of the plantation owners and managers:

> Gala day at Pln *Land of Milk and Honey*. — Yesterday the Manager of this estate, Mr. Milkenwater, gave the immigrant labourers the usual quarterly holiday, a practice now regularly established on this and most

other estates. The whole of the people sat down to lunch on the lawn in front of the Manager's house where they were waited on by many of the aristocracy of the neighbourhood including the Doctor and the Clergyman and their respective wives. Conspicuous amongst the ladies who were eager to see that the wants of the coolies were being attended to, were Mrs. Milkenwater and her two interesting daughters the Misses Milkenwater. Some little amusement was created by the coolies making use of their chairs, not in the orthodox fashion, but to squat on after their own style; and a good deal of diversion took place after the banquet was over, in hunting for the silver forks and spoons, many of which had been kindly lent for the occasion by the surrounding *élite*; the missing articles were after a time all found, these really clever jugglers, the Chinese, having artfully concealed them in the folds of their simple garments. One look at the laughing innocent faces of these talented people, was enough to convince the most sceptical that the taking of the spoons was only meant to add to the pleasure and hilarity of the day; and it was scarcely possible to refrain from giving the rogues a piece of money for their *bonhomie*, when, as the articles were shaken out of them, they archly remarked "Chinaman like 'um too much a fun." The fine coolie band of the estate trained under the special care of the head overseer, Mr. Cusshard, soon breathed sweet music to the air, and dancing commenced in right good earnest, the manager opening the Ball with Lalloober, the wife of one of the principal coolies on the estate, whilst Rhamstiukum the coolie driver led out Mrs. Milkenwater. It was wonderful to see with, what grace and precision the people treaded the mazy dance, at least to those who were not acquainted with the fact that the manager's amiable daughters, assisted by the Misses Suavetung, daughters of the Rector, had assiduously been teaching the labourers for weeks beforehand, the various figures of the various dances. The admiration which was universally bestowed on the dancers was a fitting reward for the Christian-like exertion of the ladies we have named. But, whilst many were engaged in tripping in on the light fantastic toe, others were finding their own amusement. The croquet lawn was occupied with a grand tournament between Indians and Chinese ladies and gentlemen; the latter countrymen exhibiting a knack of getting into position which the former could never attain. During the afternoon, refreshments were handed round, such as lemonade, tamarind water, fly,[1] gingerbeer, and maubee drink; these were freely indulged in by the guests, some of whom, in fun, would occasionally remark that 'rum too much better.' As luck would

1 A beverage made with yams, flavoured with lemon, which, from fermentation, causes the cork to fly off the bottle.

have it the happy day happened to be the first which the proprietor of the estate, now on a visit to the colony, ever spent on his own property, and as a matter of course, he had to be introduced to the various people. It was quite affecting to see the lord of many acres, standing like a patriarch of old in the midst of his willing servants, receiving their devoire; and it was direct to the heart, when, with the kindness of a father, he patted the coolie children on the head whilst their mother with happy tears of gratitude in their eyes, stood round, and in musical numbers, called on their offspring to bless the big Backra, and ask him for bucksheesh.[2] As the afternoon wore on, preparations were made for the marching past of the estate's "Band of Hope." This body was organized for the moral benefit of the people, and indirectly, for their temporal benefit, inasmuch as constant numbers when incapacitated for work, get a small weekly allowance, beside the help which the estate provides for them. A little delay was occasioned by the sudden indisposition of some of the prominent members, who were at once attended to by the Doctor. Poor fellows, their enjoyment had been thus curtailed by an accident that happened entirely by their own simplicity. Searching in child-like way over the manager's house they entered the pantry and mistook some brandy for some lemonade; there was general sympathy with them amongst their fellow countrymen, many of whom, sorrowing, said that they would the calamity had befallen them. Little incidents like this show the brotherly love that exists amongst these people. The sick men attended to, the Procession marched past, gay with banners of brilliant devices, on which were emblazoned appropriate mottoes and pithy texts, such as "Love your manager as yourself," "Labour cheap, labour cheerful," "A good coolie maketh a glad Planter," "A bitt a-day is a cow a-year," "No rum, no rows," "The manager's love is the best bucksheesh," and many other of a like nature. Closing up the procession came the present recipients of the Band bounty, all of whom had some little mark of the kind attention of the ladies who are the principal office-bearers of the society. The raiment of these pensioners, as may be supposed, was of the plainest kind, but a woman's hand could be seen in touches here and there. None but little clever fingers could have touched off the calabash which one wore for a cap, with a few streaks of colour and a ribbon or two, that made it look smart and gay; and it could only have been the same loving fingers that twined around the several wooden legs, wreaths of evergreens dotted with nature's flowery gems of every hue. The rest of the afternoon was spent in part-singing, in which the various overseers led the labourers; the effect of the whole choir joining in "Come in Abraham" and other

2 A Middle-Eastern word meaning a gratis amount or bonus. Also spelt "baksheesh."

well-known popular pieces was overwhelming. As the evening closed more tea was handed round, and cake; and after that the company broke up, all highly delighted with the day's entertainment."

Your obedient Servant,

JOHN FOURFOOT

[*Royal Gazette*, 19 Jul 1873]

OPIUM AND GAMBLING

In addition to participation in such organized festive occasions, there were some Chinese who indulged in opium smoking and gambling as their recreational pursuits. These habits were having an effect on the community at large.

The upsetting of a lamp by a few Chinese gamblers occasioned, last night, the destruction of property of the value of about Sixty Thousand Dollars. Since the fire in Regent-street, which in the year 1848 destroyed the premises of Mr. HUNTER, there has been no fire in the City so extensive as that which last night collected, in the immediate vicinity of the Bonded Warehouse, a great proportion of the male and female citizens of Georgetown. Within a few minutes of mid-night a room in the new range of buildings recently erected by Mr. PEQUENO, the proprietor of the hitherto well-known Grog Shop in Werk-en-Rust, was discovered to be on fire. It appears that this room had been let to some Chinese, who used it ostensibly as a shop, but really devoted it to the practices of a Chinese Hell. These men, it appeared, had been gambling last night as usual, and, by some accident, the lamp by which they were playing was upset, and the burning fluid becoming ignited the room was soon in a blaze. The Chinese, with characteristic cowardice, fled the spot without making the slightest effort to extinguish the flames. Within a few minutes of the accident, the whole range of buildings of which the roof formed a part, became one blazing mass, and before the first Engine arrived, which was brought from the Police Station on the Brick-dam, the fire had extended itself beyond PEQUENO's range of lodging rooms and had commenced its ravages upon his grog-shop.

. . . We are informed that some of the Portuguese who were seen with folded arms making no effort to save PEQUENO's property, assigned as a reason for their conduct that PEQUENO had impiously boasted that the Almighty could not make him poor, and they therefore could not sympathize with him. [*Royal Gazette*, 18 Jun 1863]

It is said that another "Hell" — as these gambling houses are termed — such as existed in the late Brass Castle, has been established near the Lunatic Asylum by some Chinese. We do not vouch for the fact, but if it be the case we hope to see the establishment broken up, and the keepers of it punished. The chief game, as we are informed, played by the Chinese, is one not unlike the well known game of *rouge et noir*. There is a small square copper box, very shallow, the bottom of which is painted white and partly black or red. The parties engaged in the game stake on one of the colours, the banker receiving and paying as the stakers hit or miss the right colours. It does not appear that the Banker has any point in his favour, and the game is therefore one of mere chance. Two Chinese accused of keeping gambling houses have been recently sent on by a Magistrate for trial at a higher court, and we may then get some more precise information on the subject. The Chinese appear to be great gamblers, but it will be a question for a Jury, what constitutes a gambling house. Where there is a building or room to which any and everybody can obtain admittance for the express purpose of gaming, there can be no doubt that such a building or room would come within the term "gambling house," but it is a query whether this term can apply in this case where a number of Chinese are in the habit of assembling among themselves for the purpose of gambling without others being admitted to take part in the game. "Keeping and maintaining a common gaming house for lucre and gain," would scarcely seem to suit such a case. However, this is a point which it will be for the Supreme Criminal Court to determine. [*Royal Gazette*, 4 Jul 1863]

There is, in New Amsterdam, a "Chinese quarter," just as there is in the Charlestown quarter of this city, and it is the favourite resort not only of Chinamen, but also of vagrant coolies, who go there to indulge in opium smoking. If these "dens" were looked up a little oftener both in Georgetown and New Amsterdam, it is possible that not only much illicit traffic in opium might be brought to light, but also that many deserters from the estates might be discovered. As to gambling, which is a favourite amusement of the Chinese, little or no attempt appears to be made to check or put a stop to it. The evil consequences arising from this habit are so serious that every effort should be made by the Government to suppress it. To say nothing of the murders to which it has given rise, how much of the desertion of the Chinese immigrants throughout the colony is to be attributed to this indulgence in it! And yet gambling saloons are not only to be found in the towns, but are regular institutions on the estates. It may be difficult or impossible to put a stop to it altogether, but it might certainly be checked and, perhaps, gradually abolished. If Chinese immigration is to be resumed, . . . it is of the highest importance that the vices of the Chinese already settled amongst us should be corrected, before they lead to the demoralisation of a better class of immigrants who may be introduced into the colony. It is well known too, that our most daring and skilful thieves are Chinamen, and it is possible that their deprecations are carried on, not for the support of life, which is an easy matter in a country like this, but to recoup the losses sustained in gambling, and to supply the requisite funds for further ventures. Taking, therefore, into consideration the many and grave evils which result from this practice, the murders, the desertions from estates, and the robberies which can be traced to it, it is not too much to say that stringent measures should be adopted to check it and to turn the ingeneous minds of our Chinese immigrants to some occupation more profitable to themselves and less prejudicial to those amongst whom they live. Although toleration may be extended to their enjoying their "*opium cum dignitale*" in their private abode, injurious to their health though this may be, yet no such toleration can be looked for or conceded in regard to the rise of gambling, the evil consequences of which are so extensive and disastrous. [*Royal Gazette*, 13 Nov 1875]

The dens of infamy in the Charlestown district carried on by the Chinese, are increasing in number and promise, before long to furnish material wherewith to mark a dark page in the colony's history. The poor, the starving, and the obscene are always amongst the visitors to these dens of iniquity — both women and men carry the few pence which they can either beg for, borrow, or steal, to be swallowed up by John Chinaman, and the visitors have to depart sadder, but by no means wiser people. It is a pity that crime should be allowed to run rampant and not an arm to be raised to suppress it, or, at least, to divert that downward tide which is leading and has led to the Lunatic Asylum, and to the gaol, and promises to lead on to the scaffold. In the face of the police, to be observed on the public highway, and close to the temples wherein the congregation assemble, are the dishonest and the desperate allowed to gather without let or hindrance. [*Royal Gazette*, 15 Nov 1884]

IN THE EYES OF THE BEHOLDER

To the people who had ready access to the media the Chinese community was viewed in different perspectives. During his visit to British Guiana in mid-1861, Rev. William Lobschied had an opportunity to inspect various Chinese communities at the estates to which they were indentured. He observed:

> There are now at Skeldon men who brought over to this Colony from 15 to 20 relations to whom they were at home a kind of Patriarch. These men sold a considerable amount of property at home and left for this place with a view to establish for themselves a new and happy home. The departure of these men under Contract would have been to them a source of vexation had not Dr. Henry, in accordance with the wishes I expressed on their behalf to Mr. Austin in China, given them their liberty and allowed them to establish a shop on the Estate. They exercise a great deal of influence among their Countrymen, and letters from them to their friends in China would induce a large number of healthy peasants to come to this Colony. It is needless to say how much such news would encourage a vast number of poor country people to follow their friends under indenture. And in order to facilitate the demarkation of the boundaries, it might be desirable for the Government to lessen the expenses for surveying the land given to the Colonists and permit them to cultivate the same until a Surveyor could be conveniently procured.
>
> INTERMARRIAGE IMMIGRANTS AND CREOLES: . . . Wherever I have made enquiries, I find them very adverse to mixing with the Creoles of this Colony. Only one instance has come to my notice, where a Chinaman who came in 1853 has married a Creole woman with whom he feels apparently happy. Another instance was mentioned to me where the Chinaman soon sent the woman away and refused to have further intercourse with her. I find everywhere that a Chinaman almost blushes, when the thought of being married to a Creole woman crosses his mind, a feeling which he in a great measure shares with the Caucasion race. . . . But a Chinaman is not so adverse to an intermixture with inferior races, as might appear at first sight. He is accustomed to look upon all coloured races as barbarians who possess neither refinement nor education and being from home not accustomed to select a Partner for himself, he finds himself in a great predicament when the desirableness of creating a pleasant home for himself assails him in moments of solitude. In Java and Singapore where the Chinese have been living for Centuries about 70 or 80 per cent are married to natives or Malays whose language they almost all speak. They have everywhere Schools, and take care of the education of their children who enjoy the benefits of education in the swamps of Siam, and the South of Borneo; as well as in the retired Gold Mines of that interesting island. In Australia where he had a more unrestrained intercourse with Europeans of low Extraction, and where

his wealth and education which in his splendid Shops, he found ample means of displaying to his own advantage there he had no difficulty in finding willing hearts to lay their future happiness in his hands and what the European women lacked in Education, he readily supplied by giving them an opportunity of accomplishing themselves in the excellent institutions around them. Seeing himself connected with a Superior race he readily divested himself of his native costume and pagan religion and the Government will find him, not only a Patriot, but ready to give to the Poor and needy. . . .

I would here respectfully ask the favor of Your Excellency to engage, for the accomplishment of the preceding object Hun Yin Fook, the present Schoolmaster and Catechist at Skeldon. He has, besides the good character he bears, been the principal means of bringing to this shore, all the people who came in the 'Dora', none of whom would have without him, and had they not left their home, there would, at so early a period, have been great difficulties in procuring at one, that percentage of families required by Government regulations. He would require only $25 per month for his and his family's support, and I am convinced that the good which his preaching, his communicating the kind intentions of this Government as well as the account of all that he has heard and seen will do among the Chinese laborers, will more than compensate the Government for the small amount expended for his salary.

. . . I would draw Your Excellency's attention to the state of the Chinese on the Estates Rose Hall, Reliance and Adelphi in Berbice, where I have reason to fear they have not been fairly dealt with. The Dwelling Houses at Reliance are particularly much neglected, and I am afraid that the mortality on this Estate must be ascribed to the utter indifference of the Manager to the Welfare of those under his care. At Adelphi I was particularly struck with the emaciated state of all the Chinese, and as these are all Country people accustomed to Agriculture, I almost suspect that advantage has been taken of their ignorance, and that they have not been able to earn money sufficient to support their own frames.

In 1870, an account was published by a visiting Englishman, Mr. John Chester, about his experiences in British Guiana. He found very little to satisfy him in the colony. The climate, hotels, people, buildings, food, and service were among the items that became the subjects of his venom. In reprinting a portion of the account, the *Royal Gazette* added the editorial comment: "We may almost say of Mr. Chester that he has walked from Dan to

Beersheba and found all barren." With regard to the Chinese, John Chester provided the following observations:

> No people can be less like the East Indian than the Chinaman. Of these last most wear their national dress, but some effect white trousers, blue jackets, and straw hats. They are pleasant fellows enough to talk to, from their cheerfulness, *bonhomie*, and self-possession; and it is hard to realise that they are the rascals they are represented to be by their masters. At one end of George Town there is quite a Chinese quarter. Wishing to purchase one or two of the beautiful jade earrings worn by the women, I one day made an excursion for that purpose. Having rejected an inferior specimen, for which an exorbitant sum was demanded, I was going away, when a young man came up and told me a friend of his had a splendid pair of jade-stone armlets. These were produced, sewn down to a bit of wood, covered with purple silk. Nothing could have been lovelier than their colour, and I was about to buy them, when my suspicions were aroused by the smallness of the sum asked. . . . I held them up to the light and detected, by the occurrence of a few tiny air bubbles, that they were made of glass. Although forgeries, they were well worthy of a place in South Kensington Museum, as exquisite specimens of imitative art.
>
> At the house of an elderly Chinaman of better class I afterwards saw a very curious armlet of real jade; the ends were carved like dragons' heads, it was doubtless of considerable antiquity. It was used as a charm for certain diseases, and in London or Paris might have fetched half of the two hundred dollars demanded for it.
>
> . . . The Chinese are in great request as labourers, and, being possessed of greater powers of endurance, can do heavier work than the natives of India. Compared with these last, they save but little money, being fond of substantial and plentiful diet, and having little care for the future. I have reason to fear that the coolies, and especially the Chinese are treated with great severity. During my stay in Demerara a local paper contained the following notice, which I insert as a specimen of many others:-
>
> "On Thursday last two Chinamen of Mahaica, who had been convicted for stealing plantains, received *thirty-nine lashes each with the cat-o'-nine tails*, at the expiry of their term of imprisonment for one month."
>
> It is difficult to believe that the larcenous Scotchman would have received forty stripes, save one; but in a country where equal justice is professed, it is hard to see why the sauce for the goose should not also be sauce for the gander.
>
> There are a considerable number of Chinese women in the colony, and their new-born babies are the most primevally old-fashioned-looking

little articles imaginable. I saw one Chinaman who had taken a negress to wife. The offspring of this union, I suspect would rival the ugliness of that very common, but most uncomely cross-brat, the child of a red-haired Scotchman and a woolly-headed black woman. But the Chinese coolies are by no means the quaintest fellow-subjects one meets with in the streets of George Town. From time to time parties of the aboriginal South American Indians, chiefly of the Arawak and Accawai tribes, come down to the cities in their canoes and corials. . . .

Transatlantic Sketches, by John Chester.

[*Royal Gazette*, 26 May 1870]

In the summer of 1876 the turmoil in California arising from resentment toward Chinese became a pressing issue all over the United States. The Chinese there were accused not only of taking away jobs by accepting excessively low wages and intolerable conditions but also of being immoral and lusting after white women; the few Chinese women who immigrated there were portrayed as low class prostitutes. Other denigrating terms were assigned to the Chinese including depraved, heathen, lawless and unclean carriers of disease. Some writers claimed them to be threats to the society and incapable of becoming citizens. Such viewpoints became known in British Guiana through news reports and personal letters. They undoubtedly stimulated those who were not pleased about the way the Chinese in the colony behaved. Amidst this, William Russell, an estate owner and member of the Court of Policy, did a survey and made lengthy notes of his observations of the Chinese in the colony which are referred to in the following article:

To anyone who will take the trouble to attend service, in the fine Church built by the Chinese in Charlestown, or the very neat chapel in front of Peter's Hall belonging to the Chinese who have joined themselves to the Plymouth Brethren, and watch the earnestness with which they attend service in their own ancient language, the feeling will force itself upon him that greater earnestness is not to be found amongst any other body of worshipers in this Colony. The contributions they have already given to procure themselves those two places of worship will compare favourably with like contributions from a similar number of people in any part of Christiandom. It is true, some little assistance was given in the way of public subscription to the Charlestown congregation, but the Peter's Hall chapel was entirely raised by Chinese contributions, and the current expenses are met with creditable regularity.

It may not be generally known that one of the most successful Chinese Merchants here is about to return to his country, and means to leave one of his partners in a large European house, as his attorney. The arrangement has been made with two of his countrymen, for the carrying on of his business, i.e. — to pay him 6 per cent. interest on the capital left in the concern, and the profits accruing from the business are to be equally divided between the two partners and the Church! Can any other Christian community point to such liberality on the part of its members?

Of the Chinaman as the head of a household, the notes speak equally as favourable. The picture of exemplary economy to be witnesssed in the Chinaman's house where every member of the family is expected, and is in duty bound, to perform some of the sub-divided industries peculiar to Chinese housekeeping, is refreshing after a contemplation of the squalor and poverty to be found in the hut of the average Coolie or Black.

. . . Mr. Russell writes: "The misinformed are under the impresssion that the large feet women introduced here are such characters as are complained of even by the Agents of the Six Companies.[3] This mistaken idea would soon be corrected if those entertaining it were to take the trouble to inspect the dwellings of the Chinese and see the collection of fine, healthy children playing about, those about 8 to 10 years of age assisting in many of the domestic duties such as fetching water for house use; and also for liquefying the manure and applying some to different plants, collecting food for the pig, which receives more attention at their hands than is believed on many native children, and labouring in various other ways, thus learning to be industrious from their earliest years. Look also at the tidy, well kept apartment, with the apparel of man and wife so well patched as to defy an expert to say what was the original fabric from which the garments were made. Again, see the women preparing the various vegetable plants, and one cannot help reverting in thought to another country where similar industry is drawn forth from the inhabitants by the inexorable demands of nature. The training soon tells on the young, and the invariable answer by the Schoolmasters to any question about the relative of their scholars is that the Chinese are much the quickest to learn."

Let us now give the notes on the nature of the Chinaman at work, either in the field, at the artisan's bench, or in the retail shop, for at any industry John attaches himself to, he manages to be successful. Alluding to them as a body, the notes say:- "The greater number of able bodied

3 The Chinese Consolidated Benevolent Association in the U.S. was also known as the Chinese Six Companies.

men and women have naturally taken themselves to agricultural pursuit and there are many Managers who point to the frugal Chinese as the pick of the labourers. As mechanics and manufacturers there are few planters who cannot point to Chinese as their most intelligent attendants on machinery, and in manufacture it is well known that the [Mongol] face has replaced the European on many of the pan stages as chief boilerman, doing the work for dollars as against pounds and wherever neat-handed work is required, there Chin is to be found. As Gardeners, the local road side markets bear testimony to their success, and Creoles, who at first disdained to purchase the manure fed vegetables of the Chinese, have got over such prejudice already, and they are now their best customers. Give a Chinese family 50 square yards of ground, and they will not only live comfortably upon it, but also save money. As Shopkeepers, it has been often said of these people that they are born hucksters; and the way in which they have gained on the retail trade of the rural districts, is enough to raise a cry from the old settled shopkeepers, similar to what has been raised by the white settlers in California against them."

[*Royal Gazette*, 27 Jul 1876]

Social Interactions

Getting along with the other ethnic groups in British Guiana was very important for the Chinese in assimilating into the society. The customs and practices of the Chinese immigrants were sometimes considered to be strange and uncivilized to the locals, giving rise to unpleasant consequences. A Chinese labourer pressed charges against the manager of an estate, an overseer and a Portuguese labourer for cutting off his queue:

> Now the operator may not have intended any harm by it, and may have looked upon the act as a capital joke, but it is not a legitimate joke to dock a Celestial's tail without leave or licence. Who would like to have his head shaved, or even his beloved moustache taken off against his will? It is true the hair will grow again, but the act would nevertheless be looked upon as a injury and an insult, and we would suspect that a Chinaman feels more than indignant at having his appendage taken off by force. As matters now stand, it is the duty of every planter who has Chinese immigrants under his care to try and make them comfortable and contented, but such an act as that we refer to is calculated to have quite the contrary effect, and may do a deal of mischief, as the insult will be felt by all the countrymen of the individual sufferer.
>
> [*Royal Gazette*, 8 Nov 1860]

On occasion there were clashes, which saw the Chinese in combat with other racial groups.

> Wong-a-sam, Hoo-sen-kam, Gumspulte, Wak-a-yan, Lang-ye-took, Ramgutty and Gopool were indicted for riot at Success.
>
> It appears that there had been some dispute between the Coolies and Chinese on plantation Success on the 6th October, which resulted in a riot between the two classes of immigrants.
>
> There were about 40 or 50 Chinese and 500 Coolies. Many of the combatants were wounded and had to be taken to the hospital.
>
> The jury found them all *Guilty*. [*Royal Gazette*, 8 Dec 1871]

The Chinese also occasionally found themselves in the middle of conflicts, and they did not display a reluctance to get involved.

> A dispute occurred between a Creole blacksmith and some of the Coolie gang, and in a short time the Coolies, mustering in force, attacked the creoles, drove them off and beat several of them. Mr. Clarke, the manager of the estate endeavoured to make peace, but he was threatened with violence, and might have suffered severely at the hands of the rioters, had he not been assisted by the Chinese, who, although only about one-sixth in number to the Coolies, interposed with their cutlasses and knives fastened to shovel-sticks. Creoles from Nonpareil and neighbouring places joined the Chinese, to keep the Coolies thoroughly in check. [*Royal Gazette*, 1 Nov 1870]

> [The Chinese] are too sensible to be led into riots which would be sure to result in their own punishment. Recent events, also, have shown that in the event of a disturbance the Chinese and Creoles would oppose the Coolies, who, with opposition from that quarter, from the Police, the troops and special constables, would be speedily defeated and crushed. [*Royal Gazette*, 10 Nov 1870]

In this incident the Chinese went to assist the Creole labourers against the Indian immigrants. There was a different scenario in December 1875 when an ugly scene developed at Pln. Wales. The black workers were noisy and boisterous when they went to collect their pay and the manager, Mr. Lorcner, Jr., declined to pay them until the afternoon. However, at the second attempt, the Creoles were even more boisterous and the manager again refused to issue their pay.

> His refusal to again pay caused him to be assaulted. He called on the Coolie gang to help but they did not respond with any alacrity. The

> Chinese were sent for who turned out *con amore* and gave the Blacks a beating. In the midst of the melee a Chinaman drove his shovel into the abdomen of a Black man, who had before that, received some wounds about the head. The Black man died and the Chinaman is in custody.
> [*Royal Gazette*, 28 Dec 1875]

The nature of these clashes seem to suggest that while some incidents may have been the result of racial animosity, another motive for involvement may have been an eagerness to participate in a ruckus. The Chinese certainly were not adverse to engaging in actions by which their behaviour, in local terms, would be called "wrong and strong."

Despite the occurrence of occasional conflicts of this kind, cooperation was common between the racial groups.

> About 12 o'clock last night the villagers and others residing on the opposite bank of the river were aroused by the bells of Plantation *Schoon-Oord* and other estates pealing an alarm, and it was soon found that one of the Logies of *Schoon-Oord* was on fire. Our informant states that it was wonderful in how short a space of time people assembled at the spot, considering the distances that many of them had to travel. . . . Hundreds of the labourers promptly offered their services in extinguishing the fire. . . . Such buckets as could be procured from the Portuguese shops were readily brought into use, and by the great exertion of the people only about 56 feet of the logie was destroyed and megass equal to 15 hhds. . . . Not only did the Creole labourers work well, but the Chinese and Coolies also exerted themselves, and the conduct of the people generally is beyond all praise. [*Royal Gazette*, 12 Aug 1863]

In contrast to the reported cowardice of the Chinese when the gambling place in Georgetown caught fire a few months earlier, the display of commitment to help on the estate could probably be due to the fact that the fire at the logie could have caused a greater conflagration that might have engulfed their own housing. The loss of the gambling room, however, did not arouse a similar urgency for them to want to take part in saving it, especially when their involvement in gambling would have made them subject to severe criticism or even to criminal charges.

In October 1865 a boiler exploded on Pln. Providence in Berbice killing 3 Creoles and 3 Coolies. The Chinese workers immediately went to provide aid:

> The Chinese gang on the estate are reported to have acted admirably, affording every assistance to those who were injured, while the other

persons employed about the place stood aloof probably fearful of another accident. [*Berbice Gazette*, 28 Oct 1865]

Cooperation was evident not only at times of disaster but also on festive occasions:

The Tadja Festival, in the West Bank District, which lasted from Saturday to Monday was conducted with the greatest order, and without disturbance of any kind. The Magistrate of the District and the Inspector of Police were both on hand in case their services might have been wanted, but there was no need of them at any time. This year the Coolies called in the aid of the Chinese to build their gaudy temples, and these ingenious fellows gave the Coolies better temples than they have ever had before. As on former occasions the black people followed the processions in thousands, and seemed to look on the festival as one designated as much for their spiritual benefit as for that of the Coolies. The ministers of the district entreated the people from the pulpits to give no countenance to the worship of idols; but the blacks found the Tadja to their taste, and declined to be dictated to in matters of religious belief. [*Royal Gazette*, 11 Mar 1873]

We hear that the black people of Pln Leonora attempted, some time in April to hold a "black Tadjah" procession, but that the immigrants, Coolies and Chinese, turned out and destroyed the temple, and dispersed the would-be processionists, giving a few of them an accidental (?) blow or two. At this Tadjah on the East Coast on the 19th and 20th of April, the usual number of black people, men, and more particularly women, were present. It will be observed that the 20th April was a Sunday, and this procession was in possession of the Public Roads from 3 till 6 o'clock, P.M. of that day and on the route had to pass the Parish Church, to the scandal of the District. [*Royal Gazette*, 10 May 1873]

Christian Influences

The influence of Christian faith had already played a role in the lives of several Chinese immigrants even before they left China because of the work of missionaries. A large group of Chinese Christians were allotted to Skeldon in Berbice and their support of the faith was noted in the 1862 report to the Guiana Diocesan Church Society.

You will notice a goodly list of subscriptions from the Chinese Christians, $30.26, and when I add that this amount has been collected

> without the least trouble, I trust the gift will be none the less acceptable to the Society. I never knew money . . . given so cheerfully.

Christianity was embraced by more and more of the Chinese immigrants as they attempted to establish themselves in the colony. Some turned to Christianity in order to become more accepted in a society based on the Christian ethic, or in other words, to behave like those who held positions of status, power and influence. This was especially so since the Chinese population was relatively small and assimilation of the prevailing customs and culture could pave the road to success. Still, the converts, and especially those of the later generations, became dedicated and faithful believers of Christianity. This conversion brought about significant changes in the social values among the Chinese. As an example, the practice of consulting with fortune tellers to determine the viability of an arranged marriage eventually fell by the wayside from the lack of a wide selection of Chinese women and as the descendants of the immigrants accepted the western concept of free choice of their partners. This however did not reduce the tendency for people to try to match-make for relatives and friends.

Although by tradition monogamy was the recognized tenet in China it was not uncommon for a man, especially one in good economic standing, to take on concubines as additional members of the family. This situation would arise particularly if the wife was unable to produce a male heir and the descendants, whether from wife or concubine, were all accepted as part of the same household. In British Guiana, however, a man who decided to maintain an extra-wife relationship found that his secondary partner would not be readily acknowledged as a part of the household after the Chinese accepted the Christian version of monogamy. This had a significant effect on those children who were born out of wedlock and who became outcasts from the family. Even so there were some Chinese men who still persisted in maintaining the tradition of having more than one wife, but now the secondary wife and her offspring became subject to rejection by the "mainstream" attitudes and only in isolated cases did they become accepted by the man's family.

> In the annual report of the Guiana Diocesan Church Society is to be found an interesting account of the missionary work that has been done under its auspices during the past year. . . . Of the progress of

Christianity among the Chinese and East Indian immigrants, the report does not say much. What little it does, does to show that the former adapt to it more readily than the latter. The Bishop in his recent charge expresses, in the following terms his experience in his visitation of last year:-

"It is impossible of course for me to have personal intercourse with all the candidates presented to me, but with those who have just come out of heathendom I always desire to have an interview before the day arrives for our solemn meeting. I was astonished by the intelligence of some of the Chinese converts, and, I may add, as the commencement of a happy sign of a future harvest, in which, as yet hardly any fruit has been gathered in, that the fellow Coolies who have been admitted into communion with us have hitherto been steady, and that I am generally greeted by them with a warmth which encourages me to believe that Christ's gospel will surely, though it may be slowly, burst forth amidst the darkness which so heavily surrounds this fine race of people."

. . . The Society maintain four Chinese and two Coolie Catechists.

[*Royal Gazette*, 27 Jun 1872]

The work of spreading the gospel was carried out by Chinese catechists who relied on texts and printed tracts brought over by the Christian converts as well as hand-made copies of such materials. The catechists typically were responsible for ministering to Chinese spread out over several estates and would make the rounds to meet with the congregation in small gatherings. One such person was How-You-Fook, who arrived on the *Dora* in 1861 and was among a large group of Christian converts who were sent to Skeldon, Berbice. He was a man of advanced age and dedicated to his religious work but succumbed to yellow fever within three years. Not long before his death he was sent to another district in Berbice from where he wrote to Mr. Farrar of the Guiana Diocesan Society:

Houston, June 18, 1864.

I am through the goodness of the Almighty, the influence of your letter, and the kindness of the Archdeacon, at present employed by the Houston and Peter's Hall Estates as a Chinese catechist, receiving $5 (month) from each estate. Other gentleman representing the Estates situated on the East Bank have also promised me further employment in the same capacity when they shall have more Chinese immigrants on their estate. I am likewise glad to inform you that there are about thirty Chinese on the Houston estate joining with us in the worship of God,

12 of whom have been baptized in China, and the rest of them, by the blessing of God may soon follow their example.

The Chinese were willing to consider Christianity, although it sometimes took a quite a bit of exertion to have them sincerely embrace the faith. O. Tye Kim (whose activities are described in the next chapter) related the obstacles in a letter to Rev. Austin, dated 1 January 1867:

> Generally we had a good attendance; the people are willing to hear, and always give us kind welcome. Taking it in a natural point of view, the Chinese in the colony are not likely to receive the word readily on account of the evil influence they are living under, and the difficulties they have to encounter — these are of various kinds, and from various sources. Opium and gambling are the two principal evils prevalent among the people; they impede their progress in temporal improvements. . . . All their spare time and minds are entirely given to the two evils. . . . We know our undertaking is great and arduous; we need much grace, spiritual as well as physical strength to go through all the hardships and trials attending work of this nature. . . . Already some twenty have come forward desiring to be admitted into the body of the Church by Holy Baptism, . . .

CHURCH BUILDING

In general the newer generations of Chinese were more accepting of the Christian faith, and as the old stock died off (some through their indulgence in opium) the trend towards Christianity became more evident. The conversion to Christianity came to a climax with the decision to establish a church specially for the Chinese community so that the services could be held in their own language.

> Opening of the Chinese Church in Charlestown.
>
> The site of the old St. Philip's Church, in the district of Charles-town, which for some years has been vacant, was in August last year, — as many of our readers will remember — the scene of a very interesting ceremony. The foundation stone of a Church for Divine Services, in the Chinese languages, was on that occasion laid by His Excellency J.R. Longden, Esq., Governor of the Colony.
>
> Last week the crowning services were celebrated, viz: the formal opening of the building, now sufficiently completed and furnished for Divine Service.

At an early hour of the day the Chinese from the suburban villages and neighbouring estates came into town, some walking, others — whole families — seated in their donkey carts. . . .

At the 11, A.M., service the little Church was over-crowded. Many of the Chinese, residing in its immediate neighbourhood and other parts of the city of Georgetown, who have hitherto shown no disposition to enter a Church — some, perhaps, only because the service was unintelligible to them — were there present. The service began with the 24th Psalm, chanted in Chinese. The Rural Dean of Demerara then read the Bishop's Licence for the celebration of the Holy Sacraments, and rites of the Church within the building. The Canticles and Hymns 87, and 160, from Hymns Ancient and Modern, were very heartily sung by the Chinese in their own tongue. The Special Lessons . . . were read by two Catechists, a part of the congregation listening with great attention, their eyes fixed upon the reader, the rest following him in their own books. Towards the close of the service the Bishop addressed the Chinese in his usual pathetic style. The address — previously translated — was read in Chinese by two Catechists, the Bishop paused twice during the delivery for the purpose. It was very interesting to mark the attention and occasional sensation of the congregation during this impressive portion of the service — one, here and there rising quietly in his place and leaning forward with eager countenance. . . .

In the portion of the work of building their Church the Chinese have evinced a most praiseworthy earnestness of purpose, intelligence and perseverance. The painting of the building was mainly their own work. A pleasing peculiarity is seen in the groups of flowers and fruits painted by the Chinese artist on scrolls, and attached to the panels between the windows. On the panel facing the entrance the scroll contains in Chinese characters the name of the Church — S. Saviour — and over the doorway a sentence of which the literal translation is "Amen. Come, worship." The Eastern end is adorned with a painted window, the gift of a lady in England through her son a Clergyman in the Colony. The altar cover is given by the Bishop's wife, and a beautifully worked pulpit frontal has been sent by another lady from England.

The Church itself is a plain but well proportioned building, consisting of Nave 50 feet by 20 feet, and North and South Aisles 50 feet by 8 feet. It is hoped soon to add a Chancel, and before long to find it necessary to extend the building westward, so zealously are the leading Christian Chinese throwing themselves into the work. The total cost of the building with enclosure of the site had been $3,408 85. For some little time the sacraments must still ministered in English, but it is confidently expected that after a moderate probation and such training as can under the circumstances be given, the Bishop will be able to select one or two from the ranks of the present active earnest-hearted Catechists on whom to lay hands. The ordinary services will be wholly in Chinese.

[*Royal Gazette*, 4 Dec 1875]

The opening of St. Saviour's Church was a triumph for the Chinese Christians and showed their determination in seeing their spiritual belief transformed into a physical place of worship. The effort and money required to complete the church were not a pittance and the *Royal Gazette*, seven months earlier, had rebuked the Christians of the privileged class for not providing significant aid to the construction of the church.

Unobtrusiveness is certainly a commendable quality, but like many commendable things it may become, in some degree, pernicious from being over-done. We are led to this reflection in relation to the Chinese Church now building in Charlestown. The public has heard nothing of it; yet it merits attention. . . . Quietly and successfully the work has gone on hitherto. . . . A few earnest-hearted Christian immigrants, in a strange land, striving with apostolic zeal for the spread of the Gospel and the dispensation of Christian Ordinances amongst their fellow countrymen, without any adequate practical evidence of sympathy from that Christian people to whose shores they have been brought, and more particularly from that class thereof for the security and increase of whose material welfare, these Chinese have been induced to leave their homes.

[*Royal Gazette*, 15 May 1875]

While St. Saviour's Church served the largest group of Chinese Christians there were other churches built through the contributions, both physical and monetary, of Chinese converts. At Plantation Peter's Hall, East Bank Demerara, followers of the Plymouth Christian Brethren sect established a chapel and in 1878 were able to gain the Rectory:

By Robert Kingsland and Joe Hubbard, transport of the north half of a piece of land in front of Plantation Peter's Hall measuring eight roods and eight feet facade from north to south, known as the "Rectory," . . . to and in favour of the said Robert Kingsland, Alfred Wrigglesworth, Wong-a-tson, No. 2,560, ex "Agra," 1862, Lung-a-on, No. 2,537 ex "Agra," 1862, Fung-a-shing, alias Chan-moon, No. 2,534 ex "Agra," 1862, Chung-a-chak, alias Wong-you-Wing, No. 3,186, ex "Sir George Seymour," 1862, Lam-a-Fuk, No. 3,121, ex "Persia," 1862, Kwong-a-Chung, alias Chow-a-Sune, No. 6,304, ex "Arima," 1865 and Chan-a-

Sho, No. 2,484 ex "Agra," 1862 for and on behalf of the congregation commonly known as Christian Brethren. [*Royal Gazette*, 8 Jun 1878]

> His Lordship the Bishop. . . attended in New Amsterdam for the purpose of opening the new "Coolie and Chinese Church," called St. Thomas. . . . The Coolie immigrants . . . are the principal contributor to the building fund, two of whom having given $200 between them. The contribution from the Chinese was merely nominal, although there were several of them present at the opening service, and seemed to have been much impressed with what they have seen and heard.
> [*Royal Gazette*, 8 Nov 1877]

> A confirmation Service was held in St. Augustine's Church, Friendship, East Coast, on Sunday afternoon, 27th ult when 24 Chinese and 11 Coolies, were duly admitted to the full privileges of the Church. . . One of the Chinese, a married woman, who along with her husband, arrived a few weeks ago on the *Dartmouth*, is a person of some education. She rendered valuable assistance to the Clergyman in Charge of the *Non Pareil* Mission by writing phonetically in the English character a translation of the Confirmation Service into Chinese whereby he was enabled to read the Service to the Immigrants in their own tongue. The same woman has a knowledge of music and says that she can play the harmonium. Amongst the Chinese who were confirmed are several who came in the *Dartmouth*. [*Royal Gazette*, 6 May 1879]

Acting on behalf of the Society for the Propagation of the Gospel, Rev. F.P.L. Josa, an Anglican minister, found himself being asked all manner of questions by his readers in England which revealed that the British people knew very little about British Guiana. He decided to write an article describing the different ethnic groups in the colony and the work of the Church among the groups. With regard to the Chinese community, he stated:

> This field of work more than any other is ripe for harvest. A good work is going on throughout the country. The Chinese are more ready to receive Christianity than the East Indians. They are most easily taught — to begin with, ninety of every hundred of our Chinese (men) can read Budha's moral code of law [which is] in every way more excellent than Manu's. And, that the Chinese are, after all, Atheists only makes it easier for the Missionary to teach them. Our Chinese in Guiana have nothing taking them back — no (heathen) priests — no temples, — nothing in this respect to nourish the memory of the associations connected to their

homes. The work has progressed so steadily that I venture to state, that at any rate in my own district, there will be no heathen Chinese left except for hardened sinners.

We have one barrier, and only one, in the way of the Gospel — that cursed opium. I have known of some moderate smokers, [some of] these I have ventured to admit into the covenant of Grace, trusting that God will give them strength to give up the obnoxious habit. I have a worthy coadjutor in my Chinese catechist — a good, holy man, I met with [in] the "buildings" where the negro-workers [live]. . . . His name is Yang-a-pat, [known as] "James." He is a Christian of many years standing and an elderly man who nearly always travels with me in my wagon, i.e. whenever I travel in this way. He is much respected by his countrymen and has done a good work. I have read to him a good deal (as he lives in my "yard" in a two-roomed range), but more especially all the prophecies which have a reference to our Blessed Saviour, and which are to be found in the four "major" prophets. He has also been very industrious, and has written with his own hands during the year several hundreds of portions of the Prayer Book such as the "Lord's Prayer" and the "Ten Commandments," &c.

There is a large body of Christian Chinese in the colony. In my own district I have baptised upwards of 200, and the work is still going on; a steady increase everywhere apparent.

I have only to mention, that although the Chinese will sing everything they [possibly] can, yet they have not the slightest [ear for] music. My Chinese teacher has got [to know] one tune (which is no tune at all that I know of); he will sing that to every thing in the Hymn-book Canticles, &c. with no exceptions. He being a married man, it is to be expected that his wife will sing a [tune] from her husband; and I can in truth say, that each member of my congregation has a tune peculiar to himself. [You can] just imagine the awful din when all the tunes are brought in one room, and [all] at the same time! (Let me add [to this] thesis, *I am supposed to be accompanying them*!!) [*Royal Gazette*, 25 Jun 1881]

CHAPTER 8

THE SHEPHERD AND HOPETOWN

O. TYE KIM ARRIVES

On 17 July 1864 Mr. O. Tye Kim arrived in Georgetown. Known in the Cantonese dialect as Wu Tai-kam, he was born to a humble family in one of the settlements along the Strait of Malacca. He attended a school run by the London Missionary Society in Singapore and later married and raised three children. Sometime about 1851-52 he embraced the teachings of Christianity and began to preach to fellow Chinese when he was not at work as a surveyor for the Singapore Government, a post he held for ten years. He became committed to spreading the faith of Christianity and accepted an offer from the Society for the Propagation of the Gospel in Foreign Parts to go to Calcutta to prepare for ordination. He left his wife and family in Singapore but on landing in Penang he found that he had missed his connecting vessel by three days. He felt this to be the interposition of Providence and set out instead for England at the invitation of the captain of the ship upon which he had embarked in Singapore. On this voyage he learnt that many Chinese had gone to British Guiana and he made up his mind to go there to minister to them.

Within a short period of time of his arrival in British Guiana O. Tye Kim managed to establish a following among the Chinese community and became well known and respected. His efforts resulted in the conversion of a significant number of heathen Chinese into Christian believers and this greatly impressed the established religious leaders. Soon enough the ministers and priests were asking their own congregations to extend not only their blessings to the newly converted but also to make monetary contributions to further propagate the Holy Word.

> The October Meeting of the Georgetown Union of Pastors and Churches was held last evening, at Providence New Chapel, Charlestown — the Rev. JOSEPH KETLEY, presiding.

Mr. O. Tye Kim, (the Chinese evangelist) was present, and gave an interesting account of his labors, since his arrival, among his benighted fellow-countrymen. These efforts have already, through the Divine blessing, produced great fruit. Some two hundred Chinese in different parts of Demerara, afford evidence of conversion to the faith of Christ, and about one-hundred-and-twenty assemble regularly each Lord's Day, in Georgetown, for the worship of God, in instruction in His Word. Mr. O. Tye Kim had found among the Christian Chinese immigrants two or three educated men qualified to render him efficient aid in carrying on his important work. One of these excels in carving Chinese characters on blocks for printing hymns, tracts, &c.

After listening to Mr. O. Tye Kim's statements, which was followed by brief addresses from some of the Ministers present, it was felt that the Chinese Mission has a strong claim upon the sympathy and the aid of the Christian people of this country. The hand of the Divine Head of the Church was devoutly recognised in raising up and directing to this Colony, one so evidently well qualified for the work of Chinese evangelization; whilst the fact that Mr. O. Tye Kim is identified with no particular denomination — is sustained by no Missionary Society — and has come out here simply to do his Master's Work and trusting in his Master's care, was looked upon as giving him a powerful claim upon the aid of all who love the Lord Jesus Christ, and the souls of men perishing for lack of knowledge of His great salvation. Under the influence of these views and feelings, it was proposed by the Revd. E.A. Wallbridge, seconded by the Rev. T.S. Gregory, and unanimously adopted by the Meeting, that an appeal be made by their respective pastors to the congregation belonging to the Union, for pecuniary aid to the Chinese Mission, and that the Venerable Chairman be requested to act as Treasurer of the funds thus raised.... [*Royal Gazette*, 28 Oct 1864]

A Chinese Settlement Proposed

In January 1865 O. Tye Kim drew up a plan to acquire some Crown land for the establishment of a Chinese Christian community. O. Tye Kim wrote a "Humble Petition" which, in typical Chinese fashion, he sent directly to the governor rather than submitting it to the Court of Policy.

Your petitioner on his arrival in this Colony remarked with surprise, that his people were not as prosperous here as those who have been an equal time in other countries; the few exceptions having for the most part become such by gambling and other disreputable means; and he has become aware in the course of his labours, the large proportion of the immigrants are in consequence dissatisfied with their condition and prospects, and are contemplating emigration on the expiration of their indentures. They have learnt that their countrymen in the neighbouring colony of Trinidad are in comparatively flourishing condition; that many there are growing rich in pursuit of trade and in the cultivation of the soil; and this knowledge has added to their discontent, and confirmed their determination to go elsewhere.

Your petitioner believes that irrespective of the loss of their labour, the departure of any considerable number of Chinese would be highly prejudicial to the interests of this Colony; as when the news become generally known in China, as would certainly be the case, Immigration thence to this Colony would entirely cease. And the continuation of the present dissatisfaction would, in the opinion of your petitioner, eventually produce the same result even if no emigration should take place. . . .

Your petitioner would enumerate among the higher advantages of the proposed scheme, the probable utilization of a large portion of the waste lands of the Colony, the consequent increase of trade and wealth, and above all, the rare opportunity which would be afforded of spreading Christianity among a people, whose natural readiness for its reception would be increased by gratitude for temporal blessings.

Your petitioner has been for twelve years Revenue Surveyor in the service of the British Government at Singapore; and is well versed in the choosing and laying out of lands. . . .

That should your Excellency be graciously pleased to grant a tract of Crown Land for the purpose above mentioned, a small sum of money would be required at the outset for the purchase of axes, saws, boats, and other necessaries, besides provisions for five months. At the end of that time your petitioner hopes and believes that the Settlement would begin to be self-supporting and would shortly afterwards become entirely so. . . .

[*Royal Gazette*, 2 Feb 1865]

Mr. O. Tye Kim had already checked out a few potential sites and recommended a tract near the Camoonie Creek, some 25 miles up the Demerara River, as the most viable location for the proposed settlement. G. William Des Voeux, in his recollections, *Experiences of a Demerara Magistrate*, lays claim to being the one who found the site, and this might not be a contradiction because, as a magistrate dealing with the estates and their employees, he may have been aware of the various tracts of Crown land in the colony. However, it was O. Tye Kim who pressed for its dedication as a Chinese settlement. His arguments and proposals in the petition found favor with Governor Hincks who was also impressed by the reputation and vision put forward by O. Tye Kim. Governor Hincks decided to seize the initiative on this issue and took it upon himself to push forward the proposition at the Court of Policy. The Governor explained that Mr. O. Tye Kim started up his ministry in a room at the old Colony House:

> He had got a congregation there of upwards of 120 who came regularly to service and some of them from considerable distances. . . . [S]ome of them came from the *Diamond*, which as members knew was a considerable distance from town, and that they had to get up at two o'clock in the morning so as to reach town by nine o'clock in time for the service. . . He had to walk from estate to estate and from town to estates; he visited the hospitals and went among the people and had been doing everything he could in every way for their welfare. . . .
>
> He thought that looking at the way in which Mr. O. Tye Kim had gone about his work it did appear as if his steps had been directed by Providence to British Guiana. [*Royal Gazette*, 2 Feb 1865]

The first time that the Governor introduced the petition at the Court of Policy the elected members, who represented the plantation owners, were not at all impressed. The argument was raised that granting of Crown lands would set a bad precedent for anyone with a righteous or noble cause who might come along asking for other tracts of land.

> Mr. CLEMENTSON strongly objected to the scheme in the planting interest believing that it would draw away from the estates labour that had cost the Colony so much and pictured to himself an encampment in the far interior "hundreds of miles from Georgetown," whither the indentured immigrants on estates would flee and whence on the approach of a policeman they would fly into the bush. Crime of all sorts would go there unpunished, unless a police force was sent with the settlers, and disease would cut them down unless hospitals and medical attention were procured. All these would cost money, and it was the duty of every man to look well to his pocket, which the honorable member affirmed to be the first guiding principle of every man's conduct.
>
> [*Royal Gazette*, 31 Jan 1865]

The Court of Policy deferred making any decision about O. Tye Kim's petition. The objections were so strongly voiced that the editor of the *Royal Gazette* felt it appropriate to join the discussion:

> We cannot but regret that the Governor's scheme for establishing a Chinese Colony or Village up the Demerara River has not found that favour at the hands of the Elective Members of the Court of Policy, which it undoubtedly merits in many respects. We certainly do not agree with Mr. CLEMENTSON in his fears that such a settlement would become a refuge for deserters from the Estates and for fugitives from justice — on the contrary we are disposed to think that, under Mr. O. TYE KIM's supervision, a kind of local police would be speedily organised, and the head of every household held responsible for what occurred within its precincts, so that any unauthorized person entering the village would be at once handed over to the nearest authorities. In place of a nest of idlers and villains we picture to ourselves rows of cottages neatly built of bamboo, surrounded for miles with fields of luxuriant rice falling beneath the sickles of a handy and industrious population in sufficient quantities to make us, in great measure, independent of our imports of that grain. [*Royal Gazette*, 2 Feb 1865]

The *Royal Gazette* was not alone in arguing in favor of the Chinese settlement:

> It is a rather rare event for all the papers on the Colony to be unanimous, but in the matter of the proposed Chinese settlement all of them are agreed that, at all events, the experiment ought to be tried, believing that is successfully carried out, it would be to the advantage of the colony at large. [*Royal Gazette*, 7 Feb 1965]

The debate in the Court of Policy continued on and off for the next week with the Governor, Chief Justice, Attorney-General, Government Secretary and Auditor-General arguing on behalf of O. Tye Kim's proposal. The four elected members representing the planting interests eventually realized that they stood in the minority in face of the strong and tenacious position generally held by the proponents. On 9 February 1865 the following resolutions were put to the vote:

> "*Resolved*, 1. That in the opinion of this Court it is expedient to establish a village of Chinese Christians on a suitable tract of Crown

land up the Demerara river, or one of the tributary Creeks thereof, to be hereafter defined by survey.

"2. That in order to carry out this object it is desirable that the village should be entitled to participate in the village loan.

"3. That His Excellency the Governor be requested to instruct the Attorney-General to prepare the necessary Ordinance, and in the meantime to appoint a Committee to superintend the arrangements for establishing the village and to receive and appropriate in behalf thereof an advance not exceeding $1,500 from the village loan, it being conditioned that such advance shall be a first charge on the Settlement, and that due provision shall be made for securing its repayment with interest."

Mr. Bascom withdrew his opposition to the scheme, on the ground of the general opinion in favour of it.

Mr. Porter said he had never been opposed to the scheme, itself of a Chinese village, but to the proposed site. . . .

Mr. Mackey expressed himself in favour of the scheme, and said he always had been in favour of it. . .

The Chief Justice objected to the settlement being exclusively a Christian settlement. He thought that all were alike entitled to any benefits that might arise from the adoption of the scheme. . . . He would not, under any circumstances, oppose the resolutions, but if the scheme were not properly matured before adoption, he would have forebodings of evil which he hoped might not be realised.

The resolutions were carried. [*Royal Gazette*, 9 Feb 1865]

A TOWN FOR HOPE

On 18 February 1865 Admiral Sir James Hope, KCB, on a tour of the colony, was invited to pay a visit to the site of the proposed settlement, in deference to his earlier involvement with China. He was accompanied by Governor Hincks and other dignitaries. The party left Georgetown at 8:30 in the morning, taking a leisurely cruise upriver on the Colonial Steamer *Berbice*. They went ashore and listened to Mr. O. Tye Kim explain his plans for development of the site where already there were some 25 Chinese who had moved there at the end of January. After the Governor had finished his speech a district magistrate proposed that the site be named "Hopetown" in honor of Sir James Hope. Following this, it would hardly have been becoming for other suggestions to be put forward and the settlement was thus duly named by unanimous agreement. An hour after landing the dignitaries reboarded their launch to enjoy a delicate lunch at the mouth of the creek.

Hopetown had a shaky start on account of persistent rains and doubts were being raised about its potential for success.

> It is said that the Chinese settlement of Mr. O. TYE KIM is not in all respects successful, nor was it to be expected that it would be. The rivers are healthy only above the point to which salt or brackish water reaches, a fact which it is well to bear in mind in dealing with this or any similar question. The Chinese settlement was made too low down the river, and we fear can never be so healthy as if a position considerably higher up has been chosen. [*Royal Gazette*, 26 Sep 1865]

However, the following month a more optimistic report was presented suggesting that the settlement appeared to have weathered the storm.

> In ordinary years there would have been three months of dry weather, during which the settlers would have been able to protect their land from the floods of the rainy season. This year, however, has been an extraordinary year. By the end of March the creek had risen to a height which it seldom reached even in July. The water surrounding the tents of the settlers who (then about 70 in number) were obliged to remove in consequence.
>
> Then came a trying time for all concerned in the success of the scheme. It had been calculated that the people would be able to subsist by burning charcoal until their provisions should come to maturity. The Chinese thoroughly understand the manufacture. Their method, however, differs greatly from that usually practised in Demerara. The Portuguese and Creole burners place the wood to be burnt in pits dug in the sand. The Chinese construct ovens of clay above ground. Now there was no clay at the place to which the settlers were compelled to remove. They were therefore compelled to learn the Creole method to which they were unaccustomed. The first attempts resulted in failure. Some of the wood was entirely consumed, and the little charcoal which was produced was of inferior quality. All the money granted by the colony had been expended in the purchase of food, tools, boats, &c., and as yet very little was being earned. Rain poured almost incessantly during March, April, May and June. All that time the settlers had a hard struggle to keep bread

in their mouths. But for the timely liberality of the Governor, who had from the beginning taken a great interest in the scheme, they could not have done so. A few lost heart and came away. This ill report caused the rumour that the settlement was a failure.

However, about the middle of July, matters began to mend. The water in the creek had fallen off sufficiently to allow of a return to Hopetown. Work then commenced in earnest. Houses were put up, trees felled, and charcoal oven built. In the three months which have elapsed since the return to Hopetown, a very large amount of work has been accomplished. About 20 houses have been constructed, all of them substantially thatched with troolies, and surrounded with deep drains. Over 50 acres of heavily-timbered land have been cleared, 18 charcoal ovens, holding each from 50 to 100 barrels of charcoal have been completed, and 12 more are in course of construction. These ovens are built of clay, with walls from three to four feet thick, and require a large amount of labour. They however, make a better charcoal than the Creole pits, and more than twice as quickly, so that the cost of erection is soon compensated.

The extent of the land cleared, over and above the other work done, is the more extraordinary in consideration of the fact that only a very few of the people were accustomed to the use of the axe, and that the timber felled was chiefly of the hardest description, mora and wallaba.

Besides the above results, over 3,000 brls. of charcoal have been made and sent to Georgetown. At the present time about 2,000 brls. are being produced per mensum, an amount which will shortly be increased to between three and four thousand when the necessary ovens are completed.

The health of the people is excellent, and their spirits have entirely recovered from their late depression. All are prospering more or less. Each able-bodied man earns from two shillings to three shillings a day, and can live well enough on a shilling, so that they will soon accumulate money. Some already own bateaux, and have purchased pigs and poultry. They feel confident of being able in a year or two to bring out their relatives from China, by which it would seem that they look upon success as certain.

The "clearings" and houses already shew a marked contrast to those of the Creoles in similar situations, both in respect of neatness and comfort. Each man has constructed substantial steps at his "water-side," at which a visitor can land without inconvenience at any time of the tide, instead of being obliged to wade through mud or totter over an unstable and slippery plank. Deep drains are cut round all the houses. Each man sleeps snugly on an India mat, and covered with a curtain to protect him from bats and insects. Considering the place, the shortness of time since the formation of the settlement, and the slender means of the people, they have made themselves wonderfully comfortable.

Fault has often been found with the location chosen for the new settlement. Some have suggested the East Coast, some the banks of the Essequebo as preferable. We on the contrary think that a better choice could not have been made. The East Coast would have one advantage. There would there have been less labour in clearing the ground. On the other hand, the carriage of crops to market would be far more expensive, and would thus deteriorate greatly from their value.

The Essequebo banks would not only have the same disadvantage, but would moreover afford no means of livelihood to the settlers while the crops were being planted and ripening.

Charcoal is so bulky in proportion to its value that its manufacture only "pays" in the immediate neighbourhood of a market. The Portuguese charcoal-burners know this well, and take out grants only in those Creeks of the Demerara which are with in easy distance from town. The Camoonie Creek is reached easily in six hours from town. The water of the Demerara is seldom too rough to allow of small boats carrying a load — a very important point. The land in the neighbourhood of Hopetown is virgin, and equal to, if not better, than any in the Colony. There are several wet savannahs near. One of them about 300 acres in extent, will be planted with rice, as soon as the weather will allow of the grass being burnt off.

There are now about 150 Chinese in the Camoonie, of whom 21 are women. Many more are anxious to proceed thither; but as every man requires support until he can produce charcoal, the limited means at the disposal of the manager do not allow of the reception of more than 7 or 8 a month. Even at this rate of increase, the population will reach a very respectable number in a few years. Then we may look for a fall in the price of vegetables, such as is already beginning to take place in charcoal.

The success of the undertaking up to this time is almost entirely owing to the extraordinary energy and 'pluck' of the manager, O. Tye Kim. He is disheartened by no failures, and daunted by no difficulties. But for him, the settlement would not have survived the trying time of the long rainy season. He rushed about from place to place to cheer, to instruct, to direct. He performed in person the different duties of preacher, surveyor, store-keeper, and general manager.

As none of the people talk sufficient English to buy and sell to advantage, he has been compelled to be perpetually on the move between

Georgetown and the settlement, travelling often at night, during the rains, and in a open boat. In a word, he has done work which would have killed a man of ordinary constitution. As he has hitherto undergone all the labour and endured no ordinary privations gratuitously, it is to be hoped that he will some day receive a substantial reward from the Colony. If the settlement proves to be a permanent success, and especially if it leads to that much desired result a free immigration of Chinese, he will have done a service to British Guiana, the value of which cannot be estimated. [*Royal Gazette*, 26 Oct 1865]

We are happy to hear that the Chinese Settlement under the management of Mr. O. Tyke Kim, is prospering. Great difficulties having had to be contended with, chiefly arising from want of capital, but there are now 200 Chinese, who are doing well. The first crop of rice is now gathered, and in about three months another large crop will be ready. The people have had no sickness, but of course the necessity of providing for the instant necessities of life, has kept the settlement back.

Surely this Colony could well afford to advance $1,000 or so to help forward so *profitable* an enterprise. Under the management of Mr. O. Tyke Kim the money would bring a bountiful return, and would certainly be repaid. [*Guiana Times*, 1 Mar 1866]

The potential for prosperity as observed at Hopetown stimulated the Chinese to look for other places to start settlements:

Among the arrivals by last week's steamer was a Chinaman, come to inspect lands on the Berbice river with a view to the establishment of a village of his countrymen similar to the one started last year in the Camoonie Creek above the sand-hills of the Demerara river. Wong-a-Wai was we understand an overseer in the settlement under Mr. O. Tye Kim; and according to his report there are a number of Chinese, not only on the Demerara river but in other parts of the Colony, anxious to try their fortunes on the Berbice. [*Berbice Gazette*, 21 Apr 1866]

We have been informed that the Chinese Settlement of Hope Town is beginning to exhibit unmistakable proofs of prosperity.

[*Royal Gazette*, 22 Sep 1866]

In his 1871 book *The Coolie. His Rights and Wrongs* Edward Jenkins wrote that in his opinion the preamble of a catalogue for the Paris Universal Exhibition in 1867 contained descriptions of the immigrant labourers which bordered on propaganda being foisted on the public by the planters. With Hopetown in existence for just two years the promotional catalogue stated:

The inhabitants have cleared about five miles on the banks of the river and its tributary creeks; they have erected dwellings in uninterrupted succession among the clearing; they have built forty ovens, at a cost of sixty dollars each, for burning charcoal, and have succeeded in reducing the price of that indispensable commodity thirty per cent. The trade had previously been monopolised by the Madeirans, who burn their charcoal in pits. The ovens are considered to be a decided improvement. The settlers have, moreover, planted ginger, sweet potatoes, plantains, and other vegetable products. They have pigs valued at one thousand dollars; they have planted one hundred and fifty acres in rice, calculated to yield six hundred bags valued at nine dollars each; the population is one hundred and seventy, of whom forty are Christians; they are well fed, well clothed, and comfortable; they have had but one death; on the other hand, there has been but one birth. They have erected a temporary chapel and school-house, of neat construction, as might be expected from them. They possess three large punts besides bateaux, and they keep up a constant trading intercourse with the capital. . . .

FLIGHT OF THE SHEPHERD

Just when things seemed to be going well for Hopetown, some unusual rumors began to circulate about O. Tye Kim.

A rumour was afloat on Saturday afternoon that Mr. O. TYE KIM had been drowned. We have not yet had any confirmation of the rumour, although it is still current, and we must therefore hope, at all events in the meantime, that it may prove to be unfounded.

[*Royal Gazette*, 9 Jul 1867]

At length something like definite intelligence has been received about Mr. O. TYE KIM. We heard it surmised, yesterday, that as two of the men who had been with him in the batteau had been seen on the Arabian Coast [Essequebo], they must have drowned him and made off with the batteau and his effects. It is now confidently stated that he himself was, a few days ago, in the Arabian Coast, and report says that after coming down the river, on the 2nd instant, he and the three men who were with him went on to the West Coast, where they remained that night, and then started at an early hour next morning for Capoey. There one of the men, the one who is said to have given the information, was paid off and left, and the others then went on to Plantation Hampton Court, where a robbery was afterwards committed. It is not at all likely that O. TYE KIM had anything to do with them, but we understand that an article belonging to one of the two men who were with him was found under such circumstances as to show that one or both had been concerned in the robbery. The Revenue Cutter, having on board Mr. Inspector JOSEPH, and ten or eleven Policemen, had been sent down in pursuit of the parties. The affair is a strange one altogether, but in all probability we shall soon be in a position to give all the particulars connected with it.

[*Royal Gazette*, 13 Jul 1867]

The Revenue Cutter has returned to town without Mr. O. TYE KIM, or any of them who were with him. [*Royal Gazette*, 18 Jul 1867]

[Re: O. TYE KIM:] It is very probable that they have crossed the Tapacooma Lake, passed down the creek leading from the bank of the lake into the River Pomeroon, and thence coasted it down to the Spanish Main. We have not heard what specific charges have been made against O. TYE KIM, but it is said that latterly his life has been immoral, and it is known that his licence was withdrawn by the Lord Bishop. His fall is a source of much regret to many, as he was looked upon as a good Christian and worthy man, and he was, accordingly, very much liked and respected, until reports got abroad which impugned his private conduct. His lapse is also a damper in respect to the establishment of any settlements under the support of the Colony.

[*Royal Gazette*, 23 Jul 1867]

Apparently Mr. O. Tye Kim had been involved in an affair with a local woman who was about to bear his child when he decided to leave the scene. There was no further news after this of the Singapore preacher.

HOPETOWN CARRIES ON

Hopetown was visited by three commissioners appointed in 1870 to inquire into the treatment of immigrants. Their official report stated:

The land, except on the very edge of the stream, was next to useless, for want of a regular system of drainage; and the wood further back appeared to be a swamp. The Chinese have built a number of houses along the bank of the creek. These houses are covered with thatch and enclosed with palm bands: the chinks between the bands have not been filled up, and the Chinese do not seem to care whether they are so or not. In other respects, the houses appear comfortable enough. They are much more roomy than the huts on the estates; and the older families appear

> to take in as lodgers the young men, who from time to time find their way thither from the plantations. One large thatched house serves for a school and chapel: small patches of potatoes, rice and ginger are planted near the banks of the creek, where the land is sufficiently dry to allow their growth. There was a schoolmaster there, when we visited the place: but the education of the children did not seem to be conducted on any regular system. There were half a dozen very intelligent boys, who could read and write a little. Besides the provision grounds already mentioned on the left bank of the creek, there were several acres of rice on land from which the forest trees had been lately cleared. A stelling and store-house on the banks of the river at Georgetown have been set apart for the accommodation of the Chinese from the settlement, when they came down to dispose of their charcoal and provisions. They are somewhat too far from Georgetown, and, in consequence, from the support of civilizing associations and rules; but that of itself would not lead us to despair of the future of Hopetown, if some means could be devised to give them a better chance as cultivators. At all events, valuable experience has been acquired for the next effort that it is deemed right to make in the same direction.

Despite his biased viewpoint Edward Jenkins was apparently pleased with what he encountered during this 1870 visit to Hopetown, describing his Chinese host as having

> a better house than I have seen inhabited by any immigrant in the colony. A spacious room, with hard earth floor, lofty pitched roof built of a strong timber frame, with bamboo slots nailed on, half an inch apart, and neatly thatched with the leaves of the Eta-palm. . . . A cackling protest indicates that Lum-A-Yung is sacrificing two chickens to the Chinese god of hospitality. Another petroleum lamp is lit, a table set, my bathing-sheet is pressed into service as a table-cloth, and in half an hour we are eating, off Worcester ware, broiled chicken, Cambridge sausages, Cincinnati ham, and drinking iced beer and St. Lucia coffee - the ice from Wenham Lake, the beer from Burton, the hosts from China, and the two white men, whose race has made this wondrous conjunction possible, swinging there in aboriginal hammocks. Was not that worth a thought?

The following personal account was also related to the commissioners by one of the Hopetown settlers:

> In my own country I was a schoolmaster. I was well taught. I heard that people were going to Demerary, and I was asked to go. Agent told

> me it was a nice place — many of my countrymen were going over: over there they had plenty of work to do — plenty money — would get rich: food was found at first, and a doctor if we were sick, and good wages. I was told the work was garden work. I thought that meant like our gardening in China. I did not think it was like the hard work in the sugar-field here. I was told, if I came, I could soon get good pay as schoolmaster, and I hired as schoolmaster. There were others like me who came in the ship. There was a doctor, some schoolmasters, some tailors, and other people who were not labourers in the fields, and who all thought they were going to work at their own trades. When we got to Georgetown we were taken out of the ship and sent to the sugar estate. At first they gave us food and rooms in houses. The rooms were dirty and not nice. Then they told us to work in the fields. We did not like it, but we had to do it. If we did not work we were brought before magistrate and fined or sent to prison. It was very hard for us. Some became sick. We could not earn enough to buy food from week to week. We had a part of our bounty, but that was soon done. Some had given so much money to friends in China, and the manager wished us to pay it back, and took it from our wages. We could not bear it any longer, so we struck and came to Georgetown. We went to the attorney — he told us we were wrong and must go back. The police took us to carry us to the steamer, and several jumped into the water. They were taken out, and went to Mr. ——. He spoke kindly to us, and sent us home, and after that they did not take our money every week. it was always very hard work. Several of my friends hung themselves because they were starving. When I was free I came up here. I want to go back to my own country.

Hopetown continued to attract more Chinese settlers and when the census was taken in 1871 there were 311 men, 123 women and 133 children for a total of 567. By April 1874, the settlement was estimated by Mr. E.G. Yewens, Inspector of Villages, to have some 800 Chinese, although he apparently included those in the surrounding settled areas. Yewens observed that the Chinese were relying primarily on making charcoal. They had abandoned rice cultivation since the birds were taking away at least half of the crop and there was difficulty in drying the rice in all seasons. Even so the settlers seemed satisfied and he wrote in his report:

> The Chinese live well, and kill twice a week, and every Chinese householder, I believe, keeps one or more pigs, which they feed in pens. I saw none running about, and they are very careful in fattening them, boiling vegetables for their use.

However, later in that same year, concerns were being raised about the effect of the Hopetown-based activities on the environment.

> Every valuable young greenheart, mora, suridanny, and silverbally tree, (some valuable for ship building,) is cut off short to the ground and made into charcoal. To come near town, at the Chinese settlement at Hopetown, Camoenie Creek, persons can easily see for themselves what a destructive clearance is made by the charcoal burners. From the riverside to the entrance of this creek, up to some distance in the Watatilla, a branch of the Camoenie, the whole country is without a tree for at least three hundred roods from the banks. So it is on the Portuguese charcoal grants higher up the river. [*Royal Gazette*, 3 Aug 1874]

There were also threatening forces from within the Chinese community itself:

> The peaceful Chinese settlement at Hopetown, Demerara River, is being ruffled out of its usual calm by the lawless conduct of some of the unbaptised settlers, who, it is supposed, are being instigated to the mischief by a well known gambler whose business has been considerably affected by the refusal of the Christian settlers to patronise his den. Two of the Christians — the Catechist and the schoolmaster — both officers supported by the Chinese themselves we understand that neither the Government nor the Church Society contributes anything to Hopetown for the propagation of religion (or education) have come to town to relate the trouble with which the Christians are being threatened, and to ask for protection. The 'heathen' Chinese have commenced an open and deliberate persecution of those of their countrymen, who have forsaken Confucius for the Gospel, and have threatened to fire their Chapel and school-house unless they cease their teaching. When John Chinaman, who is a very matter of fact and determined fellow, threatens to commit a crime, there is very little doubt that he means to keep his word, and we need not be surprised if we hear that the chapel and school-house at Hopetown have become the prey of the incendiary. But if there is time left for the police to avert the committal of the threatened crime, we owe it to these Christian settlers to make the attempt to do so. They have adapted our land and our religion, and in a double sense they have a claim upon us for protection against attacks of the lawless, more particularly, as in this case, when the danger to which they are exposed is due solely to their renouncing the faith and traditions of their countrymen; and unless

we are content to abandon all hope of seeing further converts made to Christianity it would be necessary for us to take special precautions against the proselytes being persecuted on account of their change of religion. The Hopetown case we believe to be unique of its kind, at all events we have never before heard of any manifestation of ill-will on the part of the heathen towards the Christian Chinese; but none the less on that account ought the evident disposition to initiate a system of petty terrorism be put down quickly and sternly. The presence of a few policemen on the settlement for a few days would probably have a good moral effect on the rowdies, it would show them that the Government was ready to protect the Christians and punish the molesters, and the chances are that the manifestation would frighten them out of their criminal intentions. We advise the Catechist and Teacher to communicate either directly or through those Clergymen in the city whom they have already consulted, with the Magistrate of their District, and lay the facts of the case before him, he will best be able to obtain for them the official protection of which they stand so much in need.

While on the subject of the Hopetown Settlement, we may mention, what perhaps has not yet been brought to the notice of the Government, that the settlers have expressed themselves anxious to have their settlement removed to a healthier and more favourably situated district. Hopetown, from the day when it was opened with much ceremony and gush by Sir Francis Hincks, accompanied by Admiral Sir James Hope, (after whom the settlement is called) has been condemned as a mistake, by many persons capable of giving an opinion on the subject. For one thing, it does not admit of any but the most imperfect drainage, and the settlers are liable to be, and are, flooded as regularly as the wet weather sets in. This want of drainage is a fundamental detriment to its value as a settlement, and but for the pluck and energy of the settlers — who, once settled, determined to do their utmost to make the place a home for themselves — not a soul would have been left, at this date, to represent the original settlement. They deserve credit for the industry they have displayed under very adverse and disheartening circumstances, but they have pretty well exhausted the limited resources of the district and, as a home, the place is becoming less and less desirable every day. The Chinese say that they would be grateful if the Government would transplant them from Hopetown to the East Bank of the river where there is unlimited ground suitable for their wants. Considering how very desirable it is to foster and encourage immigrant settlers who pursue a recognised industry (as these Chinese do) and how easily the Government could meet the wishes of the Hopetown people with regard to a change of site, we should suppose that the wish would only have to be mentioned to the Executive to be complied with. Let the Hopetonians lay their petition, in proper form, before their paternal Government, and we think they may depend on being treated with every kindness and consideration. [*Royal Gazette*, 2 Dec 1876]

The Church apparently managed to survive the threat from the extortion attempts but the weather took its toll and the building became tattered and worn. The decision was made to build a new Chapel and the Chinese community put up contributions to the construction. Their efforts were noticed by some Christian elders who put out an appeal for support for the worthy cause.

CHINESE SETTLEMENT CAMOONIE CREEK

The Chinese Settlers in this Creek, Members of the Church of England, have by dint of self-denial and perseverance raised amongst themselves a sum of nearly a thousand dollars. With this they have erected the frame of a new and commodious Church, roofed it in, and partially boarded up the sides. An appeal is now made to all Members of the Church and others who are ready to help those who help themselves to assist in the completion of the work so well begun.

Subscriptions will be received by the Ven. Archdeacon Wyatt. 26 April, 1881. [*Royal Gazette*, 30 Apr 1881]

THE DECLINE OF HOPETOWN

By 1891 the population of Chinese at Hopetown had dwindled to 240 people, less than half of the 567 settlers who had gone there 20 years earlier. When the supply of timber and the demand for charcoal both diminished the people began to move away.

Fredrick O. Low, the first local-born Chinese barrister-at-law later gave several reasons for the decline of Hopetown. Many were attracted to the more populous Georgetown where the opportunity for getting ahead seemed greater. The younger generations were also less inclined to till the soil or to engage in strenuous manual labour. The Chinese failed to plant permanent crops such as cocoa and coffee apparently because they were unfamiliar with these trees. Furthermore, with the land being granted as a whole unit rather than allocated to each person holding individual title, there was less motivation to engage in an agricultural venture requiring five or more years to bear fruit so that the potential of inheriting the cultivated plots never became an incentive for the later generations to remain in Hopetown.

In 1900, Ho-A-Shoo, a immigrant who had become successful in business, suggested that the Chinese settlement at Hopetown be properly drained by canals. The cost of the work was estimated to be $10,000 and Ho-A-Shoo felt that he could raise a half of it from the Chinese community. This project did not come to fruition, however, most likely because interest in Hopetown had withered away. Ho-A-Shoo did put up $250 toward the construction of a dam to enclose about 523 acres, estimated to cost a total of $500. The dam was completed on 21 May 1902 at an actual cost of $642.98.

In 1901 there were 198 Chinese recorded in Hopetown and by 1911 the population was down to 37 men and 36 women. On 11 October 1914 Cecil Clementi, Government Secretary, visited Hopetown and commented:

> The people appeared glad to see us and anxious to show us round. The whole village accompanied us, as we went "aback" of the houses to look at the cultivation, but nowhere was anything satisfactory to be seen; a few miserable plantains, a few poor cocoa bushes, untended and uncared for, was all we could observe. A paddy-field, to which we were led, was merely a clearing in the bush, the trees having been cut down, but the stumps left standing, and no attempt made to irrigate or drain; there had been no manuring, or indeed any sign of tillage. The sight was a sad one to eyes accustomed to the smiling, carefully tended rice-fields of China, with their neatly dammed divisions for conserving water, fields from which the laborious Cantonese, by unceasing toil, reap their annual reward of two rice harvests and one crop of "dry cultivation." The Hopetown settlers told us they could only raise a rice crop from the given area once in five years; but with care the land could, of course, be made much more productive. The settlement possesses no animals; not even a pig, so universal in China, was to be seen. In fact the people evidently lack the energy to make an effort to improve their condition. Most young Chinese desirous of better things, have doubtless discovered that by going to Georgetown, they can with the thrift, industry and business instincts of their race find more promising opportunities of making a living, by trade or otherwise, than Hopetown offers them. Hence only the aged, the feeble or the indolent remain in the Settlement.

CHAPTER 9

GOING FURTHER AFIELD

BECOMING FREE

After the Chinese indentured labourer had completed his term of service he became "entitled to demand and receive from the Immigration Agent-General" a Certificate of Industrial Residence to show that he was now free of indentured obligation. For a while the *Royal Gazette* printed the names of those who had become free, both Chinese and Indian, but the practice came to a halt after a few years. The following are a few abbreviated lists taken from these public announcements which show the immigrant's name, passenger number on the boat, name of the boat, and estate to which he was indentured.

Ong Chwan	44	Samuel Bodington	Malgre Tout
Yung-i	57	Whirlwind	Enmore

[*Royal Gazette*, 17 Apr 1862]

Ng-a-Yong	54	Gen Wyndham	Better Hope
Lim Kon	86	Lord Elgin 1853	Blankenburg
Zoung-a-loke	1103	Claramont 1861	Skeldon
Lui-a-wun	975	Norwood 1860	Greenfield

[*Royal Gazette*, 15 Jan 1863]

Wong-a-qui	72	Royal George	Windsor Forest
Yeung-soi-on	2835	Lancs. Witch	Versailles
Chow-a-poo	405	Persia 1862	Zeelandia
Sui-a-Sam	850	Minerva 1860	Perserverance
Shak-ng	2233	Mystery 1861	Beehive

[*Royal Gazette*, 6 Feb 1864]

The opportunity to enter into another contract of indenture was always available and some did indeed sign on for a subsequent term, typically for five years. Eventually though, even these second-term indentured Chinese labourers joined the majority who chose to make a go of it on their own away from the plantation. Of the few who remained with the estates several became headmen or drivers for the work parties, employed in these positions because of their demonstrated organizational and leadership abilities. In one case a Chinese immigrant, Pim-a-Min, had been recruited to become a driver even before leaving China. He arrived on the *Dartmouth* in 1879 and was engaged at the promised position on plantation Anna Regina for which he was paid an attractive wage of $15 per month. However, after three months he was dismissed and sent into the fields. Pim-a-Min took his grievance to court.

> The Magistrate said it was no fault of the immigrant if he was engaged in China and sent here as headman when he was not fit for the place, that he thought he was entitled to his wages as headman.
>
> Judgment was given in favour of the Plaintiff for $17 48 without costs. [*Royal Gazette*, 6 May 1880]

Pim-a-Min was fortunate to obtain some recompense for his incompetence and the estate's representative gave notice that he would appeal the verdict.

Besides suitability for the job, gaining a reputation as a stable, honest and hard-working person was a personal characteristic held in high regard, and it paid off for Yip-tak-Wo, who

> was indicted for having on the 20th August last, burglariously broken into the dwelling house of Jagadoo, a free Coolie, and stolen a box or trunk containing one chain, three silk shirts, one wrapper, one shawl, and . . . money.
>
> [The defense declared that] the prisoner was a man of established character who had been a rural constable for seven years, and a driver on the estate for a considerable term. . . . Mr. Scott, the Manager of Peter's Hall, also was called and stated that the prisoner had been employed upon the estate ever since he undertook the management in 1865; that he had latterly been employed as a driver, repeatedly as an overseer of punt loaders, was an excellent workman, and, so far as he knew, an honest man.
>
> The jury, after a few minutes consideration, returned a verdict of Not Guilty and the prisoner was discharged. [*Royal Gazette*, 6 Feb 1872]

Being a driver carried significant responsibility and the drivers were classified as Rural Constables. In official status, they joined those who were on the beat helping to maintain law and order in the villages and countryside. From time to time a list of the Rural Constables was published in the *Royal Gazette*.

Pln Wales — Chung-a-Dun
Haarlem — You-a-luck
La Jalousie — Nag-a-Man
Blankenburg — Chu-a-Chung
Met-en-Meerzorg — Ling-chung-Ping, Leong-a-Tong, Lum-a-Sak, Yung-a-Sang
De Kinderen — Ong-a-Sack
Pln Success — Tan-a-Fai, Leung-a-Fuk
Peter's Hall — Liu-Kou-Chin, Tong-You, Leung-king-chung, Yip-tak-Woo, Lang-a-Chee
Pln Morfarm — Low-a-man
Pln Perseverance — Chung-kung-tong. [*Royal Gazette*, 8 Feb 1872]

Although there were a number of Chinese Rural Constables they were in fact estate employees. Only a few Chinese took up a career in law enforcement and on occasion there were reports of situations involving Chinese police officers. In 1882 a Chinese police detective was involved with the capture of several Chinese trying to leave the colony illegally. Also in that year P.C. Ho-a-You was involved in an assault in Georgetown in which he was the alleged victim, but when he brought a charge against his assailant the case was dismissed by the court. Apparently Police Constable 416 Ho-a-You was prone to taking a beating, for in the following year he brought a charge against Jose Gomes who had "assaulted and beaten him whilst in the execution of his duty."

> Other witnesses were examined whose evidence supported the statement that the police struck the defendant several blows. At the conclusion of the case, His Worship observed that there was some doubt in the evidence, and he would give the defendant the benefit of it. The case was dismissed. [*Royal Gazette*, 14 Aug 1883]

Sugar Technologists

There were other employment opportunities on the estate particularly those related to the technology of converting the sugar cane into marketable products. The labourers who showed ability to undertake skilled and technical jobs were given training in sugar processing as well as distilling for rum production. In one case the trained employee was skilled enough to become a prime candidate for recruitment by a rival estate.

Copy.

Plantn. Wales, 13th Sept., 1877

Dear Chew, —As I know that you are free and I will require a Distiller here on 23rd instant, if you will come I'll give you six bits per day for one month, and after that I'll pay you seven bits per day to look after Distillery alone when grinding, and when not grinding you can mark packages at 4 cents each, and plenty of other work I can always find for you. If you accept of the offer write and let me know as soon as possible when you'll come. I would like you to take over work here on the 18th or 19th of this month. In haste,

I remain
Yours truly
(Syd.) F. Farnum

Yim Ying Chew, (Chinese)
Blankenburg, West Coast.

Blankenburg, 18th Sept., 1877

Dear Mayers — The original of which the enclosed is a copy having fallen into my hands, I intend publishing in both of our colonial newspapers as a specimen of Planters' morality. As you are however directly interested, I think it only fair to give you an opportunity of clearing up the matter, reserving to myself the right of publishing the entire correspondence.

I do not for one moment think Mr. Farnum consulted you before attempting to entice away the man Yim Ying Chew from here, but having evidently entrusted your interests to his keeping you are of course responsible for his acts, and that his act on this occasion is dishonourable, is evident from the fact of his having been ashamed to direct the envelope himself, but had to resort to that most questionable of "dodges" — getting some illiterate person to write the address for him; unfortunately he had not sufficiently educated "dear Chew" when here to understand the "dodge."

I shall send all the papers I may have for publication on Saturday next, 22nd Inst. In haste.

Very sincerely yours
D.C. Cameron, Jr.

B. Meyers, Esq — Pln *Wales*

Wales, 20th September, 1877

My dear Cameron — Yours of the 18th, I have received to-day. Mr. Farnum my building overseer, did not consult me before opening his correspondence with dear "Chew," had he done so I certainly should not have allowed it.

I instructed Mr. Farnum to look out for some one to work the distillery on this estate, but was not aware of his predilection for "dear Chew" until your letter *reached me* to-day. I have not yet seen "dear Chew," when I do I'll send him back to you.

Yours sincerely

(Sgd.) J.B. Mayers.

Donald C. Cameron Jnr., Esq
Blankenburg

21st

(P.S.) Since writing the above I have seen "dear Chew" and he says he prefers "dear Farnum" to "dear Cameron."

You may publish this, as it speaks volumes for Chinese Immigration to the "Magnificent Province." [*Royal Gazette*, 25 Sep 1877]

This matter of an exchange of personnel caught the eye of a reader who enjoined:

Sir, — It is reported that when Mr. Cameron discovered that his Chinese distiller had been coqueting with Mr. Mayers, he struck an attitude, and exclaimed like the dying Caesar, "Et *Chew*, Brute"!

It is the first Latin quotation, and the most successful pun of which "dear Cameron" has been guilty.

Yours truly

QUID PRO *CHEW*

[*Royal Gazette*, 29 Sep 1877]

In another situation, a Chinese who had risen in position to become head distiller made the almost fatal mistake of lighting up his product.

Explosion at La Grange.

The evidence now taken consisted of that of a Chinaman named Kow, who at the time of the accident was employed as head distiller of the estate, and who sustained such injuries thereby so to necessitate his being confined to the hospital. . . . When questioned as to the immediate cause of the explosion he admitted that it was through his fault, as he had unwittingly indulged in the silly act of taking a lighted lamp close to the machinery in which rum was being manufactured, thus causing the liquid to ignite and a portion of the machinery to explode. [He said he did not know of the danger. One person died from the explosion.]

[*Royal Gazette*, 6 May 1880]

While the opportunities for skilled technical workers were limited, the need for field labourers still remained at a very high level. In 1872 the manager of Great Diamond estate decided to go public with an offer of money and land to free Chinese who would take on another term of indenture.

VERY IMPORTANT NOTICE
TO *FREE* CHINESE OR OTHER
FREE IMMIGRANTS

The Undersigned hereby gives notice that the Immigration Agent will visit the *Great Diamond* Estate on Wednesday, the 14th instant, to pay Bounty to Re-indentured Immigrants, and that he will be prepared to receive any number up to 100 Chinese, or other *respectable* Immigrants who may be willing to enter into agreements for five years.

Half an acre of good provision land adjoining the extensive lot of land now under labourers' provisions will be allotted to each Immigrant, besides the other usual privileges.

EDMUND FIELD, Manager
Great Diamond, 2nd Feby, 1872.

[*Royal Gazette*, 8 Feb 1872]

TRAVELS TO TRINIDAD

This appealing offer of money and land must undoubtedly have caused many to sign up, although some of them had different ideas about what to do with the windfall.

Yesterday, a batch of eight Chinese Immigrants newly re-indentured in the colony were arrested on board the French Steamer, in which they had taken out passage to sail for Trinidad. It is not an uncommon occurrence for immigrants to hang about on estate till the re-indenture cheque for $50 is safe in their pockets, and then to depart to lie in hiding till the Police or the Immigration Agents bring them to light in some quarter or other, but this is the first time we have heard of their making use of the newly acquired cheque to purchase an outfit, and pay their passage to another colony. It is a fortunate thing for the planters in general that the first attempt to leave the colony clandestinely, immediately after receipt of the indenture bounty, was strangled at once, for success of the first lot might have induced others to follow suit. It seems very strange that the French Steamer Captain should have allowed these men to come on board without asking for their free tickets as he should have done; and if they did not deceive him by showing stolen tickets, he is much to blame. There would be little safeguard against shipmates, if the captains of steamers trading here, neglected the precaution to ask for the passes of all the immigrants who sought passage in their vessels; and unless the police made a point of inspecting the various steamers before their departure, a number of estates' labourers might be outside the bar before their departure might be discovered and reported at the proper quarter. No doubt the case just noticed will be fully investigated and if it is found that the Captain was really to blame he will readily deserve to be mulcted in the heaviest fine the law prescribes for the offence.

[*Royal Gazette*, 4 Jun 1872]

A number of Chinese had a strong interest in traveling to Trinidad where the environment was significantly different. In British Guiana the Portuguese, who had preceded the Chinese as indentured labourers, had now become the predominant group in merchandising and trade. However, in Trinidad there was not an established ethnic group which dominated the middle economy and the opportunities for getting ahead as shopkeepers and merchants over there were better. The majority of immigrants who had gone directly from China to Trinidad had arrived at the same time as they did in British Guiana but they were making faster progress in accumulating wealth in Trinidad.

Report from Trinidad: The Chinese, to judge from those already brought to this island, is of a more aspiring character [than the Indian immigrant]. In the great number of instances he redeems his indentured service before its expiration, and passes into employments requiring greater mental activity. Of those introduced in 1853, very few, if any, now remain in the condition of agricultural labourers. They have become shopkeepers, or they cultivate land on their own account. Already, even beyond Arima, large spaces of ground are under cultivation by the Chinese in sweet potatoes and other vegetables.

There is another broad distinction between the East Indians and the Chinese. The former is essentially parsimonious and content with a low standard of food, and with little and cheap clothing. The latter has large and more varied wants, is indulgent of his appetites and tastes, and liberal in his expenditure. His standard of food is high, his holiday dress is of rich and varied materials. He earns money not to hoard but to spend it. He differs from the Indian in one point, most important to the community, of the conditions on which he is brought into the colony. He comes not as the Coolie for a limited term of years, and with the right, on the expiration of that term, to a return passage at the public expense, but as a settler for life. [*Royal Gazette*, 25 Aug 1860]

From the *Port of Spain Gazette*: According to the General Census for 1861 the number of Chinese was 460. In reference to these the Agent-General states that they have now become incorporated with the other inhabitants of the Colony; many have married and are comfortably settled with their families; these are in almost every instance traders; not a few are comparatively affluent, and among the number is one man who has been sickly and unsuccessful as a labourer, but who now has about $4,000 acquired in retail trade, and proposes to return shortly to China. [*Royal Gazette*, 26 Jun 1862]

The government authorities in British Guiana clearly recognized the differences between the two colonies as far as the opportunities for entering into the merchandising business was concerned:

There was not the smallest doubt that there was a wide difference between the condition of the free Chinese here and the condition of the free Chinese in Trinidad. . . . [The Governor] had been in Port of Spain and he asserted that no one could help noticing the appearance of the Chinese there. They were an improving and pushing class of people. The free Chinese were in fact what the Portuguese were in this Colony when they were extremely industrious, and a thriving and prosperous class. [*Royal Gazette*, 2 Feb 1865]

The field which is open to Chinese as traders, in Trinidad, is closed to them in this colony. It is already well filled by the Industrious Portuguese population. [*Royal Gazette*, 3 Feb 1865]

WEALTHY COOLIES — Under this head the *Trinidad Chronicle* has the following: -

Atteck, a Chinaman, also a Mission shopkeeper and property holder, is considered to be worth £12,000. He is now a Christian; as is the next, also a Chinaman, Soni, alias Daniel O'Connel, reputed be worth half as much as Atteck. His wealth is also in shop and house property. [*Royal Gazette*, 1 Feb 1877]

SAUNTERING TO SURINAM

For those who had completed their indenture the possibility of going abroad had always been an option for consideration. A significant number did indeed venture abroad and the resulting loss of manpower, particularly to territories competing in the sugar trade, was considered to be a very serious matter by the plantation owners and the government. After 15 Indian labourers were caught on a Dutch Steamer headed for Surinam the government pondered the best way of trying to retain workers who were free and had every right to leave. It was curiously decided to utilize the Passengers' Act, which enabled a penalty of one hundred pounds sterling to be imposed on offenders.

> His Excellency issued a Proclamation in which it was declared that the length of the voyage of any vessel conveying passengers from this Colony to Surinam should, for the purposes of the Passengers' Act — that is, in regard to the scale of diet — be taken to be ten days. . . . The passage can always be made within two days.
>
> [*Royal Gazette*, 24 Sep 1863]

It is unlikely that this act had any great deterrent value since there continued to be a steady flow of labourers from British Guiana to Surinam, even though several had taken the return journey after discovering that the grass in Surinam was no greener.

> On the 25th, last month, nine Chinese arrived in Surinam by the Schooner Lady of the Night, with the intention of becoming field labourers. If these immigrants have closed their term of service in British Guiana, no reasonable objection can be made to their leaving here for another Colony where they have reason to believe that the labour-market is very promising, but it is not unlikely that they too will regret the change, after a time, and return to us. [*Royal Gazette*, 10 Dec 1867]

> We have recently ascertained that a large number of [Creole labourers] have left Nickerie and returned to this Colony. They report that provisions are 25 per cent dearer than in this Colony; that at times work is scarce, and not only have they have to pay for a passport in the first instance, but the frequent exhibition of it is annoying. It is well that the experiment has been made. These people have looked for greater things in Surinam, and they have found to their cost that they are better

off in their own Colony. Their experience will open the eyes of others, and lead to a good result. [*Royal Gazette*, 21 Dec 1867]

The need for labourers in Surinam became so great that the plantation owners there were willing to put up high stakes to attract labourers from British Guiana. The incentives resulted in the emergence of a recruiting system with agents being dispatched from Surinam specifically to procure labourers. These methods inevitably led some labourers into making the attempt to leave British Guiana illegally.

At the Police Magistrate's Court this morning, a Chinaman was fined $24, with the alternative of two months' imprisonment with hard labour for harbouring another Chinaman with the intention of taking him to Surinam. A Coolie and a Chinaman were charged with attempting to leave the colony without having first given a fortnight's notice to the Immigration Agent-General, as was required by the Ordinance, and were remanded till to-morrow. These immigrants form part of a lot of 24 Chinese and 14 Coolies who were captured on Saturday night last by Sergeant Birch, on board a sloop called the Prince of Wales, bound for Surinam. The practice of illegally smuggling immigrants from this colony to Surinam for a tempting reward which is not very often obtained after the immigrants have been secured there, seems to be gaining ground here, and the speculators in this illicit traffic seem at present to be many. Why only a couple of weeks ago, a schooner, having about fourteen immigrants on board, was riding at anchor ready to start for Surinam. An attempt was made to board her, but the captain, having his weather-eye open, immediately raised anchor, and in a short time was out of the reach of pursuit. [*Royal Gazette*, 17 Jun 1873]

Four more convictions were obtained in the Police Magistrate's Court to-day against Chinese for harbouring immigrants with the purpose of helping them to leave the colony surreptitiously. The fine in each case was the extreme penalty the law allows, that is twenty-four dollars. This fine in no way can be considered sufficiently heavy for the offence. Compared with the fines imposable for other offences, as for instance breach of the Reverence Laws, it is a fleabite and can scarcely be expected to act as a deterrent on men who can make double the amount of the fine by the successful shipment of one immigrant. We believe it came out in evidence in one of the cases just tried that the agreement with the Surinam people, provides a fee of forty dollars to the Agent for each man sent, and a bounty of a like amount to every immigrant who proceeds to Surinam. The business is thus made a lucrative one for the Chinese Agents, and they naturally push it with all their national vigour. Information has been received here that several Chinese are coming over on the First Dutch Steamer, provided with a large amount of specie for the express purpose of engaging immigrant labourers. These men cannot be arrested on their arrival, and it will require the utmost vigilance of the Police to intercept the departure of the people whom they are sure to prevail on by the power of money, to break their engagements with their employers here, and proceed to Surinam. To put a stop to this unfair and dishonourable traffic, it is useless appealing to the Surinam planters; the best way is to make the penalty for abducting immigrants sufficiently heavy to render the business too risky and unprofitable for the Agents to undertake it. The matter is one in every way closely connected with the interests of the Colony and the individual members of the Elective Members of the Court, that we may expect to see it receiving early attention. [*Royal Gazette*, 21 Jun 1873]

On Saturday night the 14th instant, Sergeant Birch boarded the sloop Prince of Wales while it was lying in Cordes' canal in Charlestown, and captured and detained 24 Chinese and 14 Coolies, who, in consequence of very seductive promises which had been held out to them as to wages, were about to sail for Surinam in the sloop. The defendant was not on board at the time, and has not been seen since; but it is clearly established that he was the captain of the vessel. . . . Two of the Coolies who formed part of the lot captured, and who are now in confinement at the Brick-dam Station, stated that they were to sail for Surinam the very night Sergeant Birch went on board, they having been "fooled," as one of them expressed it, into the belief that they would get "too much money" when they arrived there. [The Magistrate decided] to impose upon the defendant a penalty of $3,800, being $100 for each immigrant. . .

[*Royal Gazette*, 24 Jun 1873]

Yo-a-Fot, Yong-a-Fat and three other indentured Chinamen were charged with having attempted to leave the colony with the French steamer, without being provided with a passport. . . . The detective police officer, a Chinaman, who caught them in the attempt of leaving the colony, and to whom they gave a gold ring, as hush-price, was examined and corroborated the fact for which they were prosecuted. . . . The Magistrate quoting the law on the point, and looking at it that the defendants had come here in 1879, according to certificates from the Immigration department before him, and were leaving the colony before

> the residue of their indenture time was expired, fined each the sum of $12. [*Royal Gazette*, 26 Aug 1882]

These attempts show the lucrative rewards available to those who were plying an authorized trade with nearby countries and who switched to transporting illegal passengers. There were others who made use of more clandestine methods for which an organized network was set up for recruiting and transporting the labourers.

> It appears that boats of a sloop class, which are intended for this particular trade, generally take in cargoes of shell for estates on the East Coast, and that after discharging, they run down to some convenient point on the coast previously selected and agreed upon, where they receive large numbers of immigrants, Coolies and Chinese, who, according to previous arrangement, hang about or conceal themselves near the spot till the boat is ready. [*Royal Gazette*, 26 Jul 1873]

A glimpse of the Chinese community across the border in Surinam was given by Archdeacon Wyatt who paid a visit in April/May 1876 to the English-speaking labourers there.

> Among the congregation I observed a number of Chinese. I have since heard that they were a part of a Chinese congregation at Skeldon, who had crossed over to Dutch territory in search of work.
>
> . . . There were several Chinese present with their catechist, who had come over from Skeldon to teach his countrymen who are settled in the district. He presented three adults for baptism; I found that they could read their own language, were acquainted with the baptism service, and understood the engagements they were undertaking. It took me of course some time to satisfy myself on these points, for neither the candidates nor the catechist could readily converse in English. It is worthy of record that this catechist is working among his countrymen, trudging from estate to estate, without any fixed stipend, his only means of subsidence being such voluntary offerings as they can contribute out of their weekly earnings in the canepiece.
>
> In the Nicerie district several of the proprietors, as well as the principal managers of the estate, have all along been Englishmen; and between these gentlemen and their friends on the English side there may have been frequent exchange of visits. . . [*Royal Gazette*, 8 Feb 1877]

SAILING TO ST. LUCIA

Surinam happened to be the closest place readily accessible to those determined to go Dutch. However, other nearby countries also dangled the hope for a better life. Even the Immigration Office was involved in the exodus.

> A case of some importance to the agricultural interest of the Colony was heard to-day before the Police Magistrate of Georgetown. A Chinaman named Lung-a-yung was charged . . . with collecting and engaging seventeen Chinese, being persons of the labouring class, to proceed to another colony, to wit, St. Lucia, without being duly licenced by the Governor as an agent for that purpose. . . .
>
> It seemed that Mr. Des Voeux the Administrator of the Government of St. Lucia, sent the defendant to this colony to procure Chinese labourers to go to St. Lucia. . . . The money which was required for the payment of these people's passage was sent by Mr. Des Voeux to the Immigration Agent General, and between Mr. Des Voeux and the Immigration Agent General, the colony was deprived, in this way, of a certain amount of labourers. . . . [Lum-a-yung] went to St. Lucia some time ago and returned to the Colony on 22nd July. He came to the Immigration one day in this month . . . and said that he had some Chinese going to St. Lucia, and that he wanted some money to pay their passage with. [Mr. Crosby] . . . drew a cheque for $173.25 on the Colonial Bank. [Lum-a-yung] said that Mr. Des Voeux wanted them to teach the people how to burn charcoal, and had said that they would be able to "make railway" there. Two dollars were paid, in addition to the passage money, to each man for his own use on board the steamer (*Corsica*).
>
> Mr. Brumell held that the offense was clearly proved and inflicted a fine upon the defendant of $96, to be recovered by distress, and in default of sufficient distress, to be imprisoned for six months with hard labour. [*Royal Gazette*, 29 Sep 1874]

What was most irksome in this case was that Mr. James Crosby, the Immigration Agent-General since 1862, could have been involved. The *Royal Gazette*, in its editorial, was indignant and proposed that Crosby "be granted $600 to retire."

> Mr. Crosby himself does not deny that he was the principal agent in the matter, but shelters himself under the plea that he was *ignorant of the law*. Now considering that it is Mr. Crosby's duty to be acquainted with the law, that he himself is a lawyer, and that he has acted as a Puisne

> Judge in our Courts on more than one occasion, and for considerable periods of time, this plea of ignorance is, to say the least, a remarkable and not over credible one. That the Immigration Agent General of British Guiana should be permitted to become Emigration Agent for the Government of St. Lucia, should use his influence to entice away from the Colony labourers who have been brought here at enormous expense to the Colony, should attempt to depopulate this Colony, that St. Lucia may be populated, is altogether too monstrous an idea to be entertained for a moment. [*Royal Gazette*, 6 Oct 1874]

James Crosby managed to weather this storm and continued to hold office as Immigration Agent-General until his death in September 1880 after a long illness. In making the retrospective report for 1879, Mr. Trotter, the succeeding Immigration Agent-General, stated that passports were issued to 104 East Indians and 299 Chinese (251 men, 23 women, and 25 children) permitting them to leave the British Guiana. The annual report indicated that the passport holders were

> "supposed to have left the colony, some to visit Trinidad and Cayenne, and others to visit Surinam." We believe it is perfectly well known that the destination of the great majority, (of the Chinese, at all events) was the Surinam Goldfields, and it is notorious that a great number of other Chinese immigrants, not entitled to passports, including many who arrived only last year in the Dartmouth, have made their way thither overland, via the Correntyne Coast and Nickerie, not as Mr. Trotter implies, with the intention of paying a mere visit, but of remaining permanently if they find gold-digging sufficiently lucrative.
> [*Royal Gazette*, 2 Dec 1880]

The authorized emigration of Chinese persons from British Guiana was not filled with fanfare and from time to time the shipping reports would show the departure of a number of "Chinese" and "deckers" who were traveling economy class, or steerage. Second class passengers were given the privilege of an entry by name in the shipping announcements:

> Per Royal Mail Steamer *Corsica* on the 6th instant for Colon: Mr. Fung-a-wa, Mr. Leu-quay. [*Royal Gazette*, 23 May 1876]

> Per French Mail Steamer *Venezuela* for Surinam and Cayenne: Wong-shee-que, Pow-shee, Tong-a-pu, Lo-a-how.
> [*Royal Gazette*, 28 Feb 1878]

For Trinidad: Li-a-wing, Li-a-Kong, Ha-a-Kwai.
[*Royal Gazette*, 23 Apr 1878]

For Havana: Dr. Chung Kwook On and Mr. Cheung-hon-ting.
[*Royal Gazette*, 25 Jul 1878]

For Baltimore: 15 adult and 4 infant Chinese passengers.
[*Royal Gazette*, 23 Aug 1881]

For Jamaica: Choo-lan-Ying, Choong-a-Yang and Ng-She.
[*Royal Gazette*, 9 Mar 1882]

Travel to the Panamanian port of Colon and to Baltimore would have been chosen by those seeking to return to China via North America, although some did settle in Panama, especially after digging of the Panama Canal began in 1881. The flow of Chinese out of British Guiana continued for many years and contributed significantly to the reduction in their population. For example, in 1883 there were 20 Chinese who arrived from other countries in the region, but 251 departed the colony that year.

A number of Chinese leaving the colony chose to return to China and this induced some businessmen to offer the opportunity to organize a chartered voyage to China.

NOTICE
As it is intended to send about the end of June next
VESSEL TO CHINA

Parties desiring a Passage will be good enough to communicate with Manoel Gonsalves & Co., or I.H. De Jong, in Georgetown; or Ho-Ha-Hin, Storekeeper, New Amsterdam.

It is proposed that the same vessel will return to Demerara with Passengers and Immigration after a stay of a month in China.

Demerara 11th March, 1881

[*Royal Gazette*, 15 Mar 1881]

It is not known whether there were sufficient takers for the boat to China since no further reference of a ship departing for China was evident in the following months.

The Settlers

Those who decided to remain in British Guiana tried their hands at an assortment of ventures, but particularly in the retail trade. As mentioned in an earlier chapter, the potential for the Chinese to become important players in the middle economy had been predicted even before any of them arrived in British Guiana. In 1861, eight years after the Chinese first arrived, a traveler from England related:

> I am creditably informed of one Portuguese gentleman, who now owns two or three estates and much house property in Georgetown. He was originally an indentured agricultural labourer. Walking up and down Water Street and Queen's Road of Georgetown, we see numerous small stores owned by Portuguese, and is it too much to expect that the dollar-worshipping Chinaman will in due time get his share of the loaves and fishes? He must not, however, expect everything to be *coleur de rose*, or to obtain the advantages I have pictured without a fair amount of toil and labour. [*Royal Gazette*, 24 October 1861]

The arrival of a wave of indentured Chinese labourers in British Guiana the following year became the subject of a commentary in the *Daily Press* of Hong Kong, which predicted that the Chinese would do well even in the face of competition by the Portuguese. The *Royal Gazette* quoted the article and then extended the discussion:

> "Now in Demerara it pays well to pay Chinese to go, and if they only want a market for their labour there is an unlimited one for them. We have more than once prognosticated great results from Chinese emigration to British Guiana. We extract the following from the *Georgetown Gazette* (Demerara) of 17th Sept. last. It is a summary of the progress of the Portuguese in the colony of British Guiana. The perusal of this really surprised us — if the word "*Chinese*" had been substituted for *Portuguese* the account would have been a stereotype of the history of the former wherever they have obtained a footing. The two races will now have to enter into competition and if the Chinaman does not carry the day, his competitor must be a very different breed to any Portuguese or other European that we ever saw. The statement very fully proves the existence of the field for Chinese in that country which we stated our opinion would be found in the West India colonies generally. . . ."
>
> Here we see that the Editor of the *Daily Press*, who, from residing in China has or ought to have a good knowledge of the people, predicts that before long our Chinese Immigrants will enter into competition with the Portuguese Shop-keepers of this Colony, and probably with success. The Chinese bear the character of being not only ingenious but industrious,

but when we look at the privations to which the Portuguese dealers voluntarily submit in the way of food and clothing, the personal toil, which they undergo, and their close attention to business, it is scarcely to be credited that they can be beaten out of the field by any other people, however clever and hard-working these may be. Here and there we see a Coolie shop, but we have heard of only two or three instances in which the Coolie speculator has been able to do much more than keep his head above water. It might be different with the Chinese, but as yet they have not been tested, although one enterprising individual has established a shop somewhere in the country — we believe in Plaisance. We heard him assert, some time ago, that, if he could find support, he would import from China many articles which would find a ready market, and that he felt satisfied he would be able to drive a good trade. This is plausible enough, but we have very strong doubts whether the Chinese could venture with any great prospect of success in the particular department selected by the Portuguese. It is also a query whether the Chinese imported here are the sort of people likely to become Shop keepers; if they are, they cannot be the effective labourers which — by some sort of fiction — they are supposed to be; and if they are not, there is little chance of their verifying the prediction of the Editor of the *Daily Press*.

[*Royal Gazette*, 29 Mar 1862]

GETTING DOWN TO BUSINESS

The opinion of the *Royal Gazette* was based on the fact that the Portuguese were well established as merchants and traders and would be tough competitors to beat. The Chinese though were willing to work hard at gaining a foothold in the marketplace and were capable of adjusting to the prevailing conditions.

The Heathen Chinee.

"John" has the reputation of being a great cheat, but I am inclined to think that, in common with other races we charge with the same vice, he is what we have made him. For an example — John comes into the yard of a suburban residence one morning with his basket of vegetables. "Carbagee!" cries John, thereby meaning vegetables generally and cabbages in particular. "Well, John," says the lady of the house, coming out to his baskets, "what have you this morning?" "Ebbyting, mum," says John, showing his yellow teeth in a broad grin. The lady selects a bunch of turnips, and says: "How much John?" "Fourpenny," says John. The lady looks inexpressible shocked and drops the turnips.

"Too dear, John — much too dear. You mean twopenny. I give you twopenny; that's all — you savvie?" "No, no! Me no savvie twopenny — treepenny," holding up three bony and long-nailed fingers. And so they fence for some time, until the lady at last retrieves triumphantly to her kitchen, having secured the turnips for twopence halfpenny, and "John" moves on contentedly, knowing full well that, had he asked for twopence halfpenny in the first instance, he would have been beaten down to three halfpence. [*Royal Gazette*, 2 Sep 1885]

One example of how the Chinese coped with the challenge in British Guiana was the way they fared in the charcoal market where they went into direct competition with the Portuguese. Charcoal began to be produced by a more efficient and economical process at the Chinese settlement of Hopetown. The wood was obtained from the surrounding area by licence:

Li-wi-chi and Chung Lin — [granted wood cutting licences] for 157½ acres on the right bank of Camoenie Creek.
[*Royal Gazette*, 8 Mar 1877]

William Choung — [granted a wood cutting licence] for 200 acres on the Left Bank of Werywery Creek, Camoenie Creek.
[*Royal Gazette*, 6 Feb 1883]

A description of the production process was given by a visitor to Dunoon village, also situated on the Demerara River, not too far distant from Hopetown.

Several ranges have been built for the accommodation of labourers, and already enterprising Portuguese and Celestials have started opposition retail shops.

A short distance up the creek we found some Chinese burning coal of the estate in an *oven*, — a most peculiar contrivance, and one that I saw for the first time. It was circular in shape, built of clay, the top rising in the shape of a dome. The logs of wood are brought in at a large opening left on one side, and are closely packed *on end*. Another opening serves as a furnace, and four small holes in the roof answer for chimneys. When the oven has been well packed the large hole is blocked up, and the fire made in the quasi-furnace — the smoke and steam escaping through the apertures in the roof. The wood is thus literally baked into coal, the waste being trifling. [*Royal Gazette*, 28 Feb 1884]

The charcoal industry provided employment and wealth not only to the manufacturers but also to the woodcutters in the area, the shippers taking the product to Georgetown, and the distributors and merchants of charcoal. The Chinese even went so far as to acquire property on the riverbank in the vicinity of Georgetown where they could land the charcoal. The more efficient method of production of charcoal made it feasible for the investment in the landing dock without unduly affecting the price of charcoal in the market. The Chinese were thus able to compete successfully with the long established Portuguese merchants. The volume and price of the charcoal even made it an export commodity to islands in the Caribbean.

The competition sharpened further in 1877 when, under orders from the Municipal Council, barricades were erected preventing access to the Le Repentir Canal, a public waterway south of Georgetown. The Council had earlier made the decision that the canal needed to be filled in so as to better drain the Charlestown district of the city. Up to this time the Portuguese charcoal producers had also been shipping their product from up-river but relied on the canal to land their product close to Georgetown. Faced with the loss of access to their traditional landing sites, some Portuguese merchants wrote a petition to the Municipal Council asking that docking facilities be built:

> "We would be willing and ready to rent the dock from the proper authorities at the rate of $50 per month, payable quarterly, for a number of years, or to pay a fee of one cent per barrel or sack of charcoal landed there. Our first-mentioned offer is contingent on dock accommodation being given for fifty bateaux at a time." [*Royal Gazette*, 15 Sep 1877]

The councilors denied the petition after the following discussion:

> Mr. Abraham: What have the Chinese done?
>
> Mr. Forshaw: They have provided their own private place.
>
> Mr. Abraham: The Chinese came a long time after the Portuguese, who have been in business here so long that they ought to have done the same as the Chinese. [*Royal Gazette*, 15 Sep 1877]

Another petition was received at the same session of the Municipal Council, this one from a group of Chinese seeking permission to expand their operations beyond the Stabroek, Bourda and Cummingsburg markets in Georgetown.

Bagot Town Village, East Bank 29th August, 1877

Sir,- We respectfully beg that you will place before the Council this application of ours for licence "to sell meat in other parts of Georgetown besides the Markets," as we have the supplying of several of our fellow Chinese in Georgetown with pork, which we slaughter at our place at Bagot Town, and then dispose of the same in the City.

We are led to make this application from the marks that have been reported as being started by you on the 27th, at a meeting of the Council.

We have the honour to be, Sir
Your obedient Servants
Wow-A-Kong
Chow-a-How

The Town Clerk was instructed to inform the petitioners that they must comply with the regulations. [*Royal Gazette*, 15 Sep 1877]

The situation was updated a few years later when the Council was briefed about current state of the meat market:

The Town Clerk then read a letter from Mr. Fairbain, the Chief of the Markets, in which he stated that with regard to the sale of fresh meat, as the law stood, section 177 of the Town Council Ordinance was unworkable (there being no penalty attached for a breach of it), so that butchers' meat was being sold all over the city without license or inspection, to the injury of the butchers' business in the markets and the probable danger of the consumers. [*Royal Gazette*, 19 Jan 1882]

In the absence of definitive information it would be very presumptuous to think that the Chinese butchers, under the circumstances of a growing demand for meat and the lack of penalty for infractions of the ordinance controlling meat sales, were party to these extra-market affairs. It is left for the reader to make a conclusion about the likely behavior of the Chinese entrepreneurs.

GROWING IN GEORGETOWN

The petitioners' reference to an increasing market demand among the Chinese in Georgetown reflects the growing population of Chinese who had taken up residence in the city. The news stories related in earlier chapters reveal that the Chinese were becoming involved in growing vegetables, provisions and rice, and in raising cattle and other livestock. Stores were opened, particularly in the Charlestown district, by Chinese entering the retail business and eventually in trading and wholesale. There were jewellry shops where gold and silver were melted and poured into moulds or drawn out into threads to be worked into fine jewelry. Tailors used paper patterns to cut and measure the cloth and provided the community with hand-made suits and dresses of the latest fashion. Others left their mark through fine cabinet making skills. Restaurants, bakeries and cook-shops supplied a variety of delicacies, with roast pork and noodle dishes becoming commonplace Chinese food items that gained acceptance among the general population. Different outlets were opened to provide customers with staple provisions — plantains, rice, yams, eddoes and cassava. Chinese also operated stores selling nuts, oils and coffee as well as vegetables, meats and poultry. Chinese medicines and the still legal opium could be purchased. The Georgetown community was provided with the services of a Chinese doctor, named Chun-choi-ching, who was "a medical practitioner duly qualified according to the laws in force in the dominions of His Celestial Majesty the Emperor of China." A certain degree of prosperity became evident among the Chinese.

> As a proof of the material prosperity of the Chinese settlers, we may mention that the funeral cortege of one of their countrymen, who was buried at Le Repentir yesterday, was composed of twenty-five carriages, all filled with Chinese. [*Royal Gazette*, 15 Feb 1877]

Carriages represented a visible testimony to the growing wealth of the Chinese. A prosperous Chinese businessman hosted a grand wedding followed by a sumptuous reception, for which a few dozen carriages were employed:

> The marriage of Mr. John Lum-chun and Miss Mary Tsen-ah-Kue was celebrated yesterday at St. Philip's Church, Werk-en-Rust, in the presence of a large number of Chinese residents in the city. Rev. Canon Castell officiated, assisted by Fong-qui-sue, cathecist at St. Saviour's Chinese Church, Charlestown. The male spectators were located in the southern portion of the nave of St. Philip's, and to the females was assigned the northern part. The service was choral throughout. The prayers and exhortations were repeated after the Incumbent in Chinese by the attendant cathecist. The ceremony concluded, a procession of

carriages, about 40, headed by the newly married couple in a close brougham, went through some of the principal thoroughfares of the city, *en route* for the "Rose of Sharon" Hall, Charlestown, where a splendid *dejeuner* was provided. It is said that the preparations for the repast were on a most elaborate scale, upwards of a dozen cooks having been employed for several days. At night Mr. Leung-Wo, father of the bridegroom, gave a grand ball to his workmen.

[*Daily Chronicle*, 12 Dec 1884]

Another outward indicator of their improvement in economic status was the acquisition of property, for both residential and commercial use. Not all of the property transactions were listed in the *Royal Gazette* and the following are just a few examples of the transfer of real estate.

By James Henry Osterbede, transport of west quarter of number 72 or west quarters 87 and 88 situate in Werk-en-Rust district, city of Georgetown, county of Demerary, with a building thereon — to and in favor of Koh-ting, a Chinese. [*Royal Gazette*, 12 Feb 1867]

In June 1870 Koh-ting sold this property "to the Honourable James Crosby."

By John Gomes, transport of lot number 59 . . . in Werk-en Rust district, in the city of Georgetown . . . to and in favor of Simon Leung, a free Chinese man, No 630, ex "Thomas Mitchell," 1860.

[*Royal Gazette*, 9 Jun 1877]

Simon Leung was an interpreter for the Immigration Office and he concluded his purchase by taking out a first mortgage on his property in favor of the Portuguese Benevolent Society of British Guiana, Limited.

Three merchant ventures that became prominent in Georgetown were Ho A-Shoo Ltd., Wo-Lee & Co. and Hoahing & Co., the last enterprise being a branch of the main operations based in New Amsterdam, Berbice. Ho A-Shoo Ltd. was named after its founder John Ho-A-Shoo. He started up a small store on the Demerara River and later acquired another business at Dunoon followed by a sugar estate. His big breakthrough came when the manager of the Barima Gold Mine asked if he would open a shop to serve the mining community in a remote area near the Venezuelan border. John Ho-A-Shoo took the chance and prospered so well that he opened further shops in other mining districts. He opened his Georgetown business in 1897 and became a well-known and wealthy entrepreneur.

Wo-Lee opened for business in June 1879, dealing in Chinese and Japanese goods, and placed an advertisement in the *Royal Gazette* announcing this new establishment. Lee Lun was one of the principals behind Wo-Lee and two years later the business premises were expanded.

> By Lee Lun, transport of the south east one third lot number 2, situate in Werk-en-Rust district . . . to and in favour of the said Lee Lun, Lee Lam, Lee Kang, Lee Fook Yen, and Ah-Chung, trading together in this colony in co-partnership under the name, style and firm of Wo-Lee and Company. [*Royal Gazette*, 5 Mar 1881]

Not much later, two of the partners were successful in a judgment against Chan-a-Moon and property belong to the latter was put up for auction by the Provost Marshal in settlement.

> In behalf of Lee-Lun and Chong-Soon-Chung carrying on business in this colony in co-partnership under the firm of Wo-Lee and Company, plaintiffs, versus Chan-a-Moon (a Chineseman), at present residing in the City of Georgetown, defendant:- 12 shell toilet ornaments, 11 sandal wood boxes, 1 tortoise shell box, 46 boxes, 43 fans, 16 tooth brushes, 5 towel rings, 2 cigar cases, 7 boxes turtle ornaments, 2 paper knives, a box valentine, 6 bottles sandal wood, 1 musical box, 5 Chinese caps, 2 Chinese tea pots, 3 large looking glasses, 2 small looking glasses, 4 fans (leaf), 2 baskets, 1 pair ear rings, 1 silver ring, 1 cabinet, 7 waiters, a lot of toys, the property of the defendant Chan-a-Moon.
> [*Royal Gazette*, 27 May 1882]

The items auctioned off show the variety of goods that were available in the Chinese stores. Chan-a-Moon was himself a trader and declared insolvency, causing the rest of his estate to be later put up for sale, including a lot of Chinese haberdashery.

Wo-Lee and Company grew further with the takeover of more property in the Charlestown district of Georgetown.

> We are informed that the property known as Chinese Quarters, Charlestown, Lot 25, recently purchased at Execution Sale by R.J. McKenzie and Lee-Lun of Wo-Lee and Company, has been taken over entirely by the latter, Mr. McKenzie having disposed of his half for a consideration. [*Royal Gazette*, 24 Apr 1884]

Other businesses that became recognized in Georgetown by 1890 included Kwan-Sun-Lung & Co., Man-A-Qui, Tian-Sun-Tong & Co., Hing-Cheong Co., and Low-A-Yan & Co.

One of the young immigrants who made a name for himself in the jewellry business was Joshua U A-hing. Brought by his parents, he arrived in British Guiana in 1861 when he was 13 years old and became a driver at Plantation Versailles. He then went to Goedverwagting where he became a panboiler, responsible for preparing the cane juice for the process of crystallization. He later became chief panboiler at Plantation Schoon Ord. In 1887 Joshua purchased a jeweller's business in Georgetown and his son Manoel U-hing became an apprentice to a goldsmith. Two years later Manoel took over the management of the business and it became known as M.U. Hing, Manufacturing Jeweller, which became one of the leading jewellry businesses in the country. His advertisements promoted nugget jewellry as a specialty, as well as brooches, scarf pins, bracelets, pendants, studs, earrings, hat pins and solid chased bangles.

Alongside M.U. Hing's store was that of Chin-A-Yong, a wholesale and retail grocer, whose premises was used for storing and selling fireworks. On 22 December, 1913, a small explosion was heard followed by a much larger one coming from Chin-A-Yong's premises. The roof was blown off and the building collapsed inwards in a ball of flames, which started a huge conflagration that quickly engulfed the stores nearby, all built of wood. By the time the flames were brought under control 24 properties spread over a square area of approximately two city blocks had been consumed and 23 bodies recovered including that of Chin-A-Yong. M.U. Hing managed to escape with a black eye and injuries to his arm and leg.

Lee A-pen, who took the name Thomas Lee-A-Pen, was a goldsmith and a butcher and became well-known for his delicious roast pork.

Cabinet making establishments were opened on Lombard Street, in the Chinese Quarter, by Wong, Yeo-Ming & Co. as well as by Lam-A-Sue.

In the heat of competition between the established Portuguese enterprises and the mushrooming Chinese businesses there were others who did not make it in merchandising and became bankrupt, while still others apparently pretended to be penniless.

> [An insolvent was charged] with fraudulently concealing property belonging to his estate to the value upwards of fifty dollars. The insolvent described himself as "Lay Fart, merchant, 14, Water-street, and also trading as merchant, without any partner, at lot No. 225 Lombard-street, Georgetown, as a Chinese merchant, as Tong-fat and Co." [The property included the] stock-in trade of a shop on Pln Nonpareil, which belonged to the accused, and which he concealed by not delivering it up to the Official Assignee. . . . [He] removed a large quantity of goods from lot 14, Water-street, to the premises of one Lim-Li in the same street and there had them concealed. [He also had an] interest in the business carried on in Lombard-street under the name of Kioung-Sun-Song & Co., Chinese merchants. [*Royal Gazette*, 24 Aug 1878]

The shops doing trade in goods and foods, concentrated in the growing Chinese Quarter in the Charlestown district of Georgetown, became the most visible aspect of the entrepreneurial nature of the Chinese in the colony. At the same time several smaller enterprises, focusing on the service sector, blossomed, and, to the general public, became everyday avenues of interaction with Chinese people. Among them were laundries that delivered clothes that were hand-washed, starched and ironed and then neatly folded and wrapped in large sheets of brown paper. Tailors operated out of their homes or had small frontage outlets, sometimes being no more than a door upon which a sign was hung and behind which was a small room where a foot-pedal sewing machine or two busily worked away at creating the latest in fashionable outfits. However, the most ubiquitous representation of the Chinese presence were the small restaurants, commonly called cook-shops, where for a relatively small payment a satisfying and filling meal could be obtained. The rice or noodle dishes were the fast foods of those times and made items such as roast pork, won tun, chow mein, low mein, congee and steam buns (called "pow") popular with Chinese and non-Chinese alike.

Blooming in Berbice

Chinese businesses were also becoming active in New Amsterdam, the second largest city in British Guiana, and the capital of Berbice County. One prosperous entrepreneur was Ho

Hin who arrived in British Guiana in April 1862. He worked at Plantation Bath on East Coast Berbice where the manager Andrew Hunter recognized his ability and promoted him to become driver. Ho Hin became known as Andrew Hunter Ho-A-Hing and opened a shop on the estate. After accumulating sufficient money he started a second shop and in 1882 moved to New Amsterdam to expand his business enterprise. There he became one of the leading merchants and in 1883, because of his income status, was named as one of only two Chinese to be registered as eligible to vote in the electoral process for regional financial representative to the Combined Court. (The other eligible voter was Ho-A-Ming who generated an income exceeding $96 per year from the rental of a house in Henrietta, Leguan Island, Essequebo.) Ho-A-Hing became wealthy and well-known in the colony, and over the years acquired and sold several properties in New Amsterdam as well as a branch operation in Georgetown. He was one of the coordinators for a potential boat trip to take prospective returnees to China in 1881, and he also launched an appeal to raise money for China after a serious famine there in 1889.

Chee-A-Wai, an immigrant in 1866, set up his bakery on High Street, another major thoroughfare in New Amsterdam. Others who opened bakeries in the same street were Chee-A-Foo, John Cheong and Kok-A-Yat.

Lam-A-See, one of three Lam brothers who arrived in 1861 on the *Minerva*, became a tinsmith and also opened his business on High Street.

Edward Foo became a cabinet maker and also hung up his sign on High Street.

Besides these, there were other Chinese immigrants who were settling and becoming established in New Amsterdam:

> By Bholah, No 53 ex "Clarence" 1866, a free coolie, transport of the southern half of the back half of lot number 47 (forty-seven) situated in that part of New Amsterdam called Stanley Town, . . . to and in favor of Lamatung, a free Chinese, No 702, ex "Minerva," 1861.
>
> [*Royal Gazette*, 21 Dec 1872]

> By Jacinthe D'Andrade, transport of the southern back quarter of lot number 8, situate in that part of the town of New Amsterdam called Smythstown, . . . to and in favour of Ho-a-niu, No 2698 ex "Red Riding Hood," 1862, a free Chinese immigrant. [*Royal Gazette*, 8 Dec 1877]

> By Molky . . . a free male Indian immigrant, transport of the southern back quarter of lot number 38, situate in that part of New Amsterdam called Stanley Town . . . to and in favour of Tam-a-Wai, No. 538, ex "Thomas Mitchell," 1860, a free male Chinese immigrant and Lan-she, No. 3522, ex "Ganges," 1863, a free female immigrant.
>
> [*Royal Gazette*, 15 May 1880]

Although the Chinese shopkeepers would put in long hours and great effort into trying to make their businesses prosper, they did, at the appropriate occasion, take leave to enjoy themselves.

> On Thursday last, a Chinese wedding of considerable importance took place at the Parish Church in this town. After the ceremony was performed, Mr. Chan-a-Fook, the gentleman who took to himself a better half, entertained his friends at a sumptuous repast in Mr. Comacho's residence in the Main road, nearly all the Chinese shops in the town were closed in honour of the occasion.
>
> [*Berbice Gazette*, reprinted in *Royal Gazette*, 20 Nov 1883]

COUNTRY SHOPS

Georgetown and New Amsterdam, being the two main cities in the colony, became the places to where many Chinese migrated. Some others did decide to stay in the countryside in the years shortly after being released from indentured obligation and there they ventured into shop keeping. They bought or started up small shops, which became the source of supplies for the labourers on the plantations. They were typically general stores providing a variety of goods for the local customer — salt and sugar, flour and rice, salt fish and pickled meat, pepper and spices, nuts and peas, candies and preserves, canned and bottled foods, pills and ointments, candles and lamp oil, cigarettes and matches, needles and thread, soap and brushes, slate and chalk.

The shop owners had to apply for the appropriate business licences and some of the applications were recorded in the *Royal Gazette*.

Shops:	You-tsoi-Win	Skeldon
	Chin-kan-moi	78 Village
	Chan-a-hee	Cumberland

Opium:	Chuck-a-hoo	Hope and Experiment
		[*Royal Gazette*, 17 Mar 1870]
Shops:	Fen-Kong-Chund	Henrietta
	Kou-a-qui	Land of Plenty
		[*Royal Gazette*, 8 Apr 1871]

There was at least one person who had a chain of stores:

Shops:	Li-a-Kim	Pln Waterloo
	Li-a-Kim	Pln Maryville
	Li-a-Kim	Phoenix village
		[*Royal Gazette*, 11 Apr 1871]

These licence applications for shops are only a sampling of the many recorded for all parts of the country, although starting up in business was not always a smooth operation:

> Lee Man and Sinqui vs. M. DeCross. This was an *ex parte* suit by two Chinese to recover from the defendant, a Portuguese, $2,500, as damages for the forcible seizure and sale by the defendant of the goods in the shop at *Enmore* on the 7th February last.
>
> The plaintiff purchased from the defendant the stock-in-trade of a provision shop at pln. *Enmore* for $414 67 of which $219 67 was paid at the time, and the balance of $195 on the 29th December 1874. The licence of the shop was transferred to the plaintiffs on the 20th Novr. On Sunday the 7th February the defendant went to the plaintiffs' shop and demanded payment of $50, which the wife of the plaintiff Lee Man had borrowed from him. Lee Man told him he must wait a little while; as it was Sunday he could not get the money that day. But the defendant declared that he would not wait, forcibly ejecting the plaintiffs from the shop and locked the door on them; and on the following morning began to sell off the goods at very much less than their value.
>
> [*Royal Gazette*, 2 Dec 1875]

In addition to the issuance of shop licences the growth of prosperity among the Chinese community was made evident by licences granted for ownership of donkeys, horses, mules, carts, guns and dogs. The possession of guns and dogs reflected the owners' need for protection of property, but the use of such defensive measures required conformity with the regulations.

> Lee-a-wan, a shop keeper at Goedverwagting estate was charged by the Commissary for keeping two dogs without taking out licences for

them as required by the law. Defendant was made to pay a fine of five dollars and costs in each case, and ordered to take out the licences.
[*Royal Gazette*, 18 Mar 1882]

PROPERTY PURCHASES

As they gained more and more wealth, the Chinese business-men were able to purchase land and property in many different areas of the colony.

By Samuel Payne, lot number 168, part of plantation Rome, EBD, known as the village of Agricola, to and in favour of Chan-a-Kung, a Chinese Immigrant. [*Royal Gazette*, 15 Jan 1876]

Two years later Chan-a-Kung's lot was subdivided into two and sold off separately to Leung-a-Kai, an immigrant on the *Ganges*, and to Lung-a-On who arrived on the *Agra*.

By William Henry Burgess, . . . transport of lots numbers 81, 82, 83, 84 and 85 section A, parts of lands now known as Old Vilvogorden, situate on Great Troolie Island [Essequebo] . . . to Chang-fook, a Chinese man, No 575 ex "Dora," 1867. [*Royal Gazette*, 20 Mar 1880]

By Toolah, transport of South half of plantation Groote-en-Klyne, Uitvlugt, with all buildings and erections thereon, save and except two buildings the property of Wong-a-Wing, a Chinese man, and Francis de Sousa — to and in favor of Chee-A-Tow, a Chineseman, No. 6,579 ex Buxton Castle, 1865. [*Royal Gazette*, 28 May 1889]

The ship that brought Chee A-tow was in fact the *Bucton Castle* but the recorders of the day apparently were influenced by the better known name, Buxton, a growing village on East Coast, Demerara. The other Chinese property owner at the Uitvlugt location, Wong-A-Wing, was an interpreter at the Immigration Office.

Several property transfers took place in Berbice County:

By Thomas Julian, transport of . . . lot number 11, . . . plantation lot No. 74, . . . to and in favour of Li-a-Kwong, No. 1,559, ex "Red Riding Hood," 1861 a free Chinese immigrant. [*Royal Gazette*, 10 Aug 1878]

Li-a-Kwong ran a shop in the Berbice countryside and also consolidated his land holdings by selling a portion of plantation No. 74 to a fellow Chinese in 1879. He appeared to be doing well but unfortunately died the following year and his assets were sold off, with some of the proceeds going to pay his outstanding debts to Leong-a-hing, Ho-a-Hing, Chan-a-Yok, Wong-a-tooi, Wo-Lee & Co., and Foon-a-Aie. His remaining land and property was later bought by a fellow-traveler on the same immigrant boat:

> By the Acting Administration General of British Guiana, as representing the estate . . . [of Li-a-Kwong], deceased, transport of the north half of building number 11, northern half of section A, and the west half of provision lot number 11, northern half of section B, parts of plantation lot No. 74, Corentyne Coast, in the county of Berbice . . . to and in favour of Tsang-a-Ming, No. 1,458, ex "Red Riding Hood," 1861 a free Chinese man. [*Royal Gazette*, 20 May 1882]

One huge project in Berbice involved the purchase of extensive sections of an estate:

> The Colony of British Guiana, transport of Plantation Lot Number 72 (seventy-two) Corentyne . . . to and in favor of Chun-Ming-Tong, No 29 ex "Dora," Fan-a-Ngan, No 5,312 ex "Queen of the East," 1865, Ho-Chun-Fook, No. 466 ex "Dora," 1860, and Yan-Thow-Moi, No. 346, ex "Dora," 1860, Chinese men. [*Royal Gazette*, 4 Aug 1883]

The purchase of the plantation, which was known as Chinese Town, apparently was made in order to control the transfer of ownership because a month later the property was divided into 48 lots and sold off to various individual Indian and Chinese buyers. Among the purchasers were Tsing-a-ng; William Lee-Yin-Choi; Simon Wong-Mok-Ying (a minor); Fung-She, No. 5,293 ex *Queen of the East*, a Chinese woman; Sam-choy otherwise called Thomas; Chan-a-tak, No. 1,504 ex *Red Riding Hood*, 1861; Lee-a-Nee; Tyan-a-lok, *Casual* 1872; Chong-Yim-Sow, *Casual* 1853; Chun-a-Kwei, No. 303 ex *Dora*; Lai-a-Tsan, No. 7,405 ex *Pride of the Ganges*; Cheung-a-fook, No. 1,137 ex *Claremont*; Hung-wei-Sheng, *Casual*, 1880; and Leung-she, No. 1,416 ex *Red Riding Hood*, 1861, a Chinese woman.

Most of the Chinese started off as owners of small shops selling general goods but as they became more prosperous the Chinese built up enough economic clout to venture into businesses that had been operated by Portuguese entrepreneurs for many years, such as trade in dry goods, liquor, lumber, and hardware as well as in shipping, machinery, manufacturing, and financial services.

While the Chinese, because of their small population, did not completely take over the middle economy, as was envisioned by some pundits many years earlier, they controlled a significant portion of it and became recognized as astute businessmen capable of doing well in virtually any enterprise.

THE SECOND GENERATION

While the first generation Chinese immigrants accepted shop keeping as an improvement in their status as compared to doing physical work on the plantation they had the ambition for their children to do even better through education. In British Guiana there existed an ordinance which provided for compulsory elementary education for the children of immigrants. However, not all complied.

> Children [of Indian immigrants] are being kept from schools either to be employed on the neighbouring plantations amongst the "Creole" gangs, or to work on the provision grounds which the parents themselves are too lazy to till. We know of one estate where the Immigrant gang is under 1,300 and yet the average attendance of Coolie and Chinese children at its school is over 100. There the manager insists upon the children's attendance, and he informs us he never had any difficulty with the parents. His compulsion took a very practical form. "If you do not send your child to school you will not be allowed to keep a cow."
>
> [*Royal Gazette*, 10 Jun 1882]

The status of the scholar in China was traditionally one that was greatly respected and admired and the Chinese immigrants in the colony needed little additional incentive to convince them of the benefits of education for their children. Just two years after the first Chinese families arrived in British Guiana the children were beginning to show promise in schooling as this 1862 account of the Creole and Immigrant School at Enmore, East Coast Demerara, shows:

> There is a large list of 95 children and among them are 40 Coolies, 9 Chinese, 12 Portuguese, and 34 Creoles — the average attendance during the last quarter being 49 — very often there are more than 70 in daily attendance. . . . The Chinese are very quick . . . at figures, and about 7 of them are writing in copy books. [On Sundays] they are called

> together morning and afternoon for religious instruction, and among the most regular are the Chinese and some of the Coolies.

In some instances the Chinese community became directly involved in getting schools going in their local area through financial and physical exertions.

> A very interesting ceremony took place at Met-en-Meerzorg on Monday . . . namely the laying of the foundation stone for a Chapel School for Chinese Christians belonging to the West Coast.
>
> [*Royal Gazette*, 24 Feb 1876]

> An interesting event gathered together on Thursday, a small but earnest band of Chinese Christians, at a distant spot on the West Coast. The manager of Plnt. Met-en-Meerzorg has erected, almost entirely at the expense of the estate a small building to be used by the Chinese of the neighbourhood as a kind of chapel-school, and on Thursday it was formally opened, and a blessing sought for the furtherance of its object.
>
> [*Royal Gazette*, 9 Feb 1878]

GAINING A HIGHER EDUCATION

Obtaining an elementary education was considered a minimum expectation to allow the children of the immigrant Chinese to gain a reasonable foundation for adult life. Achieving competency in English would enable better interaction with the majority of people in the colony while an ability in mathematics would provide the necessary foundation for conducting financial transactions. Although it was desirable to have the children continue on to complete high school it was not always within the financial means of the parents. The adults had to make an economic decision between the benefits of having the children join their businesses and the merits that could be gained from the extra level of education. Still, it was regarded as a matter of pride and prestige to have at least one child in the family achieve higher education, thereby seeing someone of the next generation gain the honor of a more respected status in society compared to the immigrants themselves. In many cases the eldest child, or else the one with the greatest potential, was encouraged to keep on studying and to go on to university while the other siblings would be required to work to help the chosen one realize the family's dream. Those immigrants who had become wealthy were able to send several children abroad for further learning.

Listed below are a number of second generation Chinese, i.e. those children who were born in the colony to an immigrant parent from China, who went to the developed countries for higher education.

Simon Leung, an immigrant aboard the *Thomas Mitchell* which landed in 1860 had 10 children two of whom became barristers. Francis (1878-1916) went to Africa to carry out his profession. His brother Stanley (1892-1926) settled in Europe.

Three of Ho-A-Hing's children went to London for their higher education. Joseph, the eldest, was born in 1879 and admitted to Middle Temple in 1910 but died in 1912 before writing his final exams. His brother Isaac (1893-1945) went to Canada and when in Saint John, New Brunswick he enlisted to join the Canadian Over-Seas Expeditionary Force on 18 June 1918. It is unlikely that he went into battle before the war ended on 11 November 1918. He thereafter followed in his brother's footsteps and studied law in England. He graduated in 1919 after which he became a barrister-at-law in Singapore. Their sister Martha (1889) was at Grovesnor College and then went to Edinburgh to study medicine, after which she set up her practice in Trinidad.

Lau Shiu-t'ong was a schoolmaster in China before emigrating to British Guiana in 1860. During his service of indenture the plantation manager, David Dougall, noted that he was not suited to agricultural work and set him up to run a shop on the estate. The shop business went well and Lau moved on to Hopetown but did not fare as well causing him to try his hand at shop-keeping at other estates, but without great success. He had a family of eight children and one of them, Frederick Orlando Low, expressed an interest in pursuing a law career after being exposed to the tutorship of a solicitor. His elder brother James, who held a responsible position with Ho-A-Shoo's company, agreed and set aside a monthly allowance for him. On hearing of the ambition of the promising young man, Ho-A-Shoo and other prominent Chinese businessmen did some fund raising and a few hundred dollars was presented to Frederick. He began his studies at Middle Temple in 1905 and was called to the Bar in 1908, at the age of 27. He returned to British Guiana and became the first person of Chinese descent to practice law, becoming well known and respected in the field.

Ho-A-Shoo's eldest daughter, Susan A-sin, was born at Dunoon in 1886 and wrote her Cambridge senior examinations at Ursuline Convent in Georgetown. She went to study at Nuneham College, Cambridge in 1905 and then at Edinburgh, graduating in medicine in 1911. A sister A-ho (1891-1939) also attended the University of Edinburgh. She gained her degree in medicine in 1916 and set up her practice in Hong Kong, Jamaica and Singapore. Their brother Fung-yan (Kesker), born in 1895, went on to study agriculture at Edinburgh after which he returned to British Guiana.

William Alfred Phang (1888), the son of immigrant Pang Yee, was an electrical engineer as well as a merchant and Special Correspondent to the *Daily Argosy* newspaper. In 1947 he was elected to be a Member of the Legislative Council representing the North West District serving until 1953.

John Samuel Ho-Yow (1893), son of immigrant Sampson Ho-Yow, qualified as a sicknurse and dispenser in 1914 and then as a Chemist and Druggist in 1919, becoming the first local Chinese to gain these qualifications. After gaining experience as an employee at T.L. Rebitt's Drug Store, John Ho-Yow set up his own drug store in 1934.

Another Sicknurse/Dispenser of that period who also became a Chemist and Druggist was Benjamin Philbert Alexander Ting-A-Kee (1891-1969). He later was elected to the Kitty Village Council. One of his brothers, Cuthbert Dundonald Alexander Ting-A-Kee, became a Fellow of the International Faculty of Sciences (London) and was Chief Sanitary Inspector when he retired in 1961.

Ng Yow's two eldest sons went into shopkeeping and business while the third son, Charles W. Yow (1892), went to study medicine in Britain. He remained there to establish his medical career.

An immigrant aboard the *Thomas Mitchell* was Ho A-Lim, who was called Thomas Ho-A-Lim. His daughter Rosaline went to Cambridge to study law. There she met and married Lim Cheng Ean, and they went to live in Penang. Rosaline's brother, Philip, (1895-1980) started off as a bookkeeper working for various lawyers in Georgetown. He then went to England to study law and later took his family to London. He decided to journey to Shanghai, stopping on the way at Singapore where he could visit his sister. The Japanese invasion of Shanghai prevented him from continuing his quest and he and his family were caught in Singapore when the Japanese extended their conquest to the Malayan peninsula. Philip was a successful lawyer in Singapore and became a good friend of Lee Chin Koon. After the war ended, Philip was active in the Malayan Democratic Union, working to achieve independence from Britain. He became chairman of the MDU, which was the forerunner of the various national movements that led to independence for Singapore under the leadership of Lee Kwan Yew, the son of Philip's friend, Lee Chin Koon.

Ho Ah Loke, another son of Thomas Ho-A-Lim, graduated as an Electrical Engineer in Hong Kong. He settled in Penang, where he became famous as a film producer.

Robert Victor Evan Wong (1895-1952), the eldest son of immigrant Wong Yan-sau, studied engineering and economics at the University of Bristol and received his B.Sc. degree in 1917. His poor eyesight prevented him from serving in World War I and he returned to British Guiana to work for the civil service, designing sea walls, bridges, roads, sluices and other infrastructure projects. In 1926 he was elected to the Court of Policy, representing the Essequebo Islands. Two years later the Court became the Legislative Council through a constitutional change. He thus became the first person of East Asian descent to be elected to a national legislative body in the Americas. He was re-elected to the Legislative Council in 1934 with a campaign slogan that utilized the initials of his name: Right Vanquishes Every Wrong.

Joseph Clement Luck (1896-1981) attended Queen's College during its formative years. After unsuccessful attempts at farming, shop-keeping, gold-digging and rice-milling, he became the founder and headmaster of Central High School in Georgetown, at which he taught Latin and mathematics. Tuition fees were $3.16 per month. Starting off with an initial enrolment of 35 students in 1929 the school grew to become the largest private school in the country with a few hundred pupils who were able to gain both primary and secondary education. J.C. Luck later obtained a B.A. degree from London in 1947 as an external student.

Alice Fung-A-Ling (1897), eldest daughter of Job and Alice Fung-A-Ling, studied at Sherry's College and the School of Medicine for Women in Edinburgh. After passing the second year examinations in 1916 she returned to British Guiana because of financial reasons and began working as a nurse. In 1922 she became Assistant Matron at the Public Hospital, Georgetown. She was awarded a Gold Medal for nursing and later went to London to take examinations for general nursing, which she passed in 1927. She subsequently became the Supervisor of Best Hospital, the tuberculosis sanatorium.

Li Ya Un arrived in British Guiana as a 5-year-old boy, brought by his mother and her spouse aboard the *Zouave* in 1864. He was known as James Lee-Own and succeeded as a shopkeeper. One of his sons, Albert Lee-Own (1903-1968), qualified as land surveyor and rose to become Deputy Commissioner of Land and Mines.

There were of course many children of immigrants who did not have the opportunity to obtain a higher level of education but who were successful in business, following in the steps of their parents. In these cases the goal of having a scholar in the family was deferred for a subsequent generation. Among the later descendants a greater number of them were able to improve their level of education. Locally they were accepted into the civil service and went into accounting and teaching. Others went to the developed countries, particularly Britain, to study at various universities. The interaction with people of different countries and cultures together with the shrinking nature of the world through improved communications have made them feel less inhibited about their ties to Guyana. The Chinese immigrants who were brought over to be cane reapers now have successors spread all over the globe and involved in practically every field of endeavor.

CHAPTER 10

NAME CALLING

CHINESE CHARACTERS

In reading through this book it may have become apparent that many of the surnames of the Chinese persons invariably have one or two hyphens in them. To a native speaker of Chinese such names appear complex, confusing and even non-Chinese, while to the English-speaker they appear complex, unusual and even exotic. The surnames are indeed different from conventional Chinese family names and to understand how they came about and became a distinctive outcome of the Chinese presence in British Guiana it would be useful to first examine the nature of Chinese names.

The surname, or family clan name, of a Chinese person is the first part of his or her full name. This could be argued to be a reflection of the traditional Chinese perspective in which greater importance is placed in the family clan compared to the individual. In similar fashion, the address written on a letter in the Chinese manner would show the country first, followed by the city, district, street, house number and then the name of the individual, which reflects the logical and sequential path for locating the recipient. The Chinese way of writing dates is also from large to small — year, month, day. The order of importance is reversed in Western custom with the person's given name coming first and surname last. With different positions for placing the surname in Chinese and Western traditions the potential for misinterpretation is in place.

There were several thousand Chinese surnames in ancient times but many have become obsolete leaving some 700 or so in use today, of which 500 would account for more than 90 percent of the population. Surnames usually consist of only one syllable, although a small number of them, less than 10% of the total, consist of two syllables, e.g. Ouyang, Sima, Situ and Zhuge. The names just described are in pinyin spelling which has come into standard use in China in recent times. Pinyin is a system developed in China using the alphabet to depict Mandarin speech. The ten most frequently occurring surnames, using pinyin spelling, are Wang (written as Wong in Cantonese), Chen (Chan), Li (Lee), Zhang (Chiang), Liu (Lao), Yang (Yeung), Huang (Wong), Wu (Ng), Lin (Lam), and Zhou (Chao). These ten surnames account for some 40% of the people in China. Because of variations in local dialect, spellings such as Whang, Chin, Lei, Chang, Low, Young, Whong, Ing, Lim, and Chow have resulted for the same top ten surnames.

These different spellings raise some curiosity about the nature of the Chinese language itself. It would take a lengthy thesis to discuss this subject in depth. In brief, there are a large number of regional dialects, some of which are quite distinct from the others while some are variants of a main dialect, in much the same way as English, French, Italian and Spanish are derived from Latin. Interestingly enough the written language is commonly recognized by all, meaning that even though the people may speak diverse dialects they can read and understand the same newspaper but each would vocalize the characters differently. An approximation in English can be found in the title "lieutenant" which would become "left-tenant" in England and "loo-tenant" in the USA. This is of course a very simple example and many pronunciations in the various Chinese dialects are totally different, much more like an American looking at a building and declaring it to be an apartment whereas to a Londoner it would be flat.

Since most of the emigrants from China departed from the south the predominant language of Chinese overseas has been Cantonese along with other locally-based southern dialects such as Taishan (Toisan), Hakka, Hokkien, Teochew, and Fujian (Foochow). After World War II, Mandarin, spoken mainly in the north, became the official dialect in China with Beijing pronunciation taken as the standard.

Note that some names merge in their Mandarin and Cantonese pronunciations and this can sometimes cause misunderstanding unless the characters are examined. For example, the Mandarin names Huang (meaning yellow, and also the surname of a person who was one of the early emperors) and Wang (king) both become Wong in Cantonese. In order to write the correct Wong, it may be necessary to ask "Is it Wong the emperor or Wong the king?" This type of question is not unusual in Chinese conversation.

In most instances the Mandarin and Cantonese pronunciations for the same character are completely different and confusion can result if the dialect is not known. To illustrate, in going from Mandarin to Cantonese, Wu becomes Ng and Hu changes to Woo. The Mandarin "Wu" and the Cantonese "Woo" are similar sounds so that the dialect, or else the written form, would need to be known to get the correct surname. To complicate matters, Hu (Woo) is also written "O" or "U" with a pronunciation somewhat like "Ooh" in the English expression "Ooh and Ah." Thus the name of the founder of Hopetown has been variously written O. Tye Kim and Wu Tai-kam, reflecting the differences in local dialect for Hu Da-jin, which would be his name in Mandarin pinyin.

Individual or given names of a person are attached behind the family name, so that Lin Hong-ying (also written Lin Hongying) signifies the person named Hong-ying of the Lin family. Most Chinese personal names are made up of two combined names, although a single name is also used. However, no more than two given names are bestowed on a child, in contrast to an unlimited number of personal names in Western custom. The given names are typically chosen to denote desirable attributes — intelligence, strength, virtue, sincerity; or things from nature — swan, wind, summer, lotus; or great expectations — happiness, health, wealth, victory, or just about any beneficent characteristic projected for the infant. Traditionally, the first of the two given names is the generation name, which is shared by siblings, while the last name is the specific name for the individual. Thus Wen An-fu, Wen An-li and Wen An-ping might be the names of three brothers and sisters of the Wen family. However, the sharing of the same ending name by siblings can also occur, e.g. Soong Ai-ling, Soong Ching-ling and Soong Mei-ling who are three well-known and influential sisters of the Soong family.

TRANSLATION TROUBLES

Several methods were devised to render Chinese into an alphabetic form during the nineteenth century but they did not have a consistent basis in their approach. This resulted in different spellings for the same Chinese word depending on whose system was being used. In addition, the sound that was represented by a certain spelling could be pronounced in a different way if another system of Romanization were applied. As an illustration, the name McKay in English can be pronounced in two ways. The sound of the last syllable "Kay" can rhyme with either "bay" or otherwise with "sky." Furthermore, a similar sounding surname can be spelt "MacKay." Thus the spoken name does not tell the listener the way it should be spelt, and conversely, seeing the name in print does not inform the reader the way it should be pronounced. In comparable fashion Chinese names written with the English alphabet have in some cases become transformed from their original sounds and, in other cases, subject to different ways of pronunciation.

Thomas Wade was one of the English scholars to develop a system of Romanization for Mandarin which has become a widely accepted standard for many generations right through to modern times and a brief examination of his approach can show some interesting consequences. Some of Wade's choices for the depiction of Chinese words have caused the evolution of both misinterpretations as well as new interpretations. As an example, for the Chinese sound "tee" he used the notation "T" followed by an apostrophe thereby producing spellings T'ing, T'in, T'ien, etc. For the "dee" sound Wade also used the letter "T" but without an apostrophe resulting in Tang, Ting and the like, whereas the correct pronunciations of these words in Chinese are more like the English words "dang" and "ding." Thus the spiritual/philosophical belief written in English as Taoism should correctly be vocalized as "Dow-ism." Similarly, the increasingly popular food item tofu is in fact more like "dough-foo." For a reader of English who is unfamiliar with Wade's system there would be no indication of the difference in pronunciation between T'ang and Tang. To further complicate matters, the spelling "Tang" is also the written form in a local dialect for a surname that Wade would show to be "Teng." This is the same surname as the former Chinese leader Deng Xiaoping, whose name was written Teng Hs'iao-ping before the pinyin system was adopted. Thus Tang is a spelling variation of Teng and Deng.

The sounds "bee" and "gee" are depicted in Wade's system by the letters "p" and "k." Ignoring the nuances of local dialect for the moment, this produces the spelling "pe" for the sound "bay" and "king" for the sound "jing" (as in "jingle"), which together becomes Peking as the English written form for the spoken word "Bay-jing." The currently used pinyin spelling is "Beijing."

Dash It All

The various attempts at Romanization have taken on an added degree of complexity by the practice in English of using hyphens for tying together connected or closely associated items. While a single hyphen would seem to have been reasonable for linking the two given names of a person, the use of hyphens became so liberal that it became the subject of comment in the September/ October 1884 issue of *The Chinese Recorder*, a missionary bi-monthly periodical published in Shanghai:

On Romanizing Chinese Names.

DEAR SIR,

Is it not a pity that the good sense which foreign writers possess often leaves them when they undertake to write Chinese names? It seems as though that abominable hyphen which is peppered into or sandwiched between Chinese names on all occasions, when written with Roman letters, insists upon a space for its useless body. A man who would never think of writing in English John-henry-smith, no sooner gets hold of Mr. Wang, which is the Smith of Chinese names, than he writes him out Wang-ping-chi. Whoever thought of writing Man-ches-ter in English? But the gentleman who would be ashamed to so write the name of a foreign city does not hesitate to write Chen-tu-fu. This perpetual use of hyphens and small letters in romanized Chinese names is much more objectionable when the names of books are given. How does this look in English; A treatise-on-trees-and-plants-of-the-united-states-of-america? Yet how is it better than Nan-fang-tsao-mu-chwang?

Does this need more than the briefest mention to show up its ridiculousness and barbarity? Sz Macheng would turn over on his grave if he knew that western doctors of law and divinity were writing him down as Sï-ma-cheng and his country as Ta-tsing-kwoh and his book as Shi-ki and so on to the end. Is it not common sense to say in general, that the hyphen should not be used in romanizing Chinese, except in those instances where it would be naturally used in English and that the names of cities, provinces, rivers, mountains, and so forth are simply so many polysyllables, and should be written continuously; *e.g.* the city of Nanking is in the province of Kiangsu, and upon the Yangtsz river; the names of individuals should begin with capital letters, *e.g.* Chang Pei Lin not Chang-pei-lin. Am I wrong? If so please set me right. If I am right *nota bene* and oblige yours truly,

A READER

The hyphenation approach — dash it all — would not have seemed particularly unusual to the Englishman whose language is full of multiple hyphenated expressions. Some examples are commander-in-chief, mother-in-law, will-o'-the-wisp, fly-by-night, across-the-board, under-the-counter, black-and-blue, tongue-in-cheek, spick-and-span, hand-to-mouth, man-of-war, and a whole lot more. There are also several comparably styled geographical names such as Newcastle-under-Lyme, Southend-on-Sea Henley-in-Arden, Stratford-upon-Avon. In Guyana, in the vicinity of Georgetown are Werk-en-Rust and Vreed-en-Hoop, names that were adopted from the Dutch words meaning "work and rest" and "peace and hope." In the countryside can be found similar compound names including Met-en-Meerzorg, Tuschen-de-Vrienden, Zorg-en-Vlyt, Hoff-van-Aurich. In the Dutch language their words would not be hyphenated in the manner in which they were compromised by the English.

The practice of adding hyphens to the names of Chinese indentured immigrants was started by the British officials at the emigration houses in China who copied the format proposed by resident scholars of Chinese. The custom continued in British Guiana where, taking the process a step further, the full name of an individual in many cases became the compounded hyphenated surname for subsequent generations.

The matter does not end there. Besides calling a person by the individual's name, there is also a familiar or more informal form of address, particularly in southern China, in which the prefix "A-" (pronounced "ah") is attached to the person's given name. Thus, before becoming the Heavenly King, Hung Hsiu-ch'uan would have been called A-ch'uan by his family and friends. In English, this practice is comparable to attaching the suffix "-ie" or "-y" to a name so that Frederick becomes Freddie, or dad daddy. These familiar forms of address — mommy, auntie, granny, Archie, Maggie, Tommy, Annie, Jenny, Johnny, etc. — are commonplace in the English-speaking world. Interestingly enough, English also uses the prefix "A-" to modify the meaning of the attached word, thereby creating such words as across, akin, alive, amend, anew, asleep, await, away, and so on.

There is yet another complication since, in the Cantonese dialect, the same sound "Ah" is also a word meaning second place, runner-up, secondus, next in succession, junior. From the records of the Chinese immigrants in British Guiana there are a significant number of people with the name "A" meaning second position. The given names of Soo A-cheong mean "second position" and "length," inferring long life or extensive ability. In spoken Cantonese, the distinction between A-cheong, meaning Second Cheong, and the familiar form of address is made by a different tone or inflection placed on the syllable "A."[1] This distinction is lost in the Romanization of the name.

Soo A-cheong's son Soo Sam-kuan would have been called A-kuan in the informal manner of address and he thus became known as A-kuan of the Soo family or Soo A-kuan. This transformed name became the origin of the surname Sue-A-Quan which was thereafter carried by his descendants. In this case the given name Sam (meaning three or third) became substituted by the colloquial "A-" prefix. This modification has become fairly commonplace among the Chinese immigrants in a manner similar to U.S. president James Carter's request that he be known as Jimmy Carter.

When a commission was dispatched from China in 1874 to investigate the conditions of Chinese immigrants in Cuba it recorded complaints from numerous Chinese labourers. In the report are many persons with the middle name "A" — Wu A-kuang, Liu A-shou, Lo A-chi, Su A-hai, Chang A-lin, Ho A-ying, Li A-wu, Feng A-kai, Lin A-pang, etc. In every single one of these names, the Chinese character for the middle name "A" has been transformed into the term of informal address. However, the surnames are not linked together by hyphens with the given names to produce double hyphenated names as occurred in British Guiana.

Soo A-cheong's family name is "Su" in pinyin spelling. The surname Su is said to have been conceived more than 3,000 years ago by the son of a regional emperor, Zhuanxu, who apparently was himself conceived by the emperor of China through His Majesty's influence on one of his lay subjects. The original Su lived in today's Henan province and his clan fled to the south to escape the Mongols in the 13th century. The surname became commonplace in southern China and ranks among the lower part of the top fifty most prevalent surnames. The Su surname

---

1 There are four tones in Mandarin and six tones in Cantonese, and a different tonal inflection changes the meaning of the word. There is no equivalent in English, but a sense of the nature of the tones can be obtained from the word "why" in the following sentences: "Have you wondered why?", "Why not?", "Don't ask me why.", "Why! Never!"

can thus be traced to a single person (of light blue blood), and in similar fashion Soo Sam-kuan became the unique source of the name Sue-A-Quan, although as the result of cultural and language transformations beyond his control. The Westernized spelling "Sue" is an accurate rendition in English pronunciation, although variants of the same clan name are also common including, So, Soo, Siu and Seow. The unusual surname Sue-A-Quan can mislead the reader into thinking that an error was made in trying to depict "Sue A. Quan," (i.e. a woman of the Quan clan) or else that it was an example of poor handwriting with marks looking like dashes slobbered in between the name.

WHAT-A-NAME

There are a considerable number of double-hyphenated surnames with "A" in the middle which have become commonplace in Guyana. Among them are Chan-A-Shing, Chee-A-Tow, Cheong-A-Shack, Chin-A-Loy, Choo-A-Fat, Chow-A-Shing, Chu-A-Kong, Chuck-A-Sang, Chung-A-Hing, Fung-A-Ling, Ho-A-Hing, Hu-A-Kam, Lam-A-Tung, Lee-A-Sam, Leung-A-Low, Low-A-Sue, Ng-A-Fook, Sue-A-Chung, Ting-A-Kee, Wong-A-Wing, and Woon-A-Tai, and these comprise just a small selection of the compound names derived from differing Chinese family clan surnames. Some of them, like in the evolution of the name Sue-A-Quan, have come about from the changing of the middle name. Two other examples of this kind of transformation are Fung-A-Fat derived from Fung Kung-fatt and Low-A-Chee which was originally Lau Yun-chay.

Another form of conversion came about by the insertion of the familiar form of address "A-" where it did not exist before. Records show that one immigrant arrived on the *Minerva* in 1860 bearing the name Seow Sam and departed with a different one, the name on his gravestone in Georgetown being "Seow-a-Sam."

There are other double hyphenated names such as Fung-Kee-Fung, Ho-Sing-Loy, Man-Son-Hing, where the full original names of the immigrants were recorded with added hyphens and became the surnames for their descendants. There are also surnames which have a single hyphen — Lee-Own, Lou-Hing, Mook-Sang, Too-Chung, Woo-Ming, Woon-Sam, etc. Some of these are the full names of persons who carry a single given name, such as Woo-Ming where "Woo" is the family name and

"Ming" the given name. In other cases, they are the ancestor's personal names which have become detached from the clan name. This has arisen from the English practice of putting surnames last, thereby giving the impression that the last part of the Chinese name is the surname. This was the case for Chung Tiam-fook, some of whose descendants now carry the surname "Tiam-Fook," although they originate from the Chung family clan. Similarly, descendants of Ho Ten-pow are known as Ten-Pow or Tenpow and the later generations of Tsoi Mook-sang carry the Mook-Sang surname.

Finally, there are some Chinese surnames which were correctly passed on to descendants and do not carry any of the complicated transformations just described. A few examples are Chan, Chin, Chung, Lam, Lee, Li, Low, Wong, Yhap, Yow and Young. However, even in these cases there are varying spellings of the same clan surname, such as Cheong and Chung, Low and Lowe, Yhap and Yip, Yong and Young.

In old Chinese tradition women were regarded as being subservient to men and the three transitions in life that females could expect were to fulfill their obligations first to their fathers, then to their husbands, and finally to their sons. On becoming married the woman became a part of the husband's household. From then on she would be referred by her original clan name along with the title "Shee," meaning "belonging to the clan of," equivalent in sense to "née." Thus a girl named Chin Mei-lan at birth would be known as Chin Shee after marriage. This accounts for the numerous instances of women previously described with the name Shee (sometimes written "She"). In modern China a married woman retains her full name given at birth and the married couple is known by the linking of his and her individual names in people's memories or in written records. Their children would carry the father's surname, although this practice has its exceptions.

ANGLICIZED NAMES

The Chinese immigrants to British Guiana were inevitably influenced by local customs and, in an English speaking environment, would have accepted the English names bestowed upon them by their plantation managers, religious leaders and other persons in authority. Many new arrivals were not only given English personal names such as John and Mary but also new surnames. There were several Chinese who became known by surnames such as Alexander, Bridges, Gillette, Hebert, Isaacs, Milner, Porter, Russell, Stokes, and Tanner through this renaming process.

There were also surname changes derived from the English personal names assigned to the Chinese. For example, an immigrant with the surname Lam was assigned the name Mark so that he was referred to as Mark Lam. It was not unusual in those days for him to be addressed as Mr. Mark as a sign of respect. This courteous form of address was commonly used especially so for a person holding a position of higher ranking than others around him, such as being a driver on the plantation or a shopkeeper. In this way the descendants of "Mr. Mark" became known by the surname Marks. This evolutionary process has given rise to several personal names becoming surnames — Aaron, Benjamin, Cyril, James, John, Joseph, Marks, Paul, Phillips, Samuels, Thomas.

A few surnames have also emerged as variations of the Chinese name. One story goes that at a marriage ceremony the presiding minister asked the name of the Chinese bridegroom and, being uncertain about what he heard, the minister wrote down "Layne." The original surname is not known but appears in archival records as Len, which is most likely the Mandarin surname Lin. In another story an immigrant with the surname Quan is said to have been an older person and, as is the Chinese custom, was called "Old Quan" as a term of respect, which in Chinese would be "Lo Quan." This evolved into the surname Loquan — an interesting contrast to the emergence in Western tradition of "son" names such as Carlson, Davidson, Johnson, Stevenson, etc.

LINEAGES

With only 15% of the Chinese immigrants being women and the majority of the men not having the inclination to form an inter-racial marriage with the local people the population of Chinese in British Guiana declined over the years as the men died without progeny. While 13,541 immigrants arrived between 1853 and 1879 only about 3,000 remained at the turn of the century. The ratio of males to females then reached a balance which thereafter sustained their numbers. There were therefore extensive inter-marriages between the remaining Chinese families. Because of close association among the members of the Chinese community it is not uncommon to find siblings of one family married to siblings of another even after a few generations. In several instances there have also been marriages between cousins, although they are usually not first cousins. Later generations of locally-born Chinese adapted to the culture and customs of the land and did not feel as obligated to confine their search for marriage partners to only members of the Chinese community.

In an examination of human relationships of this kind it is inevitable that there are instances where the recorded parents are not the biological parents, including cases where the children are adopted. Furthermore, there are children sired by persons listed in the lineage charts, but who were not brought up as part of the formal family group of one of the parents. They have been euphemistically called "outside children" in common parlance. These occurrences exist in any extensive family clan, regardless of nationality, social status, economic well-being, or era.

The process of gathering the information has sometimes been very challenging since the recollections of people, places and events have not always been consistent. An even greater challenge appeared when written documents revealed apparent discrepancies. The birth certificates of my father and his brother indicate different mothers. While this is quite possible from a biological perspective it does not correspond with family history or physical evidence, and on closer examination it turns out that the mother's maiden name shown on my uncle's certificate is in fact the name of her father-in-law. Such errors have turned up in several instances caused by misunderstandings arising from insufficient knowledge of English and of the questions asked by the person inscribing the document. This confusing situation has been compounded by the practice of births often being reported to the registrar by family or friends (frequently by the midwife or nurse) who unwittingly provided incorrect information that became a part of the written record.

The record keepers themselves have created errors by writing down what they thought they heard using a spelling which they felt appropriate at that moment. One person's name appears as Man-Yok-Shin, Man-Yuk-Shang and Min-Fok-Shin in records written on different occasions. The errors even include date entry foul-ups where a child is shown to be baptized before being born. The old documents have also been the source of inconsistencies from the fact that the entries were all written by hand and the quality of the handwriting has not always been of exemplary nature. This has sometimes presented a formidable challenge in correctly reading the original name. Chin sometimes looks like Chan or Chiu while Liu has the appearance of Lin or Lui, and Leung takes on the disguise of Loung.

NAME LIST

The following is a listing of some of the commonly occurring surnames of Chinese who trace their ancestry to the original batch of indentured immigrants during the period from 1853 to 1879. It includes the names of some of the original immigrants and their descendants who are known at the time of printing. The spellings of the names are those that have become the more generally acknowledged versions although variations in spelling do exist. Although regional variations in dialect do occur the surnames are considered mainly by the Cantonese pronunciation. An attempt has been made to relate them their equivalent Mandarin versions in pinyin spelling, recognizing that some inaccuracies would arise because there are cases where the written Chinese names of the original immigrants are not precisely known.

Aaron: This immigrant of the Li family (pronounced "lie") was given the personal name Aaron which then became the surname for his descendants, while some kept the Chinese surname Li.

Ahing: Chan Hing arrived on the *Corona* in 1874 with his wife Wong Shee (known as Rachel) and were allocated to Plantation Bel Air, East Coast Demerara. One of their three sons took the name John Ahing and later emigrated to Trinidad. His descendants carry the Ahing surname. Rachel subsequently married Tang A-tsoi and bore six sons who grew up in Trinidad.

Alexander: See Ting-A-Kee.

Appin: William Appin was an interpreter at the Immigration Depot. The original Chinese surname had not been determined.

Au-Young: Also written Au-Yeung this is one of the rarely occurring Chinese surnames with double syllables. The Mandarin equivalent is Ouyang.

Benjamin: This surname is attributed to Wong-A-Wa, who was known as William Benjamin Wong-A-Wa and then William Benjamin. He was a catechist in Berbice.

Bridges: The surname Bridges was given to a yet unidentified Chinese immigrant and is believed to originate from W.F. Bridges, a plantation owner who was a member of the Combined Court in the 1880s. Nathaniel Bridges, a son of the Chinese immigrant named Bridges, emigrated to Venezuela and then Trinidad.

Chai: This surname can be derived from two Chinese characters. In Mandarin, one is spelt Cai and the other Chai.

Cham-A-Koon: See Sue-A-Quan.

Chan: The surname Chan is the Cantonese for the second most commonly occurring surname, which in Mandarin is Chen. Other spellings for the same clan name are Chang, Cheung and Chin. Among those maintaining the original Chinese surname Chan are the descendants of Chan Qui, and Chan Moon, an immigrant aboard the *Agra* in 1862. See also Ahing, Chan-Choong and Daniels.

Chan-A-Shing: The surname comes from the immigrant Chan A-shing who had the personal name Joseph.

Chan-A-Sue: The family name is believed to be derived from the immigrant Chan A-sue who became a shopkeeper and rum shop owner in Essequebo. He married Maria Wong, who was also born in China, and their descendants carry the surname Chan-A-Sue. There is an unrelated person with this surname, Paul Chan-A-Sue, who immigrated from China and became a catechist at St. Saviour's Church in Georgetown.

Chan-Choong: Chin Chan-Choong was a doctor in China and is said to have been recruited to serve the needs of the Chinese community in British Guiana. He had four children, some of whom carried the Chinese surname Chin while others became known by Chan-Choong. Some later generations have changed to using Chan as the surname.

Chang: This spelling is most widely used for the fourth prevalent Mandarin surname Zhang, although is also occurs for the clan names Chen and Zheng. An alternate spelling is Choong.

Chao: See Chow.

Chee: A Cantonese version of the Mandarin name Chi (pronounced like the ending "ch" in "church"), as well as She. These are less frequently occurring family names. See also Chee-Yan-Long.

Chee-A-Fat: This surname is most probably derived from the immigrant Chee A-fat.

Chee-A-Kwai: Believed to be derived from an immigrant named Chee A-kwai.

Chee-A-Nam: Likely originating from immigrant Chee A-nam.

Chee-A-Tow: She A In was immigrant #6579 from Poon Yu who arrived on the *Bucton Castle* in 1865. The surname in Mandarin is Xie, meaning "thanks." He was allotted to Plantation Peter's Hall. He changed his name officially to Chee A-tow on 15 May 1889. He was a shopkeeper and acquired property and land at Uitvlugt, West Coast Demerara, in the 1880s where he raised a family of 16 children.

Chee-A-Wai: Chee A-wai immigrated his wife Ho Shee on the *Pride of the Ganges* and arrived in July 1866. He established a bakery in New Amsterdam. His descendants later emigrated to Trinidad.

Chee-Yan-Long: This family name comes from Jacob Chee-Yan-Long the son of Chee A-mow who was a catechist with the given name Abraham. Jacob married Ethel Lee-Own and their descendants are known as Chee-Yan-Long or Chee.

Chen: This Mandarin name is more commonly encountered overseas as the Cantonese variations Chan and Chin.

Cheong: The surname is also spelt Cheung and Chung, equivalent to the Mandarin Zhang, the most prevalent Chinese surname. One Cheong family comes from Cheong A-hoi who was also known as Matthew Murray Cheong and whose descendants have the names Cheong or Murray-Cheong. See also Chang and Gillette.

Cheong-A-Hoi: The surname is derived from Cheong A-hoi. He was also known as Matthew Murray Cheong-A-Hoi.

Cheong-A-Shack: This family surname is believed to be derived from immigrant Cheong A-shack.

Cheung: Usually a spelling variation of Cheong, although some families trace their origin to the Chen clan.

Chin: Several Chinese families from Guyana have the surname Chin which can be from the second most popular surname Chen (in Mandarin) or the somewhat less commonly encountered Qian which ranks towards the lower part of the top 50 Chinese surnames. Descendants from the Chin-A-fat, Chin-A-Kow, Chin-A-Yong and Chin-Chung families have resumed the use of the Chin surname. See also Ching, Choy and Stokes.

Chin-A-Fat: Most likely derived from the immigrant Chin A-fat, the compound surname is carried by some descendants while others have assumed the Chin surname.

Chin-A-Pow: The Chin-A-Pow name is more prevalent in Surinam, where is it spelt Chin-A-Paw. Some of Chin-A-Pow's descendants are also known as Humphreys.

Chin-A-Yong: Chin-A-Yong was a businessman whose establishment on Lombard Street was the origin of a great fire in December 1913. His children carry the Chin surname.

Ching: This spelling can be derived from a few possible clan names. Sometimes encountered as a variation of Chin, it could also be equivalent in Mandarin to Cheng, Zheng (pronounced "jung" as in "jungle") or Qin (pronounced "chin").

Cho: The Cantonese version of the Mandarin surname Cao (or Ts'ao in the Wade system).

Choo: See Chu.

Choong: See Chang.

Chow: Also written as Chao and Chau this can be the equivalent of the Mandarin Zhao (pronounced "jow" as in "jowl"), the tenth most commonly occurring Chinese surname, or else Zhou (pronounced "Joe").

Choy: This Cantonese name is the same as the Mandarin name Cai (pronounced "ts-eye"), one of the top 50 surnames. However, one family derives its surname from the personal name of the immigrant Chin Choy.

Chu: Also written Choo, this name is equivalent in Mandarin to either Zhu (pronounced "Jew"), which is among the top 15 commonly occurring Chinese surnames, or else Chu.

Chu-A-Kong: Most likely originating from the immigrant Chu A-kong. Many descendants have changed to the surname Kong.

Chu Cheong: Chun A-cheung, also called John Chu Cheong, was nine years old when he was brought by his mother on the *Queen of the East* in 1865. His descendants are known by the surname Chu Cheong as well as John.

Chuck: Also written Chuk, this surname becomes Zhuo (pronounced "Jew-oh") in Mandarin.

Chuck-A-Sang: Believed to be derived from an immigrant named Chuck A-sang.

Chuck-A-Tai: Born about 1845, Chuk Fook became known as Thomas Chuk-Fook but his son was named Chuk A-tai from whom the surname Chuck-A-Tai (or Chuk-A-Tai) originated.

Chung: Although existing mainly as a variation of Cheong the surname Chung can also be equivalent to Zhong in Mandarin, a much less frequently occurring surname. J.T. Chung was the commonly used by John Too-Chung, son of To Cheung. The ancestors of some Chung families are Chung-Lee-Pow and Chung-Kim-Sue. See also Ho Ten-pow.

Chung-A-Fook: Derived from William Chung-A-Fook, a son of Chung Kam-sow, who originated from Tung Koon and arrived with his wife Wong Shee aboard the *Pride of the Ganges* in 1866.

Chung-A-Hing: Most likely originating from the immigrant Chung A-hing.

Chung-A-Kung: This surname originates from Peter Chung-A-Kung, another son of Chung Kam-sow and Wong Shee, who came on the *Pride of the Ganges.*

Chung-A-Ming: Family history has it that the original immigrant Chung-A-Ming arrived in the1870s and was given the personal name James. He married an Indian girl named Lakia and had two sons, Richard and Thomas James Chung-A-Ming. James opened up a liquor store, hotel and grocery in the Corentyne district. Some of his descendants are known by the surname James.

Chung-Tiam-Fook: Cheung Tiam-fook was three years old when he and an older brother, Cheung A-ki, were brought by their father Cheung Cheung-man from Tung Koon. They were on the *Pride of the Ganges*, arriving in July 1866 in British Guiana. The younger son took the name Peter George Chung-Tiam-Fook and became a prosperous merchant dealing in provisions and liquor. By the time of his death in 1948 his children were managing diverse business operations in New Amsterdam and Georgetown. His descendants are known by the name Chung-Tiam-Fook but mainly by the surname Tiam-Fook.

Cyril: See Ng-A-fook.

Daniels: An immigrant of the Chan family clan also became known by the surname Daniels.

Evan Wong: See Wong Mook.

Ewing-Chow: Born in Shun-tak, Guangdong province, Chau Luk-wu is reported in Cecil Clementi's book to have traveled with his wife Mack Shee on the *Dora* which landed in Georgetown in April 1860. They were assigned to Plantation Peter's Hall, some 7 miles from Georgetown. However, all the immigrants on the *Dora* were allotted to plantations in Berbice. Archival records show that Chau Luk-wu was in fact an immigrant on the *Red Riding Hood* in 1860, and arrived five days after the *Dora*. His wife, Mack Shee, was the former wife of Chan A-sy, who arrived as a couple aboard the *Ganges* in 1863. Chan A-sy and Mack Shee had a daughter before Mack Shee married Chau Luk-wu. Chau worked in the fields while his wife was later able to earn a bit extra as a herbalist and acupuncturist by providing medical services to the Chinese workers, although payment usually came in the form of garden vegetables, eggs and chickens. About 1876, Chau took ill and a year later he died leaving Mack Shee with a daughter of 12 and a son, Chow Loi, who was 9 years old. Mack Shee felt that her son was old enough to become a wage earner. The young lad was bright and keen at sports and this made a favorable impression on both his primary school principal, Miss Hewlings, and Rev. D. Ewing, the Anglican minister. They encouraged him to pursue his studies after he finished working at the nearby Chinese shop where his ability with English and Chinese was very useful. Chow Loi embraced Christianity and when he was baptized took the name David Johnstone Ewing-Chow. The religious conversion created a rift between his mother and himself lasting for several years during which time David became an entrepreneur tailor and shopkeeper. He married Emily Leung and the surname Ewing-Chow was carried by their 11 children, although some later descendants have reverted to the original Chinese surname Chow. David's elder sister married Wong T'in, who was also known by the surname Kam, and bore three children taking the Kam name. After his death she married Samuel Low and had three daughters.

Foo: This surname can be derived from different Chinese written characters that have Fu as the Mandarin equivalent. Some people with the Foo surname are also descended from Tong Foo.

Fung: There are several families with the surname Fung, the Cantonese version of the Mandarin surname Feng, which is among the top 50 Chinese surnames. Among those bearing this surname are the descendants of Fung A-pan, an immigrant on the *Whirlwind* in 1860, and Fung A-man, who arrived on the *Arima* in 1865. There are also other Fung families whose surname is equivalent to the Mandarin name Hung, which in Hakka dialect is pronounced Fung (see Fung-A-Fat and Hung Khui-syu).

Fung-A-Fat: The family traces its ancestry to the Hung clan, this surname being made famous by the exploits of Hung Hsiu-ch'uan, Heavenly King of the Taiping Rebellion. The Hakka pronunciation of Hung is Fung and thereby generated the spelling Fung for the family. One of the immigrants to British Guiana was Hung Kung-fat, a passenger on the *Dartmouth* in 1879, whose name was transformed into Fung-A-Fatt and from whom the family name is derived. Most of the descendants are now known by the simpler spelling Fung-A-Fat and some others have resumed the use of the root Hakka surname Fung.

Fung-A-Ling: Fung A-ling was born about 1839 and became known as Job Fung-A-Ling. He married Rosa Chin-A-Kou and had 4 children.

Fung-Fook: The surname is believed to originate from the immigrant named Fung Fook.

Fung-Kee-Fung: Fung Kee-fung arrived in British Guiana via another country and thus is shown in immigration records to be a "Casual." His son, known as Joseph Fung-Kee-Fung, was born about 1858 and became established at Windsor Forest, West Coast Demerara. He married Martha Kwok, daughter of Kwok Fok-un, who continued the management of the family's plantation holdings and shops after his death in 1914. They had 11 children known by the surname Fung-Kee-Fung.

Fung-Teen-Yong: Fung-A-Pan, an immigrant from Poon Ye was aboard the *Whirlwind* in 1860. He married Yung Shee and they had nine children, one of them being Isaac Fung-Teen-Yong, better known as "G.P." Fung.

Gillette: An immigrant with the surname Cheong became known as John Alexander Smith Gillette. Some descendants are known by the surname Smith-Gillette and others by Gillette.

Hebert: An immigrant of the Leung clan was given the name Hebert by a religious minister of the same name, and this has become the surname for his descendants.

Hew: See Hugh.

Hing: The Hing family name is derived from different immigrants including Phang Hing, U-Hing (on the *Chapman* in 1861), and Wong A-hing (*Sea Park*, 1861).

Ho: The Mandarin equivalent of this name, ranking among the top 50 surnames, is He (pronounced "huh"). Ho A-Kai and Ho A-yee are among those whose descendants have the surname Ho.

Ho-A-Hing: Ho Hin was born in Sam Shui, Guangdong Province and left China aboard the *Red Riding Hood* in 1862 at the age of nineteen. Assigned initially to Plantation Eliza and Mary in Berbice he later was transferred to Plantation Bath where the manager Andrew Hunter promoted him to be a driver. Ho Hin became known as Andrew Hunter Ho-A-Hing and opened a shop on the estate. Ho-A-Hing prospered and then moved his operations to New Amsterdam where he be-came a wealthy and well-known businessman with branch stores in Georgetown. He married Ruth Tang in 1880 and had 12 children carrying the Ho-A-Hing surname. One branch of the family in Singapore has since changed to the spelling Hoahing.

Ho-A-Kai: The surname Ho-A-Kai is believed to be derived from the original immigrant Ho A-kai. Some later generations are known as Ho.

Ho-A-Lim: Family accounts say that Ho A-lim and his brother were out for a stroll in their native village of Pok Loh when they were kidnapped and shipped to British Guiana aboard the *General Wyndham* in 1859. Ho A-lim survived the journey but his brother was taken off when the boat docked at a refueling port in the Strait of Malacca. Known as Thomas Ho-A-Lim, he had 13 children, one of whom, Philip. studied law and became Chairman of the Malayan Democratic Union after World War II.

Ho-A-Shoo: Sometimes also written Ho-A-Shu, there are two unrelated Ho-A-Shoo families. One is believed to originate from Ho A-shoo and his descendants became established in Bagotville, West Bank Demerara. The other is derived from Ho A Shau who was immigrant #6567 on the *Bucton Castle* in 1865. Cecil Clementi incorrectly states that he arrived on the *Corona*. His name became John Ho-A-Shoo and he gained his wealth through shops he opened in the remote gold and diamond fields. He married Marie Wong Fung-kiu, daughter of his business partner Wong A-yong, and they had 8 children who took the surname Ho-A-Shoo.

Ho-A-Yun: Born about 1844, Ho A-yun immigrated on the *Sebastopol* in 1861. He became known by the name James Ho-A-Yun and was twice married. His first wife bore him six children and his second, Eliza Young, daughter of Yang A-Pat, had one son. The children took the surname Ho-A-Yun, although some are also known as Ho-Yun.

Ho-Chan: Possibly comes from an immigrant named Ho Chan.

Ho-Chung: The surname is believed to originate with an immigrant named Ho Chung. See also Ho Ten-pow.

Ho-Chung-Qui: See Ho Ten-pow.

Ho-Sing-loy: Ho Sing-loy was known as Samuel Henry Ho-Sing-Loy. He became an interpreter at the Immigration Depot. The Ho-Sing-Loy surname was continued by his descendants, with some also known as Loy.

Ho-Ten-pow: Ho Ten-pow was better known as John Ho-Ten-Pow. With his first wife he bore two children, the son having the name Benjamin Ho-Chung-Qui from whom the sur-names Ho-Chung, Chung and Ho-Chung-Qui have been derived. John Ho-Ten-Pow and Charlotte Tanner Lam then had 13 children, the descendants taking the surnames Ho-Ten-Pow, Ten-Pow and Tenpow.

Ho-You: Ho You is the likely originator for this surname.

Ho-Yow: Believed to originate from Ho Yow who was a lad of 15 when he arrived in 1865. In 1890 he married Henrietta Lam, daughter of Ananias Lam-A-Poo and they had six children.

Ho-Yun: See Ho-A-Yun.

Hugh: Also written Hew the spelling Hugh may have come into being because of its closeness to the English name of the same spelling. This surname can be derived from either Hu (either Cantonese or Mandarin) or else Qiu (pronounced "chew.") The family name is also carried by descendants of Yu Kong-ku, with the Yu surname being transformed into Hugh.

Hugh-Yow: The original immigrant of this family is understood to be from the Hui clan.

Hui: This is one of the top 20 surnames and becomes Xu (pronounced somewhat like "shoe") in Mandarin.

Humphreys: A Chinese immigrant of the Wong clan is understood to have been renamed Humphreys. One of his daughters married Chin-A-Pow but some of their children are also known by the surname Humphreys.

Hung: This is the surname of the family clan from which came Hung Hsiu-ch'uan who declared himself Heavenly King of the Taiping Kingdom. Written Hong in Mandarin the surname is pronounced Fung in Hakka dialect and it is by the latter version that descendants are better known. See Fung-A-Fat and Hung Khui-syu.

Hung Khui-syu: The son of Hung Jen-kan, who became the Shield King of the Taiping Heavenly Kingdom, Hung Khui-syu escaped to Guangzhou Province after the collapse of the Taiping Rebellion. There he continued to teach Christianity in the countryside, but when persecution by the vengeful imperial troops became dangerously close he was given protection in Hong Kong by European missionaries. The surname Hung is pronounced Fung in Hakka dialect so that he was also know as Fung (or Foong) Qui-sue. He married Tsen A-lin, a girl from Shanghai who was going to be sold off by her parents but was taken into the care of missionaries. He taught for a while under the auspices of the Basel missionaries and emigrated to British Guiana aboard the *Dartmouth* in 1879, along with his wife and three children. He served as a catechist and became an overseer at Plantation Diamond, East Bank Demerara and a pastor at St. Saviour's Church in Georgetown. He had three more children and later left for Trinidad with his expanded family.

Isaacs: At his baptism, Lee A-Shoo (see below) was given the name Isaacs by the attending minister, Rev. Isaacs. Some of the later generations thus became known by the surname Isaacs.

James: See Chung-A-Ming and Ng-Yow.

John: Lam A-tung, an immigrant aboard the *Minerva* in 1860, was given the name John. His descendants thus became known by the surname John. However, in 1927, his son Augustus John made a legal application for his name to be changed to Augustus John Lam, thus reviving the original Lam surname. In similar fashion the descendants of John Chu Cheong became known by the surname John.

Joseph: See Ng-A-pu.

Kam: This surname is the Cantonese form of the Mandarin surnames Gan and Jin. Chan A-kwong, an immigrant on the *Genghis Khan* in 1862 was also known by the surnames Kam and McLean. See also Wong T'in.

Kong: This meaning of this Cantonese surname is river and is written as Jiang in Mandarin. Several members of the Kong clan arrived aboard the *Dora* in 1860. They originated from Sin Own, just north of Hong Kong. See also Chu-A-Kong.

Koo: One of the rarer Chinese surnames, the Mandarin form of which can be Gu (pronounced "goo") or Qiu (pronounced "chew"). Another variant of the Koo name originates with Kow

A-ping, a native of Kwei Chow, who immigrated on the *General Wyndham* in 1859, and also from Kow Cook-hong.

Kow: See Koo.

Kum: This name becomes Jin (pronounced "gin") in Mandarin. Two Kum twin brothers arrived on the *Red Riding Hood* in the 1860s one of whom, Kum Tai-yi, was given the name Timothy. His twin brother became known as McLean Kum with descendants carrying the McLean surname.

Kwang: Kuang is the Mandarin spelling for this clan name, which is also pronounced Kong in Cantonese. Also derived from the personal name of immigrant Ng A-kwang.

Kwok: This is the Cantonese pronunciation for Guo in Mandarin and is among the top 20 most frequently occurring surnames. The descendants of immigrant Kwok Fok-ng, who sailed on the *Ganges* in 1863, and his wife Victoria Phang Shee carry the surname Kwok, pronounced "coke."

Lai: See Li.

Lam: The ninth most prevalent Chinese surname, Lam is also written as Len, Lim, Lin and Lum and is the equivalent of Lin in Mandarin. Among the ancestors of Lam families are Lam-A-Poo (*Pride of the Ganges*, 1866), Lam A-tung (*Minerva*, 1860), Lam A-yow (*Minerva*, 1860), and Lum Cha (*Mystery*, 1861). See also John and Marks.

Layne: Immigrant Len A-yook is believed to be of the Lin clan. His son's name was changed to the more English version Layne when he was registered to be married to Mary Chin, daughter of Chin Chan-Choong. The Layne surname was then carried on by their descendants.

Lee: The Lee clan name, spelt Li in Mandarin, is the third most frequently occurring Chinese surname. The descendants of Lee-A-Choi (*Saldanha*, 1861), Lee Lam-cha (*Montmorency*, 1861) and Li-A-Tak (also written Lee-A-Tak) (*Agra*, 1862) are among those who carry the Lee surname.

Lee-A-Shoo: The name is believed to be derived from Lee A-shoo, an immigrant of 15 years who landed in 1865. He and his wife Mary raised four children who were known by the surnames Lee-A-shoo and Isaacs (see above).

Lee-Own: Chinese written characters show the name to be Lee A-On (Li Ya-an in Mandarin). He arrived as a 5-year-old with his mother on the *Zouave* and allotted to Canefield in Berbice. In adulthood he became a successful shop-keeper. He married

Agatha Ng-A-Fook with whom he had 14 children carrying the surname Lee-Own.

Leow: The Leow surname is a dialect variation of the Mandarin name Liu, but different from the other Liu clan name that becomes Low in Cantonese.

Leu: See Lieu.

Leung: Ranking among the top 30 most popular Chinese names, Leung is the Cantonese equivalent of Liang in Mandarin. One of the Leung clan immigrants arrived on the *Thomas Mitchell* in 1860. He became known as Simon Leung and worked as an interpreter for the Immigration Office until his death in 1906. He married Mary Gemon and had 16 children, most of whom emigrated to Panama when excavation of the canal began. See also Hebert.

Leung-A-King: Leung A-king arrived on the *Sea Park* in 1861. He was a catechist on West Coast Demerara and also a shopkeeper. He was also known as James Leung-A-King and married Sarah Green. Their six children were known by the surname Leung-A-King.

Lewis: Lu A-tak, an immigrant aboard the *Queen of the East* in 1865 was otherwise known as Arthur Lewis, and the Lewis surname continued with his descendants.

Li: Pronounced "lie" this Cantonese name is also written Lai and, like Lee, has Li as the equivalent Mandarin spelling but is a different written character, not as prevalent. See also Aaron.

Li-A-Ping: A native of Sun Tak, Li A-ping arrived on the *Red Riding Hood* in 1861. He was allotted to Haarlem, West Coast Demerara. Descendants carry the Li-A-Ping or Liaping surname.

Lieu: This name is equivalent in Mandarin to either Liao or Liu, the second of which has also become Low.

Liu: This surname ranks fifth among the most prevalent surnames and becomes Lao or Low in Cantonese.

Loh: A spelling variation of Low.

Loo: There are four different characters written as Lu in Mandarin, which would be equivalent to Loo or Lou in Cantonese. Two of the four Lu clan names occur among the top 50 most prevalent surnames. Loo Tong-chu was one of the original immigrants whose descendants carry the Loo surname. See Lewis.

Loquan: It is said that the original immigrant was named Quan but because he was somewhat older that his compatriots he was addressed as Lo Quan meaning "Old Quan" as a form of respect. This evolved into the surname Loquan.

Lou-Hing: It is handed down that immigrant Lou Hing lived in Essequibo and died leaving a daughter and son as orphans who were known by the surname Lou-Hing.

Loung: This is equivalent to the Mandarin Long (pronounced "lung"). It is reported that some Loung families are actually Leung, the transformation coming from a misreading of the name written in English.

Low: Also written as Lau, Lowe and Loh this Cantonese name is commonly associated with Liu, one of the top 10 Chinese surnames. The descendants of Lau Shiu-t'ong are known by Low. See also Lieu.

Low-A-Chee: Lau Un-che (also written Lau Yun-chay) was a native of Thong Kun who traveled aboard the *Dora* in 1860. He married Mary Kok and had 7 children who carried the surname Low-A-Chee.

Low-A-Sue: A native of Hong Kong, Low A-sue was known as William Low-A-Sue. He married Lydia Aaron and their children assumed the Low-A-Sue surname.

Lowe: An alternative spelling of Low. The descendants of Low A-yong, immigrant aboard the *General Wyndham* in 1859, are known by the surname Lowe.

Loy: Also written Loi or Louie, the name becomes Lei (pronounced "lay-ee") in Mandarin. See also Ho-Sing-Loy.

Luck: The equivalent in Mandarin is Luo (pronounced "loo-oh"). It is said that Luck Kim-hee was recruited by a Chinese person who had returned to China from British Guiana. Born about 1855, he traveled on the *Dartmouth* in 1879. He became a shopkeeper and raised a family of 13 children who took the Luck surname.

Lui: A variation of Loy. Some Lui surnames may also have arisen from a misinterpretation of the surname Liu when written in English.

Lyen: This surname originates from immigrant Lui A-kwong who arrived as immigrant #1010 on the *Norwood* in 1860.

Mack: Mak is another written form for this Cantonese name, which is Mai (pronounced "my") in Mandarin.

Man: Also written Mann, the name becomes Wan in Mandarin. Another possibility is a dialect variation of the Cantonese Mun which would be Man in Mandarin.

Man-Son-Hing: Mun Son-hing traveled on the *Mystery* in 1861 accompanied by his wife Fung Shee and son Man Yuk-shang. He became the originator of the Man-Son-Hing (or Manson-Hing) family line.

Marks: One family named Marks is derived from Lam A-yow who was one of three Lam brothers who arrived on the *Minerva* in 1860 and allotted to Berbice. Lam A-yow was given the personal name Mark and his descendants thereafter have carried the surname Marks. The members of the other Marks family, who became established in Demerara, are understood to take their name from an immigrant who was given the name William Mark.

McLean: Chan A-kwong, who arrived on the *Genghis Khan* in 1862, was one of a few Chinese immigrants known by the surname McLean, apparently taking the name of a minister or estate manager. See Kum.

Milner: A Chinese immigrant named Wong Che-nyow, assigned to a plantation in Berbice, was bestowed with the name Peter Milner when he was baptized by the Seventh Day Adventist minister, Peter Milner.

Ming: See U A-ho.

Mook-Sang: See Tsoi-Mook-sang.

Murray-Cheong: See Cheong-A-Hoi.

Ng: Sometimes written Ing, this Cantonese name is the popular surname Wu in Mandarin.

Ng-A-fook: Archival records show that Ng Fook was the name that Moo Kow Ten, #339 on the *General Wyndham,* chose for his son. It is likely that the family surname is in fact Ng and that Moo was an erroneous entry made by the scribe. The son was born in Lusignan in 1869 and was known as John Cyril Ng-A-Fook and later became a successful businessman. Some of the children of John Cyril and his wife Tamar Lee became known by the surname Cyril while others have retained the full name Ng-A-Fook as the surname.

Ng-A-Kien: Most likely derived from the immigrant Ng A-kien.

Ng-A-Kwang: Descendants of Ng-A-Kwang carry his full name as a surname or else are known as Kwang.

Ng-A-pu: Given the name John Joseph, Ng A-pu's children with his wife Mary Li, daughter of Aaron Li, became known by the names Ng, Ng-A-Pu and Joseph.

Ng-A-Qui: Believed to be derived from an immigrant named Ng A-qui.

Ng-See-Quan: This name is said to be derived from the original immigrant Ng Sue-quan of the Ng family clan. Later generations are also known by Quan.

Ng-Yong: Wilfred Samuel Ng-A-Yong, a son of Ng-A-Fook, was the originator of the Ng-Yong surname.

Ng-Yow: Immigrant Ng A-yow was given the names James Solomon. Although his children carried the surname Ng-Yow, the second son became better known as Henry James and the third son, who became a doctor practicing in England, took the name Charles Yow. While the son of Henry James continued with the family name James, the daughters were known by the surname Ng-Yow.

Paul: One of the families known by the surname Paul is derived from the given name of Paul Fung-A-Yu. Another family is said to originate from immigrant Su A-sam. See also Tong Shun.

Phang: Equal to Pang or Peng in Mandarin, the latter occurs among the top 50 frequently occurring surnames. The surname Phang is carried by descendants of Phang Hing as well as Phang Yee, immigrant No. 2764 on the *Lancashire Witch*.

Phang-Hing: The descendants of Phang Hing became known by all three possible surnames — Phang, Hing and Phang-Hing.

Phillips: An immigrant named Lo A-mun (also known as How Sam) was given the name John Tait Phillips and his descendants are known by the surname Phillips.

Poon: This Cantonese name is written as Pan in Mandarin. Poon A-chin arrived on the *Queen of the East* in 1865 and married Ham Siow, an immigrant on the *Lady Elma Bruce* which landed in August 1862. They raised seven children taking the Poon surname.

Quan: Also written Kuan or Kwan the name becomes Guan in Mandarin. Because Quan occurs as the ending part of the compound surnames Ng-See-Quan and Sue-A-Quan, some later generations of these families have adopted Quan as the surname. See also Loquan.

Richards: An immigrant of the Choong clan is understood to have been given the personal name Richard. His descendants in Trinidad are known by the Richards surname.

Sam: This is the Cantonese or Hakka pronunciation for the surname Cen (pronounced "tsen") in Mandarin.

Scott: Shim Gott was born in the 1840s in Sun Wai, Guangdong Province. After immigrating to British Guiana he later left to make his fortune in Trinidad. He had a successful beginning in merchandising and it is said that Shim Gott next wanted to enter the liquor business but he found that the colonial authorities did not readily issue licences to those with unconventional names. Thereupon he changed his name to Thomas Scott. His success continued with his son William Henry Scott who built a thriving empire with a variety of business activities including trading, retailing, manufacturing and real estate.

Seow: The surname Seow is a variation of the surname Soo. Born in Canton in 1839 Seow Sam immigrated aboard the *Minerva* in 1860. He was assigned to Plantation Perseverance in Berbice and became known as Phillip Seow-a-Sam. He later became a shopkeeper, married Mary Wong Shee and raised a family of 10 children, some of whom carry the surname Seow-Sam and others Seow.

Seow-Sam: See Seow.

Shim: This surname in Mandarin becomes Shen. See also Scott and Thomas.

Siung: After Hung Khui-syu (see above) took his family to Trinidad, his eldest son Hung Ken-siung became known as Henry Siung. This surname was also carried by Henry's younger brother Samuel and his descendants.

Stokes: Chin Sin-qui, passenger on the *Claramont* in 1861, was born about 1843 and was assigned to Plantation Enmore, East Coast Demerara, managed by Mr. Stokes. He became known as Chin-Qui-Stokes and rose to the position of head distiller on the estate. His descendants continue to carry the surname Stokes although some have reverted to the original Chinese surname Chin.

Sue: Also written as Seow, Siu, Soo and Sui, the surname in Mandarin is Su and ranks among the top 50 most prevalent surnames. Some of the descendants of Ching-A-Sue also use Sue as their surname.

Sue-A-Chung: Believed to originate from an immigrant named Sue A-chung (or Sue Cheong), the family became established as shopkeepers in Sisters Village, West Bank Demerara.

Sue-A-Quan: Soo A-cheong was 60 years old when he embarked on the *Corona* in December 1873. He was accompanied by his 37-year-old wife Yau Shee and son Soo Sam-kuan, a boy of nine. The family was allotted to Plantation La Grange, West Bank Demerara but Soo-A-cheong quit working as an indentured labourer a year later. Soo Sam-kuan was baptized by a church rector named Henry John May. This raises the possibility that Soo Sam-kuan's family name could have become May since he was affectionately called "Old May." However, his descendants carry a variation of his full name, i.e. Sue-A-Quan. Henry Sue-A-Quan became a shopkeeper in Essequebo, and married Mary Ho, daughter of Ho-A-Yee. He moved to Met-en-Meerzorg at the turn of the century and raised a family of seven children. In 1915 he is shown to be involved in some real estate transactions at Vergenoegen, a few estates from Met-en-Meerzorg. Some later generations have changed their surname to Quan and Qan (as in Qantas).

In addition to his own family Henry Sue-A-Quan took care of a young boy John Chum-A-Kun who had been brought from Surinam by an aunt who was also accompanied by her two daughters. The aunt had hoped to marry off a daughter to one of Henry's sons but a match did not occur. The young Chum-A-Kun was then left with Old May who showed him the basics of shop-keeping and treated as a member of the Sue-A-Quan family. In adulthood he became known as John Cham-A-Koon.

Tan: The Tan surname is spelt and pronounced the same way in Cantonese and Mandarin.

Tan Tat: Derived from the immigrant Tan Tat who was born about 1841 and became known as John Tan Tat.

Tanner: This surname is said to have been given to an immigrant of the Lam family by a minister named Tanner. Another person with the Tanner surname was an immigrant who arrived about 1861. He was called Thomas Tanner but he hails from the Leung clan. He died in April 1911 leaving a widow but no descendants.

Tang: The surname Tang in Cantonese sounds closer to "dang" as in the word "dangle" and the written English form came about through the use of the letter "T" to depict the "dee" sound in early attempts at writing Chinese using the alphabet. In Mandarin the pinyin spelling is Deng and the surname is among the top 30 most prevalent names. Most of the Tangs are descendants of Tang A-chi, a native of Hok San, who arrived with his wife on the *Red Riding Hood* in 1861. Another Tang family comes from Tang A-tsoi, who came on the *Brechin Castle* in 1865. Tang A-tsoi married Rachel Wong Shee (a former spouse of Chan Hing) and the family later emigrated to Trinidad. One of

Tang A-tsoi's grandsons, Norman, was elected Mayor of Port-of-Spain (1948–1950).

Thomas: A passenger on the *Corona* in 1874, Shim Chin was given the name Thomas. He married Mary Chee-A-Wai, and Thomas became the family surname for most of his descendants, although some returned to the original Chinese surname Shim.

Tiam-Fook: See Chung-Tiam-Fook.

Ting-A-Kee: The surname Ting is more correctly pronounced "Ding" which is the Mandarin spelling. Ting A-kee is believed to have been a young lad when he arrived in British Guiana. He was adopted by William Alexander who gave the boy the same surname. Some of the later generations were known as Alexander but a reversion to the surname Ting-A-Kee was subsequently made. Ting A-kee gained success through charcoal making operations and also opened up grocery and rum shops.

Tjin: The "Tj.." spelling reflects the Dutch way of inscribing the Chinese pronunciation that would be written as "Ch.." in English. Thus Tjin would become Chin in English. Tjin-A-Fat and Tjin-A-Lin are some examples of Tjin clan members.

Tjon: The surname Tjon occurs in several families such as Tjon-A-Kien, Tjon-A-Mann, Tjon-A-On, Tjon-A-Yong, Tjon Hing and others. Tjon is the equivalent in Dutch for Cheong or Chung in English and reveals that the original immigrants have connections with Surinam, the Dutch colony east of Guyana.

Tong Shun: The Cantonese surname Tong becomes Tang in Mandarin spelling and ranks among the top 50 Chinese surnames. The son of Tong Shun was named Paul Tong-A-Shun, also written as Paul Tung-Shun, and his descendants are known by the surname Tung-Shun as well as Paul. Some Tong descendants carry the surname Foo (See Foo).

Too: The surname Too is more correctly pronounced like the English word "do" and is written Du in Mandarin. The surname is one of the top 50 most frequently occurring surnames.

Too-Chung: To Cheung was 10 years old when he arrived with his mother, Chea Shee, aboard the *Ganges* in 1863. The compound Too-Chung surname is carried by his descendants.

Too-Kong: To Kong-sing, also called John Too-Kong, is the son of To A-fun, who landed in 1862 on the *Red Riding Hood.* John Too-Kong's descendants carry the surname Too-Kong.

Tsoi: The Mandarin form of this surname is Cai (pronounced "ts-sigh") and is one of the top 50 most prevalent surnames.

Tsoi-Mook-Sang: In 1866, Tsoi Kan-ui and his wife arrived with two sons, Tsoi Shui-fung and Tsoi Muk-shang aboard the *Pride of the Ganges*. The family came from Tung Koon and was allotted to Plantation Friends in Berbice. The younger son became known as James Tsoi-Mook-Sang and lived to be 80 years old, by which time he had become a well-known businessman in New Amsterdam. His descendants carry the surname Mook-Sang although several have the original Chinese surname Tsoi as one of their personal names.

Tung-Shun: See Tong-Shun.

U A-ho: A family consisting of U A-ho, his wife Loo Shee and four children, U A-kat, U A-hing, U A-ming and a girl who was given the name Grace Woo traveled on the *Chapman*, arriving in June 1861. U A-ho was born about 1826 in San Wui, Guangdong Province and he took his family abroad after his home was robbed by Taiping rebels. The family was assigned to Plantation Ogle. The surname written as U is the same as Woo or Wu so that one of the sons became known as U-Hing or Woo-A-Hing and the other Woo-Ming or U-Ming. Subsequent generations are also known by the surnames Ming and Hing. Loo Shee's second husband was Li A-tak, an immigrant who arrived on the *Agra* in February 1862, with whom she had a daughter Edith, who married the immigrant Ting-A-Kee, and a son George Lee.

U-Hing: See U A-ho.

U-Ming: See U A-ho.

Wan: See Woon.

Wong: This widely occurring Chinese name is the Cantonese version of two distinct Mandarin surnames, Wang, which is the most prevalent surname, and Huang, which ranks seventh. Families carrying the surname Wong include the descendants of Wong-A-Choi (who married Lydia Aaron), Wong-A-Fook (*Corona*, 1874), Wong A-lam (*Red Riding Hood*, 1861), Wong A-lam (*Sevilla*, 1865), Wong A-qui (*Dartmouth*, 1879), and Wong-A-Yong. See also Humphries.

Wong Mook: Wong Mook arrived on the *Dartmouth* in 1879 with two sons and a daughter. The family was assigned to Plantation Great Diamond, East Bank Demerara. The elder son Wong Yan-cheung became known as Joseph (also called John) Wong-En-Chung and he married Ida Seow, daughter of Phillip Seow-Sam, with whom he bore 10 children bearing the Wong surname. The younger son Wong Yan-sau was given the name Evan Wong and was a good scholar. He made a favorable impression on Rev. Robert Wylie who took him away from the plantation to the vicarage in Georgetown and subsequently to Enmore, East Coast Demerara. After a brief stint as interpreter for the Immigration Depot, Evan Wong opened a shop in Golden Grove, East Bank Demerara but packed up in the days of the gold rush to go off to Essequibo to stake his claim near the Omai mines. He fell ill, however, and returned to Georgetown. With help from his brother he started over in a shop at Plantation Diamond. He fortunes changed after this and he later acquired three estates devoted to rubber, cocoa, coffee and coconuts. He was then able to purchase the Omai mines, and branched out into the timber and sawmill industries. He married Sara Leung and their 12 children carry the surname Evan Wong.

Wong T'in: Wong T'in was born about 1838, a native of Poon Yu, and arrived on the *Red Riding Hood* in 1861. He became a shopkeeper in Anna Catherina, West Coast Demerara. He assumed the surname Kam and married the daughter of Mack Shee (see Ewing-Chow).

Woo: Ranking among the top 20 commonly found Chinese surnames the Cantonese Woo is also written as O, U and Wu and in Mandarin becomes Hu which is pronounced "who."

Woo-A-Hing: See U A-ho.

Woo-Ming: See U A-ho.

Woo-Sam: Believed to be derived from an immigrant named Woo Sam who became established as a businessman in Berbice.

Woon: Also written Wan and Wen this Cantonese name is equivalent to Wen (pronounced "when") in Mandarin.

Woon-A-Fook: Also known as Simon Woon-A-Fook, Woon Fook was a shopkeeper married to Maria the daughter of Len A-yook.

Woon-Sam: Le A-pan, #269 on the *Whirlwind* in 1860 is shown in archival records to have legally changed his name in 1889 to Wong A-sam. This then morphed into Woon-Sam. He became a shopkeeper in Essequebo and known as George Woon-Sam. He married Jane Kong, daughter of Kong Foong-chin, who was born aboard the *Dora* three days before landing at Georgetown in March 1860.

Yan: One family with the surname Yan derives the name from James Ku A-nyan, born in 1866 to immigrant Ku Mak-sun, who came on board the *Brechin Castle* in 1865.

Yang-A-pat: Immigrant Yang A-pat, #1529 on the *Saldahna*, became known by the name James Yang-A-Pat. He was a catechist on East Coast Demerara and also a shopkeeper. He married Rhoda Chung and had seven children known by the surnames Young-A-Pat and Young.

Yau: See Yow.

Yee: Descendants of immigrant Ow Yee, known as Gideon Ow-Yee, carry the surname Yee.

Yhap: Also spelt Yap, this is a Cantonese variation of Yip. Descendants of immigrants Yhap Chow, Yhap Young-sau, and Yip A-tow are known as Yhap.

Yhip: A variation of Yip.

Ying: This name has the same spelling in Mandarin.

Ying A-tseng: Born in San Hui, Guangdong Province Ying A-tseng traveled with his wife Kong Shee and daughter on the *Ganges* in 1863. They were assigned to Plantation La Belle Alliance, Essequibo. Their descendants are known by the surname Ying.

Yip: Although this surname occurs more frequently as Yhap among the Chinese from Guyana, the pronunciation in Cantonese is closer to Yip (also spelt Yhip). The name becomes Ye (pronounced "yeah") in Mandarin and ranks among the top 30 surnames. Some Yip descendants are derived from Yip Li-king, an immigrant on the *Red Riding Hood* in 1860.

Yong: See Young.

Young: Also spent Yeung, Yong and Yung, the spelling Young may have become more dominant because of its closeness to the sound of the English word describing "youth." The Mandarin equivalent is Yang, which is the sixth among the common surnames in China.

Yow: The Cantonese name Yow (or Yau) can be equivalent in Mandarin to You (pronounced "yo" as in "yoke") or Qiu (pronounced "chee-yew"). Henry Sue-A-Quan's mother, Yau Shee, comes from the Qiu family clan. See also Ng-Yow.

GOING INTERNATIONAL

Recent generations of the offspring of the Chinese indentured immigrants have spouses who are of many different races and nationalities. These inter-racial bonds have occurred not only in Guyana but more particularly in other countries to where the descendants of Chinese Guyanese have now migrated. This has resulted in a host of new surnames with an international flavor. They include Arrizza, Bacchus, Cezair, DaCosta, Erickson, Fernandez, Gradsky, Hoffberg, Iwakoshi, Jungst, Kachorowshi, LaCroix, McKenzie, Neilsen, O'Toole, Pillac, Queva, Rajack, St John, Taljit, Van Alts, Wishropp, Yedid and Zollna.

The descendants, bearing both Chinese and non-Chinese surnames, continue to blossom and flourish in countries all over the world perhaps with little knowledge of the events affecting their ancestors, the cane reapers. It is for them that this story has been told.

Red Riding Hood, 720 tons, was built in London as a tea clipper and launched in August 1857. She carried a total of 954 Chinese indentured immigrants from Canton to Georgetown in 1860, 1861 and 1862. *F.J. Lambert* oil painting done in China in the 1860s.

Corona, 1200 tons, was built in Dundee in 1866 and conveyed 320 convicts to Western Australia that year. She carried 388 Chinese immigrants to British Guiana in 1873. [© National Maritime Museum, Greenwich, London]

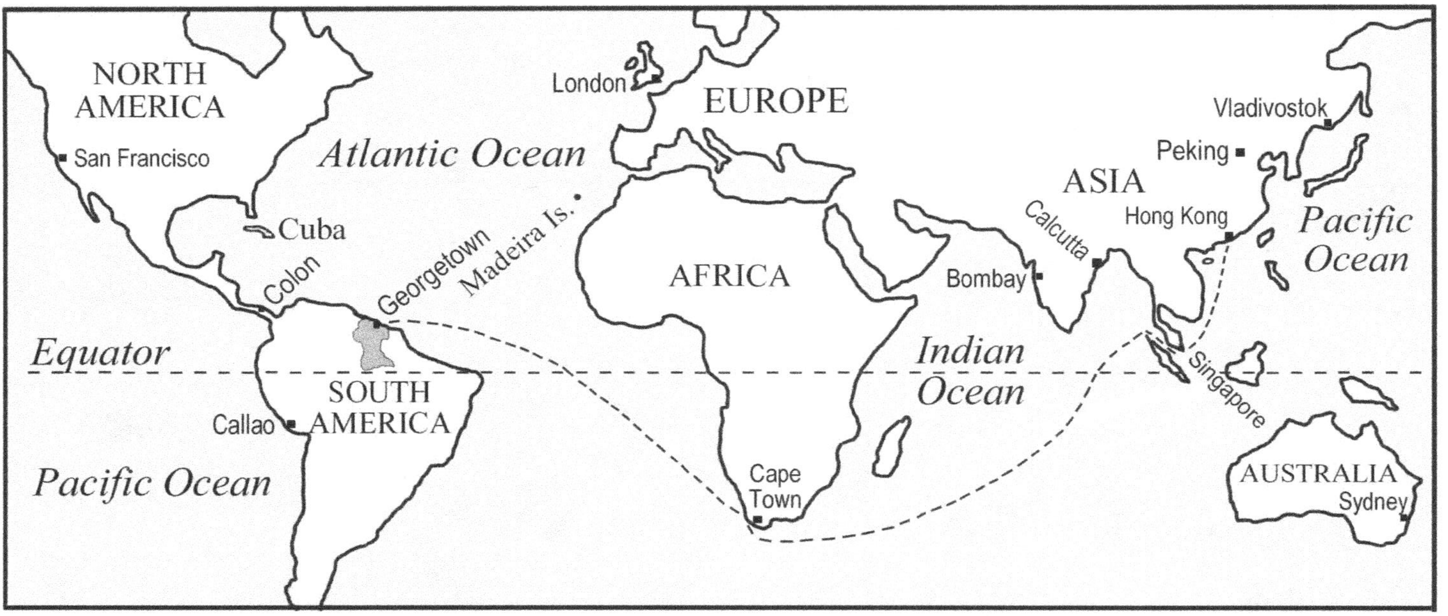

Sailing route between Hong Kong and Georgetown used by the immigrant ships. Stops were made at Singapore and Cape Town to re-supply the ships. Between 1853 and 1879, a total of 39 boats took 13,541 Chinese immigrants to British Guiana, the journey lasting between 2 and 6 months.

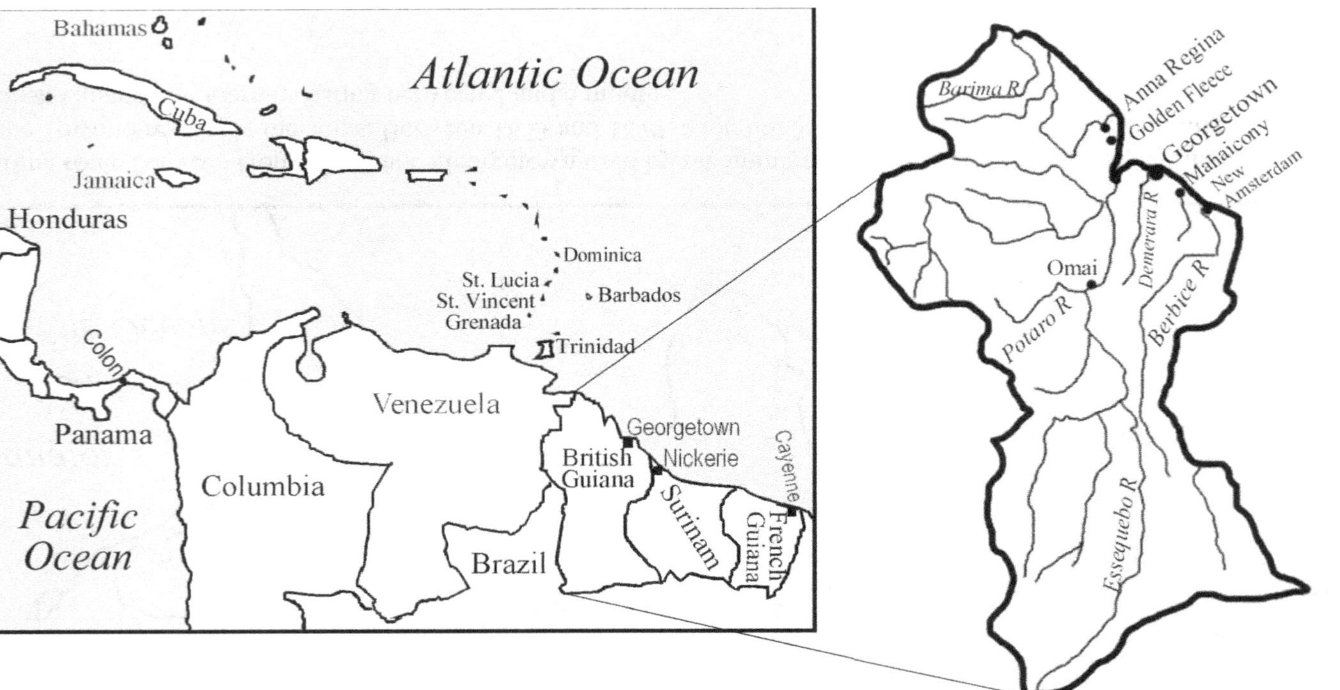

The Caribbean Region and the Guianas.

Guiana means “Land of Many Waters.”

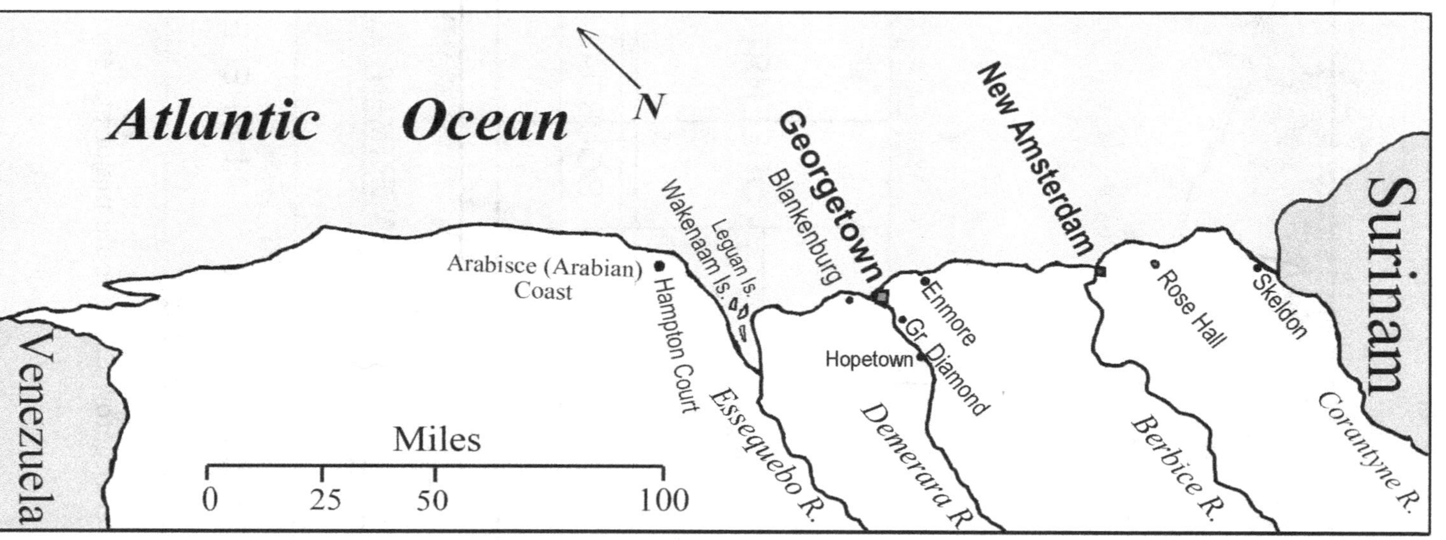

North Coast of British Guiana. The sugar plantations were located on the coastal strip of fertile land and along the banks of the major rivers. Names of the sugar estates are listed in the Appendix.

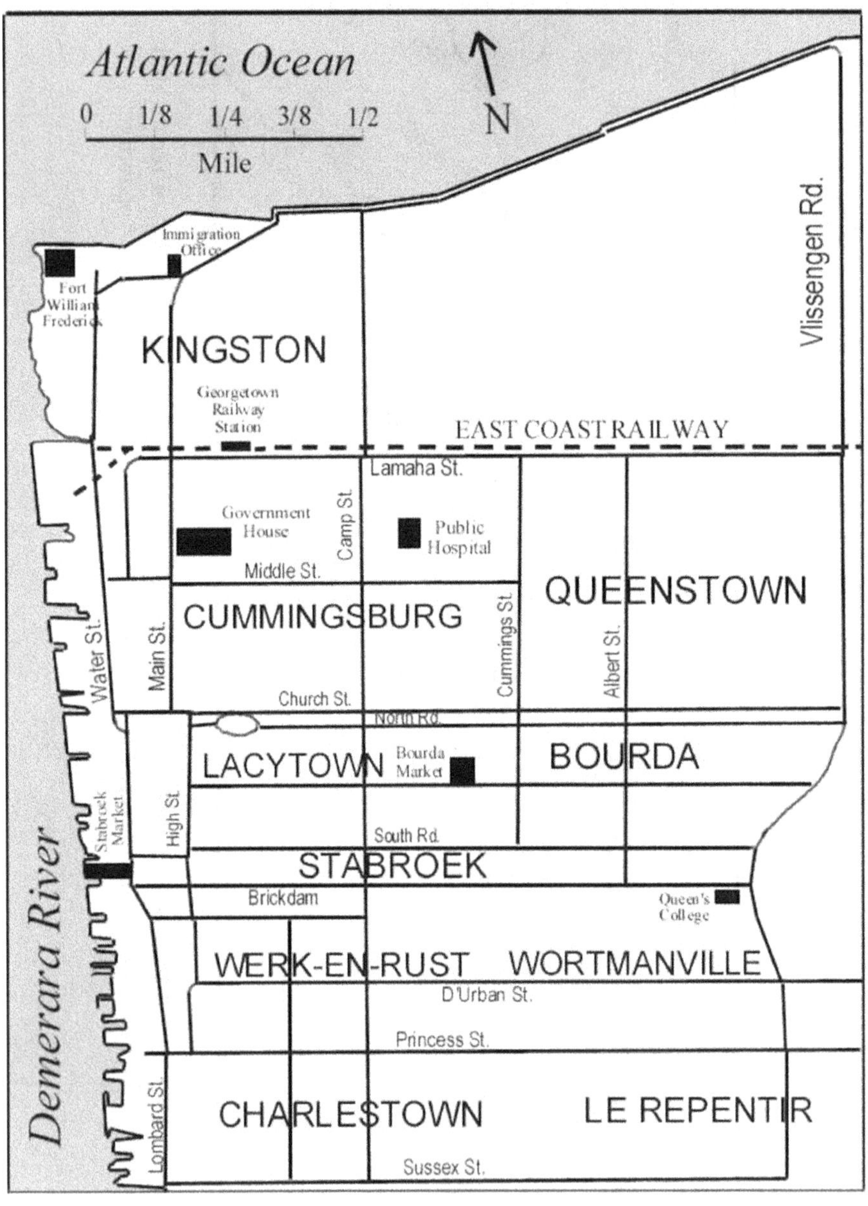

Districts of Georgetown and some major streets.

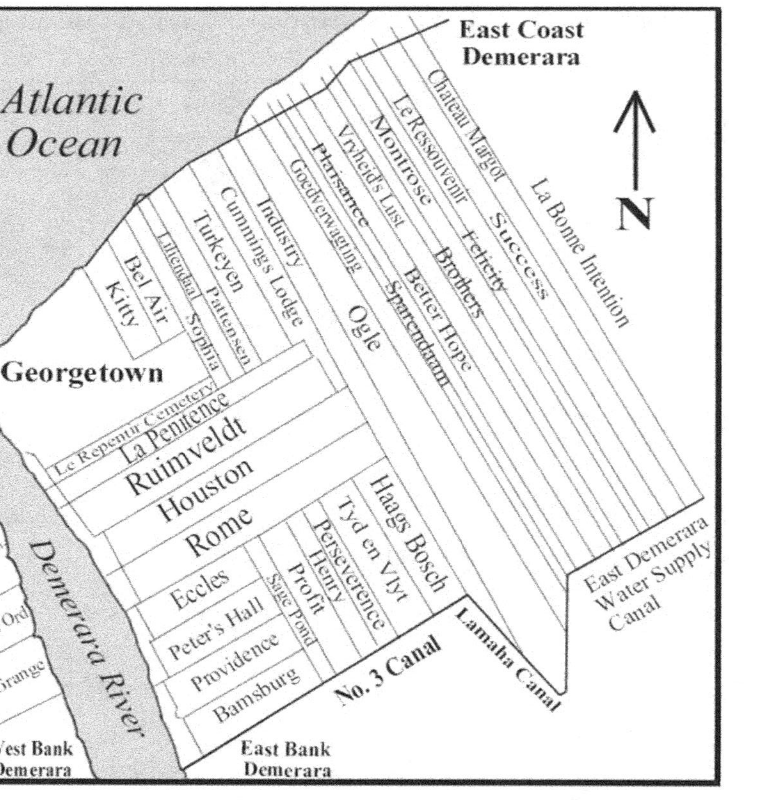

Sugar estates in the vicinity of Georgetown.

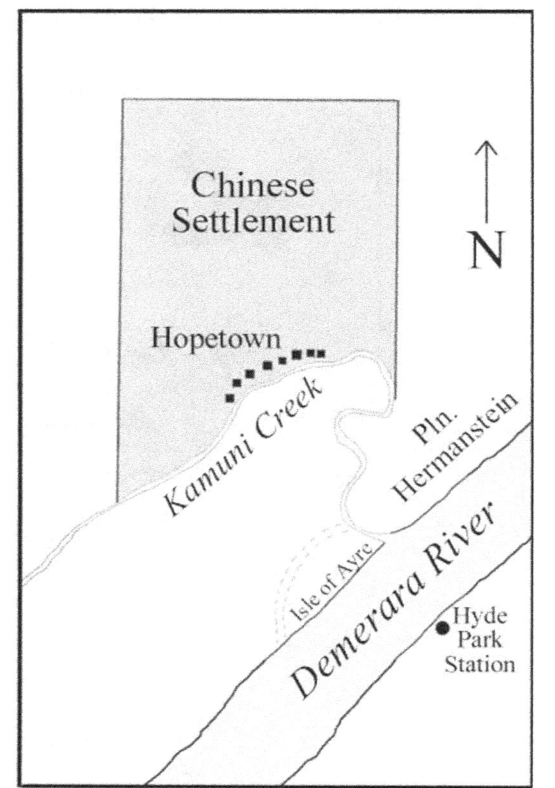

Hopetown, located about
25 miles from Georgetown.

Activities at the estate manager's house. *The Coolie. His Rights and Wrongs*, by Edward Jenkins, 1871.

Depiction of a hospital facility. *The Coolie. His Rights and Wrongs*, by Edward Jankins, 1871.

No. 29

BRITISH GUIANA — IMMIGRATION DEPARTMENT.

Temporary Certificate of Industrial Service.

Ord. 4 1864 Sec. 91

~~Immigration Office~~ La Belle Alliance the 26 day of September 1872

The Bearer Kong she F No. 3797 ex Ganges 1863

is entitled to demand and receive from the Immigration Agent-General a Certificate of Industrial Service which he can obtain on application for that purpose, at the Immigration Office, Georgetown; and meanwhile this Certificate is to be considered a Ticket of Leave.

Father's Name Kong a-yee

Age on arrival 39

Height

Bodily Marks Small scar centre of forehead

Immigration Agent-General

Temporary Certificate

No. 29

The Temporary Certificate of Industrial Service served as an interim document for those who had completed their service of indenture. This one was given to Kong She, who arrived with her husband Ying A-tseng on the *Ganges*.

18 80

BRITISH GUIANA, COUNTY OF Demerara

IMMIGRATION DEPARTMENT.

CERTIFICATE OF FREEDOM issued to Infant Immigrants who were Infants on introduction, or born in the Colony.

This is to Certify that the Chinese Immigrant hereunder described and who has never been under Indenture of Service is exempt from all legal liability to labor under the Immigration Ordinances of the Colony.

No. 87 Dated Friday 9th July 1880

Name of Immigrant, Sex, No. designated, name of Ship, year of arrival, if under one year of age on introduction, previous to the 1st July, 1873, and never under indenture of service.

Name of Immigrant, Sex, date of birth, if born in the Colony previous to the 1st July, 1873, and never under indenture of service. A-chow F Creole born on the Leonora Estate in 1868. Birth Register No. 273 – 1868

Name of Immigrant, Sex, date of birth, if born in the Colony since 1st July, 1873. 29th Aug 1867

Name of Immigrant, Sex, No. designated, name of Ship, year of arrival, if under 10 years of age on introduction since 1st July, 1873.

Name of Father of Immigrant, age on arrival, No. designated, name of Ship, and year of arrival. Poong-loong M No. 5394 Earl of Windsor 1862

Name of Mother of Immigrant, age on arrival, No. designated, name of Ship, and year of arrival. Soo-she F No. 4385 Earl of Windsor 1862

REMARKS.

NOTE.

Immigrants under 10 years of age require no Certificate of Freedom, as they are under no legal obligation to work.

James Crosby
Immigration Agent-General

This Certificate of Freedom was issued to A-chow, daughter of Poong-loong and Soo-she, immigrants on the *Earl of Windsor* in 1862. A-chow (Catherine) later married Nathaniel Ying, son of Ying A-Tseng.

Notice of Birth

For the Manager of any Plantation or Estate, Superintendent of any Woodcutting Establishment or Farm, and the Governor, Superintendent or other Resident Officer of any Gaol or any School, Reformatory, or other Public or Charitable Institution.—These Notices should be sent as soon as possible after the Birth, and the Sick Nurse or some competent Person should attend and sign the Registers at intervals of Two Weeks upon any day that may be arranged with the Registrar.

1. Where and when born. Ninth May 1883 Hopetown
2. Name, if any. Isaac-Sam
3. Sex. Boy
4. Name and Surname of Father and other Description* Sui-a-Sam Chinese
5. Name and Maiden Surname of Mother and other description* Mary Sam Chinese
6. Rank or Profession of Father. Farmer

Signature or Mark of Informant. Sui-a-Sam Chinese Father Hopetown.

Date.

Witness (Where a Mark is make by Informant)

* State whether Father and Mother are white, coloured, or black, European, Creole, West Indian, Portuguese, Chinese, Coolie, African, or Indian.

BRITISH GUIANA,

Immigration Department,

16th Feby 1899

No. 210.

The ~~Indian Immigrant~~ Chinese Bearer Isaac Sue Male,

Born ~~years on arrival~~, ~~No.~~ 1883 ~~189~~ of British Guiana

~~never having been under indenture to any~~ Estate in British Guiana, is at liberty to leave the Colony at any time he may desire to do so.

F.h. Sue-Sam 850 Minerva 1860.

[signature]

Immigration Agent General.

C. K. Jardine, Printer to the Government of British Guiana. 4,718—R.O. 7,227.

The Notice of Birth in 1883 for Isaac Seow (left) shows his name as Isaac-Sam and his father's name as Sui-a-Sam. When he left for Trinidad in 1899, his name on the emigration permit (above) was inscribed as Isaac Sue, with the name Sue-Sam for his father who was immigrant No. 850 on the *Minerva* in 1860. Family members are now known by the surnames Seow and Seow-Sam.

164

BAPTISMS solemnized in the Parish of *Saint George S. Saviour's Church* in the County of *Demerara* in the Year 18*82*.

[margin note]	When Baptized.	Child's Christian Name.	Parents' Name: Christian.	Parents' Name: Surname.	Abode.	Quality, Trade, or Profession.	By whom the Ceremony was Performed.
[illegible] 千里達	1882 April 19th No. 105	得其亞 Zacchens	陳秀 Chun	Sou Chinese adult	Charlestown	Barber	Henry Thomas Stamp Castell Incumbent S. Philip's Church
	1882 April 19th No. 106	大辟 David	陳必 Chun	Put Chinese adult.	Charlestown	Carpenter	Henry Thomas Stamp Castell Incumbent S. Philip's Church
[illegible]	1882 April 19th No. 107	打馬士 Thomas	廖同 Leu	Young Chinese adult.	Georgetown	Barber	Henry Thomas Stamp Castell Incumbent S. Philip's Church
1886 回唐	1882 April 19th No. 108	威廉 William	謝榮 Philip ~~Hannah~~ & Martha	Tsa Comm	Mahaica	Shop Keeper	Henry Thomas Stamp Castell Incumbent S. Philip's Church
1886 回唐	1882 April 19th No. 109	約瑟 Joseph	謝順 Philip & Martha	Tsa Comm	Mahaica	Shop Keeper	Henry Thomas Stamp Castell Incumbent S. Philip's Church
1886 回唐	April 19th No. 110	革順 Gershom	謝奇勝 Philip & Martha	Tsa Comm	Mahaica	Shop Keeper	Henry Thomas Stamp Castell Incumbent S. Philip's Church
[illegible] 月廿[illegible]故	May 31st No. 111	奄馬 Emma	Tong Qui Sue En Bin	Catechist's wife	Charlestown	Catechist	Henry Thomas Stamp Castell Incumbent S. Philip's Church
	June 27th No. 112	馬利亞 Maria (adult)	[illegible]	林[illegible] Father's name. Both parents Coolies.	Charlestown	—	Henry Thomas Stamp Castell Incumbent S. Philip's Church

The preceding page shows page 14 of the baptismal records at St. Saviour's Church for the year 1882.

The Chinese characters accompanying the child's Christian name are transliterations of the English names, such that, in re-translation they would sound like Twoh-mah-suh for Thomas and Ma-lee-ya for Maria. The predominance of biblical names is a common occurrence among the relatively recent Christian converts, being appropriately advised by their established religious leaders.

The entry in the margin alongside No. 105 is from a later date showing that Zaccheus Chun Sou departed for Trinidad in 1887, the year being inscribed using an ancient Chinese style of notation.

The first three entries on the page are for the baptism of adults indicating that Christianity was embraced by the indentured labourers as they settled in their new land.

The surnames written in English for the first three persons illustrate the difficulties of conversion from the Chinese pronunciation. The Chinese surname in No. 105 and No. 106 are written as Chun but this name is more commonly known as Chan or Chin, as well as Chen. The surname Leu in No. 107 occurs more often as Liu, and sometimes Lui, although the latter spelling may be a misreading of the name written in English. The marginal entry states that Thomas Leu Tong succumbed to disease in 1885.

Three children of Philip and Martha Tsa Comm (Will, Joseph and Gershom) were brought from Mahaica, East Coast Demerara for baptism at St. Saviour's Church. The family returned to China in 1886.

Foong Qui Sue, son of the Shield King of the Taiping Rebellion, and his wife En Bin had a daughter Emma who was baptised in 1882 but she died on 21 August 1884. Foong Qui Sue was a cathecist at St. Saviour's Church.

Entry No. 112 is for Maria, an adult of Indian descent who converted to Christianity, most likely through her husband Lam Hing-cheong. His title and relationship are shown in Chinese characters. The name of Maria's father, written in Hindi, is Dilonkas.

...3108. BRITISH GUIANA.

COPY FROM THE REGISTER OF BIRTHS IN DIVISION No. Twenty Eight DISTRICT "N" IN TH[E]
COUNTY OF Demerara IN THE YEAR 1899

When and Where born.	Name, if any.	Sex.	Name and Surname of Father and other Description	Name and Maiden Surname of Mother and other Description	Rank or Profession of Father.	Description Signature, and Residence of Informant	When Registered.	Signature of Registrar.	Baptismal Names if added after Registration of Birth
Ninth May Eighteen Hundred and Ninety Nine M' M' Zorg	James	Boy	Henry Sue-a-Quan Native Chinese Descent	Mary Sue-a-Quan (born Sue-a-Chunk) Native Chinese Descent	Shop-keeper	Henry Sue-a-Quan (Father) M' M' Zorg	Fifteenth May 1899	J. B. Liverpool Registrar	James Alexander 5th April 1939

JOB 5.4.39

CERTIFIED A TRUE COPY.

Fee 60 Cents.

April

Deputy Registrar General.

Birth certificate for James Sue-A-Quan, the author's uncle, hand copied in 1939 from the original document dated 1899. His mother's maiden name, which should be Ho, is inscribed as Sue-A-Chunk, which is her father-in-law's name. Errors such as this have crept into official documents when the person reporting the information failed to understand the questions asked in English.

Page 1764

BAPTISMS solemnized in the Parish Church of St Mark Enmore in the County of Demerara in the Year 1865

When Baptized.	Child's Christian Name.	Parents' Name. Christian.	Surname.	Abode.	Quality, Trade, or Profession.	By whom the Ceremony was performed.
1865 June 18th No. 1764	Henry May Chinese child	Sue Cheong & Sue	She	Enmore Estate	Parents intentional Labor on Enmore	Henry Holton May Rector of St Peters Leguan and Offg Minister.

Extracted from the Register-Book of the above Parish Church the 21st Day of June 1865 Henry Holton May Offg Mint.

This 1865 baptismal certificate for Henry May Sue Cheong was handed down to the author's family. Although the author's grandfather, Soo-A-cheong, was named Henry and affectionately called "Old May," there are inconsistencies in the date, location and also the wife's name, showing that this document is in fact not for the author's ancestor. This illustrates some of the difficulties faced in reconciling the information for Chinese immigrants when only English versions of their names are available.

Li-A-Tak (seated right), who immigrated on the *Agra* in 1862, poses for a photo with his wife Loo Shee (seated left), who arrived on the *Chapman* in 1861. Behind them are their son George Lee and his wife Maria. Completing the picture are the first four children of George and Maria – Rebecca, Katie, Victorine and Aldewyn. Loo Shee was previously married to U A-ho and bore seven children altogether with her two husbands. Her descendants now exceed 1,600 in number and live in different countries all over the world. (Photo ~1901). *Andy Lee.*

Family of Matthew and Mary Wong (granddaughter of U A-ho and Loo Shee). Back row (L to R): Johanna, Peter, Christine. Front row (L to R): Evaline, Matthew, Ivy, Mary, Walter (1908). *Margot DaCamara.*

Family of David and Emily Ewing-Chow. Standing: Mary (Moy), James, Elizabeth (Tingsie), Joseph, Rachel (Quannie), Jerimiah (Jerry). Seated: Solomon, Emily, David Johnstone, Rebecca (A-lan). Front: Robert, Charles, Nathaniel. *John Ewing-Chow.*

Judy Fung.

The Fung-A-Fat family has the same clan name as the Taiping Heavenly King, Hung Hsiu-ch'uan. Fung is the Hakka pronunciation for Hung. At the back stands Hung Kung-fatt, better known as Charles Fung-A-Fatt.

John Ewing-Chow.

James Ewing-Chow with his grandmother Mack Shee, a Chinese doctor who arrived in April 1860. (~1914)

Immigrant Ho Ten-Pow had three spouses with whom he fathered fifteen children. Here eight of his children gather with their mother Charlotte Tanner Lam. Clockwise from top left: Ivan, Edgar, George, Edwin, Victor, Leonard, Rose, and Henry. Most descendants are known by the surname Ten-Pow. *Whitney Ten-Pow.*

Robert V. Evan Wong (L), grandson of Wong Mook, immigrant aboard the *Dartmouth*, married Cheuleen Ho-A-Shoo (R), daughter of Ho Shau. Robert's brother Vivian married Cheuleen's sister Elizabeth. *Sally Bors.*

Marriage between Walter Chee-A-Tow and Pearl Sue-A-Quan, backed by their parents T.M. and Ivy Chee-A-Tow (L) and William and Johanna Sue-A-Quan (R). Walter's brother Stanley married Pearl's sister Elsie, a not unusual occurrence of double sibling marriages, even after four generations. *Margot DaCamara.*

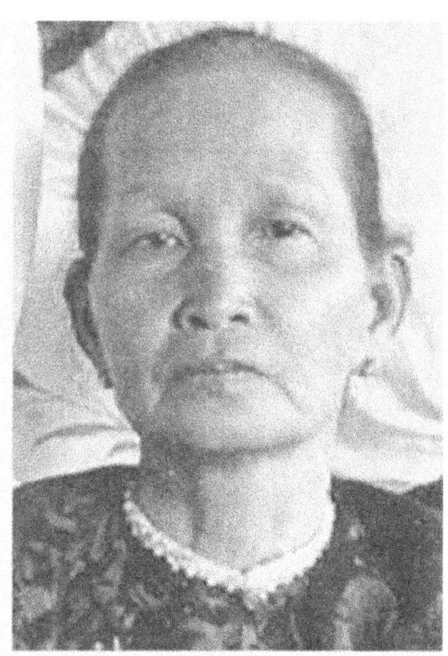

L: John Alexander Smith-Gillette is the son of an immigrant with the surname Cheong. Most descendants carry the Gillette surname. *Donna Chan.*
R: Wong Fung-kiow (Maria), wife of successful businessman John Ho-A-Shoo, originated from Surinam (1918). *Katy Wong.*

L: Wong Foong (Annie) married Luck Kim-hee, an immigrant aboard the *Dartmouth. Chris Lam.*
R: Joseph Clement Luck-A-Fat, popularly known as J.C. Luck, is the seventh of twelve children of Luck Kim-hee and his wife Annie. *Andy Lee.*

Edward Lou-Hing (L) and his wife Elizabeth Woon-Sam (R) are the author's maternal grandparents. Elizabeth's mother, Jane Kong, was born aboard the *Dora*, three days before arriving in Georgetown. *Roderick Sue-A-Quan.*

George Young (L), is the son of cathechist Yang-A-Pat, who was on the *Saldanha* in 1861. He married Lucretia Marks (R). Lucretia's grandfather, Lam A-yow, arrived on the *Minerva* in 1860 and given the personal name Mark. His descendants carry the surname Marks. *Rita Lou-Hing.*

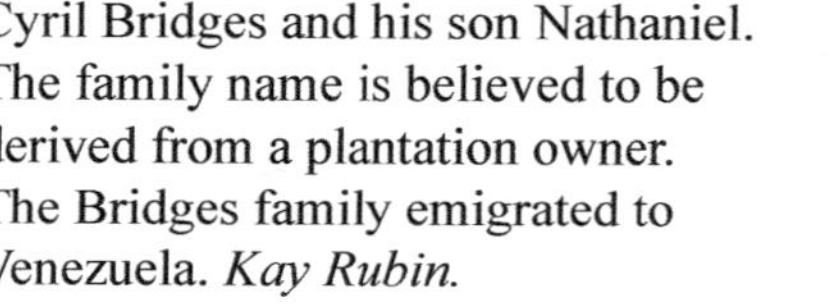

Cyril Bridges and his son Nathaniel. The family name is believed to be derived from a plantation owner. The Bridges family emigrated to Venezuela. *Kay Rubin.*

Sarah Chin-A-Yong, nee Fung-A-Fat, with her youngest son Abraham. After her husband died in the great George-town fire of 1913 Sarah and her two sons moved to Jamaica. *Judy Fung.*

Lily Woon-Sam (L) was one of many Chinese who emigrated to Trinidad. Her niece, Marie Lou-Hing, a sister of the author's mother (R), married James Sue-A-Quan. *Roderick Sue-A-Quan.*

Maria Chan-A-Sue, nee Wong, arrived in British Guiana as a child. She is the ancestor of all who carry the surname Chan-A-Sue. *Joe Pierre.*

Phoebe Fung-A-Shing appears in traditional Chinese dress. Her father Wong-A-Lam was an immigrant on the *Red Riding Hood* in 1861. *Patsy Layne.*

Elaine Fung-A-Ling

Sandi Wong-Moon

Local-born Chinese readily adapted to the British standards of custom and dress. L: Sisters Rosa Fung-A-Ling and Ellen Lee-A-Chung (nee Chan) pose with Ellen's daughter in fine Victorian attire. R: Josephine Wong-A-Wing, who married Samuel U-Ming, wears a dress with a narrow waist and high collar, the fashion of the 1900s.

Chung-A-Ming was given the name James and his family became known by the surname James. His son Thomas (above) was the owner of various transportation enterprises in the Corentyne, Berbice. *Les Bovell.*

Isaac "G.P." Fung-Teen-Yong gained wealth and status from cocoa estates in Essequibo. *Laura Hall.*

Matron Alice Fung-A-Ling became Supervisor of Best Hospital for tuberculosis patients. *Elaine Fung-A-Ling.*

Thomas James Chung-A-Ming, dressed in a white suit and standing ahead of the horse, was the owner of a bus company serving the Corentyne area. The photo was taken in front of his house. *Les Bovell.*

Central High School, located on Smyth Street, Werk-en-Rust, was founded by J.C. Luck. The initial enrollment in 1929 was 35 students. *Andy Lee.*

NOTICE.

THE UNDERSIGNED

HAVING resumed Business as GOLD and SILVERSMITH, at Lot No. 4, Lombard Street, cautions the public against purchasing goods said to be of his manufacture, unless the disposer of the Jewellery is provided with a printed copy of this intimation or a written authorization from me.

PHILIP-HOW-KAM-CHAY,
Gold & Silversmith.

May 3rd, 1879.

Wo-Lee and Co.

RESPECTFULLY intimate to the Public that their new premises at Lot 4 Lombard Street, third door south of HARRISON's Agency and Inquiry Office, being now completed they are enabled to offer as they now do a choice assortment of miscellaneous Chinese and Japanese GOODS, as well as their unequalled TEAS, at prices to suit the times.

June 7th, 1879.

SILVER SMITH.

WOUNG-A-CHOW,

GOLDSMITH

AND

SILVER SMITH,

LOMBARD STREET, (WATER SIDE, OPPOSITE NO. 12 LAMP,

BEGS to inform the Ladies and Gentlemen of Georgetown and Country, that he keeps a Stock of GOLD & SILVER BRACELETS, RINGS, LOCKETS CHAINS, &c., &c., and he will make anything to order. Goods are guaranteed in quality, and if found not of pure Silver or Gold, they will be taken back, and double the money given for them.

Come and see his Stock.

June 12th, 1879.

Sam-Yung-Tai,

FURNISHES of his own manufacture, Silver and Gold Bracelets, Broaches, Rings, etc., of exquisite manufacture both as to quality and design, and equal to European manufacture, at the most reasonable rates, consistent with quality and workmanship. His shop is immediately opposite to HARRISON's Agency and Inquiry Office. SAM-YUNG-TAI invites inspection of his stock of Jewelry.

June 21st, 1879.

Advertisements for products and services offered by Chinese businessmen began to appear in the *Royal Gazette* in the late 1870s.

C. S. CHUNG & CO., LTD.,

4 or 6, Water Street, Werk-en-Rust,

PROVISION, LUMBER, OPIUM AND GANGE

MERCHANTS;

DEALERS IN

WALLABA POSTS, PALING and VAT STAVES, SHINGLES,

AND ALL

Building Materials.

The sale of narcotic products such as opium and cannabis (in the form of bhang and gange) was legal to the beginning of the 20th century. The daily amount allowed to be sold to an individual was limited by law.
British Guiana Almanac and Directory, 1906.

APPENDIX

Table A1. Statistics for Chinese Immigrant Ships.

Table A2. Estates and Villages.

Table A3. Distribution of Chinese Immigrants.

Table A4. Contract of Indenture.

Table A1. Statistics of Chinese Immigrant Ships

Year of Arrival	Name of Ship	Tons	Whence	Date of Departure	Date of Arrival at Georgetown	Duration of voyage in days	Number Actually Embarked						Number Disembarked at Georgetown					
							Men	Women	Boys	Girls	Infants	Total	Men	Women	Boys	Girls	Infants	Total
1853	Glentanner	615	Amoy	1/9/52	12/1/53	134	305	- -	- -	- -	- -	305	262	- -	- -	- -	- -	262
"	Lord Elgin	354	"	23/7/52	17/1/53	177	115	- -	39	- -	- -	154	57	- -	28	- -	- -	85
"	Samuel Boddington	669	"	25/11/52	4/3/53	98	308	- -	44	- -	- -	352	260	- -	40	- -	- -	300
1859	Royal George	608	Hong Kong	8/12/58	29/3/59	110	300	- -	- -	- -	- -	300	254	- -	- -	- -	- -	254
"	General Wyndham	865	"	15/2/59	13/5/59	84	461	- -	- -	- -	- -	461	450	- -	- -	- -	- -	450
1860	Whirlwind	978	"	24/12/59	11/3/60	78	304	56	7	4	1	372	304	56	7	4	1	372
"	Dora	854	"	9/1/60	3/4/60	84	207	120	31	16	11	385	207	117	31	16	12	383
"	Red Riding Hood	720	Canton	22/1/60	8/4/60	75	298	12	4	- -	- -	314	297	10	4	- -	- -	311
"	Minerva	829	Hong Kong	9/2/60	23/5/60	96	233	65	8	2	2	310	230	65	8	2	2	307
"	Thomas Mitchell	578	Canton	23/2/60	9/6/60	107	252	- -	- -	- -	- -	252	252	- -	- -	- -	- -	252
"	Norwood	819	Hong Kong	10/3/60	23/7/60	135	269	52	3	4	3	331	259	48	3	4	3	317
1861	Sebastopol	938	Canton	23/12/60	28/3/61	95	283	45	4	1	- -	333	282	42	4	1	- -	329
"	Red Riding Hood	720	"	19/1/61	13/4/61	84	259	48	3	- -	4	314	256	47	3	- -	4	310
"	Claramont	634	Hong Kong	1/1/61	13/4/61	103	188	87	6	1	- -	282	188	86	6	1	1	282
"	Saldanha	1557	"	4/2/61	4/5/61	86	428	69	3	- -	- -	500	421	67	3	- -	1	492
"	Chapman	750	Canton	27/2/61	9/6/61	102	238	57	6	- -	2	303	230	53	6	- -	1	290
"	Mystery	1074	Hong Kong	3/3/61	9/6/61	97	316	41	1	1	1	360	295	39	1	1	1	337
"	Montmorency	660	"	14/3/61	27/6/61	105	271	18	- -	- -	1	290	265	17	- -	- -	1	283
"	Sea Park	835	Canton	18/3/61	7/7/61	112	236	52	4	1	- -	293	221	40	2	- -	- -	263
"	Whirlwind	977	Hong Kong	9/4/61	31/7/61	114	307	51	1	4	2	365	298	47	1	4	2	352
"	Lancashire Witch	1386	"	23/3/61	5/8/61	131	425	28	6	- -	2	461	398	26	6	- -	3	433

Table A1. Statistics of Chinese Immigrant Ships - Cont'd

Year of Arrival	Name of Ship	Tons	Whence	Date of Departure	Date of Arrival at Georgetown	Duration of voyage in days	Number Actually Embarked						Number Disembarked at Georgetown					
							Men	Women	Boys	Girls	Infants	Total	Men	Women	Boys	Girls	Infants	Total
1862	Agra	714	Canton	26/11/61	15/2/62	80	249	36	2	- -	- -	287	249	35	2	- -	1	287
"	Earl of Windsor	738	Hong Kong	4/12/61	17/3/62	104	178	141	2	3	1	325	172	124	2	2	3	303
"	Red Riding Hood	720	Canton	19/1/62	11/4/62	80	271	47	7	1	- -	326	270	45	7	1	1	324
"	Persia	1683	Hong Kong	19/3/62	10/7/62	112	405	112	9	5	- -	531	404	107	9	5	- -	525
"	Lady Elma Bruce	920	Amoy & Swatow	29/4/62	15/8/62	102	349	33	3	- -	- -	385	349	32	3	- -	- -	384
"	Sir George Seymour	730	HK, Canton & Swatow	1/4/62	20/8/62	142	281	38	5	- -	- -	324	256	29	4	- -	- -	289
"	Genghis Khan	1208	do.	2/5/62	20/8/62	110	406	97	4	2	3	512	385	86	4	2	3	480
1863	Ganges	839	Canton	4/4/63	29/6/63	85	293	100	12	4	4	413	286	92	12	4	2	396
1864	Zouave	1323	"	19/12/63	28/2/64	70	337	157	15	3	5	517	336	151	14	1	7	509
1865	Brechin Castle	537	"	18/10/64	26/1/65	100	187	78	5	- -	- -	270	186	76	5	- -	2	269
"	Queen of the East	1226	Whampoa	5/1/65	18/4/65	103	362	112	14	2	- -	490	358	107	13	2	1	481
"	Sevilla	598	"	8/3/65	22/6/65	106	204	93	14	- -	1	312	199	91	13	- -	2	305
"	Arima	691	"	31/3/65	18/7/65	109	271	59	13	- -	- -	343	249	50	12	- -	- -	311
"	Bucton Castle	886	"	30/4/65	28/8/65	120	266	74	10	- -	3	353	252	60	9	- -	4	325
1866	Light Brigade	1214	Amoy	18/1/66	14/4/66	86	488	4	- -	1	- -	493	482	4	- -	1	- -	487
"	Pride of the Ganges	641	Whampoa	31/3/66	31/7/66	122	259	29	16	1	- -	305	256	29	16	1	- -	302
1874	Corona	1200	"	23/12/73	23/2/74	78	314	40	26	5	3	388	313	40	26	5	4	388
1879	Dartmouth	915	Hong Kong	24/12/78	17/3/79	81	437	47	18	5	9	516	436	47	18	5	9	515

Table A2. Estates and Villages.

The following is a listing of the estates, towns and villages in British Guiana showing the constabulary districts. Published in the *Royal Gazette*, 9 December 1884.

Georgetown and Suburbs

Brick Dam District: Georgetown | Lodge Village | Wortmanville | Thomas

East Coast Demerara

Kitty District: Kitty Village | Bel Air

Sparendaam District: Liliandaal | Sophia | Turkeyen | Cumming's Lodge | Industry | Ogle | Goedverwagting | Sparendaam | Plaisance | Better Hope | Vryheid's Lust | Brothers | Montrose | Felicity | Le Resouvenir

Beterverwagting District: Success | Chateau Margot | La Bonne Intention | Beterverwagting | Triumph | Mon Repos

Vigilance District: Good Hope | Lusignan | Annandale | Buxton | Friendship | Vigilance | Bladen Hall | Strathspay | Nonpareil | Enterprise

Belfield District: Bachelor's Adventure | Paradise | Enmore | Haslington | Golden Grove | Naboclis | Cove and John | Victoria | Belfield | Hope | Duchfour | Two Friends | Ann's Grove | Clonbrook

Mahaica District: Beehive | Greenfield | Grove | Unity | Spring Hall | Mahaica | Helena | La Bonne Mere | Melville | Cane Grove

East and West Bank Demerara

Providence District: La Penitance | Ruimveldt | Meadow Bank | Houston | Rome | Agricola | Eccles | Bagot's Town | Peter's Hall | Providence | Haags Bosch | Canal No. 3 | Herstelling | Farm | Covent Garden | Great Diamond | Golden Grove | Craig | New Hope | Friendship

Toevlugt District: Vive-la-Force | Vriesland | Patentia | Hababoe Creek | Wales | Good Intent | Belle View | Sisters | Canal No. 2 | La Retraite | Toevlugt

Vauxhall District: Nismes | Bagotville | Canal No. 1 | La Grange | Schoon Ord

Vreed-en-Hoop District: Goed Fortuin | Versailles | Malgre Tout | Klein Pouderoyen | Vreed-en-Hoop | Best | Nouvelle Flanders | Unica

West Coast Demerara

Fellowship District: Haarlem | Windsor Forest | La Jalousie | Blankenburg | Den Amstel | Fellowship | Hague | Cornelia Ida

Stewartville District: Anna Catherina | Leonora | Stewartville | Uitvlugt | Zeeburg | De Willem | Met-en-Meerzorg

Vergenoegen District: De Kinderen | Zeelugt | Tuschen-de-Vrienden | Vergenoegen | Philadelphia

Table A2. Estates and Villages. - Continued

Essequebo Coast, Wakenaam and Pomeroon

Aurora District: Good Hope | Spring Garden | Aurora | Hibernia | Vilvoorden

Suddie District: Pomona | Huis t'Dieren | Riverstown | Airy Hall | Tiger Island | Adventure | Onderneeming | Belfield | Maria's Lodge | Johanna Cecilia | Zorg | Golden Fleece | Perseverance

Capoey District: Cullen | Abram Zuil | Annandale | Zorg-en-Vlyt | Hoff-van-Aurich | Union | Queenstown | Taymouth Manor | Affiance | Columbia | Aberdeen | Three Friends

Anna Regina District: Land of Plenty | Mainstay | Reliance | Bush Lot | Anna Regina | Henrietta | Richmond Hill | La Belle Alliance | Lima | Coffee Grove | Danielstown | Sparta | Windsor Castle | Hampton Court | Devonshire Castle

New Amsterdam

Strand District: New Amsterdam | Sheet Anchor

East and West Bank Berbice

Sisters District: Providence | Glasgow | Edinburgh | Everton | Belle Vue | Rotterdam | Lonsdale | Sisters | Friends | Kootberaad | Dieutichum | De Kinderen | Busee's Lust | Highbury | Light Town

Schepoet District: Ma Retraite | Mara

Corentyne Coast

Albion District: Pln. Albion | Villages, Farms and Settlements from Maryberg to and inclusive of Rose Hall.

Whim District: Pln. Port Mourant | Villages, Farms and Settlements from Pln. Port Mourant to and inclusive of Maida.

Tarlogie District: Villages, Farms and Settlements from Maida to Heversham.

No. 51 District: Villages, Farms and Settlements from Heversham to No. 58.

No. 63 District. Villages, Farms and Settlements from No. 58 to Stockholm or No. 74.

No. 79 District: Pln. Eliza and Mary | Pln. Skeldon | Villages, Farms and Settlements from Stockholm or No. 74 to Corentyne River.

Table A2. Estates and Villages. - Continued

In addition to the above, the following estates are listed alphabetically by Cecil Clementi in his 1915 book "The Chinese in British Guiana."

Essequebo Mainland: Better Hope | Hoff van Holland
Essequebo Islands: Bankhall | Caledonia | Endeavour | Friendship & Sarah | Hamburg | Maryville | Moorfarm | Palmyra | Retrieve | Sophienburg | Success | Waterloo | Zeelandia
West Coast Demerara: Groenveldt
West Coast Berbice: Bath | Cotton Tree | Hope & Experiment
Berbice River: Blairmont
East Coast Berbice: Adelphi | Canefield | Goldstone Hall | Smythfield | Smithson's Place

Table A3. Distribution of Chinese Immigrants
From Clementi

	District	Males	Females
Immigrants allotted to estates on:	Essequebo Mainland	1,334	256
	Essequebo Islands	945	211
	West Coast Demerara	2,295	375
	Demerara River	1,985	345
	East Coast Demerara	3,118	446
	West Coast Berbice	225	17
	Berbice River	374	78
	East Coast Berbice	565	123
	Corentyne River	424	147
	Total allotted:	11,295	1,998
	Unallotted	74	39
	Deaths, &c.	97	38
	Total:	11,466	2,075

Table A4. Contract of Indenture

1155			*5713*
1156	Ship *Corona*	No. *402*	*5714*
1157			*5715*

Agreement between *Soo a cheong* native of China and THEOPHILUS SAMPSON, Esq., Acting as Agent for the Government of the Colony of British Guiana in the West Indies. Whereas the said T. Sampson has opened an Emigration Office at Canton for obtaining coolies for the Colony of British Guiana, I the said *Soo a cheong* agree to go on board ship and to go the British Guiana and there to work on the terms set forth below.

1.- I agree to work in British Guiana as I may be directed by the Government Immigration Agent or for any person to whom he may transfer this Contract.

2.- The period of service is five years commencing from the day I begin to work, or if on my arrival I be too ill to work then it shall commence eight days after my recovery.

3.- I agree to do any kind of work that I may be lawfully directed to do, whether in town or country, in fields, in factories, in private houses &c.

4.- I shall not be required to work on Sundays unless I be employed as a domestic servant or to take care of cattle; in such case, and in all cases in which it is the local custom to do so, I must work on Sunday. In all other cases my time during Sunday shall be entirely at my own disposal.

5.- A day consists of 24 hours and I may not be required to work more than nine and a half hours in one day. If I work more than nine and a half hours one day, I may work an equal length of time less on another, or if not, then my employer shall compensate me.

6.- At the end of the five years service my master will give me $50 in lieu of a return passage to China. If at the expiration of the term of the contract I do not wish to return to China, and if the Authorities of the place still permit me to reside in Guiana, in that case my master shall give me the $50 stipulated in the Contract for my own use; but if I wish to enter into another agreement for five years, half of the above sum namely $25 will be given to me by my master as a bonus, and at the end of the second five years the original sum of $50 will be paid to me in lieu of a return passage to China.

7.- If after arrival I become incurably ill so as to be unable to work, my master shall at once pay me the fifty dollars to assist me to return to China, if my master does not do so I may petition the Authorities who shall on their part recover the money for me.

8.- Wherever I may work or in whatever family I may be employed, I must obey the lawful regulations there in force; on the other hand should I at any time feel aggrieved at the conduct of my master towards me, all reasonable facility shall be afforded me, for laying my complaint before the proper officers of the Colony.

9.- When the contract shall have been signed and I have embarked, I cannot again return to the shore; if urgent business requires me to do so, I must first obtain the consent of the said Theophilus Sampson and then I may do so.

10.- It is distinctly agreed that this contract binds the Coolie to go as a labourer to no other place than to British Guiana.

11.- During the five years beginning on the day agreed in the Contract the wages shall be four dollars a month or the equivalent in Gold, for which my master shall be responsible. The wages shall be paid every month and shall not be allowed to fall into arrear.

12.- Every day, food will be issued as follows; 8 oz. salt meat and 2½ lbs. of other articles, all of which shall be good and wholesome.

13.- In case of illness, medical attendance and medicines and proper food will be provided free of expenses till recovery; no matter what such medical expenses may amount to, the master may make no deduction on account of them from the coolie's wages.

14.- Each year there will be given me one suit of clothes and one blanket.

15.- Passage to British Guiana will be provided by the said Theophilus Sampson.

16.- The said Theophilus Sampson will provide to the Emigrant the sum of *nil* dollars or the equivalent in gold for the use of his family. This sum shall be repaid by the Emigrant in British Guiana to the holder of the Contract by deductions from his wages at the rate of one dollar a month till it all be repaid, but no further deductions from wages may be made. No debt that may be incurred by the coolie during the voyage, or in British Guiana, may be construed into a lien on his services, or availed of to prolong the period of service specified in this contract.

17.- On embarkation three suits of clothes and every thing necessary for the voyage will be provided for the emigrant free of expense to him. The clothes and articles thus provided to be considered a free gift. The coolie is to enjoy their use and is not to be called upon to return them.

18.- While he is working in British Guiana he shall enjoy the protection of the law of the place; on his return however to China, this protection will be abrogated.

19.- I the said coolie now agree that my wages shall be four dollars a month and I declare my willingness, before my departure, to go to British Guiana, it is therefore understood that hereafter if I hear or ascertain that the labourers in British Guiana receive more wages than myself, I must still be satisfied with the wages and other compensating advantages secured to me by this Contract.

All the foregoing clauses were clearly understood and were read and explained before the Contract was signed; both parties being willing and fully understanding the terms, cannot hereafter complain that they were in ignorance thereof. This Contract is signed in English and a Chinese translation is annexed, as a proof, each party holding a copy.

Tung Cho *12* year *10* moon *22* day *11th December* 187 *3*

{Wife Yau She 38 sui}[1] *{Soo a cheong}*

{Son Soo Sam kuan 9 sui}

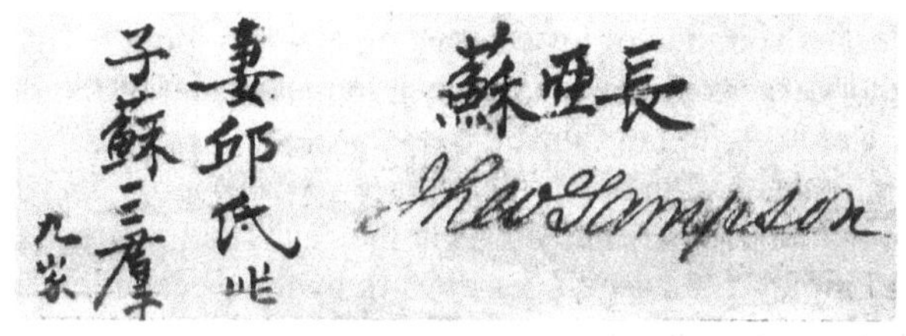

Theo Sampson

This done in duplicate, each of the parties aforesaid retaining one copy, at Canton, on the *11th* day of *December* in the year of our Lord 187*3*, in the presence of the undersigned, who declares that this Contract has been signed willingly, and with full knowledge of the contents, by the emigrant labourer named herein.

[Signature of Emigration Officer]
Emigration Officer

To this contract is appended the 8th 9th 10th 14th and 22nd clauses of the convention of 22 articles agreed to in 1866 by the Tsung Li Yamun in reference to coolie Emigration, they run as follows -

Article VIII.- The contracts shall specify: 1st The place of destination and the length of the engagement. 2nd The right of the Emigrant to be conveyed back to his own country and the sum which shall be paid at the expiration of the contract to cover the expense of his voyage home and that of his family should they accompany him. 3rd The number of working days in the year and the length of each day's work. 4th The wages, rations, clothing and other advantages promised to the Emigrant. 5th Gratuitous medical attendance. 6th The sums which the Emigrant agrees to set aside out of his monthly wages for the benefit of persons to be named by him should he desire to appropriate any sum to such a purpose. 7th Copy of the 8th, 9th, 10th,

1 The words enclosed in curly brackets { } indicate written Chinese characters. In Chinese, a person is reckoned to be one year old at the time of birth, so that 38 sui would correspond to 37 years by the Western practice for counting birthdays.

14th and 22nd. Articles of these regulations. Any clause which shall purport to render invalid any of the provisions of this regulation is null and void.

Art. IX.- The term of each emigrant's engagement shall not exceed five years, and at the expiration of which, the sum stipulated in the contract shall be paid to him to cover the expense of his return to his country. In the event of his obtaining permission to remain without an engagement in the colony, this sum will be paid into his own hands. It shall always be at the option of the emigrant to enter into a second engagement for five years, for which he shall be paid a premium equivalent to one half the cost of his return to China. In such a case the sum destined to cover the expense of his return home shall not be paid until the expiration his second engagement. Every emigrant who shall become invalided and incapable of working, shall be allowed, without waiting for the expiration of his contract, to claim before the legal Courts of the Colony, or territory where he may be, payment on his behalf of the sum destined to cover the expense of his return to China.

Art. X.- The Emigrant shall in no case be forced to work more than six days out of seven, nor more than nine hours and a half in the day. The Emigrant shall be free to arrange with his Employer the conditions of work by the piece or job, and all extra labour undertaken during days and hours set apart for rest. The obligation on holidays to attend to cattle or to do such service as the necessities of daily life may demand shall not be considered as labour.

Art. XIV.- Any sum handed over to the emigrant before his departure shall only be regarded in the light of a Premium upon his engagement. All advances upon his future wages are formally forbidden except in the case of their being appropriated to the use of his family, and the Consul will take special pains and provide against their being employed in any other way. Such advances shall not exceed six months wages and shall be covered by a stoppage of one dollar per month until the entire debt shall have been paid. It is absolutely forbidden whether on the voyage or during the emigrant's stay in the Colony or Territory in which he may be employed to make any advances to him in money or kind payable after the expiration of his engagement. Any agreement of this nature shall be null and void and shall give the creditor no power to oppose the return of the Emigrant to his country at the time fixed by the contract.

Art. XXII.- In the distribution of emigrants as labourers, the husband shall not be separated from his wife, nor shall parents be separated from their children under fifteen years of age. No labourer shall be bound to change his employer without his consent, except in the event of the factory or plantation upon which he is employed changing hands.

The above are such of the clauses of the Convention of 1866 that should enter into the Contract and should be considered as binding upon both parties.

* * * * * *

Received an advance of nil *dollars on account of wages for the use of my family, and a bonus of* ten *dollars for myself, and a gratuity of* twenty five *dollars for my wife* Yau She *and* one *child* {Soo a cheong}

* * * * * *

I agree to employ Soo a cheong upon the terms stated above.

[Employer's representative]

I certify that the labourer whose name appears above has been allotted by His Excellency the Governor of British Guiana, to plantation La Grange , and that the signature was acknowledged in my presence.

James Crosby
Immigration Agent General of British Guiana

Copy of the contract of indenture for Soo A cheong, accompanied by his wife Yau She and son Soo Sam kuan, dated 11th December, 1873.

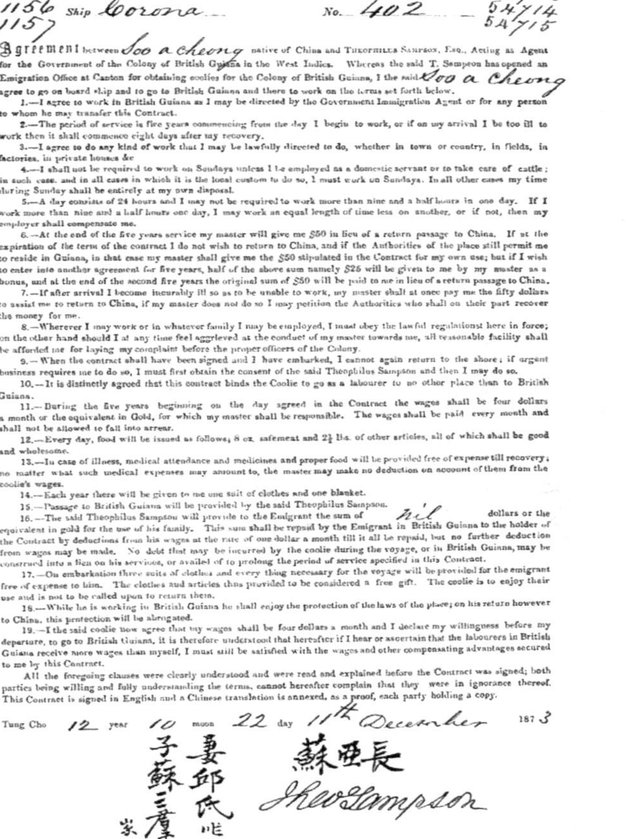

1155
1156 Ship Corona — No. 402 — 54713
1157 — 54714
54715

Agreement between Soo a cheong native of China and THEOPHILUS SAMPSON, ESQ., Acting as Agent for the Government of the Colony of British Guiana in the West Indies. Whereas the said T. Sampson has opened an Emigration Office at Canton for obtaining coolies for the Colony of British Guiana, I the said Soo a Cheong agree to go on board ship and to go to British Guiana and there to work on the terms set forth below.

1.—I agree to work in British Guiana as I may be directed by the Government Immigration Agent or for any person to whom he may transfer this Contract.

2.—The period of service is five years commencing from the day I begin to work, or if on my arrival I be too ill to work then it shall commence eight days after my recovery.

3.—I agree to do any kind of work that I may be lawfully directed to do, whether in town or country, in fields, in factories, in private houses &c

4.—I shall not be required to work on Sundays unless I be employed as a domestic servant or to take care of cattle; in such case, and in all cases in which it is the local custom to do so, I must work on Sundays. In all other cases my time during Sunday shall be entirely at my own disposal.

5.—A day consists of 24 hours and I may not be required to work more than nine and a half hours in one day. If I work more than nine and a half hours one day, I may work an equal length of time less on another, or if not, then my employer shall compensate me.

6.—At the end of the five years service my master will give me $50 in lieu of a return passage to China. If at the expiration of the term of the contract I do not wish to return to China, and if the Authorities of the place still permit me to reside in Guiana, in that case my master shall give me the $50 stipulated in the Contract for my own use; but if I wish to enter into another agreement for five years, half of the above sum namely $25 will be given to me by my master as a bonus, and at the end of the second five years the original sum of $50 will be paid to me in lieu of a return passage to China.

7.—If after arrival I become incurably ill so as to be unable to work, my master shall at once pay me the fifty dollars to assist me to return to China, if my master does not do so I may petition the Authorities who shall on their part recover the money for me.

8.—Wherever I may work or in whatever family I may be employed, I must obey the lawful regulations here in force; on the other hand should I at any time feel aggrieved at the conduct of my master towards me, all reasonable facility shall be afforded me for laying my complaint before the proper officers of the Colony.

9.—When the contract shall have been signed and I have embarked, I cannot again return to the shore; if urgent business requires me to do so, I must first obtain the consent of the said Theophilus Sampson and then I may do so.

10.—It is distinctly agreed that this contract binds the Coolie to go as a labourer to no other place than to British Guiana.

11.—During the five years beginning on the day agreed in the Contract the wages shall be four dollars a month or the equivalent in Gold, for which my master shall be responsible. The wages shall be paid every month and shall not be allowed to fall into arrear.

12.—Every day, food will be issued as follows; 8 oz. saltmeat and 2½ lbs. of other articles, all of which shall be good and wholesome.

13.—In case of illness, medical attendance and medicines and proper food will be provided free of expense till recovery; no matter what such medical expenses may amount to, the master may make no deduction on account of them from the coolie's wages.

14.—Each year there will be given to me one suit of clothes and one blanket.

15.—Passage to British Guiana will be provided by the said Theophilus Sampson.

16.—The said Theophilus Sampson will provide to the Emigrant the sum of nil dollars or the equivalent in gold for the use of his family. This sum shall be repaid by the Emigrant in British Guiana to the holder of the Contract by deductions from his wages at the rate of one dollar a month till it all be repaid, but no further deduction from wages may be made. No debt that may be incurred by the coolie during the voyage, or in British Guiana, may be construed into a lien on his services, or availed of to prolong the period of service specified in this Contract.

17.—On embarkation three suits of clothes and every thing necessary for the voyage will be provided for the emigrant free of expense to him. The clothes and articles thus provided to be considered a free gift. The coolie is to enjoy their use and is not to be called upon to return them.

18.—While he is working in British Guiana he shall enjoy the protection of the laws of the place; on his return however to China, this protection will be abrogated.

19.—I the said coolie now agree that my wages shall be four dollars a month and I declare my willingness before my departure, to go to British Guiana, it is therefore understood that hereafter if I hear or ascertain that the labourers in British Guiana receive more wages than myself, I must still be satisfied with the wages and other compensating advantages secured to me by this Contract.

All the foregoing clauses were clearly understood and were read and explained before the Contract was signed; both parties being willing and fully understanding the terms, cannot hereafter complain that they were in ignorance thereof. This Contract is signed in English and a Chinese translation is annexed, as a proof, each party holding a copy.

Tung Cho 12 year 10 moon 22 day 11th December 1873

妻邱氏 子蘇三糜 蘇亞長

Theo Sampson

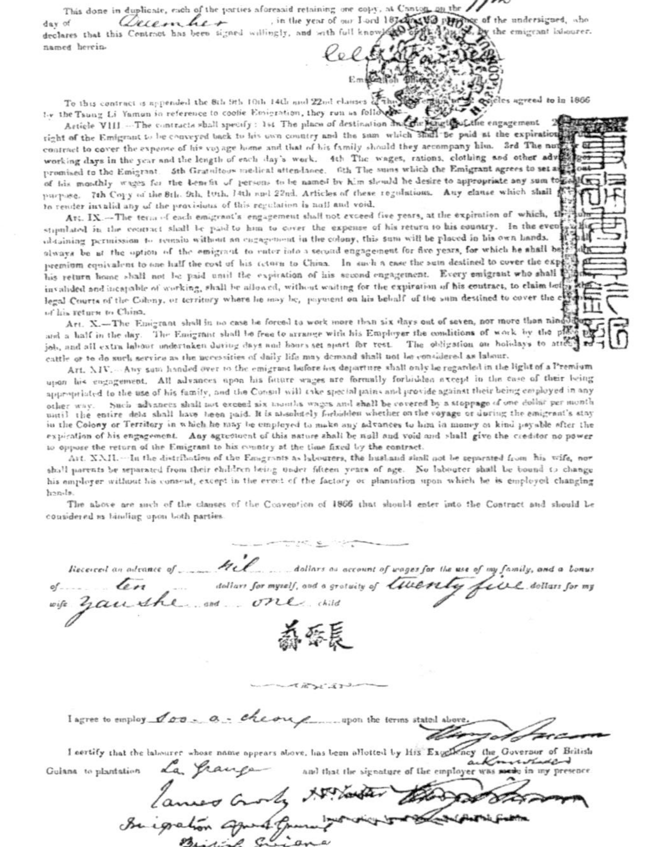

This done in duplicate, each of the parties aforesaid retaining one copy, at Canton, on the *11th* day of *December*, in the year of our Lord 187[illegible] presence of the undersigned, who declares that this Contract has been signed willingly, and with full knowledge [illegible], by the emigrant labourer named herein.

[illegible signature]

Emigration Officer.

To this contract is appended the 8th 9th 10th 14th and 22nd clauses of the [illegible] articles agreed to in 1866 by the Tsung Li Yamun in reference to coolie Emigration, they run as follows:—

Article VIII.—The contracts shall specify: 1st The place of destination and the length of the engagement. 2nd [illegible] right of the Emigrant to be conveyed back to his own country and the sum which shall be paid at the expiration [illegible] contract to cover the expense of his voyage home and that of his family should they accompany him. 3rd The number of working days in the year and the length of each day's work. 4th The wages, rations, clothing and other advantages promised to the Emigrant. 5th Gratuitous medical attendance. 6th The sums which the Emigrant agrees to set apart out of his monthly wages for the benefit of persons to be named by him should he desire to appropriate any sum to [illegible] purpose. 7th Copy of the 8th, 9th, 10th, 14th and 22nd. Articles of these regulations. Any clause which shall [illegible] to render invalid any of the provisions of this regulation is null and void.

Art. IX.—The term of each emigrant's engagement shall not exceed five years, at the expiration of which, the sum stipulated in the contract shall be paid to him to cover the expense of his return to his country. In the event of [illegible] obtaining permission to remain without an engagement in the colony, this sum will be placed in his own hands. [illegible] always be at the option of the emigrant to enter into a second engagement for five years, for which he shall be [illegible] premium equivalent to one half the cost of his return to China. In such a case the sum destined to cover the exp[illegible] his return home shall not be paid until the expiration of his second engagement. Every emigrant who shall [illegible] invalided and incapable of working, shall be allowed, without waiting for the expiration of his contract, to claim before the legal Courts of the Colony, or territory where he may be, payment on his behalf of the sum destined to cover the expense of his return to China.

Art. X.—The Emigrant shall in no case be forced to work more than six days out of seven, nor more than nine [illegible] and a half in the day. The Emigrant shall be free to arrange with his Employer the conditions of work by the piece [illegible] job, and all extra labour undertaken during days and hours set apart for rest. The obligation on holidays to attend to cattle or to do such service as the necessities of daily life may demand shall not be considered as labour.

Art. XIV.—Any sum handed over to the emigrant before his departure shall only be regarded in the light of a Premium upon his engagement. All advances upon his future wages are formally forbidden except in the case of their being appropriated to the use of his family, and the Consul will take special pains and provide against their being employed in any other way. Such advances shall not exceed six months wages and shall be covered by a stoppage of one dollar per month until the entire debt shall have been paid. It is absolutely forbidden whether on the voyage or during the emigrant's stay in the Colony or Territory in which he may be employed to make any advances to him in money or kind payable after the expiration of his engagement. Any agreement of this nature shall be null and void and shall give the creditor no power to oppose the return of the Emigrant to his country at the time fixed by the contract.

Art. XXII.—In the distribution of the Emigrants as labourers, the husband shall not be separated from his wife, nor shall parents be separated from their children being under fifteen years of age. No labourer shall be bound to change his employer without his consent, except in the event of the factory or plantation upon which he is employed changing hands.

The above are such of the clauses of the Convention of 1866 that should enter into the Contract and should be considered as binding upon both parties.

Received an advance of nil *dollars as account of wages for the use of my family, and a bonus of* ten *dollars for myself, and a gratuity of* twenty five *dollars for my wife* Yau she *and* one *child*

蘇亞長

I agree to employ Soo - a - cheong upon the terms stated above.

[signature]

I certify that the labourer whose name appears above, has been allotted by His Excellency the Governor of British Guiana to plantation La Grange and that the signature of the employer was ~~made~~ acknowledged in my presence

James Crosby — Immigration Agent General, British Guiana

[signatures]

BIBLIOGRAPHY

Several books and papers were examined in preparing this account and the following were particularly useful:

Beeching, Jack, "The Chinese Opium Wars," Hutchinson of London, 1975.

British Parliamentary Papers, miscellaneous records.

British Guiana Royal Gazette, miscellaneous issues.

"Chinese Emigration. The Cuba Commission. Report of the Commission sent by China to Ascertain the Condition of Chinese Coolies in Cuba," Shanghai, 1876.

Crawford Campbell, Persia, "Chinese Coolie Emigration," Frank Cass & Co. Ltd., London, 1923.

Chang Hsin-pao, "Commissioner Lin and the Opium War," Harvard University Press, Massachusetts, 1964.

Clarke, Prescott and J.S. Gregory, "Western Reports on the Taiping," Croom Helm, London 1982.

Clementi, Cecil, "The Chinese in British Guiana," The Argosy Co., Georgetown, 1915.

Cooke, George W., "China: being '*The Times*' special correspondence from China in the years 1857-1858," G. Routledge & Co., 1858.

Des Voeux, G. William, "Experiences of a Demerara Magistrate," Vincent Roth (Ed.), The Daily Chronicle Ltd., Georgetown, British Guiana, 1948.

Forbes, Archibald, "Chinese Gordon. A succinct record of his life," George Routledge and Sons, London, 1884.

Graham, Gerald S., "The China Station, War and Diplomacy 1830-1860," Clarendon Press, Oxford, 1978.

Hahn, Emily, "China only yesterday: 1850-1950," Doubleday &Co., Inc., Garden City, New York, 1963.

Hall, Laura Jane, "The Chinese in Guyana: The Making of a Creole Community," Ph.D. thesis, University of California, Berkeley, 1995.

Hsu, Immanuel C.Y., "The Rise of Modern China," Third Edition, Oxford University Press, New York, 1983.

Irick, Robert L., "Ch'ing Policy Toward the Coolie Trade 1847-1878," Chinese Materials Center, Taiwan, 1982.

Jen Yu-wen, "The Taiping Revolutionary Movement," Yale University Press, 1973.

Jenkins, Edward, "The Coolie. His Rights and Wrongs," George Routledge and Sons, New York, 1871.

Kirkpatrick, Margery, "From the Middle Kingdom to the New World," Margery Kirkpatrick, Georgetown, 1993.

Kwok Crawford, Marlene, "Scenes from the history of the Chinese in Guyana," Demerara Publishers, Georgetown, 1989.

Lin Shan, "Name your baby in Chinese," Heian International, Inc., Union City, California, 1988.

Look Lai, Walton, "Indentured Labor, Caribbean Sugar," Johns Hopkins University Press, Baltimore, 1993.

Look Lai, Walton, "The Chinese in the West Indies 1806-1995: A Documentary History," The Press, University of the West Indies, Kingston, 1998.

Low, Frederick O., "Hopetown Chinese Settlement," Timehri, September 1919.

McGregor, David R., "The Tea Clippers. Their History and Development 1833-1875," Conway Maritime Press, 1983.

Millett, Trevor M., "The Chinese in Trinidad," Inprint Caribbean Ltd., Port of Spain, 1993.

Morse, Hosea B., "In the Days of the Taipings," The Essex Institute, Salem, Massachusetts, 1927.

Morse, Hosea B., "The International Relations of the Chinese Empire," 1917.

Spence, Jonathan D., "God's Chinese Son: The Taiping Heavenly Kingdom of Hong Xiuquan," W.W. Norton & Co., New York, 1996.

Stewart, Watt, "Chinese Bondage in Peru," Duke University Press, Durham, N.C., 1951.

Sue-A-Quan, Trev, "Cane Ripples: The Chinese in Guyana," Cane Press, Vancouver, BC, Canada, 2003.

Sue-A-Quan, Trev, "Cane Rovers: Stories of the Chinese-Guyanese Diaspora," Cane Press, Vancouver, BC, Canada, 2012.

Takaki, Ronald, "Strangers from a Different Shore. A History of Asian Americans," Penguin Books, New York, 1989.

Tan, Thomas Tsu-wee, "Your Chinese roots," Heian International, Inc., Union City, California, 1987.

Trollope, Anthony, "The West Indies and the Spanish Main," 1859. Republished by Alan Sutton Publishing Ltd., Gloucester, 1985.

Wang, Sing-wu, "The Organization of Chinese Emigration 1846-1888," Chinese Materials Center, Inc., San Francisco, 1978.

About the Author

Trevelyan A. Sue-A-Quan was born in November 1943 in Georgetown, Guyana. He is the great-grandson of an indentured labourer who had embarked with his wife and son aboard the ship *Corona* at Canton. They arrived at Georgetown in February 1874 after 78 days at sea. The family was allotted to La Grange sugar cane plantation on the Demerara River.

Many of the second-generation descendants of these Chinese field workers became shopkeepers, including Soo Sam-kuan the author's grandfather. In the process of cultural assimilation his name became transformed into Henry Sue-A-Quan thus initiating the distinctive family surname.

Trev Sue-A-Quan's generation was the one that typified the transition from shopkeeping to professions based on higher education. His brother and sister both graduated from Edinburgh, Scotland and became chief surgeon and mathematician/computer specialist, respectively. Trev attended Queen's College in Georgetown and attained B.Sc. and Ph.D. degrees in Chemical Engineering at the University of Birmingham, England. He immigrated to Canada in 1969 but then pursued a career opportunity with a major oil company in Chicago where he was engaged in research in petroleum processing and fossil fuel utilization. Eight years later Trev headed East — to Beijing, China, becoming Senior Research Engineer at the Coal Science Research Center. He spent five years there and in 1984 returned to Canada with his wife and son. They now make their home in Vancouver.

The interest in Trev's family history came from a curiosity about the circumstances that caused his great-grandfather to leave his native land. Almost 20 years after obtaining a copy of his ancestor's contract of indenture Trev has applied his training in analytical research to compile this comprehensive account of the experiences of the first Chinese immigrants in Guyana.

www.ingramcontent.com/pod-product-compliance
Lightning Source LLC
Chambersburg PA
CBHW070551270326
41926CB00013B/2270

9780973355734